UNCLE SAM'S
CHRISTIAN PATRIOTS

UNCLE SAM'S CHRISTIAN PATRIOTS

A personal, political and Religious Discussion of
September the 11th, War and Peace
and Freedom and Oppression

GLEN STANISH

ReadersMagnet, LLC

Uncle Sam's Christian Patriots: A personal, political and Religious Discussion of September the 11th, War and Peace and Freedom and Oppression

Published in the United States of America
ISBN Paperback: 979-8-89091-135-3
ISBN Hardback: 979-8-89091-136-0
ISBN eBook: 979-8-89091-137-7

ReadersMagnet, LLC
10620 Treena Street, Suite 230 | San Diego, California, 92131 USA
1.619. 354. 2643 | www.readersmagnet.com

Cover design by Tifanny Curaza
Interior design by Dorothy Lee

TABLE OF CONTENTS

DEDICATION

This book is dedicated to my wife Joy, and my children, Mariel Catherine and Harrison Matthew, whom I love more than I could ever say.

This book is also for those everywhere who are committed to contributing all that they can, to provide for a condition of peace, for as one who was once said, "... And is not peace... basically a matter of human rights..."

"Deliver me, O Lord, from evil men;
preserve me from violent men,
Who plan evil things in their hearts;
they continually
gather together for war."
(Psalms 140:1-2, NKJV)

"If you see the oppression of the poor, and the violent perversion of justice and righteousness in a province, do not marvel at the matter; for high official watches over high official, and higher officials are over them."
(Ecclesiastes 5:8, NKJV)

NEW ACKNOWLEDGMENTS

I would like to express gratitude to ReadersMagnet Publishing for giving *Uncle Sam's Christian Patriots* a new and further opportunity to flourish. Uncle Sam's was originally published in 2006. However, the original publisher, Tate Publishing, ultimately withdrew and dissolved.

As I resumed my former career after writing the text, I put the book on the shelf for a while as airline flying is a full-time gig. I was hoping to someday revisit the chance of re-publishing and still believed the subject matter, September the 11th, was significant and therefore vital to be maintained in the public conversation.

In late 2022, I received a pleasant and welcome phone call from Val Arian, Senior Publishing and Marketing Consultant from ReadersMagnet. She informed me that ReadersMagnet was interested in republishing Uncle Sam's Christian Patriots. As I had recently retired from United Airlines, I thought this may be a good time to go for it. We talked extensively about the composition of the book and the process for issuance and eventually came to the decision of republishing the book.

Since then, I have worked closely with Yani Lynn and Leenie Sabayo, Author Relations Officers at ReadersMagnet. They have been extremely helpful throughout the process of minor editing of the text, production, and the design and development of the website.

And so, I would like to convey deep appreciation for ReadersMagnet and for all their professional staff for their support and assistance.

This book, Uncle Sam's Christian Patriots, A Personal, Political and Religious Discussion of September the 11th, War and Peace, and Freedom and Oppression, is still in essence the first edition, with scarcely any changes and mere minor editing. The original content is intact and included and I nevertheless stand by every word.

Although this coming September, it will have been 22 years since the tragic event of 9/11, it still rings true that we should "never forget 9/11."

And what is most important to remember about 9/11, like the assassination of JFK, among other chronicled historical events, is that the official story is nothing more than poppycock and rubbish. 9/11 was a Zionist "false flag" event, to be blamed on Muslim terrorists. It was in fact conducted by Zionist Israel and their like-minded, unfaithful, deceitful co-conspirator traitorous allies and agents in the United States. It benefitted Israel by derailing entirely the "peace process," the international, multi-lateral attempts to solve the Mideast crisis and establish a Palestinian State, the long planned and now some would say impossible and therefore obsolete two-state solution. It was a declaration of war against the peacemakers and the nations involved in the peace process and was a notice to those that Zionist goals to establish an exclusive Jewish state that reaches from the Euphrates to the Nile, will continue with the help of Special Forces and Secret Services like the Mossad and the CIA by the fruits that they produce.

The event was a fabricated lie and a false cause for a war against Iraq, a strong Mideast sovereign nation that posed no threat, had no WMD, but needed to be weakened for the benefit of Israel.

And for the United States' Military-Industrial complex, whose faithless CEOs and their agents, would also lobby the Federal government in order to procure giant defense and weapons spending contracts, to satisfy their investors who have no principle when it comes to interest and dividends.

But on a brighter digression, it has exposed the complicity and cowardice of the mainstream press. On almost every topic the opposing press reports, the CNN and MSNBC types, versus the Fox types, they take completely different sides and spin for their masters and subjects, the conservative or progressive bent so demanded. Except for 9/11, they are in perfect harmonious lockstep. Inexplicable.

But in contrast to dubious cowards who should have stepped up and whistleblown, many heroic authorities have come forward. There are many individuals and organizations, such as Religious Leaders, Military Leaders, Architects, Engineers, Pilots, Firefighters, Politicians and countless others with expertise who have rendered what they can to help reveal 9/11 truth.

And for current and future generations, who may select to recognize which abominable representation they may urgently need to shun, and which sovereign to confirm their allegiance, substance to scrutinize.

And so, 9/11 is still significant. And all indebtedness and acknowledgment to ReadersMagnet for helping to keep the catastrophic woe in the public eye and discourse.

ACKNOWLEDGMENTS

In the course of writing this book, it became apparent and self-evident to me that this project would not have been possible without the generous help and support of so many others and whom I would like to give proper thanks and acknowledgment to here.

In January of 2000, I was a First Officer or co-pilot with Trans World Airlines. I loved my profession and career at TWA. As a flight officer, one meets many interesting people and fellow crewmembers. On transcontinental flights, in order to help pass the time, along with enjoying beautiful scenery, pilots and crewmembers often engage in conversation.

On a particular trip, we call them pairings, I was fortunate to have flown with, or been paired up with Captain Jeff Walters. During this time at TWA, discussion of the TWA 800 "accident" was a common subject of discourse. I remember throughout the trip talking to Jeff about the accident and other topics such as the assassinations of President Kennedy and Martin Luther King, and politics in general.

As we conversed, Captain Walters asked me by chance, if I was a subscriber to *The Spotlight*, a small Washington, DC based newspaper best described as populist, nationalist and constitutionally conservative. I told him I was not and as he carried a couple of recent issues; he loaned them to me for my review.

On our layover in Oklahoma City, I reviewed these issues of *The Spotlight* and soon contacted the subscription department. *The Spotlight* had since gone through some business adjustments of their own, which is a story in and of itself, but re-emerged as *American Free Press*.

Since initially becoming a subscriber in January of 2000, I have continued to subscribe and have found this newspaper to be an invaluable source of information on both current events, and as details emerge through further research and disclosures, historical events as well.

A fellow subscriber, Mr. George Munger, wrote a letter to the editor and I think his letter best describes the quality and the importance of this publication. He wrote:

"The first time I ever saw a copy of American Free Press was in the minister of energy's office of a major Middle Eastern country. I asked the minister why he was reading a small U.S. paper like *American Free Press.* He said, 'Mr. Munger, we learn more about what the U.S. government is doing in the world from this paper than we do from our own intelligence department.'

That was interesting, but I did not think much more about it until some months later while in a major Southeast Asian country and saw it again in the office of one of that country's senior administrators. When questioned about it, these gentlemen gave me substantially the same answer."

And so, I would like to thank Captain Jeff Walters for introducing me to *The Spotlight* and *American Free Press.*

And I would also like to thank the entire *American Free Press* staff.

But some in this organization I would particularly like to recognize.

Many thanks go to Mr. Christopher Bollyn for all his coverage of September the 11th, for all his personal correspondence throughout the research for this book, and for joining me at the Johnson County White River Library for our little 9/11 presentation. Many of Mr. Bollyn's articles were extensively used and are cited throughout this text. He is certainly one of the most honest and knowledgeable investigative reporters who has thoroughly covered and truthfully reported on the events of 9/11.

I would also like to thank Michael Collins Piper of *American Free Press.* I first contacted Mike on December 22, 2004, after I had started working on this book. I had been a student as well as a fan of Mr. Piper since reading his work *Final Judgement,* considered by many researchers to be the pinnacle or the capstone of research on the assassination of President John F. Kennedy. Mike has been an inspiration as well as a source of encouragement. And his one piece of advice I frequently considered throughout this project was "finish the book." Thank you, Mike.

I would also like to thank Mr. Greg Szymanski, who has also covered and continues to report break-through material concerning the catastrophe of September the 11th. The full truth of this matter is still emerging.

Thanks also go to the editor of *American Free Press,* Mr. Chris Petherick, for putting me in touch with Christopher Bollyn.

And many thanks also go to Mr. James P. Tucker, Mr. Charley Reese, and to Mr. Vince Ryan. And again, many thanks to the entire *American Free Press* organization.

I would also like to thank Dave vonKleist and Joyce Riley, along with William Lewis, for their masterpiece of a 9/11 documentary, *911 In Plane Site,* and for providing a copy to both the Air Line Pilots Association and the Allied Pilots Association. Thank you also Dave and Joyce for having me as a guest on your program, *The Pour Hour*. It was truly an honor.

I'm sorry I could not get more from the ALPA or the APA. This is still very difficult for me to understand.

Many thanks go to Mr. Phil Jayhan for all he has done for the 9/11 truth movement. Phil Jayhan is the founder and web host for the web site www.letsroll911.Org. This site is without a doubt one of the most active web sites for 9/11 research and is a convenient one-stop location for researchers and truth seekers alike. As new material is added and updated daily in the forum sections with references and sources attached, depending on the significance of these contributions, some are put on the front page of the website. As new information or sources come forward, you can be safely assured it will be covered and reported on Letsroll.

I would also like to thank the following forum members for their contributions and exchanges: tocarm, mason-free party, Locotus, lookawaydixie, Ducati 749, hdhntr, kaha, TapirSaver, enigs, RedPillNeo, bradwww, Jack Blood, Agent Orange, SoldieroftheLord, Icke, robpriv, The Surgeon, ryandinian, Zerohour, coffeelover, Ike Ono Klast, aelphaeis_mangarae, nibls66, doogal, Exclusive, Penny, Sinister Dick Cheney, Izzy, ThouShaltnotKill, adnaj, The Revolutionist, nukuler, Endgame, and all the others with the possible exception of Perry Logan.

Many thanks also go to fellow aviators, airline captains and good friends.

Thanks to Captain Rod Ennis, Boeing 757 Fleet Manager at ATA Airlines. Rod was my primary flight instructor more than 20 years ago. Thanks, Rod, for teaching me how to fly, for your friendship, your input and your help in getting other ATA staff to look at this subject matter.

Thanks to Captain Mark Kesling. Mark was one of the first fellow airmen to sit down and view *911 In Plane Site* with me. He burned a copy or two and shared them with other airline people.

Thanks, Mark, for your friendship. We have been friends since our days at Purdue. We were groomsmen in each other's weddings, and we have flown together in aircraft ranging from Piper Tomahawks to trips in the Boeing-737 at ATA.

Many thanks also go to Captain Don Hein. I met Don at ATA. He is a neighbor and a friend. Don and I flew several trips together at ATA. He is an exemplary airman and a superb Captain; someone I would fly with anytime. He makes every trip enjoyable, and promotes a harmonious cockpit, which contributes more to safe operations than anything in the manuals. Don was the first fellow pilot I shared *911 In Plane Site* with, and he also was one of the first to read and review this manuscript. Many thanks, Don.

I cannot thank Dr. Richard Tate of Tate Publishing and the entire Tate Publishing staff enough. From the first contact I had with Tate Publishing, Dr. Tate said he was interested in the subject matter and the book. After sending to him a part of the book, Tate Publishing offered a beneficial relationship and they have helped and encouraged me throughout this project and have been there throughout the production process. As this was my first book, Tate was truly an answer to my prayers. Their generous assistance and support have been more than any writer could hope for and as a new author, made this project go as smoothly as possible.

And most importantly, thank you to my family. In the last three years, as a contributing factor of 9/11, many thousands of airline employees have suffered setbacks to their careers. Many have lost their jobs, their retirement and pensions, lost wages and benefits and any sense of security and stability. Going through these kinds of hardships can be very difficult on families, marriages and relationships. My wife and children have literally held me up through these tough times; it has indeed been burdensome, and I am sorry for the frustrations, the setbacks and the uncertainty. But with God's help, we still have each other, we still depend on each other, and we still love each other more with every passing day. But I could not have done this without you. Thank you, Joy, Mariel and Harrison.

And principally, Heavenly Father, through your Son, Jesus Christ, all things are possible.

"I never consider a difference of opinion in politics, in religion, in philosophy, as cause for withdrawing from a friend."

Thomas Jefferson

INTRODUCTION

I most certainly and honestly believe, that sometime in the not too distant future, it will become widespread and common knowledge that the events of September the 11th, 2001, were either an "inside job," designed, engineered and committed at the highest levels of our own United States federal government, or were designed, engineered and committed by a very large and "in control" rogue element within this same federal government, and was used as a pretext, a false cause, and a lie, to invade two natural resource rich foreign countries, to further pursue and expand an empire, and as part of the "war on terror," or, more appropriately, the "war on freedom," was used to frighten the American people so they would allow the infringement of their civil liberties and their constitutional rights, to allow for closer monitoring and further oppression.

This story and these facts are slowly emerging despite the suppression and the censorship of our mainstream media. Many researchers, truth seekers, investigative reporters, authors, both retired and active military men and women, technical experts, and even former President George W. Bush administration officials are now coming forward with credible and convincing information that is chiseling away the deceitful cover story of September the 11th, and that will soon expose the evil perpetrators of this massive crime against humanity. The social, geo-political and even biblically prophetic fallout of these developments is not yet known but will also be played out over the course of time.

For example, in June of this year (2005), the CSPAN II network twice aired a *Book TV* program featuring Professor, Theologian and Author David Ray Griffin, who said: "For many Americans, the idea that we are living in a country whose own leaders planned and carried out the attacks of 9/11, is simply too horrible to entertain. Unfortunately, however, there is considerable evidence for this view."[1]

And Mr. Kevin Ryan, a former Underwriters Laboratory Inspector, recently had this to say about September the 11th:

"Anyone who honestly looks at the evidence has difficulty finding anything in the official story of 9/11 that is believable. It's not just one or two strange twists or holes in the story; the whole thing is bogus from start to end. In my previous job I was in a position to question one part, the collapse of three tall buildings due to fire...

The three WTC buildings in question weren't all designed the same and weren't all hit by airplanes. The only thing they seemed to have in common were relatively small and manageable fires, as indicated by the work of firefighter's right up to the moment of collapse. From the government's report we know that only a small percentage of the supporting columns in each of the first two buildings were severed and that jet fuel burned off in just a few minutes.

To follow the latest 'leading hypothesis,' what are the odds that all the fire proofing fell off in just the right places, even far from the point of impact? Without much test data, let's say it's one in a thousand. And what are the odds that the office furnishings converged to supply highly-directed and (somehow) forced oxygen fires at very precise points on the remaining columns? Is it another one in a thousand? What is the chance that these points would then all soften in unison, and give way perfectly, so that the highly dubious "progressive global collapse" theory could be born? I wouldn't even care to guess. But finally, with well over a hundred fires in tall buildings through history, what are the chances that the first, second and third incidents of fire-induced collapse would all occur on the same day? Let's say it's one in a million. Considering just these few points, we're looking at a one in a trillion chance, using generous estimates and

1 David Ray Griffin, CSPAN II, Book TV, June 2005.

not really considering the third building (no plane, no jet fuel, different construction)."[2]

In my previous job, I, like Kevin Ryan and many others, was also in a position to question other parts of the official story of September the 11th.

I was an airline pilot, and my employer was American Airlines, one of the two airlines whose aircraft were allegedly used as missiles and flown into the World Trade Center Towers, the Pentagon, and the countryside of Shanksville, Pennsylvania. I was employed formerly with Trans World Airlines, but TWA was acquired by American Airlines in April of 2001, so I was laboring for American Airlines on 9/11.

On one occasion, several months after September the 11th, I was reading an article in my favorite newspaper, *American Free Press*, by investigative journalist Mr. Christopher Bollyn. In the article, it stated that according to many eyewitnesses and survivors at both the Pentagon and Shanksville aircraft crash sites, there wasn't any evidence that Boeing 757s had actually crashed at these locations. Many witnesses reported never seeing any pieces of wreckage from these 200,000+ pound Boeing-757s

As I was reading this article, I thought that that was very difficult for me to believe. You see, as airline pilots and flight crewmembers, we are required by the Federal Aviation Administration, the FAA, as part of our training with the airlines to become qualified flight crewmembers, to cover what is called C.R.M., or Cockpit Resource Management, or Crew Resource Management. This is required for new hires and as part of the annual required recurrent training for airline pilots.

This training is the study of airline accidents and incidents, their contributing causal factors, and what we as crewmembers could have done differently to have prevented a particular type of accident or incident. During the classroom instruction, we are always shown videos, or photos or slides, or other video news coverage of these accident sites and the one constant is that after

2 Kevin Ryan, "Former Underwriters Laboratory Inspector Speaks out on 911 Once Again" June 9th, 2005, www.911wasalic.com, 7/16/05.

an airline accident, large pieces of aircraft wreckage remain. Let me just give you a couple of examples.

TWA 800 was a Boeing 747 that departed New York's John F. Kennedy airport bound for Paris, France in the summer of 1996. During its departure, climbing through 14,000 feet or so, it allegedly suffered a "freak" catastrophic center wing tank fuel explosion; the aircraft came apart in midair and came crashing down into the Atlantic Ocean. Do you think it was hard to find any large pieces of wreckage from this aircraft? Not at all. In fact, the entire aircraft was recovered and almost completely rebuilt in a Calverton, New York hangar. Hardly any metal was missing at all.

When I was flying for a USAir Express carrier many years ago, USAir lost a Boeing 737 in the Pittsburgh suburb of Aliquippa, Pennsylvania. The Boeing-737 allegedly suffered a hard-over rudder condition that caused the aircraft to roll over on its back, it became uncontrollable, or there was not enough altitude to recover control of the aircraft and it slammed into the terrain at a very high rate of speed and descent. Again, many large pieces of aircraft wreckage remained, the usual wreckage: jet engines, large, virtually indestructible landing gear, fuselage, wings, tail, seats, luggage, etc. And I considered several other accident sites and again, the one constant when a large Boeing airliner hull is lost, large pieces of wreckage remain. Boeing 757s and 767s do not "disintegrate" to the molecular level. Boeing 757s and 767s do not "vaporize." And Boeing 757s and 767s do not "liquefy" to be absorbed by Mother Earth or the Pentagon. Boeing indeed constructs a tough airframe.

And so, after reading Mr. Bollyn's article, I thought it would be worthwhile to contact the newspaper and the reporter. I called *American Free Press* and spoke with the Editor, Mr. Chris Petherick. I told him my background and he had Mr. Bollyn, the author of the article, contact me. I spoke with Mr. Bollyn for several minutes discussing these things and he took my name and address and had Mr. Dave vonKleist forward to me a copy of *911*

In Plane Site, a documentary DVD about the September the 11th attacks that Mr. vonKleist had produced.

After viewing *911 In Plane Site*, I was shocked, stunned and saddened. I couldn't believe what was presented in this documentary, or, I didn't want to believe it, yet it was all so undeniable, put together from news coverage like CNN, FOX, ABC, NBC, CNBC, MS-NBC, and all the other news agencies during and just days after 9/11.

I must admit, during the next few days I had some emotional moments. There is a reason they say, "the truth hurts," or that it is the "ugly truth" or that it is the "harsh, cold reality." But the truth of the matter of September the 11th was beginning to penetrate. And as you become aware of the truth of 9/11, you will also feel the whole range of emotions. You'll be angry, you'll be saddened, and you'll be shocked and stunned. But it will hurt, and you will mourn. You will mourn over the loss of your country, or the loss of what you for so long innocently presumed was your country.

As I dealt with this blow, I felt like I needed to share this information. I had to tell somebody, anybody, everybody, all the while still hoping that this evidence was wrong. I loaned the documentary to a minister at a local Methodist Church that we had attended and where our children had gone to day care. We later discussed the video, and he didn't see what I was hoping he would see. He said he liked President Bush and that he thought John Kerry was not good for the country because, "Who would take a camera to war in Vietnam?"

I shared the documentary with several school administrators and teachers here in the local community where my children go to school. I never really got much of a response other than that standardized reading test scores were what was more important now.

But when I started showing it to fellow airline pilots, most of them were supportive and agreed that there was probably a lot more to the story of 9/11.

I began a professional relationship of sorts with Chris Bollyn and Dave vonKleist. I thought that large airline labor groups should be made aware of this information. As I was a member of both of the largest airline pilot labor groups, I recommended that the Allied Pilots Association and the Air Line Pilots Association should be provided a copy of the documentary and that the President of ALPA, Captain Duane Woerth, and the Director of Communications at the APA, Mr. Gregg Overman, would be good contacts for *American Free Press*. Mr. vonKleist forwarded to Captain Duane Worth and Mr. Gregg Overman a copy of *911 In Plane Site*, and I tried to follow up with emails and phone calls to these professionals. These interactions are further described in the appendix section of this text.

But I also contacted the local governing councils, referred to as MECs or Master Executive Councils, of the various airlines. I called the MEC offices of Alaska Airlines, Allegheny Airlines, America West Airlines, American Eagle, and ATA Airlines, who was my employer after I was furloughed from American Airlines due to the fallout in the industry after 9/11. I contacted Atlantic Southeast Airlines, Comair, Continental, Delta, FedEx, Independence Air, Hawaiian Airlines, Kitty Hawk Aircargo, Mesaba, Midwest Express, Northwest, Piedmont, Polar Air Cargo, PSA, another one of my former airlines, Spirit, Trans States, United, and US Airways and some other airlines which are not represented by ALPA, like Southwest Airlines.

And again, these interactions are further described in the Appendix section of this text. But it was the inconsistencies of these aircraft disasters at both the Pentagon and the Shanksville, Pennsylvania locations, evidenced by the lack of wreckage or a debris field, Mr. vonKleist's documentary "911 In Plane Site" and Mr. Bollyn's articles that prompted me to conduct further research and eventually to writing this book.

As I conducted further research for this book, I was made aware of a website, www.letsroll911.Org. I cannot more highly recommend to the readers a thorough tour of this site and a viewing of *911 In Plane Site*.

But as I became a forum member on this website, I received this message from a United States soldier currently serving in Iraq and I would like to share it with you, the readers:

"Whats up F/O? (That is my forum username. It stands for First Officer, my last position with American Airlines and ATA.) Yeah, I'm currently deployed to Iraq. I'm in the Army Reserves. My home is Nashville, TN. Titanville... Cashville... etc. I'm slated to be here until November [2005]. It stinks to spend 365+ days of my time over here with thousands of people dead based on lies and corrupt reasons. All stemming from an attack carried out by our own people on Sept. 11. I already felt horrible because I didn't agree with the war, was skeptical and suspicious about what's going on, hated having to leave home and college for a year and other personal struggles, but it was multiplied when I started researching this stuff on a daily basis. I felt like complete do-do for a month. Believed it but couldn't believe it. Couldn't believe that I signed up to wear this uniform for THIS. Thought I signed up for college funds (which are there) and to support the capture of the foreign perpetrators.

To get these perpetrators, I thought the military would conduct mostly small-scale operations to target Al Qaeda and Bin Laden and then that would be it. Because to get "terrorist" groups, you would have to play their game. These groups supposedly keep a low profile and work behind the scenes. Therefore, you would have to do the same to combat that. Small scale covert operations to target them specifically and preserve the safety of the innocent civilian population. Suddenly, here we are bombing and invading two countries, with possibly a third one on the way (hopefully not), and killing thousands of civilians so they can be "liberated." So I'm like HOLD UP! This makes no sense. Found the truth and now I know what's going on. PNAC [Project for the New American Century, further discussed and covered in text] calls for the expansion of military bases and acquisition of resources in Mid East countries that aren't so friendly; therefore, an entire country and its government must be accused of terrorism, WMD and tyranny to warrant military action and the overthrow of its government.

College graduation postponed for two extra years because of two deployments and the "war on terror" is a bogus lie. To tell the truth, I don't even care to use the benefits of the Army and government in the future. I'm too disgusted right now. What I want is my life back and this conspiracy to come to an end. Let the true perpetraitors face their penalties. Hah hah!! Sorry for the rant but its how I feel. Talk to you later."[3]

"Kickster"

I haven't yet responded to "Kickster." I just hope and pray that he comes home soon, alive and in one piece.

But many other military men and women are becoming aware of the truth of 9/11. On the 4th of July, we took our family to a 4th celebration in Franklin, Indiana, my wife's hometown. While we were there, an Indiana National Guard unit was there and I had the opportunity to speak with a recruiter, a former United States Marine who had already finished a tour in Iraq. We got to talking about the "inside job" nature of 9/11 and he informed me that in fact, many service members are becoming aware of this painful reality.

And now, just recently, a former chief economist in the Labor Department during President George W. Bush's first term announced his belief that the official story about the collapse of the World Trade Center is "bogus," saying it is likely that a controlled demolition destroyed the twin towers and adjacent building 7.

Morgan Reynolds, Ph.D., a former member of the Bush team who also served as director of the Criminal Justice Center at the National Center for Policy Analysis, said: "If demolition destroyed three steel skyscrapers at the World Trade Center on 9-11, then the case for an 'inside job' and a government attack on America would be compelling."[4]

---

3 Kickster, Personal Message, http://letsroll911.Org Forum Message, 7/16/05.

4 American Free Press, June 27, 2005, p. 1.

Reynolds, who is now a professor emeritus at Texas A&M University, believes it was "next to impossible" that 19 Arab terrorists alone outfoxed the mighty U.S. military.

"If the official wisdom on the collapses is wrong as I believe it is, then policy based on such erroneous engineering analysis is not likely to be correct either. The government's collapse theory is highly vulnerable on its own terms. Only professional demolition appears to account for the full range of facts associated with the collapse of the three buildings.

"More importantly, momentous political and social consequences would follow if impartial observers concluded that professionals imploded the WTC. Meanwhile, the job of scientists and engineers and impartial researchers everywhere is to get the scientific and engineering analysis of 9-11 right."

However, Reynolds said, "getting it right in today's security state" remains challenging because he claims explosives and structural experts have been intimidated in their analysis of the collapse of 9/11.

During a subsequent interview with *American Free Press*, Reynolds went even further, stating, "One fact is irrefutable, those buildings were blown up."

"Number one, I am a citizen, and a thinker," Reynolds said, but above all, Mr. Reynolds is a highly-credentialed former Bush administration official who is willing to challenge the seriously flawed official version.[5]

And so, there we have it. And many, many more accounts from fire professionals on the scenes, survivors, eyewitnesses and other technical experts who have shared their experiences, their stories, their accounts, and their professional opinions are covered throughout this manuscript.

But this book is not just about September the 11th. As the title indicates, it is also a political and historical, as well as a religious discussion of war and peace, and freedom and oppression. It is about the universal nature of political corruption that I believe most of us would freely acknowledge. But it also covers the depths

5 Ibid.

of this political corruption and its insidious and devastatingly disastrous results.

And this is not just a problem for the United States; it is an international problem, global in scope, and something that all common people of the world are going to have to take a long and hard look at and determine if this is the order of things they would like to continue to support. And if not, is neglecting the problems going to help or make them go away, or would becoming more informed, active and vigilant possibly be in order? As Mr. Kevin Ryan has stated, "We have to see that terrorism is actually much worse than we feared, because the terrorists are in charge."[6]

But this book is also about personal beliefs and searches for answers as to why there is so much terrorism and war, and who seems to benefit and profit from it. Why have we deviated so far from our nation's founders' most basic guiding principles and ideals for our country and for future generations of Americans, so that our country could survive as a republic? Why should I or my children join an organization, supported by the state, that would require and command us to engage in an activity, like killing someone, when this would be a violation of the most basic principles we as Christians hold dear and which is commanded to us by a much Higher Authority.

And this book is also about dissent. Not just my dissent, but dissent as being a legitimate and proper role of a loyal and patriotic U.S. citizen. As Robert F. Kennedy said in 1968: "Those who now call for an end to dissent moreover seem not to understand what this country is all about. For debate and dissent are the very heart of the American process. We have followed the wisdom of ancient Greece: 'All things are to be examined and brought into question. There is no limit set to thought... How else is error to be corrected, if not by informed reason of dissent...?'

... We dissent not because it is comforting, but because it is not-because it sharply reminds us of our true purpose... So if we are uneasy about our country today, perhaps it is because we are

6 Kevin Ryan.

truer to our principles than we realize... We say with Camus, 'I should like to be able to love my country and still love justice...'

Our country is in danger, not just from foreign enemies, but above all from our own misguided policies... This is a contest, not for the rule of America, but for the heart of America..."[7]

And as this contest continues, the stakes have never been higher than they are right now.

But this book is also about hope. Hope for justice and hope for peace and freedom. And one is dependent on the others. It is about hope for better tomorrows and hope for a better world for our children. It is about hope for a more peaceful world where all are engaged in peace and enjoying its benefits, and none are engaged in enforcing a "conditional peace" or combating to attain an "honorable peace." It is about what very little one can do, but what very much many can do, to provide for a condition of peace; it is about what guiding principles we can pass along to our children, for Jesus said: "Put up again thy sword into his place: for all they that take the sword shall perish with the sword" (Matthew 26:52, KJV).

At this time and in these conditions of international and inter-religious relations, I think it would be appropriate and wise to review and retain the words of Robert F. Kennedy, who said: "Let us dedicate ourselves to what the Greeks wrote so many years ago: to tame the savageness of man, and make gentle the life of this world. Let us dedicate ourselves to that, and say a prayer for our country and our people."[8]

---

7 RFK-Three Speeches, The Fieldston School, Department of History, www.ecfs.org/Projects/fieldston57/since40/units/unit4/supplements/RFK_3speeches.html, 1/13/05.

8 Ibid.

"When a man who is honestly mistaken hears the truth, he will either quit being mistaken or cease to be honest."

Author unknown

CHAPTER ONE
Beware of False Prophets

On Monday, September 10th, 2001, I was on the second day of a four-day domestic trip with American Airlines. My former employer, TWA, after having a brief period of financial success and growth after the TWA 800 accident, had had another period of hardship and was acquired by American Airlines in April of 2001. So now, I was a First Officer or co-pilot on the MD-80, or the "Super 80" if you were an "American Original," based in St. Louis, Missouri.

After arriving at the Dallas-Ft., Worth International Airport (DFW) from St. Louis (STL) on flight 657, my Captain, Tom Battle from Colorado, and I went to the layover hotel in downtown Ft. Worth. The hotel was now called the Ft. Worth Radisson but used to be known as the Texas Hotel. After the next day's events, it just seemed a little weird that that hotel was the same hotel where President John F. Kennedy spent his last night on the eve of his assassination back on November 22nd, 1963, in Dallas, Texas.

We arrived at the hotel around 10:00 p.m. or 2200 for you military types. As is usual and customary, after a long and grueling four-leg day of airline flying, Tom and I decided to go have a cold beer or two. And since Monday Night Football was on, we had time to enjoy the second half. We found a nice little sports bar type of place near the hotel to watch the game, quench our thirsts, and unwind a bit before calling it a day.

The next day, Tuesday, September the 11th, 2001, we did not have to get up too early. We were scheduled to leave DFW for Washington, D.C. via St. Louis later in the afternoon, around 4:00 p.m., or 1600 for you military types.

I did not have to set the alarm for an early departure, so I just woke up around 8:30 a.m., or 0830 for you military types. Ok, I'll stop with that. Anyway, I got out of bed, dragged a comb across my head, turned on the morning news, and then proceeded to make the morning coffee. While making coffee, the TV news was announcing that an airplane had crashed into one of the World Trade Center towers.

I grabbed my coffee and went back to the TV to watch the news. The cameras were now in position and you could see the fire and the smoke billowing out of the North Tower, or Building 1 of the World Trade Center.

At the time, surfing through the various news channels, they were all reporting basically the same thing, that they didn't know what type of aircraft had hit the building, possibly a Cessna, or a Piper, or a Beechcraft. A short time later, it was reported that it was in fact an airliner, and one of ours, American Flight 11, a Boeing 767, departing Boston Logan, destined for Los Angeles.

For the next few hours, I watched the rest of the day's events unfold. Another alleged airliner crashed into the South Tower of the World Trade Center. Then another aircraft had struck the Pentagon. And then, another crashed in Shanksville, Pennsylvania, enroute to the nation's capital.

Tom, my Captain, called me at some point during these events and asked me if I was watching "this shit." I told him that I was, and he said," I don't think we're going anywhere today, especially D.C."

Throughout the rest of the day, and the next, we had to evacuate the hotel twice because of bomb threats.

We did find out surprisingly quickly by the fancy footwork of our F.B.I. that it was a terrorist group, Al Qaeda, led by our former ally, Osama Bin Ladin, who was responsible for these heinous attacks and massive crimes against humanity in our country.

Throughout the next few weeks and months, we were informed that Iraq had also played a major part in these attacks and that we, as a country, were going to have to wage a long and aggressive war on terrorism and go wherever we needed to go. Our leaders also informed us that Iraq, Iran and North Korea constituted an axis of evil, something like the old empire of evil, the Soviet Union, back during the Cold War days. I deduced then that we must be a part of the axis of good.

Now we also had launched a war against terrorism in Afghanistan, and we were told that we were in hot pursuit of Osama bin Ladin. President Bush said we were going to "smoke him out" of the caves of Tora Bora. But we also kept hearing about Iraq's weapons of mass destruction, and how we needed to launch an aggressive, pre-emptive war against Iraq as part of the long global war on terror before one of our cities went up in the form of a "mushroom cloud," like Hiroshima or Nagasaki, Japan at the end of World War Two.

Just before our attack on Iraq to make the world safe from terrorism, our family went to a church service in our hometown of Greenwood, Indiana.

We had attended this church as visitors a few times. It seemed like a nice Christian church, and we had inquired about membership there.

I remember that Sunday. Part of the sermon was about the impending war in Iraq, a sermon about "justified war." The associate minister was addressing the congregation at the Community Church of Greenwood that day, and I remember him saying that our impending attack on Iraq was justified. That according to principles he cited, this would be a justified war.

I couldn't really believe what I was hearing there in the sanctuary. As I listened to the minister discuss what I gathered was this church's official position of pro-war, I wanted to just get up and leave. I looked around the congregation and as the minister spoke, I could see many people listening intently and nodding their heads in agreement. I thought as this minister was proposing this "justified war," that he surely had considered all the wartime atrocities that would certainly go along with it. And as this was a Christian church, I wondered what passages in the Bible, and specifically the New Testament, he may have used to support this position. And I couldn't think of any. I don't ever remember Jesus Christ discussing a concept of "justified war."

I did remember, however, reading in the Book of James, chapter four, verses 1 and 2, in the New Testament about the causes of war. How lust and covetousness for another person's or nation's land, property, wealth or resources are the causes of war. I had to ask myself who seemed to be the aggressor in this case, and therefore, who might be guilty of coveting.

I also wondered, as this minister preached about this church's position of justified war, if this minister was familiar with numerous other teachings of Jesus. When Jesus was teaching on the mountain in St. Matthew, chapter five, verses 43, 44 and 45, Jesus said: "Ye have heard that it hath been said, Thou shalt love thy neighbor and hate thine enemy. But I say unto you, Love your enemies, bless them that curse you, do good to them that hate you, and pray for them which despitefully use you and persecute you; That ye may be the children of your Father which is in heaven ..."(Matthew 5:43-45, KJV).

Or again, in St. Matthew, chapter ten, verse 16, Jesus said: "Behold, I send you forth as sheep in the midst of wolves: be ye therefore wise as serpents and harmless as doves." (Matthew 10:16, KJV).

Harmless as doves, He said, wise as serpents.

I wondered if this associate minister and if many in the congregation, who seemed to be in agreement with him, were familiar with St. Matthew, chapter 26, verse 52: "Then said Jesus unto him, Put up again thy sword into his place: for all they that take the sword shall perish with the sword" (Matthew 26:52 KJV), and what they may have understood this to mean and how it should apply to their lives today.

To me, if this is not a divine command, I don't know what is.

There were also the Commandments: Thou shall not kill, and Thou shall not covet, which again, according to the Book of James, is the cause of war. And the golden rule: Do unto others, as ye would have them do unto you.

I also recalled President Dwight D. Eisenhower's farewell address to the Nation. The president discussed how "American makers of plowshares could, with time and as required, make swords as well."[9] He said: "But now we can no longer risk emergency improvisation of national defense; we have been compelled to create a permanent armaments industry of vast proportions. Added to this, three and a half million men and women are directly engaged in the defense establishment. We annually spend on military security more than the net income of all United States corporations.

"This conjunction of an immense military establishment and a large arms industry is new in the American experience. The total influence-economic, political, and even spiritual-is felt in every city, every Statehouse, every office of the Federal government...

"... In the councils of government, we must guard against the acquisition of unwarranted influence, whether sought or unsought, by the military-industrial complex. The potential for the disastrous rise of misplaced power exists and will persist.

"We must never let the weight of this combination endanger our liberties or democratic processes. We should take nothing for granted. Only an alert and knowledgeable citizenry can compel the proper meshing of the huge industrial and military machinery of defense with our peaceful methods and goals, so that security and liberty may prosper together."[10]

When I thought about President Eisenhower's address, about the total influence, "even spiritual" he said, I wondered if that associate minister's personal portfolio may have contained securities from Boeing, Lockheed Martin, Northrop Grumman, Raytheon, General Dynamics, Bechtel or maybe even Haliburton.

Looking back, as I remember sitting in that sanctuary, listening to the associate minister talk about how our upcoming attack on the sovereign nation of Iraq-a country which had never attacked us, never threatened to attack us, yet only vowed that it

---

9 Military Industrial Complex Speech, Dwight David Eisenhower, 1961 http://coursea.matrix.msu. edu/~hst306/documents/indust.html.

10 Ibid.

would attempt to protect and defend itself and its citizens-how many in the congregation seemed to hang on to his every word.

I recalled another passage in the New Testament. In St. Matthew, Chapter seven, verses 15 and 16, Jesus said: "Beware of false prophets, which come to you in sheep's clothing, but inwardly they are ravening wolves. Ye shall know them by their fruits..." (Matthew 7:15-16, KJV). And in St. Matthew, Chapter 24, verse 11, Jesus said: "And many false prophets shall rise, and shall deceive many" (Matthew 24:11, KJV).

Many will be deceived, by many false prophets. Not a couple, not a few, but many. Please ask yourselves, could you be deceived? Maybe just a little bit fooled? No? Well, if you are Christian, and if you believe in the Gospels, and that Jesus is truthful, then one must admit that yes indeed, one could certainly be fooled. And this is hard to do. No one likes to be deceived.

When I look back on the events of September the 11th, and my reactions to them, sitting in that hotel room in Ft. Worth watching the "news," I do remember a strong feeling of disbelief, kind of a state of shock. But the more I learn about the events of 9/11 and the subsequent wars to make the world safe from terrorism, the more I think I understand that disbelief. Something inside just said that this wasn't right. This didn't make sense. I kept shaking my head in disbelief.

When we finally left Dallas on Saturday the 15th of September, it was kind of surreal. Hardly anybody was at the airport. The terminal looked like a ghost town. I had a new Captain that day, Mike Ettle. During the Captain's briefing, he instructed me to place the cockpit crash ax where I could get to it quickly, just in case we would have to fight to the death an evil Islamic extremist, fundamentalist hijacker. Looking back now, I think maybe I had been a little bit fooled, if not downright deceived.

When I finally got home to Greenwood, Indiana, I couldn't stop hugging my wife and kids.

In an article in a Memorial Day 2004 issue of the nationalist and populist newsweekly *American Free Press*, a United States Marine Corps General's views on war and its causes were reviewed.

The late Major General Smedley Darlington Butler (1881-1940), a highly decorated U.S. Marine Corps hero and winner of two Congressional Medals of Honor, had this to say about war:

"War is just a racket, something that is not what it seems to the majority of the people. Only a small inside group knows what it is about.

It is conducted for the benefit of the very few at the expense of the masses. I believe in adequate defense at the coastline and nothing else. If a nation comes over here to fight, then we'll fight. I wouldn't go to war again as I have done to protect some lousy investment of the bankers.

There are only two things we should fight for. One is the defense of our homes and the other is the Bill of Rights. War for any other reason is simply a racket.

There isn't a trick in the racketeering bag that the military gang is blind to. It has its "finger men" to point out enemies, its "muscle men" to destroy enemies, its "brain men" to plan war preparations, and a "Big Boss": Super Nationalistic Capitalism.

It may seem odd for me, a military man, to adopt such a comparison. Truthfulness compels me to.

I spent 33 years and four months in active military service as a member of this country's most agile military force, the Marine Corps. I served in all commissioned ranks from Second Lieutenant to Major-General. And during that period, I spent most of my time being a high-class muscle man for Big Business, for Wall Street, and for the Bankers. In short, I was a racketeer, a gangster for capitalism.

I suspected I was just part of a racket at the time. Now I am sure of it. Like all the members of the military profession, I never had a thought of my own until I left the service. My mental faculties remained in suspended animation while I obeyed the orders of higher-ups. This is typical with everyone in the military service.

I helped make Mexico, especially Tampico, safe for American oil interests in 1914. I helped make Haiti and Cuba a decent place for the National City Bank boys to collect revenues in. I helped in the raping of half a dozen Central American republics for the benefits of Wall Street. The record of racketeering is long.

I helped purify Nicaragua for the international banking house of Brown Brothers in 1909-1912. I brought light to the Dominican Republic for American sugar interests in 1916. In China I helped to see to it that Standard Oil went its way unmolested.

During those years, I had, as the boys in the back room would say, a swell racket. Looking back on it, I feel that I could have given Al Capone a few hints. The best he could do was operate his racket in three districts. I operated on three continents."[11]

It has been said that communism is the exploitation of man by man; Capitalism is the reverse.

I wonder what Marine Corps General Butler's response would be today if he could look at our Patriot Acts One and Two and our Homeland Security Act and see how they have decimated our Bill of Rights, one of only a couple of reasons he cited for going to war.

And so, a 33 years of service, highly-decorated and ranked Marine Corps General, hero, winner of two Congressional Medals of Honor, referred to war as a racket. And so, the rather obvious question becomes then, to what lengths would those who engage in the war racket profession go to gain wealth and riches by fraudulent means?

To answer that question, lets look at a book, *Body of Secrets, Anatomy of the Ultra-Secret National Security Agency*, written by James Bamford, author of *Pretext for War* and *The Puzzle Palace*:

"Since the administration of President John F. Kennedy had come into office, the extreme right wing within the military had grown significantly, not only in numbers, but also in decibels.

According to secret and long-hidden documents obtained for *Body of Secrets*, the Joint Chiefs of Staff drew up and approved plans for what may be the most corrupt plan ever created by the United States government.

---

11 American Free Press, Weekly Newspaper, Washington, DC, Memorial Day Special, 2004, p. B.4.

In the name of anticommunism, the U.S. military's Joint Chiefs proposed launching a secret and bloody war of terrorism against their own country in order to trick the American public into supporting an ill-conceived war they intended to launch against Cuba.

Codenamed "Operation Northwoods," the plan, which had the written approval of the Chairman and every member of the Joint Chiefs of Staff, called for innocent people to be shot on American streets; for boats carrying refugees fleeing Cuba to be sunk on the high seas; for a wave of violent terrorism to be launched in Washington, D.C., Miami, and elsewhere. People would be framed for bombings they did not commit [bearing false witness]; planes would be hijacked. Using phony evidence, all of it would be blamed on Fidel Castro, thus giving the Chairman of the Joint Chiefs of Staff, General Lymen Lemnitzer, and his cabal the excuse, as well as the public and international backing they needed to launch their war.

The idea may have actually originated with President Eisenhower [who forewarned us about the military industrial complex] in the last days of his administration. With the Cold War hotter than ever, and the recent U-2 scandal fresh in the public's memory, the old General wanted to go out with a win.

He wanted desperately to invade Cuba in the weeks leading up to John F. Kennedy's inauguration; indeed, on January 3rd, Ike told General Lemnitzer and other aids in his Cabinet Room that he would move against Castro before the inauguration if only the Cubans gave him a really good excuse. Then, with time growing short, President Eisenhower floated an idea. If Castro failed to provide the excuse, perhaps, he said, the U.S. "could think of manufacturing something that would be generally acceptable." What Ike was suggesting was a pretext, a false reason, and a lie. A bombing, an attack, an act of sabotage, would be carried out secretly against the United States, by the United States. Its purpose would be to justify the launching of a war. It was a dangerous suggestion by a desperate president.

Although no such war took place, the idea and the methods were not lost on General Lemnitzer. But he and his partners in crime were frustrated by President Kennedy's [forthright] refusal to authorize their plan, and angry that Castro had not provided an excuse to invade."[12]

"Operation Northwoods" called for a war in which many patriotic Americans and innocent Cubans would die [violent,] senseless deaths-all to satisfy the egos of twisted generals back in Washington, safe [and cozy] in their taxpayer-financed homes and limousines."[13]

"One idea seriously considered involved the launch of John Glenn, the first American to orbit the earth. On February 20, 1962, Glenn was to lift off from Cape Canaveral, Florida on his historic journey. The flight was to carry the banners of America's virtues: truth, freedom, [justice], and democracy into orbit high over the planet. But General Lemnitzer and his Chiefs had a different idea. They proposed to General Landsdale, that should the rocket explode and kill Glenn, 'the objective is to provide irrevocable proof that... the fault lies with the Communists et al Cuba [sic].' This would be accomplished, General Lemnitzer continued, by 'manufacturing various pieces of evidence which would prove electronic interference on the part of the Cubans.' Thus, as NASA prepared to send the first American into space, the Joint Chiefs of Staff was preparing to use John Glenn's death as a pretext, a lie, to launch a war."[14]

"Among other [wicked] plots the Chairman, General Lemnitzer and the other United States military Chiefs recommended was, 'a series of well coordinated incidents to take place in and around' the U.S. Navy base at Guantanamo Bay, Cuba. This included dressing friendly Cubans in enemy Cuban military uniforms and then have them start riots near the main gate of the base. Others would pretend to be saboteurs inside the base.

---

12 James Bamford, "Body of Secrets," Doubleday, New York, pp. 82-83.

13 Ibid. p. 83.

14 Ibid. p. 84.

Ammunition would be blown up, fires started, aircraft sabotaged, and mortars fired at the base with damage to installations."[15]

The suggested operations grew progressively more outrageous. The United States Chairman of the Joint Chiefs of Staff, General Lymen Lemnitzer and his staff [partners in crimes against humanity] came up with an extremely sinister plan. "We could blow up a U.S. ship in Guantanamo Bay and blame Cuba," they proposed. "Casualty lists in U.S. newspapers would cause a helpful wave of national indignation."[16]

Thomas Jefferson once expressed that "the newspapers are the first of all human contrivances for generating war."[17]

The United States Generals seemed to have no limit to their [demonic] fanaticism: "We could develop a Communist Cuban terror campaign in the Miami area, in other Florida cities and even in Washington,"[18] they wrote.

I'm sorry; I can't wait any longer. You all know where this is leading anyway don't you? I'm just wondering, and wondering if you're wondering yet, if today's Secretary of Defense, Donald Rumsfeld and his Chairman of the Joint Chiefs of Staff, may have considered a terror campaign in Washington, D.C. and other U.S. cities, like maybe, say, New York? We'll get back to this very soon.

Continuing now with General Lemnitzer and Operation Northwoods:

'We could sink a boatload of Cubans en route to Florida (real or simulated) ... We could foster attempts on lives of Cuban refugees in the United States even to the extent of wounding to be widely publicized.'

Bombings were proposed, false arrests, hijackings: 'Exploding a few plastic bombs in carefully chosen spots, the arrest of Cuban agents and the release of prepared documents substantiating

---

15 Ibid.

16 Ibid.

17 Maureen Harrison and Steve Gilbert, Editors, "Thomas Jefferson, In his Own Words" Excellent Books, p. 8.

18 Bamford, p. 84.

Cuban involvement also would be helpful in projecting the idea of an irresponsible government.

Advantage can be taken of the sensitivity of the Dominican Air Force to intrusions within their national airspace. "Cuban" B-26 or C-46 type aircraft could make cane burning raids at night. Soviet Bloc incendiaries could be found. This could be coupled with Cuban messages to the Communist underground in the Dominican Republic and "Cuban" shipments of arms which would be found, or intercepted on the beach. Use of MIG type aircraft by U.S. pilots could provide additional provocation.'[19]

When Uncle Sam comes calling, you may want to do your country and your fellowman a favor and consult first with a Higher Authority; for which master will you serve?

"Hijacking attempts against civil air and surface craft could appear to continue as harassing measures condoned by the Government of Cuba."[20]

Hmmm. Hijacking of civil aircraft, staged terror campaigns on U.S. cities. Fidel Castro, Osama bin Ladin, Saddam Hussien, General Lymen Lemnitzer, President Eisenhower, President Bush, Donald Rumsfeld, 1962, 2001. What is past is prologue.

Stay with me please; it really gets better here soon.

"Among the most elaborate [and satanic] schemes was to 'create an incident which will demonstrate convincingly that a Cuban aircraft has attacked and shot down a chartered civil airliner en route from the United States to Jamaica, Guatemala, Panama or Venezuela. The destination would be chosen only to cause the flight plan route to cross Cuba. The passengers could be a group of college students off on a holiday, or any grouping of persons with a common interest to support chartering a non-scheduled flight.'"[21]

"General Lemnitzer and the Joint Chiefs worked out a complex and [demonic] deception: An aircraft at Elgin Air Force Base would be painted and numbered as an exact duplicate for a civil

19 Ibid. p. 85.

20 Ibid.

21 Ibid.

registered aircraft belonging to a CIA proprietary organization in the Miami area. At a designated time, the duplicate would be substituted for the actual civil aircraft and would be loaded with the selected passengers, **all boarded under carefully prepared aliases** (emphasis added). The actual registered aircraft would be converted to a drone (a remotely controlled unmanned aircraft). Take off times of the drone aircraft and the actual aircraft will be scheduled to allow a rendezvous south of Florida.

From the rendezvous point, the passenger carrying aircraft will descend to a minimum altitude and go directly into an auxiliary field at Elgin Air Force Base where arrangements will have been made to evacuate the passengers and return the aircraft to its original status. The drone aircraft meanwhile will continue to fly the filed flight plan. When over Cuba, the drone will be transmitting on the international distress frequency a "May Day" (emergency) message stating he is under attack by Cuban MIG aircraft. The transmission will be interrupted by destruction of the aircraft, which will be triggered by radio signal. This will allow ICAO (International Civil Aviation Organization) radio stations in the Western Hemisphere to tell the United States what has happened to the aircraft, instead of the U.S. trying to 'sell' the incident."[22]

"In the final sentence of his letter to Secretary of Defense Robert McNamara, General Lemnitzer made a grab for even more power, asking that the Joint Chiefs be placed in charge of carrying out Operation Northwoods and the invasion of Cuba."[23]

"About a month after submitting Operation Northwoods, the Joint Chiefs of Staff met in the 'tank,' as the JCS conference room was called, and wrote a tough memorandum to Secretary of Defense McNamara. "The Joint Chiefs of Staff believes that the Cuban problem must be solved in the near future. Further, they see no prospect of early success in overthrowing the present communist regime either as a result of internal uprising or external political, economic or psychological pressures. Accordingly, they

22 Ibid. pp. 85-86.

23 Ibid. p. 86.

believe that military intervention by the United States will be required to overthrow the present communist regime."[24]

What General Lemnitzer was proposing was definitely not freeing the Cuban people, especially considering the General's methods. The Cuban people were largely in support of Castro. What the General was proposing was imprisoning the Cuban people in a United States military-controlled police state. "Forces would assure rapid essential military control of Cuba. Continued police action would be required," the good General wrote.[25]

Because of the secrecy and illegality of Operation Northwoods, all of these details remained hidden for forty years. General Lemnitzer may have thought that all copies of the relevant documents were destroyed. Brigadier General David W. Gray's meticulous notes were the only detailed official records of what happened within the Joint Chiefs of Staff during that time.[26]

General Lemnitzer also had no problem lying to Congress. When asked if he knew of any Pentagon plans for an invasion of Cuba, he said he did not. Yet detailed JCS invasion plans had been drawn up even before John F. Kennedy was inaugurated.[27]

Another demonically evil plan of the United States military brass was "to deliberately create a war between Cuba and any of a number of its Latin American neighbors. This would give the U.S. military an excuse to come in on the side of Cuba's adversary. Among the nations the military brass of the United States suggested was Jamaica, and Trinidad-Tobago. Both of these nations were members of the British Commonwealth. By secretly attacking them and then falsely blaming Cuba, the United States could lure England into a war."[28]

The war designers, engineers and creators even suggested secretly paying someone in the Castro government to attack the

---

24 Ibid. p. 87.

25 Ibid.

26 Ibid. p. 88.

27 Ibid.

28 Ibid. p. 89.

United States. "The only area remaining for consideration then would be to bribe one of Castro's subordinate commanders to initiate an attack on the U.S. naval base at Guantanamo." This act, bribing a foreign nation to launch a violent attack on an American military installation, is treason, pure and simple."[29]

> *"Behold, the wicked brings forth iniquity; yes, he conceives trouble and brings forth falsehood."*
>
> (Psalms 7:14, NKJV)

> *"For look! The wicked bend their bow; they make ready their arrow on the string that they may shoot secretly at the upright in heart."*
>
> (Psalms 11:2, NKJV)

Imagine your U.S. government, using your hard-earned tax dollars to pay a foreign country to attack your beloved country and countrymen. That way, your hard-earned tax revenue donation would go towards the purchase of all types of military hardware: bombs, missiles, and aircraft of the attack, fighter and bomber variety, ships, tanks, guns, ammunition, submarines and personnel carriers. Then we, or your government, along with your sons and daughters used as cannon fodder, could lay waist to that country, killing and maiming for life thousands of innocent civilians, destroying their homes and public infrastructure, sacrificing our own sons and daughters in the pursuit of exploiting that nation's land and natural resources for private profit. Then, of course, we would have to go back in and rebuild that country with private contractors, also known as war profiteers, who are in good with the current administration. You know, the ones that made generous donations to the campaign. Of course, these expenditures would again come from public funds from of course, you're hard-earned

29 Ibid.

tax dollars. It comes full circle. This is called taking from the poor and middle class and giving to the rich, or the transfer of wealth.

In May of 1963, Assistant Secretary of Defense Paul H. Nitze, sent a plan to the White House proposing another satanic plan whereby American pilots would fly dangerous, unnecessary low-level reconnaissance missions, with the expectation that they would be shot down, thus provoking a war.[30] This sounds like the provocative no fly zone operations we had over Iraq after Gulf War one. The Assistant Secretary of Defense, Paul H. Nitze, did not, however, volunteer to be an airman on one of these ridiculously provocative missions.

It can be said that General Lemnitzer was dangerous, but he wasn't alone. Far from it, in fact. Operation Northwoods had the support of every single member of the Joint Chiefs of Staff as well as other senior Pentagon officials.

Assistant Secretary of Defense Paul Nitze argued in favor of provoking a phony war with Cuba. The fact that the most senior members of all branches of the United States military services and the Pentagon could be so out of touch with the meaning of democracy, truth and justice, and the American way, would be hidden for four decades.

Looking back now, Operation Northwoods, or a page out of the same play book was probably used to launch the United States into the war with Vietnam. More than 58,000 Americans and more than 2 million Vietnamese were killed in that war.

It has long been suspected that the 1964 Gulf of Tonkin incident, the catalyst that led to the United States long war in Vietnam, was largely staged or provoked by U.S. officials in order to build congressional and public support for the war with Vietnam."[31]

Robert S. McNamara, former Secretary of Defense under Presidents Kennedy and Johnson, writing in his book *In Retrospect, The Tragedy and Lessons of Vietnam* wrote: "On November 9th, 1995, as the second edition was going to press, I learned in a

30 Ibid. pp. 89-90.

31 Ibid. p. 90.

meeting in Hanoi with General Vo Nguyen Giap, North Vietnam's Defense Minister during the war, that the presumed attack on August 4th, 1964, did not occur," referring to the alleged attacks by North Vietnamese patrol boats against U.S. destroyers in the Tonkin Gulf, which resulted in the Tonkin Gulf Resolution and the massive build up and deployment of U.S. troops.[32]

Defenders and sympathizers of the Pentagon have always and will continue to deny any charges of official misconduct or deceit, no matter what evidence or proof to the contrary is laid in front of them. However, in light of the Operation Northwoods documents, it is irrefutably clear that deceiving the public and trumping up wars for Americans to fight and die in was standard, approved policy at the highest levels of the Pentagon."[33]

This policy can go at least as far back as 1898, when an explosion aboard the battleship Maine in Havana harbor killed 266 U.S. sailors. This explosion sparked the Spanish American war. Incited by that deadly blast, more than one million men volunteered for "patriotic" duty. Media spin, known in those days as yellow journalism, was able even then to excite patriotic blood lust.[34]

"[However], in 1975, an investigation led by Admiral Hyman Rickover examined the data recovered from a 1911 examination of the wreck of the Maine, and concluded that there had been no evidence of an *external* explosion."[35]

Again, the obvious question then before us now is, is this standard approved policy of the Pentagon still in effect today? I'm just wondering now, if the mindset and the tactics of the Pentagon, or the senior personnel in the Defense Department, or of the Joint Chiefs of Staff, have changed much in the last 40 some years. Has there been a big shake up at the Pentagon? Has there been a large revision to the textbooks and course

---

32 Robert S. McNamara, "In Retrospect," Vintage Books, New York, p. 128.

33 Bamford, p. 91.

34 Ibid. p. 84.

35 Nafeez M. Ahmed, "The War on Freedom," Media Messenger Books, p. 331.

materials in the military academies or the advanced war colleges, or required courses for military promotion? Or maybe, has the material become even more aggressive, fascist, dare I say Zionist, and imperialistic? Remember that you can have an empire, or you can have a republic; but you cannot have both.

When I consider the many choices of career paths young men and women pursue, and their drives and ambitions, I am led to conclude that people normally choose their careers by the love or the ambition for the job or activity.

I know when I speak for myself; I can safely say I speak for many in my chosen profession. Airline pilots enjoy flying, pure and simple. Flying gets in your blood and I can say without exception that airline pilots are professionals. They love providing the smoothest flights they can for their passengers. And if they can get a nice grease job landing, all for the better. So, in short, pilots pursue a professional career of flying because they simply enjoy flying.

I think the same can be said for teachers. Mostly they care for children. They work hard to provide the best learning environment they can to facilitate the educational process. In short, teachers enjoy the classroom, they love children, and they enjoy teaching.

Medical doctors, I believe, pursue their careers also because they enjoy it or because they get a sense of satisfaction from it. Caring for their patients, providing the best medical care and treatment they can, whether they are general practitioners, surgeons, or pediatricians, is part of the personal drive for their profession. I believe this is also true for nurses, physical and occupational therapists, and all other health care providers. They genuinely care for their patients.

Professional musicians, I'm sure enjoy music and providing entertainment. Whether it's the drums, my personal favorite, guitar, piano, flute, trumpet or saxophone, I believe most professional musicians chose their profession because they love music, and they enjoy entertaining.

And I know that I love all kinds of music: rock and roll, jazz, live blues, gospel, classical in the early morning on the way to the airport. It's all good; well, I do have some reservations about rap. Have you heard some of those lyrics?

Policemen and firemen enjoy their work for the most part, keeping their communities safe. Designers, whether interior, exterior, or fashion all enjoy designing. Builders enjoy building; landscapers enjoy landscaping. Preachers enjoy preaching. Authors enjoy writing. And this all makes perfect sense to me.

But the one profession that I still have questions about is that of a professional soldier. Does he or she love soldiering, and if so, then does he or she love war? And if this were the case, to what lengths would they go to create their chosen work environment? Is there something about mass destruction and killing and big things that go boom that is appealing to the new recruit as well as the Chairman of the Joint Chiefs of Staff?

I think the answer lies in the preceding discussion, and the lengths to which these Generals would go to design by pretext, engineer, provoke or create by false cause a war.

And I think the answer also lies in the following discussion that was provided by General James Mattis.

While I was working on a subsequent chapter of this manuscript, sometime in February of 2005, a news item caught my attention that seemed to answer some of the questions I had about the appeal of being a soldier.

According to an audio recording, Marine Corps General Mattis stated: "Actually, it's a lot of fun to fight. You know, it's a hell of a hoot ... It's fun to shoot some people. I'll be right up front with you, I like brawling."[36]

General Mattis, who according to the Commandant of the U.S. Marine Corps, General Mike Hagee, "... often speaks with a great deal of candor..." also stated, "You know, guys like that, (referring to Afghan men) ain't got no manhood left anyway. So it's a hell of a lot of fun to shoot them."[37]

---

36 Yahoo News, "Marine General Counseled Over Comments," 2/4/05.

37 Ibid

> *"The Lord tests the righteous, but the wicked and the one who loves violence His soul hates."*
>
> (Psalms 11:5, NKJV)

> *"Deliver me from the workers of iniquity, and save me from bloodthirsty men."*
>
> (Psalms 59:2, NKJV)

These remarks are attributed to the same General Mattis who is now the commanding General of the Marine Corps Combat Development Command in Quantico, Virginia, where he is in charge of and responsible for developing ways to better train and equip marines.

Among fellow Marines, General Mattis is regarded as a fighting general and an expert in the 'art' of warfare. His comments evoked laughter and applause from the audience. General Mattis was speaking during a panel discussion hosted by the Armed Forces Communication and Electronics Association, a spokeswoman for the General said.

Nihad Awad, Executive Director of the Council on American-Islamic Relations, responded to General Mattis's remarks by stating, "We do not need generals who treat the grim business of war as a sporting event. These disturbing remarks are indicative of an apparent indifference to the value of human life."[38]

> *"To do evil is like sport to a fool, but a man of understanding has wisdom."*
>
> (Proverbs 10:23, NKJV)

According to an April 11th, 2005 issue of *American Free Press*, a former U.S. Army Corporal, Timothy McNiven, an outspoken critic of the president's handling of 9/11, who is also a 29 year U.S. Defense Department operative still under contract to the

38 Ibid.

government, said he has received a number of death threats after releasing information that his military unit in 1976 was commissioned by Congress to create the perfect terrorist plan to level the World Trade Center with airplanes and box cutters.

McNiven claims the threats were transmitted by email and "snail mail" from unknown origins in what he calls an ongoing harassment campaign to keep him quiet about the U.S. government-sponsored "perfect terrorist plan," almost identical to what happened on September the 11th. McNiven, however, disregarded the threats, telling his story to *American Free Press.*

Besides personal threats, he also claims other members of his military unit, including a man named Sergeant Riggs, were also threatened.

Riggs and the other more than 100 members of McNiven's unit have not come forward or spoken publicly yet about his claims.

McNiven told AFP, "I am just one of the enlisted men who took part, but I can confirm it took place and our plan was just like what went down on 9-11. There were about 100 people from my unit involved and I am actively seeking help to find them."

"Sergeant Riggs told me one day that he and others had their wives and children threatened by the U.S. government with retaliatory acts if they were to release their information to the media. But he said if I could break the censorship and get to the media first, he then would come forward and tell what he knows," McNiven said.

The Congressionally-commissioned study, assigned to 2/81st Field Artillery, U.S. Army, stationed in Strasbourg, Germany in 1976, specifically devised the scenario of the twin towers being leveled by Middle Eastern terrorists using commercial airliners and plastic box cutters to bypass security.

McNiven first went public with the hidden purpose behind the congressional study in an affidavit included in a 9-11 related federal conspiracy (RICO) lawsuit filed against Bush and others by Mrs. Ellen Mariani on September 12, 2003. (More will be said about this case in a subsequent chapter.)

The published version of the Congressionally-commissioned study was to identify security lapses and shortcomings and submit corrective measures to lawmakers. However, McNiven now claims the real purpose of the study was to brainstorm how to pull off the perfect terrorist attack using the same 9-11 scenario.

To further support his story and to silence and discredit critics, McNiven has successfully passed a credible lie detector test regarding his participation in the study as well as other specific orders given to him by his superiors, he has testified in a sworn affidavit contained in the federal 2003 RICO lawsuit filed against Bush, and he has provided the names of the men in his U.S. Army unit.

The head of the 1976 mock terrorist plan was Lieutenant Michael Teague of Long Island, who was given specific orders by military higher-ups to use the twin towers as the terrorist target.

McNiven said he has been unable to contact Lieutenant Teague, but was interested in his opinion now that "the 9/11 attacks happened the way we planned them in 1976."

"I remember Lieutenant Teague changed the scenario of the supposed study from a 100 story building to the twin towers," recalled McNiven, emphasizing that Teague was acting on specific orders from unknown superiors.

He then said he thought it was very strange to be asked to devise a plan to blow up your own hometown. "But as I watched the twin towers collapse on the morning of September 11th, I realized I was watching the very same thing we devised in 1976."

Since that ominous realization, McNiven has devoted his life to alerting the American public about the similarities between 9/11 and the Congressionally-commissioned study. Without much success, his story is being ignored by politicians and the mainstream media alike.

When explaining why he is trying to bring this story to the American people, McNiven claims he is still following a direct military order given to him more than 25 years ago. "During the course of the terrorist plan we were devising, I made the statement to Lieutenant Teague that if the World Trade Center was ever attacked like we planned, I'd go public. I was then physically assaulted and told never to reveal anything we were doing regarding the twin towers."

However, about a week later, a strange turn of events occurred. For no apparent reason, McNiven claims his superiors completely changed their minds.

"I was given the direct order that if the twin towers were ever attacked the way we discussed in the 1976 study, I was to do everything in my power to bring the similarities to the attention of the American people. I have no idea why they changed their minds, but I was then emphatically told that this order was never to be rescinded-never-because those who would rescind it, would be the very same people who turned against the American people.

Besides taking a lie detector test to verify his story, McNiven has made public a detailed list of about 40 names of those who took part in the congressional study/terrorist plan, including Colonel Robert Morrison, Major Joe Dipiero, Sergeant Middleton, Sergeant Arroyo and many others.

"There were also people from the Defense Department and the Central Intelligence Agency who were also monitoring the study, but I wasn't able to get their names," he added.

"I am willing to take additional polygraph exams to prove I am telling the truth until other participants in the study come forward."[39]

> *"Therefore each of you must put off falsehood and speak truthfully to his neighbor, for we are all members of one body."*
>
> (Ephesians 4:25, NIV)

As we proceed with subsequent chapters of this text, please keep Operation Northwoods and U.S. Army veteran Timothy McNiven's testimony in mind. We will refer to these periodically as we proceed with this study.

---

39 American Free Press, April 11, 2005, p. 4 and March 21, 2005, pp. 1,7.

CHAPTER TWO

Which Come to You in Sheep's Clothing

In April of 1962, President John F. Kennedy made the following remarks before a group of 49 Nobel Prize Winners: "I want to welcome you to the White House. I think this is the most extraordinary collection of talent, of human knowledge, that has ever been gathered together at the White House, with the possible exception of when Thomas Jefferson dined alone."[40]

Thomas Jefferson and his wonderful words for a Republic to live by:

Peace and friendship with all mankind is the wisest policy.

History in general only informs us of what bad government is.

If there be one principle more deeply rooted than any other in the mind of every American, it is that we should have nothing to do with conquest.

Wars and contentions indeed fill the pages of history with more matter. But more blest is that nation whose silent course of happiness furnishes nothing for history to say.

The spirit of this country is totally adverse to a large military.

Had the doctrines of Jesus been preached always as pure as they came from his lips, the whole civilized world would now have been Christian.

Having seen the people of all other nations bow down to the earth under the wars and prodigalities of their rulers, I have cherished the opposites, peace, economy, and riddance of the public debt.

We wish not to meddle with the internal affairs of any country.

---

40 Maureen Harrison and Steve Gilbert, Introduction.

Peace with all nations and the right which that peace gives us with respect to all nations, are our object.

Our first and fundamental maxim should be never to entangle ourselves in the toils of Europe.

I know of no safe depository of the ultimate powers of society but the people themselves.

It ought to be supplicated from heaven by the prayers of the whole world that at length there may be on earth peace and good will toward men.

Our citizens may be deceived for awhile and they have been deceived; but as long as the press can be protected we trust them for light.

What all agree in is probably right; what no two agree in is most probably wrong.

Under difficulties I have ever found one and only one rule, to do what is right, and generally we shall disentangle ourselves almost without perceiving how it happened.

Delay is preferable to error.

The boisterous sea of liberty is never without a wave.

It is incumbent on every generation to pay its own debt as it goes.

The God, who gave us life, gave us liberty at the same time.

We are not afraid to follow the truth wherever it may lead, nor to tolerate any error so long as reason is left free to combat it.

To inform the minds of the people and to follow their will is the chief duty of those placed at their head.

Our liberty depends on the freedom of the press, and that cannot be limited without being lost.

I tremble for my country when I reflect that God is just.

The newspapers are the first of all human contrivances for generating war.[41]

On Alliances:

I sincerely join you in abjuring all political connection with every foreign power; and though I cordially wish well to the progress of liberty in all nations, and would forever give it the

41 Ibid. pp. 3-12.

weight of our countenance, yet they are not to be touched without contamination from their other bad principles. Commerce with all nations, alliance with none, should be our motto.[42]

On Corporations:

I hope we shall take warning from the example of England and crush in its birth the aristocracy of our moneyed corporations which dare already to challenge our Government to trial, and bid defiance to the laws of our country.[43]

On the National Debt:

We are ruined, Sir, if we do not overrule the principle that "the more we owe, the more prosperous we shall be," that a public debt furnishes the means of enterprise, that if ours should be once paid off, we should incur another by any means however extravagant.[44]

On Foreign Entanglements:

Determined as we are to avoid if possible wasting the energies of our people in war and destruction, we shall avoid implicating ourselves with the powers of Europe even in the support of principles which we mean to pursue. They have so many other interests different from ours that we must avoid being entangled in them.[45]

On Peace:

Never was so much false arithmetic employed on any subject, as that which has been employed to persuade nations that it is in their interest to go to war. Were the money which it has cost to gain, at the close of a long war, a little town, or a little territory, the right to cut wood here, or to catch fish there, expended in improving what they already possess, in making roads, opening rivers, building ports, improving the arts and finding employment

---

42 Ibid. p. 359.

43 Ibid. p. 369.

44 Ibid.

45 Ibid. p. 378.

for their idle poor, it would render them much stronger, much wealthier and happier. This I hope will be our wisdom.[46]

On Truth:

Truth will do well enough if left to shift for herself. She seldom has received much aid from the power of great men to whom she is rarely known and seldom welcome.[47]

On Captives:

But is an enemy so execrable, that though in captivity, his wishes and comforts are to be disregarded or even crossed? I think not. It is for the benefit of mankind to mitigate the horrors of war as much as possible. The practice, therefore, of modern nations, of treating captive enemies with politeness and generosity, is not only delightful in contemplation, but really interesting to all the world, friends, foes and neutrals.[48]

On Tyranny:

Human nature is the same on every side of the Atlantic, and we will be alike influenced by the same causes. The time to guard against corruption and tyranny is before they have gotten hold of us. It is better to keep the wolf out of the fold than to trust to drawing his teeth and talons after he shall have entered.[49]

On the Peoples Rights and Duties Concerning Despotic Regimes:

Prudence indeed, will dictate that Governments long established should not be changed for light and transient Causes; and accordingly all Experience hath shewn, that Mankind are more disposed to suffer, while Evils are sufferable, than to right themselves by abolishing the Forms to which they are accustomed. But when a long Train of Abuses and Usurpations, pursuing invariably the same Object, evinces a Design to reduce them under absolute Despotism, it is their right, it is their Duty,

---

46 Ibid. p. 403.

47 Ibid. p. 416.

48 Ibid. p. 364.

49 Ibid. p. 417.

to throw off such Government, and to provide new Guards for their future Security.[50]

Please allow me a short digression here as I feel this is the proper location to insert text from James 5, Verses 1-6:

> *"Now listen, you rich people, weep and wail because of the misery that is coming upon you. Your wealth has rotted, and moths have eaten your clothes. Your gold and silver are corroded. Their corrosion will testify against you and eat your flesh like fire. You have hoarded wealth in the last days. Look! The wages you failed to pay the workmen who mowed your fields are crying out against you. The cries of the harvesters have reached the ears of the Lord Almighty. You have lived on earth in luxury and self-indulgence. You have fattened yourselves in the day of slaughter. You have condemned and murdered innocent men, who were not opposing you. "*
>
> (James 5:1-6, NIV)

On the Necessity of Maintaining Large Standing Armies:

A statement has been formed by the secretary of war, on mature consideration, of all the posts and stations where garrisons will be expedient, and of the number of men requisite for each garrison. The whole amount is considerably short of the present military establishment. For the surplus, no particular use can be pointed out. For defense against invasion, there number is as nothing; nor is it conceived needful or safe that a standing army should be kept up in times of peace for that purpose.[51]

You see, Thomas Jefferson was very much aware of the consequences of keeping a massive armed force and its potential for abuse at the hands of the worst element of society-the plutocracy.[52]

---

50 Ibid. pp. 47-48.

51 American Free Press, Memorial Day Special, 2004, p. B.3.

52 Ibid.

These are the same concerns as expressed generations later by Dwight D. Eisenhower when he warned us against the "disastrous rise of misplaced power" by the military-industrial complex.

Our nation's founding fathers had much common advice for future generations of American citizens and office holders alike, concerning large standing armies, war and peace, freedom and oppression, and foreign entanglements and alliances.

George Washington's Farewell Address to the nation in 1796 had many preeminent parting words of advice for future generations. Some of the most pertinent for this discussion follow:

"Hence, likewise, they will avoid the necessity of those overgrown military establishments, which under any form of government, are inauspicious to liberty, and which are to be regarded as particularly hostile to republican liberty.

Towards the preservation of your government, and the permanency of your present happy state, it is requisite, not only that you steadily discountenance irregular oppositions to its acknowledged authority, but also that you resist with care the spirit of innovation upon its principles, however specious the pretexts. One method of assault may be to effect in the forms of the Constitution, alterations which will impair the energy of the system, and thus to undermine what cannot be directly overthrown. [An appropriate example of this would be the Patriot Act, and the Homeland Security Act.] Observe good faith and justice towards all nations; cultivate peace and harmony with all.

... Nothing is more essential than that permanent, inveterate antipathies against particular nations, and passionate attachments for others should be excluded; and in place of them, just and amicable feelings towards all should be cultivated. The nation which indulges towards another a habitual hatred or a habitual fondness is in some degree a slave. It is a slave to its animosity or to its affection, either of which is sufficient to lead it astray from its duty and its interest...

So likewise, a passionate attachment of one nation for another produces a variety of evils. Sympathy for the favorite nation, facilitating the illusion of an imaginary common interest in cases where no real common interest exists, and infusing into one the enmities of the other, betrays the former into a participation in the quarrels and wars of the latter without adequate inducement or justification. It also leads to concessions to the favorite nation of privileges denied to others which is apt doubly to injure the nation making the concessions; by unnecessarily parting with what ought to be retained, and by exciting jealousy, ill-will, and a disposition to retaliate, in the parties from whom equal privileges are with held. And it gives to ambitious, corrupted, or deluded citizens, (who devote themselves to the favorite nation), facility to betray or sacrifice the interests of their own country, without odium, sometimes even with popularity; gilding, with the appearance of a virtuous sense of obligation, a commendable deference for public opinion, or a laudable zeal for public good, the base or foolish compliance of ambition, corruption, or infatuation.

Against the insidious wiles of foreign influence (I conjure you to believe me fellow citizens) the jealousy of a free people ought to be constantly awake, since history and experience prove that foreign influence is one of the most baneful foes of republican government.

Excessive partiality for one nation and excessive dislike of another cause those whom they actuate to see danger only on one side, and serve to veil and even second the arts of influence on the other. Real Patriots who may resist the intrigues of the favorite are liable to become suspected and odious, while its tools and dupes usurp the applause and confidence of the people, to surrender their interests.

The great rule of conduct for us in regard to foreign nations is in extending our commercial relations, to have with them as little political connection as possible.

It is our true policy to steer clear of permanent alliances with any portion of the foreign world... Harmony, liberal intercourse with all nations, are recommended by policy, humanity and interest."[53]

And James Madison, our fourth president, in August of 1793, had this to say about war's detrimental effect on liberty:

"Of all the enemies to public liberty war is, perhaps, the most to be dreaded, because it comprises and develops the germ of every other. War is the parent of armies; from these precede debts and taxes; and armies, and debts, and taxes are the known instruments for bringing the many under the domination of the few. In war too, the discretionary power of the Executive is extended; its influence in dealing out offices, honors, and emoluments is multiplied; and all the means of seducing the minds, are added to those of subduing the force, of the people... [There is also an] inequality of fortunes, and the opportunities of fraud, growing out of a state of war... No nation could preserve its freedom in the midst of continual warfare...

The powers proposed to be surrendered to the Executive were those which the Constitution has most jealously appropriated to the legislature...

The Constitution expressly and exclusively vests in the Legislature the power of declaring a state of war... the power of raising armies..."[54]

And so, the very founders of our great republic laid the strong foundation with some of the most important policies, advice and wise counsel they shared in common: Friendship with all nations, favoritism towards none, warnings against large military establishments, neutral foreign policies, avoidance of conquest, and no meddling in the internal affairs of foreign nations. Commerce and liberal intercourse with all nations, alliances with none. Cultivate peace and harmony with all, and advice concerning war's detrimental affect and negative impact on our liberties.

---

53 The Avalon Project, Washington Farewell Address, 1796, www.yale.edu/lawweb/avalon/washing.htm.

54 Ahmed, "The War on Freedom," p. 329.

And every Independence Day, our current and surviving presidents, congressmen and other "public servants" make a public and ceremonial display of acknowledging our founding fathers and their great wisdom, foresight, wise counsel and advice, and how they laid the cornerstones and foundations for our great republic. To pay executive and legislative lip service is one thing, but it seems when it comes to our current policies, especially our foreign policies, we have come so far as to seem to totally ignore and disregard our founding fathers' advice, to the point that the very foundations of our republic and great nation have been shaken, if not shattered and obliterated. And when the foundation crumbles, the rest usually comes down with it.

And just like the collapse of the World Trade Center towers on September the 11th, we may discover that the complete disregard to our nation's founders' wise council, advice and foresight, more than likely, may have been a contributing, if not, a direct causal factor.

As you read the following discussion, I ask you again to please keep "Operation Northwoods," discussed in Chapter One, in mind. And please also keep our nation's founders' advice in mind as we proceed with this study.

An article in *American Free Press* by investigative reporter Christopher Bollyn, entitled "9-11 Mysteries Remain," discussed how three years after the events of 9-11, half of the residents of New York City believe U.S. leaders had foreknowledge and consciously failed to act to prevent the disasters, while two out of three want a new investigation.

In the first survey of public opinion about allegations of U.S. government complicity and whitewashing of the events of 9-11, a Zogby International poll found that fewer than two in five New Yorkers believe the official 9-11 commission "answered all of the important questions about what actually happened on 9-11." One in two New York City residents say that senior government officials "knew in advance that attacks were planned on or around Sept. 11th, 2001 and that they failed consciously to act."[55]

55 American Free Press, September 20, 2004.

Going even further, there is a growing number of Americans who believe the events of 9-11 were an "inside job," according to Bollyn of *American Free Press*. Supported by evidence aired by independent researchers outside of the mainstream press, the public is becoming increasingly aware of the questionable quality of the official 9-11 explanation.

Photographs from the Pentagon and the World Trade Center are analyzed in a recently released video documentary entitled *9-11 In Plane Site*, produced by Dave vonKleist of the radio program "The Power Hour" based in Versailles, Missouri.

Mr. vonKleist says that examination of the videos of the United Airlines flight 175 and the American Airlines flight 11 planes striking the twin towers in slow motion suggests that the attacks were a military operation. Careful analysis of the video indicates the planes appear to be equipped with missile pods attached to the undersides. Mr. vonKleist argues that incendiary missiles can be seen being fired immediately before impact with the buildings.

The most compelling images from the *9-11 In Plane Site* documentary are of the aircraft that is said to be United Airlines flight 175 as it crashes into the South Tower. According to the producer, these photographs, taken from four different angles, all seem to indicate that the plane is a Boeing 767-300 military tanker with a missile pod attached to its underside between the wings, not a shorter Boeing 767-200, as claimed. (Please see www.911inplanesite.com and www.letsroll911.org

Mr. vonKleist said that this evidence supports the theory that United Airlines flight 175 and American Airlines flight 11 landed at Stewart International Airport/Air Force Base, where they crossed as they approached New York City, and that weaponized planes replaced them and continued their flights to the twin towers.[56]

Remember in the Operation Northwoods plan, part of that planned pretext for war called for creating a scenario where a military drone aircraft, armed with a remote-controlled

56 Ibid. October 18, 2004.

detonation explosive device, and painted to look exactly like a civilian commercial aircraft, would be substituted for the civilian aircraft which would divert to Elgin Air Force Base while the drone aircraft continued to its destination. While over Cuba, the military drone would be exploded by remote control in order to convince the American public and the Congress that we had been attacked by Cuba. The similarities are alarming.

Remember also the testimony of U.S. Army veteran Timothy McNiven and his description of the 1976 Congressionally-commissioned study of the perfect terrorist plan involving commercial airliner crashes into the World Trade Center towers.

Returning to 9-11, as television cameras broadcast live images, millions of viewers watched the second plane strike the South Tower at about 9:03 am. The second plane is said to be United flight 175, hijacked by Arab terrorists with box cutters.

The video images, however, do not support this version. There are a number of anomalies that indicate that the plane that struck the South Tower may not have been a passenger jet at all.

These images can be seen on videos of the WTC attacks, for example the CNN production *America Remembers.* A slow-motion viewing of the images reveals, as seen as the plane banks to the left before striking the South Tower, on the underside of the aircraft, between the wings, a cylindrical object. Is it a missile pod?

A former pilot with United Airlines who has flown the Boeing 767-200, the same type as United 175 on 9-11, told *American Free Press* that the cylindrical object is not a normal part of the aircraft. The official version, he added, is a "fairy tale, pure Hollywood."

Slow motion viewing reveals that immediately before plunging into the tower, the pod on the bottom of the plane releases a white object that enters the building with a white flash before the nose of the plane pierces the façade, reported the United Airlines pilot. The flash is reflected on the plane's fuselage indicating a separate event.

A similar flash is seen in the video of American Flight 11 striking the North Tower. In this case, the flash occurs before the plane hits the North Tower.

The flashes are thought to be evidence that the planes that struck the World Trade Center towers were military drones that carried incendiary high explosive missiles to cause the huge explosions. These massive explosions were intended to destroy evidence of the planes and create the spectacle and logical pretext for the controlled demolition of the towers that followed.[57]

After I watched the Dave vonKleist produced documentary video *9-11 In Plane Site*, Dave asked me to email him my reactions and comments. The selected comments are included as follows:

Dear Mr. vonKleist,

I wanted to thank you again for the DVD. I told you I would get back with you with my input about the object that appears on the bottom side of the B-767 that struck the South tower.

Looking at the video in slow motion, as the plane approaches the tower; you can see the foreign object under the right wing, near the wing root, or inboard. As the plane approaches the tower, towards the aft area of the object, it appears to get larger, with a white appearance, then that area becomes somewhat smokey. This occurs just before the flash appears in the video. I believe this is indicative of something being launched from that foreign object.

As far as that flash of light being a "static discharge" as reported by some, the B-767 as well as all airliners have attached to the aft areas of the flight controls, the wings, the rudder, what are called static wicks that are attached to dissipate static charges that may develop on the aircraft.

Normally, when an aircraft becomes statically charged, the pilots can hear this static in their radios as static interference. In my 20 plus years of flying, the only time an aircraft has been statically charged enough to cause radio static interference was when we were flying for extended periods of time through areas of precipitation. This can cause an aircraft to become statically charged, just like rubbing your comb on wool. And since 9-11 was

57 Ibid.

a nice day and all these aircraft flew through precipitation-free skies, I seriously doubt the "static discharge" possible explanation for the source of the flash as seen in the video.

I would also like to address the pieces of debris that come out the other side of the tower after it was hit. The aircraft wreckage combined with other building debris is losing speed and momentum, which would be expected when a thrust force is removed from a flying object. When thrust is removed-in this case, the loss of jet engine thrust-the opposing horizontal force, which is drag, becomes the greater force, which causes this debris to decelerate. Also, as the force of lift is also decreased or removed from a flying object-in this case, the loss of functioning wings-the opposing vertical force, which is gravity or weight, becomes the greater force which causes this debris to begin falling towards the earth. This applies to just about all debris except for one piece that seems to still have its own thrust force acting on it and pushing it and which appears visibly in the video as a white plume of what appears to be missile exhaust from the attached thrust source. This piece of debris seems to continue on its straight flight trajectory without any noticeable trace of a drag or gravity force acting on it, slowing it down and causing it to fall towards the earth like all other pieces. This seems to be the case for as long as the video shows this before the video stops.

Anyway Dave, I did share the DVD with another pilot friend of mine yesterday who was affected by it. Don, my friend, had never really considered the "inside job" nature of 9-11. But after viewing the DVD and discussing the evidence, I think he now considers the probabilities. Anyway, I'll still try and share this with as many of my pilot friends and others as I can. Thanks Dave, Merry Christmas.

I can not more highly recommend that one purchase and view this documentary. If you have the CNN video America Remembers in DVD form, just slow the footage down to 1/8 or 1/16 if you can. Or even better, just step through the DVD with the pause/still button.

It's amazing the details that become rather obvious in slow motion. As you step through the footage, as the aircraft pierces through the South tower, you can see where the cockpit enters, where the engines enter, where the wings enter, and where the fuselage enters. Now as you "step" through this footage, notice where the pod was attached to the fuselage. As the aircraft pierces the façade, you can also see an enlarged area on the bottom right of the fuselage, a larger torn area of façade, similar to where the engines penetrated. If the fuselage were smooth in this area, i.e., no missile pod, this area of façade penetration would be smooth and even like the rest of the fuselage.

Also, as you step through the footage as the aircraft approaches the South Tower from the side view, you can see the entire right side of the aircraft light up due to this missile launch. The aircraft approaches in the shadow of the smoke from the North Tower, so this bright reflection lighting up the entire right side of the aircraft is not associated with sunlight reflection and it looks exactly like the launch sequence of a missile from any military attack or fighter jet.

There are other indications that the plane was not United 175. A hole is seen on the underside of the plane near the tail, which appears to be the boom port for the refueling line of a Boeing 767 military tanker, said vonKleist.

Eyewitnesses, including a reporter from Fox News who saw the aircraft, reported seeing a windowless plane that did not look like a commercial jet. The Fox reporter said the plane had a round, blue logo painted near the front.[58]

I wonder if there was a white star in the middle of that round blue logo.

There are many problems with the official explanation of the crash of American Flight 77 at the Pentagon also.

American Flight 77, a Boeing 757 with 64 passengers out of a possible 289, allegedly took off from Washington Dulles International Airport, IAD, destined for Los Angeles, LAX, also on the morning of September the 11th.

58 Ibid.

At 8:47, despite having its transponder turned off by the "hijackers," air traffic controllers could see that American 77 had reversed course over West Virginia and was heading back to the East Coast.[59]

The transponder on board all commercial aircraft is an avionics unit that is used to respond to air traffic control interrogation radar. When a flight crew receives their clearance from air traffic clearance delivery or ground control, after giving its route, initial altitude and expected cruise altitude, and ATC departure control radio frequency, the flight crew is told to "squawk" a four-digit discreet code. This code is put into the transponder and when the flight is aloft, the transponder responds to ATC radar. This provides the air traffic controller with the airline's flight number, current altitude and its current position, called a data block. The air traffic controller uses this information to safely separate aircraft as part of the services that ATC provide.

When an aircraft that does not have a transponder, or an aircraft with the transponder turned off is aloft, air traffic control can still see the aircraft as a primary target, except where primary radar coverage is out, which happened to be the case in the area of the Northeast Sector where these 9-11 flights transversed.[60] It appears as a blip on the radar screen and can still be tracked by primary radar, again if primary radar is up in a particular area or sector.

As an example, years ago, when I was flying light Cessna and Piper aircraft, sometimes we would fly one with either no transponder or an inoperative transponder. Upon initial contact with air traffic control, we would simply state, "Negative transponder." The controller would then ask our approximate position and current heading or compass direction. After replying, the controller would then instruct us to turn to a new heading or direction. As the controller observed your primary target change course on his or her radar screen, the controller would state

59 Jim Marrs, "Inside Job, Unmasking the 9/11 Conspiracies," Origin Press, San Rafael,CA, p.2.

60 "911-Holes in the Radar," www.team8plus.org/the-movement/radar/Radar.htm, 10/2/05.

that they, ATC, had positive radar contact on your flight, and could then provide standard ATC services. So, an aircraft with the transponder turned off can still be tracked by ATC where primary radar coverage is available.

On December 7th, 2004, I decided to call a good friend of mine who I used to work with years ago when I was in college. We worked together at UPS, throwing freight as it were, part-time. I had to finance flight training somehow.

Roger, my friend, became an air traffic controller and has been employed as a center controller at Indianapolis Center for about 15-20 years now.

I told Roger what I was working on and asked him if he had heard any suspicious type of remarks concerning the events of 9/11 from any of his peers or coworkers. He said he had not, but that the Indianapolis Center controller who worked or tracked American 77 had been given some time off for stress and that he did in fact pass away from what Roger remembered as a heart attack, having never returned from his stress leave. Roger also said that he and most of his peers felt that the events of 9/11 were not a result of an inside conspiracy, but were probably the result of not expecting the unexpected. He did say, however, that it wouldn't surprise him much if he were to later find out there was more to 9/11 than what he had been told, and that he thought it was kind of weird that his coworker never returned, having passed away.

I then asked him about radar coverage in the West Virginia, Southeast Ohio area, and he said there were probably a lot of non-radar environments at the lower altitudes in those areas, due to mountainous or high terrain.

He did also state when asked that a B-757 with its transponder turned off would still appear as a primary target and that its data block would still accompany the primary target due to computer generation. I then asked Roger if a B-757 diverted to an alternate airport, with its transponder turned off, and then another aircraft took off from an approximate location without a transponder, therefore also a primary target in primary radar coverage, could a controller tell any difference from these targets. In other words, if a B-757 diverted to an alternate airport, and if a global hawk or any other type of drone aircraft or cruise missile was launched from a similar location, could a controller easily assume that the new primary target (drone aircraft or cruise missile) was the old primary target (B-757) that reappeared on radar, after having lost the old (B-757) primary target due to lack of radar coverage in the mountainous terrain? Roger answered in the affirmative, that indeed, a controller would not be able to tell the difference and could easily assume a new (drone aircraft or cruise missile) primary target could be the old (B-757) primary target that was temporarily lost on radar due to terrain or other factors.

Roger and I continued our conversation, discussing families, kids, sports, etc. I then asked Roger if he would please give me a call if he ever hears any remarks from his coworkers at Indianapolis Center concerning 9/11. He said he certainly would.[61]

I called Roger again shortly after this to ask him if he would speak to Christopher Bollyn of *American Free Press*, who by now I had spoken with several times. I was hoping Roger would just speak to Chris, who said he'd like to ask him a few questions. Unfortunately, Roger chose not to speak with Chris as described in this correspondence with Mr. Bollyn:

Chris,

Roger, my ATC friend called. I asked if he would be willing to talk with you. I told him you were a nice guy and everything. Anyway, Roger declined. He said he'd been on the wrong side of management with a couple of operational errors. Blah Blah Blah. That he has 8 or 9 years until retirement, etc. He did say that NATCA (National Air Traffic Controllers Association) might be a good source. He said they're in DC. Sorry Chris. I thought Roger would be willing to talk. I even asked if he remained anonymous if that would work. Still declined. Anyway, I'll still try and get you and Eric (Hufschmid) some good photos. If there is anything else I can do please let me know. Thanks. Take Care.

Glen

61 Interview, Mr. Roger Lucas, Air Traffic Control Specialist.

Glen (and Eric),

This is what we have come to expect. Americans are too afraid to speak out when it comes to 9/11 and mass murder. They don't want to lose their pensions, etc. This is the BIGGEST obstacle to finding the truth. How does it go? All that it takes for evil to conquer is that good men do nothing.[62]

Chris Bollyn

At about 9:35 on the morning of 9/11, American flight 77, with its transponder turned off, allegedly began making a complicated 270 or more degree descending, steep spiraling turn. At 9:40, it reportedly crashed into the west side of the Pentagon, penetrating three of its five rings of offices, killing 185 persons.[63]

Why NORAD chose not to scramble fighter/interceptor aircraft from Andrews Air Force Base, which is 10 miles away, but instead chose to dispatch interceptors from Langley Air Force Base which is 130 miles away is worth contemplating, especially when one considers that air defense around Washington, DC is provided mainly by fighter planes from Andrews Air Force Base in Maryland, near the DC border. The DC Air National Guard is also based there and is equipped with F-16 fighter jets, according to a National Guard spokesman.[64]

It is thus clear that combat-ready fighters assigned to the protection of Washington DC did not do anything at all for about an hour and a half, although it was known that American 77 was heading to DC.[65]

Indeed, Andrews Air Force Base, which is tasked with air defense around DC, houses two combat-ready squadrons served by hundreds of full-time personnel. The 121st Fighter Squadron of the 113th Fighter Wing, equipped with F-16 fighters, and the 321st Marine Fighter Attack Squadron of the 49th Marine Air Group, Detachment A, equipped with F/A, Fighter Attack,

62 Email from Christopher Bollyn, American Free Press.

63 Marrs, p. 3.

64 Ahmed, p. 154.

65 Ibid. p. 155.

-18 fighters comprise the aerial defense over the nations capitol that allow its citizens to sleep soundly at night. According to the authoritative U.S. military information website, DC Military, "... as part of its dual mission, the 113th provides capable and ready response forces for the District of Columbia in the event of a natural disaster or civil emergency."[66]

In other words, Andrews AFB, an active facility had at least two combat-ready squadrons designated for capable and ready response whose task was to defend DC in the event of a natural disaster or civil emergency.[67]

As an independent researcher on the events of 9/11 points out, "The media should have demanded to know the truth about why fighter jets assigned to protect Washington DC didn't scramble an hour before the Pentagon was hit."[68]

He asks: "Since planes were flying into buildings, and since Washington, DC was the city most likely to be the next target, why would planes be scrambled all the way from Langley AFB, 129 miles away as late as 9:30? Why wouldn't they be scrambled from Andrews AFB, 10 miles from the Pentagon at around 8:50, when the military knew that a hijacked plane had hit the World Trade Center?"[69]

It seems appropriate at this time to review standard procedure and the U.S. Air defense system's response to civil aircraft that may have departed from their flight plans. A clear example of this routine procedure is the FAA's (Federal Aviation Administration) response when the Lear jet chartered by golf professional Payne Stewart deviated from its flight path while the pilots failed to reply to Air Traffic Control by radio. MS-NBC reported that, "pilots are supposed to hit each fix with pinpoint accuracy. If a plane deviates by 15 degrees, or two miles from that course, the flight controllers will hit the panic button... when golfer Payne

66 Ibid.

67 Ibid.

68 Ibid. p. 156.

69 Ibid.

Stewart's Lear jet missed a turn at a fix, heading north instead of west to Texas, F-16 interceptors were quickly dispatched."[70]

CNN reported: "Several Air Force and Air National Guard fighter jets plus an AWACS radar control plane helped the FAA track the runaway Lear jet and estimate when it would run out of fuel."[71]

ABC News reported that: "First a fighter jet from Tyndall, Florida was diverted from a routine training flight to check out the Lear jet. Two F-16s from another Florida base then picked up the chase, later handing it over to two Air National Guard F-16s from Oklahoma, which handed it over to two F-16s from Fargo, North Dakota."[72]

It should be reiterated that standard procedures also require controllers to immediately alert the military to scramble fighter jets if an aircraft deviates from its flight path and communication between the plane and air traffic control is lost. This should occur whether the situation is Payne Stewart's Lear jet deviating off course due to incapacitated pilots, or singular or multiple, near simultaneous, major airline hijackings, such as occurred on 9/11. [73]

The well-known example of Payne Stewart's Lear jet also gives an idea of the acceptable time periods of a routine air response. Remember, on 9/11, there was hardly a response at all.

From the official National Transportation Safety Board accident report, the following timeline details the routine response times:

9:19 am. Payne Stewart's Lear jet departs.

9:24 am. The Lear jet's pilots respond to an instruction from ATC.

70 Ibid. p. 146.

71 Ibid.

72 Ibid. p. 147.

73 Ibid. p. 148.

9:33 am. ATC radios another instruction and receives no reply from the pilots. For the next 4 and ½ minutes, ATC tries to re-establish radio contact with the pilots.

9:38 am. Having failed to re-establish two-way radio contact, the controller calls in the military. Note that the controller did not seek, nor did he require the approval of the President of the United States or anyone else. It is standard procedure, followed routinely, to call in the Air Force when radio contact is lost with a private or commercial passenger jet, or when a private or commercial airplane departs from its flight plan or during any similar circumstance.

9:54 am. Sixteen minutes elapsed time total. An F-16 reaches the Lear jet at 46,000 feet and conducts a visual inspection of the Lear jet.[74]

Please remember that amount of elapsed time: 16 minutes.

Now the official U.S. government explanation of the dire failure to protect the nation's capitol, Washington DC, can be found in excerpts from an NBC News conference with Vice President Dick Cheney. Journalist Tim Russert: "What's the most important decision you think he (President Bush) made during the course of the day (9/11)? Dick Cheney: "Well, the-I suppose the toughest decision was the question of whether or not we would intercept incoming commercial aircraft... We decided to do it."[75]

Cheney had created the impression to the audience that the U.S. military required presidential authorization to scramble fighter jets to intercept American flight 77 before it hit the Pentagon. But we have just seen that no authorization is required or expected. It is standard operating procedure to scramble interceptors immediately to any aircraft suspected of hijacking or other similar emergency.[76]

74 Ibid. pp. 148-149.

75 Ibid. p. 157.

76 Ibid.

According to Air Force standard procedure, presidential approval is only required for *shooting down* a civilian aircraft. Therefore, the idea that the interception of the incoming commercial aircraft by fighter planes was "the toughest decision" to be made on presidential authority is a contradiction of the rules recorded in FAA documents, which clearly establish that fighter jets intercept private and commercial aircraft as a matter of routine and therefore was most likely, an attempt by the Vice president to misinform the public."[77]

Of course, this would not have been the first time in U.S. history for such an occurrence. Remember Bill Clinton, "I did not have sexual relations with that woman..." or George H.W. Bush, "Read my lips..." or Richard Nixon, "I am not a crook..." There could, of course, be many more examples.

So, contrary to what the vice president implied, and as documented here, jet fighter interceptions are followed through automatically, and on a mandatory basis, such as during hijackings and other emergencies.[78]

So, then the obvious question that must be asked by the American people and the international community is, why did no fighter aircraft scramble for interception when American flight 77 was hijacked, between 8:50 and 8:55 a.m., and the time the plane smashed into the Pentagon at 9:41 a.m., a total of 46 to 51 minutes elapsed time, when Payne Stewart's Lear jet was intercepted and visually sighted in a grand total of 16 minutes?

The answer most probably lies in the idea that the Pentagon brass, the Directors of the CIA and FBI, the National Security Council, the Secretary of State, and the President and Vice President, did not need a junior Lieutenant F-16 pilot and flight officer interfering with the creation of the cover story and the illusion of September the 11th by witnessing and then reporting that what actually hit the Pentagon, was in fact, not an American Airlines Boeing 757.

77 Ibid.

78 Ibid.

"They have all turned aside, they have together become corrupt; there is none who does good, no, not one."

(Psalms 14:3, NKJV)

"I have hated the assembly of evil-doers, and will not sit with the wicked."

(Psalms 26:5, NKJV)

"Do not gather my soul with sinners, nor my life with blood-thirsty men, In whose hands is a sinister scheme, and whose right hand is full of bribes."

(Psalms 26:9, 10, NKJV)

Let's continue our discussion and research for the support for these answers. Mrs. April Gallop was at work inside the Pentagon's west side when it was struck by a flying object on 9/11. Mrs. Gallop was getting ready to take her infant son to day care when an explosion rocked the Pentagon. "I thought it was a bomb," she recalled. "I was buried in rubble and my first thought was for my son. I crawled around until I found his stroller. It was all crumpled up into a ball and I was very afraid. But I heard his voice and managed to locate him. We crawled out through a hole in the side of the building. Outside they were treating survivors on the grassy lawn."[79]

Mrs. Gallop said while she was in the hospital, men in suites visited her more than once. "They never identified themselves or even said which agency they worked for. But I know they were not newsmen because I later learned that the Pentagon told news reporters not to cover survivors' stories or they would not get any more stories out of there. The men who visited all said they couldn't tell me what to say, they only wanted to make suggestions. But then they told me what to do, which was to take the victim

79 Marrs, p. 26.

compensation fund money and shut up. They also kept insisting that a plane hit the building. They repeated this over and over. But I was there and I never saw a plane or even debris from a plane."[80]

It is well worth noting here that the FBI confiscated all the security videos in the vicinity of the crash within minutes, including video from the Sheraton Hotel adjacent to the Pentagon.[81] This hotel is where we used to layover on overnights with TWA. This location provided a fairly convenient walk across the Pentagon property to Arlington National Cemetery, a sightseeing and walking tour I took on a couple of DC layovers. It was reported that when the FBI arrived to take this security camera footage, hotel employees were in the process of watching what actually struck the Pentagon and were warned by federal agents not to discuss what they saw.[82]

Other security camera footage confiscated came from Virginia Department of Transportation highway sign-mounted cameras and from a convenience store and gas station located adjacent to the Pentagon.[83] Sometime later, the Pentagon released a mere five frames from one of their security cameras, which showed a barely discernable object slamming into the building, followed by a huge fireball.[84]

One of the major mysteries concerning the Pentagon crash centers on what exactly happened to American Flight 77, a Boeing 757 carrying 64 passengers. According to official sources, the entire plane was consumed inside the walls of the Pentagon. Yet almost 4 years after 9/11, no one has produced any photographs of B-757 fuselage, jet engines, seats, luggage, main landing gear or other distinctly identifiable and recognizable parts of a B-757.[85]

---

80 Ibid.

81 Ibid. p. 27.

82 American Free Press.

83 Ibid.

84 Marrs, p. 27.

85 Dave vonkleist, "911 In Plane Site," Documentary DVD.

This is extremely difficult for me to believe. Throughout my flying career, flying regional turboprop aircraft for USAir Express, flying DC-9 and MD, "Super-80" turbojet aircraft for TWA and American Airlines, and my current position flying B-737-800s for ATA, I have been very concerned about aircraft and airline accidents and their causes.

As flight crewmembers, we are required as part of our training with the airlines, both as new hires and during our FAA required annual recurrent training, to cover C.R.M., or Cockpit or Crew Resource Management. This training covers airline accidents and incidents, their causal factors, and as crew members, what we could or should have done differently to have prevented the type of occurrence studied.

Take for example the TWA 800 accident, a B-747 which had just departed New York's JFK International Airport bound for Paris, France. Supposedly, the aircraft suffered a catastrophic freak center fuel tank explosion, came apart in mid air at an altitude of about 14,000 feet and came crashing down into the Atlantic Ocean off Long Island. Now I am of the understanding there may be more to the story of the cause of the TWA 800 accident, including the possibility of a terrorist missile attack or a U.S. military training test gone awry. Regardless, the B-747 suffered an explosion in the air and came crashing down into the Atlantic.

Do you think distinctly identifiable pieces of that aircraft were hard to find? Well, the NTSB, the US Navy, the Coast Guard, the FBI, and the FAA were able to recover just about the entire aircraft and completely rebuild it in a Calverton, New York hangar.

And what about the USAir Flight 427 accident, a Boeing 737 that crashed in the Pittsburgh suburb of Aliquippa, Pennsylvania during its arrival from Chicago, ORD. I remember that night. We were out flying for USAir Express, sitting in operations in Philadelphia, waiting to go to Erie, and then to Pittsburgh. Evidently, the B-737 encountered a hard over rudder condition, a definite flight control problem. The aircraft became uncontrollable, rolled over on its back, and spun into the ground at a high rate of speed and descent.

Was there any problem finding distinctly visible and identifiable pieces of the USAir B-737? Not at all, Aerial photographs of the wreckage clearly show landing gear, pieces of the wing and tail with flight controls still attached, pieces of luggage, aircraft seats and human remains were also found.

How about the Delta L-1011 that crashed at DFW during thunderstorm activity that encountered unrecoverable windshear and microburst activity. You could still see the entire tail section, charred a bit, along with other wreckage that was distinctly identifiable as pieces of that particular L-1011.

How about the United DC-10 that crashed in the cornfields of Iowa. Again, yes indeed, distinctly identifiable parts remained, and survivors also lived to tell their stories. But again, aircraft parts, power plants, landing gear, large pieces of fuselage, airframe, luggage, seats and human remains were found at the crash site and were all positively identifiable.

There was a crash on a Holloween night a few years ago of an American Eagle ATR turboprop aircraft in Northern Indiana, holding at the time in icing conditions, waiting for traffic congestion at Chicago, OHARE (ORD), to clear up. The aircraft's wings iced up; the aircraft stalled and became uncontrollable and spun into the ground at a very high rate of speed and descent. Again, aircraft wreckage and human remains were recovered.

There was a Valuejet DC-9 that crashed in the Florida everglades, caused by an uncontrollable fire in the forward cargo hold. The DC-9 came crashing into the Everglades on its attempted return to the departure airport. This time too, believe it or not, aircraft wreckage remained and was concluded to have come from that specific DC-9. There is always a large debris field when a large airliner crashes.

Just one more example before we review what retired United States Air Force Colonel George Nelson has to say about this matter.

On February 1, 2003, the Space Shuttle Columbia, approximately 40 miles above Texas, descending on its atmospheric re-entry at approximately 12,000 miles per hour, broke up due to structural failure, apparently caused by pieces of foam insulation from one of the rocket boosters striking the leading edge of the left wing on lift off. Wreckage of the shuttle and the remains of the seven astronauts were strewn across miles of countryside. Again, both pieces of the Columbia Space Shuttle and human remains of the astronauts were found and determined to be from that particular mission and spacecraft.

But yet, American Airlines Flight 77, a Boeing 757 with 64 souls on board, which allegedly crashed into the Pentagon, left absolutely no identifiable pieces of B-757 wreckage. No pieces of heavy, strong main and nose landing gear, and there should be a total of ten wheels, 2 on the nose gear, and 4 on each main landing gear truck. No pieces of wings, tail, fuselage, flight controls, flaps, large turbofan engines, cockpit seats, passenger seats, position lights, luggage, mail or freight were found which were distinctly identifiable as part of a B-757 or that came from American Airlines flight 77.

Yes indeed, water does vaporize; but I think we can safely and positively conclude from the above discussion that Boeing 757s, or any other large transport category type aircraft, do not vaporize. They do not liquefy, they do not melt, they do not oxidize, and they do not disintegrate to the molecular level, even when crashed into terrain or buildings at 400 to 500+ miles per hour.

But let's carefully consider what Colonel George Nelson, United States Air Force (retired) has to say about this subject matter. In an article entitled, "911 and the Precautionary Principle: Aircraft Parts as a Clue to their Identity," he writes:

"The precautionary principle is based on the fact that it is impossible to prove a false claim. Failure to prove a claim does not automatically make it false, but caution is called for, especially in the case of a world-changing event like the alleged terror attacks of September 11, 2001. The Bush administration has provided no public evidence to support its claim that the terror attacks were the work of Muslim extremists or even that the aircraft that struck their respective targets on September 11, were as advertised. As I will show below, it would be a simple matter to confirm that they were. Until such proof is forthcoming, the opposite claim must be kept in mind as a precaution against rushing to judgement: the 911 hijackings were part of a black operation carried out with the cooperation of elements in our government.

In July 1965 I had just been commissioned as a Second Lieutenant in the U.S. Air Force after taking a solemn oath that I would protect and defend the Constitution against all enemies, foreign and domestic, and that I would bear true faith and allegiance to the same. I took that oath very seriously. It was my constant companion throughout a thirty-year military career in the field of aircraft maintenance.

As an additional duty, aircraft maintenance officers are occasionally tasked as members of aircraft accident investigation boards and my personal experience was no exception. In 1989, I graduated from the Aircraft Mishap Investigation Course at the Institute of Safety and Systems Management at the University of Southern California. In addition to my direct participation as an aircraft accident investigator, I reviewed countless aircraft accident investigation reports for thoroughness and comprehensive conclusions for the Inspector General, Head Quarters Pacific Air Forces during the height of the Vietnam conflict.

In all my years of direct and indirect participation, I never witnessed nor even heard of an aircraft loss, where the wreckage was accessible, that prevented investigators from finding enough hard evidence to positively identify the make, model and specific registration number of the aircraft-and in most cases the precise cause of the accident. This is because every military and civilian passenger-carrying aircraft have many parts that are identified for the safety of flight. That is, if any of the parts were to fail at any time during a flight, the failure would likely result in the catastrophic loss of aircraft and passengers. Consequently, these parts are individually controlled by a distinctive serial number and tracked by a records section of the maintenance operation and by another section called plans and scheduling.

Following a certain number of flying hours, or, in the case of landing gears, a certain number of take off-and-landing cycles, these critical parts are required to be changed, overhauled or inspected by specialist mechanics. When these parts are installed, their serial numbers are married to the aircraft registration numbers in the aircraft records and the plans and scheduling section will notify maintenance specialists when the parts must be replaced. If the parts are not replaced within the specified time or cycle limits, the airplane will normally be grounded until the maintenance action is completed. Most of these time-change parts, whether hydraulic flight surface actuators, pumps, landing gears, engines or engine components, are virtually indestructible. It would be impossible for an ordinary fire resulting from an airplane crash to destroy or obliterate all of those critical time-change parts or their serial numbers. I repeat, impossible.

Considering the catastrophic incidents of September 11, 2001, certain troubling but irrefutable conclusions must be drawn from the known facts. I get no personal pleasure or satisfaction from reporting my own assessment of these facts.

American Airlines Flight 77.

This was reported to be a Boeing 757, registration number N644AA, carrying 64 people, including the flight crew and five hijackers. This aircraft with a 125-foot wingspan was reported to have crashed into the Pentagon, leaving an entry hole no more than 65 feet wide. [And this was after the outer wall collapsed, about 45 minutes after impact from the aircraft. Before the outer wall collapsed, the only hole in the side of the Pentagon was a 14-to-16-foot hole.]

Following cool-down of the resulting fire, this crash site would have been very easy to collect enough time-change equipment within 15 minutes to positively identify the aircraft registry. There was apparently some aerospace type of equipment found at the site but no attempt was made to produce serial numbers or to identify the specific parts found. Some of the equipment removed from the building was actually hidden from public view.

... It seems only that all potential evidence was deliberately kept hidden from public view. The hard evidence would have included hundreds of critical time-change aircraft items, plus security videotapes that were confiscated by the FBI immediately following each tragic episode.

With all the evidence readily available at the Pentagon crash site, any unbiased rational investigator could only conclude that a Boeing-757 *did not* (emphasis added) fly into the Pentagon as alleged."[86]

In late January 2005, I shared the documentary *911 In Plane Site* with a good friend of mine. He had been my primary flight instructor more than 20 years ago. He was now employed with ATA Airlines as the B-757 Fleet Manager. His name is Captain Rod Ennis. After viewing the documentary, Rod shared some of his observations with me. To the best of my recollection, Rod said, concerning American 77, that at an absolute minimum, "the two engine cores should have remained,"[87] referring in part to the compressor and the hot sections of the engines, consisting of the combustion chambers, the turbine sections and the exhaust nozzles. You see, the fires burning on the inside of a large turbojet or turbofan engine are a lot hotter under near perfect high-pressure conditions, than any exterior fire resulting from an aircraft crash.

To further support our position; let's consider CNN reporter Jamie McIntyre's comments as he reported from the Pentagon on September the 11th, 2001. He said, "From my close-up inspection, there is no evidence of a plane having crashed anywhere near the Pentagon. The only site is the actual side of the building that is crashed in, and as I said, the only pieces left that you can see are small enough that you can pick up in your hand. There are no large tail sections, wing sections, fuselage, nothing like that anywhere around which would indicate that the entire plane

86 George Nelson, Physics 911, www.physics911.net/georgenelson.htm, 5/14/05.

87 Interview, Captain Rod Ennis, B-757 Fleet Manager, ATA Airlines.

crashed into the side of the Pentagon, and then caused the side to collapse. Now even though if you look at the pictures of the Pentagon, you see that the floors have all collapsed. That didn't happen immediately. It wasn't until almost about 45 minutes later that the structure was weakened enough that all of the floors collapsed."[88]

Other eyewitness accounts of the alleged American Airlines Flight 77 crash into the Pentagon differ entirely from the official reports. Steve Patterson told the *Washington Post* that day, "The airplane seemed to be able to hold between eight or twelve persons."[89]

Tom Siebert said, "We heard something made the sound of a missile, then we heard a powerful boom."[90] Mike Walter excitedly questioned CNN, "A plane, a plane from American Airlines? I thought, that's not right, it's really low. And I saw it. I mean, it was like a cruise missile with wings."[91]

Air Traffic Control specialist Danielle O'Brien told ABC news, "The speed, the maneuverability, the way he turned, we all thought in the radar room, all us experienced air traffic controllers, that that was a military plane."[92]

The speed, the maneuverability, the size of the aircraft reported by several eyewitnesses and air traffic controllers, the sound of a missile instead of jet engines, all have prompted many people with their thinking caps on to conclude that what struck the Pentagon was nothing less than some sort of winged aircraft or cruise missile painted to resemble an American Airlines jet.

In a Tom Flocco News article dated May 27, 2005, it was reported that two civilian defense contractor employees said that U.S. Air Force defense contractors brought in A-3 Sky Warrior aircraft under cover of darkness to be completely refitted and

88 Jamie McIntyre, CNN, 9/11/01.

89 Marrs, p. 29.

90 Ibid.

91 Ibid.

92 Ibid.

modified at the Fort Collins-Loveland Municipal Airport in Colorado.

Widely available FEMA photographs taken shortly after the attacks clearly show that the few aircraft parts found at the Pentagon belonged to a smaller aircraft similar to a modified A-3 Sky Warrior and not an American Airlines B-757.

The defense contractor employees, who requested anonymity for personal safety reasons and fear of job retaliation, told former ArkansasRepublican and Independent presidential candidate hopeful Karl Schwarz, "the Air Force brought in separate teams to do top-secret military work... and we were told by our bosses not to discuss what we had seen with anyone."

Schwarz said, "There are about 150 retired and active U.S. military and federal intelligence officers who will come forward and testify regarding government involvement in the September 11 attacks, but only if there is a serious criminal grand jury."

The 16-foot entry hole at the outside façade of the Pentagon on 9/11 has been the subject of countless questions by those who say the hole was caused by an air-to-ground missile fired from a small military jet rather than impact damage from a Boeing 757.

The employee witnesses said that separate teams refitted the A-3 Sky Warriors with updated missiles, Raytheon's Global Hawk unmanned aerial vehicle (UAV) remote control systems, fire control systems, engines, transponders, and radio-radar-navigation systems, a total makeover, seemingly for an operation more important than use as a simple missile testing platform for defense contractor Hughes-Raytheon.

The Hughes division manufactures air-to-ground missiles, and the Raytheon division maintains the last few A-3s except for 2-4 Air Force jets, while also manufacturing the Global Hawk UAV remote control systems.

Some of the most conclusive evidence to support that the damage to the façade of the Pentagon was caused by a missile rather than the alleged B-757, other than the single, pre-collapse 14-to-16-foot circular hole: there is no indication of evidence where a B-757's wings and tail sections penetrated. Just above the small hole, where the elevated vertical tail section allegedly entered, the windows were completely intact. This was also the case adjacent to the hole where the wings allegedly penetrated: virtually no damage and completely intact windows. This relatively small, single circular hole damage to the Pentagon is completely inconsistent with the type of damage that was caused to the façade of the South Tower of the World Trade Center. There, one can easily decipher the outline and damage created where the 767 completely penetrated the building."[93]In addition, as previously mentioned, is the complete lack of conclusively identifiable B-757 wreckage that USAF Colonel Nelson documented should have been abundantly present. Could this be why Defense Secretary Donald Rumsfeld mentioned a missile when discussing the Pentagon attack? On October 12, 2001, he told Parade Magazine, "Here we're talking about plastic knives, and using an American Airlines flight filled with our citizens, and the missile to damage this building..."[94]

As an airline pilot with more than 20 years of experience, more than 12,000 hours of flight time and more than 5,600 hours in large transport category turbojet powered aircraft, I can tell you that this alleged maneuver, a 7,000 ft. steep spiraling descent at 400-500+ miles per hour, exceeding the Boeing 757's maximum operating speed by 100-200 or more miles per hour, would be an extremely difficult maneuver, even for a comparably experienced and qualified pilot. But by someone who unsuccessfully demonstrated private pilot rated flying skills in order to rent a single engine Cessna, and who had no flight experience in large transport category jets, this would be an impossible maneuver.

A Boeing 757's cockpit warning systems would be extremely distractive, overspeed warnings and loud commands from the Ground Proximity Warning System, GPWS, commanding all sorts of corrective commands such as: "Whoop Whoop Pull Up, Too Low Gear, Too Low Flaps, Sink Rate Pull Up, Terrain

93 Tom Flocco, "Witnesses Link Missile to Small Military Jet Parts Found at Pentagon," May 27, 2005 www.tomflocco.com/modules.php?name=News&file=article&sid=110&mode=&order=0&thold=0.

94 Marrs, p. 29.

Terrain Pull Up, and Clack Clack Clack Overspeed." All of these warnings in the cockpit would have been extremely loud and distractive. As the aircraft reportedly struck the Pentagon with world class precision at 400-500+ miles per hour, exceeding the maximum operating speed of the Boeing 757 at sea level by 100-200 or more miles per hour, the aircraft's controls would have become heavy and sensitive, making the aircraft difficult to precisely control. I believe most impartial airline pilots would confirm this. So yes indeed, this official cover story is a stretch, exceeding the breaking point and the limits of sound reasoning.

Captain Russ Wittenberg, retired airline pilot from United Airlines and who also flew previously for Pan Am, who was also rated on the Boeing 757/767, had this to say about Flight 77: "757s don't go that fast (530 mph at sea level according to the NTSB). The airplane will just not do that. It's exceeding its airspeed and mach speed limitations." When asked about the reported sharp descending turn, he replied, "The airplane just won't perform those maneuvers. The only air vehicle that could perform that would be a high-performance fighter jet, a remote-controlled jet powered drone, or a cruise missile." Captain Wittenberg further explained, "The white flash in the Pentagon video is the explosion of a high energy explosive."[95]

Other air traffic control specialists reported other disturbing developments. One ATC specialist from another Northeast sector revealed to a 9-11 widow that FBI threats were made of both a personal and career nature: "You are ordered never to speak about what you saw on your screen during the attacks; and if you do, things will not go well for you and your family."[96]

There are still other problems with this episode. One larger piece of wreckage was found in the entry hole, but the public was kept from closely observing what appears to be a sheared-off piece of wing from a much smaller jet than a Boeing 757.[97]

95 American Free Press.

96 Tom Flocco.

97 Ibid.

A group of military personnel and federal officials in suits were photographed tightly covering that piece of wreckage with a blue tarp and then carrying it away to a waiting truck. No reporters or independent aircraft experts have been permitted to examine any of the recovered aircraft parts and no subpoenas have been issued to hear public grand jury testimony from these public servants.[98]

Other government officials, who looked more like FBI agents than rescue workers, were also photographed moving evidence around shortly after the crash, but none have testified as to whether they were planting evidence or removing it from a mass murder crime scene.[99]

We will shortly return to the anomalies of the alleged hijackers, but ladies and gentlemen, at the beginning of this discussion, I asked you to please keep in mind the details of Operation Northwoods. Let us review some of the evil plans that U.S. General Lemnitzer and his entire Joint Chiefs of Staff had in store for the American public in their quest for war with Cuba, and the strong similarities in regard to the 9/11 attacks: Manufacturing pieces of evidence, terror campaigns in the Washington, DC area, hijackings against civilian aircraft, arming and exploding by remote control drone aircraft which had been painted to look exactly like U.S. civilian commercial aircraft, careful handling of passengers with pre-selected aliases, etc. The similarities are alarming. Enemies inside the gates? Insidious foreign influence?

> *"Deliver me from the workers of iniquity, and save me from blood-thirsty men."*
>
> (Psalms 59:2, NKJV)

In the November 8, 2004 issue of *American Free Press*, investigative reporter Christopher Bollyn reported that some of the pieces of the alleged wreckage of American 77 could not

98 Ibid.

99 Ibid.

be identified as 757 pieces and had been suspected to be from another aircraft type altogether. A picture of a piece of a small turbine engine, approximately three feet in diameter and found at the Pentagon was published in his paper last year. Some observers claimed that the small turbine wheel could have come from the APU or the Auxiliary Power Unit in the Boeing 757.

All large turbojet airliner type of aircraft have an APU. It is a small turbine engine that provides electrical power for the aircraft, bleed air from the compressor section for the air conditioning systems and compressed air for starting the turbofan engines of an airliner. Normally you can hear the APU running as you board an airliner. You can distinguish its sound from the main jet engines. It is a quieter, but higher pitched sound of a small turbine engine.

An engineer with the Arizona-based manufacturer of the APU told *American Free Press* that the piece was "no part of an APU."

The fact that that piece of jet engine was found next to insulation and housing that match in diameter indicates that it came from a small jet engine of similar size. This proves that a jet engine of between 3 and 4 feet was found at the Pentagon crash site. The opening diameters of a Boeing 757's turbofan engines are closer to 9 feet.

When AFP first published photos of these unexplained pieces of wreckage more than a year ago, the question was raised whether they could be from an unmanned aerial vehicle (UAV), such as the Global Hawk or modified A-3.

For those of us who believe a smaller aircraft or unmanned drone such as the Global Hawk or A-3 was involved in the Pentagon attack, identifying the piece in the photo could prove what kind of aircraft hit the building.

The Global Hawk is a single engine drone that uses a Rolls Royce Allison Engine, hand built near my hometown, in Indianapolis, Indiana. The AE3007H engine has a diameter of 43.5 inches. Because the Global Hawk is a surveillance drone, the engine is contained in a heavily insulated housing, which makes it extremely quiet. This corresponds with eyewitness Steve Riskus, who said he was within 100 feet of the aircraft. Asked what he heard, he said he did not "recall hearing anything." If a B-757 flew at high speed, 400-500+ miles per hour over an eyewitness, the sound would be deafening.[100]

I must include here that many eyewitnesses reported seeing an American Airlines jet. But let me just say, in my experience working for the airlines for almost 20 years now, most of the traveling public does not recognize one aircraft type from another. For example, commuting to St. Louis for years, many traveling professionals who traveled as much as I did would ask me what type of aircraft we were flying on. Most could not tell a DC-9 from an MD-80 to a B-727 to an EMB-135 to an A-320 to an L-1011 to an MD-11 to a CRJ to a B-717 to a G-4 to a B-737 to an A-340 to a B-767 to an A-310 to an EMB-145 and on and on. And this is not surprising. As much as I enjoy boating, I am not an owner or frequent operator. I therefore would not be able to tell one type of watercraft from another. With this aircraft traveling at speeds greater than 500 miles per hour, considering the very brief moment or two that this aircraft was observed by witnesses before it slammed into the side of the Pentagon, I believe it would be difficult for witnesses other than airline or aviation professionals to correctly identify this aircraft.

Also, considering that this was a shockingly unbelievable event and the likelihood of traumatic stress of varying degrees affecting these eyewitnesses, I believe it is quite likely that those who observed an aircraft painted in familiar American Airlines livery could have easily and erroneously misidentified this aircraft and reported that what they witnessed was an American Airlines B-757. And this would be even more likely after these witnesses were informed by the media of official announcements that an American Airlines Boeing 757 had crashed into the Pentagon.

But the fact that no evidence of a Boeing 757 at the Pentagon crash site has been publicly confirmed, along with the discovery of parts from a much smaller engine, provides even further

100 American Free Press, November 8, 2004.

convincing evidence that what struck the Pentagon could not have been a Boeing 757 at all. But could a Global Hawk or similar aerial vehicle such as a modified A-3, or other cruise missile type in our arsenal, altered in such a way as to resemble in appearance an American B-757, armed with a warhead, have been what actually struck the Pentagon, as reported by many witnesses?

A radiation expert and a high-ranking Army major who once headed the Pentagon's depleted uranium project, contends that the Pentagon was hit by a missile, not a commercial jetliner, adding that high radiation readings after the strike indicate depleted uranium also could have been used.[101]

"... I am highly knowledgeable in causes and effects related to nuclear radiation contamination. What happened at the Pentagon is highly suspicious, leading me to believe a missile with a depleted uranium warhead may have been used," said Ms. Leuren Moret, who has spent a lifetime working in the nuclear field as a staff scientist at the Livermore Nuclear Weapons Laboratory in California.[102]

The missile theory is also backed up by Army Major Doug Rokke (ret.), a Ph.D. physicist and military expert. "When you look at the whole thing, especially the crash site void of airplane parts, the size of the hole left and the fact the projectile's impact penetrated numerous concrete walls, it looks like the work of a missile," said Major Rokke. "When you look at the damage, it was obviously a missile."[103]

Transportation Secretary Norman Mineta testified under oath before the commission on the September 11th terrorist attacks in mid 2003. He gave the following account of his experiences on the morning of 9/11:

After stating that he had arrived in the Presidential Emergency Operating Center shortly after the South Tower of the World Trade Center had been struck, Mineta testified, "During the time that the airplane was coming in to the Pentagon, there was a

101 American Free Press, September 12, 2005, p. 7.

102 Ibid.

103 Ibid.

young man who would come in and say to the vice president, 'The plane is 50 miles out. The plane is 30 miles out.' And when it got to 'the plane is 10 miles out,' the young man also said to the vice president, 'Do the orders still stand?' And the vice president turned and whipped his neck around and said, 'Of course the orders still stand! Have you heard anything to the contrary?' Well, at the time, I didn't know what all that meant... This was the flight that came into the Pentagon..."[104]

The strange conversation between Cheney and the "young man" as related by Transportation Secretary Mineta prompts puzzling questions indeed. Specifically, what were the orders?[105]

Of course, if American flight 77 did not hit the Pentagon, even more questions arise. What happened to the plane and its passengers? Could it have been ditched into the Atlantic Ocean as suggested by some?[106]

It had been reported by *USA Today*, that according to the Coast Guard, three jets out over the Atlantic Ocean were sending distress signals on 9/11.[107]

Any number of things could have happened to it, if it existed at all. But clean up and mop up operations are usually more easily accomplished and completed than other principal components of covert black operations used as pretexts for war.

Former Republican Karl Schwartz further stated that "... the '757-crashed-into-the-Pentagon' is a Bush lie."[108]

> *"These six things the Lord hates, yes seven are an abomination to Him: A proud look, a lying tongue, hands that shed innocent blood, a heart that devises wicked plans, feet that are swift in running to evil, a false witness who speaks lies, and one who sows discord among brethren."*

104 Marrs, p. 30.

105 Ibid.

106 Ibid. p. 31.

107 USA Today, August 13, 2002.

108 Tom Flocco.

(Proverbs 6: 16-19, NKJV)

There was one more alleged aircraft incident that occurred on 9/11 that we should review before proceeding on to the problems of the hijackers.

The fourth airliner, United Flight 93, another Boeing 757, this one reportedly with 45 passengers on board, departed Newark International Airport (EWR) bound for San Francisco International (SFO) and had also been allegedly hijacked on 9/11.

United States Air National Guard Director, Major General Paul Weaver, stated that no Air National Guard or other military planes were scrambled to chase the fourth hijacked airliner, United Flight 93. I would say this borders on the criminally negligent, if not the criminal. Three hijacked commercial planes had already crashed into the World Trade Center and the Pentagon, yet no military aircraft were scrambled to at least intercept the fourth hijacked plane, a plane which allegedly crashed in Pennsylvania almost an hour and a half after the first tower was hit.[109] At least this is part of the official story.

Downplaying the dire implications of the complete absence of interceptors being scrambled in accordance with FAA and Department of Defense rules, United States Deputy Defense Secretary Paul Wolfowitz stated that "the Air Force was tracking the hijacked plane that crashed in Pennsylvania on Tuesday after other airliners slammed into the Pentagon and World Trade Center and had been in a position to bring it down if necessary."[110]

Wolfowitz also explained that "any military intervention would have been the decision of President George W. Bush." But this was not entirely true.

Maybe this was Wolfowitz's attempt to misinform the public. But the facts have already been stated. The Air Force should have immediately scrambled military aircraft to intercept United 93, yet the Director of the U.S. Air National Guard confirmed that

109 Ahmed, p. 160.

110 Ibid.

no aircraft at all were scrambled, in direct violation of the Guard's own rules governing methods of emergency response."[111]

The issue here is not whether the US Air Force was monitoring United Flight 93, which it certainly should and would have been, but why the mandatory procedure of scrambling fighter jets to at least intercept the plane were not followed. As the *New York Press* commented incredulously, "So why was it not brought down, or at least intercepted? Three key buildings had been attacked, and there is still no emergency?"[112]

The answers to these questions may not be particularly satisfactory to someone who truly wants to believe and is entirely conditioned to believe in the credibility of their own federal government and their stated goals of keeping the American people safe.

American Free Press visited Somerset County Pennsylvania to look into some of the questions concerning United Flight 93, which allegedly turned over and crashed in a refilled strip mine between Lambertsville and Shanksville, Pennsylvania.

One question again is what happened to the physical wreckage of the plane? Where is the ever-present large debris field? Remember Pan Am Flight 103, the B-747 that was blown up over Lockerbie, Scotland and the huge piece of cockpit that remained on the Lockerbie countryside?

"There was no plane," Mayor of Shanksville Ernie Stull said. "My sister and a good friend of mine were the first ones there. They were standing on a street corner in Shanksville talking. Their car was nearby, so they were the first here, and the fire department came. Everyone was puzzled because the call had been that a plane had crashed. But there was no plane," Mayor Stull said.

"They had been sent here because of a crash, but there was no plane?"

AFP asked.

"No, nothing. Only this hole," said the Mayor.[113]

111 Ibid.

112 Ibid.

113 American Free Press, September 20, 2004.

Shall we review again here and now how there is *always* identifiable wreckage at a crash site of an airliner, that 100 tons of metal does not melt or vaporize or liquefy or oxidize?

Again, USAF Colonel George Nelson said: "Aerial photos of the alleged crash site were made available to the general public. They show a significant hole in the ground, but private investigators were not allowed to come anywhere near the crash site. If an aircraft crash caused the hole in the ground, there would have been literally hundreds of serially-controlled time-change parts within the hole that would have proved beyond any shadow of doubt the precise tail number or identity of the aircraft. However, the government has not produced any hard evidence that would prove beyond a doubt that the specifically alleged aircraft crashed at the site. On the contrary, it has been reported that the aircraft, registry number N591UA, is still in operation."[114]

"Eyewitness Nena Lensbour, who had prepared lunch for the workers at the scrapyard overlooking the crash site, was the first person to go up to the smoking crater. Nena Lensbouer told AFP that the hole was five to six feet deep and smaller than the 24-foot trailer in her front yard. She described hearing an explosion, like an atomic bomb, not a crash.

Lensbouer said she called 911 and stayed on the line as she ran across the reclaimed land of the former strip mine to within 15 feet of the smoking crater. She said that she did not see any evidence of a plane then or at anytime during the excavation at the site."[115]

Other eyewitness accounts contradict the official version of events surrounding the crash of United 93. One of the key elements omitted from the official version is the mysterious white jet seen by at least six eyewitnesses, according to *The Independent*. [116]

114 George Nelson.

115 American Free Press, September 20, 2004.

116 Ibid. October 4, 2004.

Eyewitness Susan Mcelwain described to the reporters a white jet she saw "less than a minute before the Flight 93 crash rocked the countryside." The small white jet passed over Mcelwain's car and disappeared over a hilltop, nearly clipping the tops of trees lining the ridge."[117]

"It came right over me, I reckon just 40 or 50 feet above my minivan," she told *The Mirror*. "It was so low I ducked instinctively. It was traveling really fast but hardly made any sound. Then it disappeared behind some trees. A few seconds later, I heard this great explosion and saw this fireball rise up over the trees, so I figured the jet had crashed. The ground really shook. So I dialed 911 and told them what happened," Mcelwain said.[118]

"I heard nothing about the other attacks, and it was only when I got home and saw the TV that I realized it wasn't the white jet, but flight 93. I didn't think much more about it until the authorities started to say there had been no other plane. The plane I saw was heading right to the point where Flight 93 crashed and must have been there at the very moment it came down," she said.[119]

"There was no way I imagined this plane. It was so low it was virtually on top of me. It was white with no markings... The FBI came and talked to me and said there was no plane around... But I saw it, and it was there before the crash, and it was 40 feet above my head. They did not want my story-nobody here did," Susan Mcelwain said.[120]

Two other eyewitnesses, Dennis Decker and Rick Chaney, told *The Bergen Record* they saw a white jet at the time of the crash. "As soon as we looked up, we saw a mid-sized jet flying low and fast. It appeared to make a loop or part of a circle, and then it turned fast and headed out," they said.[121]

---

117 Ibid.

118 Ibid.

119 Ibid.

120 Ibid.

121 Ibid.

Another omitted observation is that people in the immediate area of the crash site reported hearing a missile, rather than a Boeing 757 jetliner. Tim Lensbouer, who was working in the scrapyard next to the crash site, told AFP what he heard. "It sounded like a missile followed by a huge explosion. It was whistling real loud, and then there was a loud bang."[122]

Again, the Mayor of Shanksville, Mayor Ernie Stull, told a local newspaper in November 2001, "I know of two people-I will not mention names-that heard a missile. They both live very close, within a couple of hundred yards... This one fellow has served in Vietnam and he says he's heard them and he heard one that day." [123]

Other problems with the official story of United Flight 93 are the initial news reports that said it had diverted to Cleveland, Ohio. A well-documented AP story quoting United Airlines CEO James Goodwin and the Mayor of Cleveland, Michael R. White, was posted on the web site of Cincinnati's WCPO-TV, an ABC affiliate. The report stated:

"A Boeing 767 out of Boston made an emergency landing Tuesday at Cleveland Hopkins International Airport due to concerns that it may have a bomb aboard said Mayor Michael R. White.

White said the plane had been moved to a secure area of the airport and was evacuated. United identified the plane as flight 93. The airline did not say how many people were aboard the flight.

United said it was also "deeply concerned" about another flight, Flight 175, a Boeing 767, which was bound from Boston to Los Angeles.

On behalf of the airline, CEO James Goodwin said, "The thoughts of everyone at United are with the passengers and crew of these flights. Our prayers are also with everyone on the ground who may have been involved.

---

122 Ibid.

123 Ibid.

United is working with all the relevant authorities, including the FBI, to obtain further information on these flights," he said.[124]

How can United Airlines Flight 93 crash in Shanksville, Pennsylvania at 10:00 am, then divert to Cleveland almost two hours later? How can the Mayor of Cleveland receive such erroneous information? Wouldn't the ATC Tower Chief in Cleveland, along with all the Cleveland Center and Cleveland approach controllers who worked this flight know the true identity of this flight? How about the emergency personnel that interviewed the Captain of that flight in order to make their required reports? Wouldn't they have gotten the correct flight number from the Captain and other flight crewmembers? You bet they would. Does anyone else here smell a rat?

Keeping the Operation Northwoods plan as precedent in mind, the admission by Major General Paul Weaver that no military aircraft were scrambled to at least intercept United Flight 93 in spite of established and required procedures to do so, and considering the account of Mayor Stull of Shanksville concerning the lack of any aircraft wreckage, does this not lead some to doubt, or at least question the official story?

Please ask yourselves, would it be difficult to convict the official alleged perpetrators of the crimes of September 11th considering these documented contradictions of the evidence? Has reasonable doubt been established? And if so, should we look elsewhere for the responsible parties?

Remember the old saying: Things are seldom as they seem; skim milk masquerades as cream.

John Carlin of *The Independent* wrote about United Flight 93, "There are most certainly a number of important unanswered questions. The shortage of available facts did not prevent the creation of an instant legend, a legend that the U.S. government and the U.S. media were pleased to propagate, and that the American public have been eager, for the most part, to accept as fact."[125]

124 Ibid. April 4, 2005.

125 Ibid. October 4, 2004.

So far, I might add. Hey, if Fox News or CNN or Dan Rather report it, it must be gospel... right?

Again, USAF Colonel George Nelson: "With all the evidence available at the Pennsylvania crash site, it was most doubtful that a passenger airliner caused the obvious hole in the ground and *certainly not* (emphasis added) the Boeing 757 as alleged."[126]

When one begins to look at the background and the current activities of the alleged hijackers, a long series of disturbing questions arise concerning them also.

On September 12, 2001, FBI Director Robert Mueller announced some astonishingly swift investigative police work. "We have, in the last 24 hours, taken the passenger manifests and used them in an evidentiary manner, and have successfully, I believe, identified many of the hijackers on each of the four flights that went down."[127]

Yet not one of the accused hijackers' names appeared on the passenger lists made public by American or United Airlines. And if this account is true, how did the FBI learn the names of five of the hijackers and obtain their photographs the day of the attacks?[128]

The fact is, seven of those named as the culprits in the attacks were soon found alive and well in the Middle East.

Saudi pilot Waleed al-Shari was identified by the U.S. Justice Department as one of the men who crashed American Flight 11 into the North Tower of the World Trade Center. But a few days later, Waleed al-Shari contacted authorities in Casablanca, Morocco, to proclaim that he was not dead yet, in fact he was very much alive and played no part in the 9/11 attacks. He said he did train as a pilot in the United States but left the country in September 2000, to accept gainful employment as a pilot with Saudi Arabian Airlines.[129]

---

126 George Nelson.

127 Marrs, p. 17.

128 Ibid.

129 Ibid.

Another man identified as one of the hijackers of American Flight 11, Abdulaziz al-Omari, also turned up alive in the Middle East. According to *Knight Rider News Service*, Abdulaziz al-Omari had once attended Aerospace Medical School at Brooks Air Force Base in Texas.[130]

Abdulaziz told the *BBC News* that he lost his passport visiting Denver Colorado and also stated, "I couldn't believe the FBI put me on their list. They gave my name and my date of birth, but I am not a suicide bomber. I am here and I am alive. I have no idea how to fly a plane. I had nothing to do with this."[131]

Saeed al-Ghamdi, who had once attended the Defense Language Institute in Monterey, California, was another suspect identified as a hijacker of United Flight 93. He was reported alive and well working as a pilot in Saudi Arabia. "You cannot imagine what it is like to be described as a terrorist-and a dead man-when you are innocent and alive," said al-Ghamdi, who was given a holiday by his airline in Saudi Arabia to avoid arrest.[132]

There are many unsettling questions concerning the story of alleged American Flight 77 hijacker, Hani Hanjour. It is widely known that this young Saudi had a history of great difficulties in his efforts to learn to fly. As late as August 2001, just one month before 9/11, he was unable to rent a Cessna 172 due to lack of ability to demonstrate suitable flying skills. According to *Newsday*, flight instructors Sheri Baxter and Ben Connor took the soft-spoken Hanjour on three test runs in the second week of August and found he had trouble controlling and landing the single engine Cessna 172. Marcel Bernard, Chief Flight Instructor at the flight school at Freeway Airport in Bowie, Maryland, refused to rent Hanjour a plane without more lessons, despite the fact he had a commercial pilot license and a logbook, which indicated he had six hundred hours of flight experience.[133]

---

130 Ahmed, p. 98.

131 Marrs, p. 17.

132 Ibid. pp. 18-19.

133 Ibid. pp. 19-20.

I have come to suspect the license and the logbook of Hanjour were probably part of the deceptive cover story used by our black operators to convince the public that Hanjour would have been capable of pulling that aerobatic stunt flying maneuver into the Pentagon.

Dr. Thomas R. Olmstead, a psychiatrist and former Navy officer, filed a Freedom of Information Act request with the Armed Forces Institute of Pathology, which had responsibility for identifying all victims in the Pentagon reportedly killed by American Flight 77. "No Arabs wound up on the morgue slab," noted Dr. Olmstead. "However... additional people not listed by American Airlines sneaked in. I have no explanation for these extras." The airline listed fifty-six persons on Flight 77 yet the Armed Forces Institute listed sixty-four.[134]

As *American Free Press* has pointed out, a case has been built largely in the media that Muslim terrorists hijacked the planes and flew them into the World Trade Center and the Pentagon. And in the eye of the public, much of the government's case against the 19 Muslim Arabs named as suspects rests on copies of a suspicious and possibly spurious five-page letter, handwritten in Arabic, which has turned up in three different locations. The document, however, raises more questions than it answers, leading one expert to say, "It could be the greatest falsification in history." 135

A law enforcement official described the letter to the press as a "spiritual instruction manual" giving the terrorists step-by-step instructions for their suicide mission and preparing them spiritually for death. The document contained a mission checklist and instructions for mental and spiritual preparation, the official said, speaking on condition of remaining anonymous, according to *USA Today*.[136]

One copy was found in Mohammed Atta's suitcase, which mysteriously was left behind at the airport in Portland, Maine.

134 Ibid. p. 19.

135 American Free Press, September 23, 2004.

136 Ibid.

Another copy was found at the Shanksville, Pennsylvania site, and a third was found in the car of one of the suspects.[137]

Muslim scholars and specialists question the authenticity of the letter, saying the phraseology and style are "un-Islamic." "This is not the way Muslims speak or think; there is a mysterious element here, and the FBI knows it for sure," said Mohammed Hurub, a Muslim scholar from Bethlehem.[138]

If the letter, which is described as "part theological, part mission statement" is genuine, "then the men who murdered more than 7000 (sic) innocent people believed in a very exclusive version of Islam, or were surprisingly unfamiliar with their religion," said Robert Fisk, a Middle East expert.[139]

The problem first arises in the opening lines of the letter, "In the name of God, the most merciful, the most compassionate... in the name of God, of me, and of my family." No Muslim would include his family in such a prayer but, would mention the Prophet Mohammed immediately after he mentioned God, Fisk said.[140]

The letter urges the reader to recite the Morning Prayer and then goes on to quote from it. A devout Muslim would hardly need to be told of his duty to say his prayers and would certainly not need to be reminded of the text of those prayers. It is as if a Christian would have to be reminded of The Lord's Prayer, said Fisk.[141]

Numerous other puzzling stories have emerged about Mohammed Atta, the alleged mastermind of the hijackers. Besides a copy of the previously discussed document, Atta reportedly left behind in his parked car two suitcases containing other incriminating material, including his passport, his driver's license, his last will, a copy of the Koran, flight simulation manuals for Boeing aircraft and a note to other hijackers. But why take

137 Ibid.

138 Ibid.

139 Ibid.

140 Ibid.

141 Ibid.

suitcases on a suicide mission? And if the suitcases were used to present the appearance of a normal tourist or businessman, why leave them behind?[142]

CNN reported on September 16, 2001, "In New York, several blocks from the ruins of the World Trade Center, a passport authorities said belonged to one of the hijackers was discovered a few days ago, according to Police Commissioner Bernard Kerik. That has prompted the FBI and police to widen the search area beyond the immediate crash site." What happened to the passport and this story? Both seemed to have disappeared.[143] Some suspicious researchers smelled planted evidence, a tactic which General Lemnitzer discussed using in the Operation Northwoods plans, remember?

Author David Ray Griffin quoted an unnamed high level intelligence source as saying what was on many peoples' minds, "Whatever trail was left, was left deliberately-for the FBI to chase."[144]

Furthermore, in light of media stories concerning Atta's personal effects, such as a Koran, flight school materials and suicide notes, why did FBI director Mueller, on April 19, 2002, in a speech to the Commonwealth Club in San Francisco, declare that the hijackers "left no paper trail?"[145]

In the days following September 11th, many major media pundits correctly pointed out that a ragtag bunch of fanatics could not have successfully pulled off the large-scale and well-coordinated attacks by themselves. They must have had the sponsorship of some state, they argued.[146]

Before moving on to why the September 11th attacks took place, I would like to explore the collapse of both World Trade Center towers as well as Building 7.

142 Marrs, p. 20.

143 Ibid. pp. 20-21.

144 Ibid. p. 21.

145 Ibid.

146 Ibid. p. 22.

Investigative journalist and author of *Inside Job, Unmasking the 9/11 Conspiracies*, Jim Marrs asks, "Why, according to several experts and numerous independent observers, did the destruction of the World Trade Center Towers appear more like a controlled implosion than terrorist-caused destruction?"[147]

Such questions concerning the collapse of the towers were advanced by experts in demolition and fire fighting immediately, only to die in the subsequent media blitz of "official pronouncements." Many people, experts and laymen alike, wondered why the South Tower collapsed first when it was not as extensively damaged as the North Tower, which burned for almost 90 minutes before its collapse.[148]

Frank A. DeMartini, the World Trade Center Construction Project. Manager, missing since 9/11, was interviewed and recorded on January 25, 2001. He had this to say about the World Trade Center tower's construction: "The building was designed to have a fully loaded B-707 crash into it. That was the largest plane at the time. I believe that the building could probably sustain multiple impacts of jetliners because this structure is like the mosquito netting on your screen door, this intense grid. And the jet plane is just a pencil puncturing that screen netting. It really does nothing to that screen netting."[149]

Numerous sources have claimed that bombs, rather than planes, caused the collapse of the World Trade Center towers.

Mr. Van Romero, Vice President for Research at the New Mexico Institute of Mining and Technology and a former Director of the Energetic Materials and Testing Center, said televised images of the collapse of the WTC towers suggested that explosives were used to create a controlled demolition. "My opinion is based on the video tapes, that after the airplanes hit the World Trade Center there were some explosive devices inside

147 Ibid p.32.

148 Ibid.

149 Anthony J. Hilder, "The Greatest Lie Ever Sold," Documentary DVD.

the buildings that caused the towers to collapse," Romero told the Albuquerque Journal on September 11, 2001.[150]

Ladies and gentlemen, we'll get back to Romero's comments here shortly. I just ask you all to trust your own eyes and your own instincts. Sometime in May of 2005, I pulled out my own copy of the CNN 9/11 documentary, *CNN Tribute, America Remembers* DVD and watched it. If you have a copy, you may want to retrieve it in order to view it again. Shortly after watching it, I posted my remarks on the Letsroll911.Org website, on the "911 and The World Trade Center (WTC) Chain of Evidence" forum:

Phil, Enigs, and all:

I was watching the *CNN Tribute, America Remembers* yesterday. In Chapter 3, "Catastrophe in New York," at DVD counter position 17 minutes, 1 second, this would be in the first minute of Chapter 3, and there is a view of both towers. The tower on the left I believe is the South tower due to the lower smoke layer.

The left building has two sides exposed due to camera position angle. The left side of the left building is in the sunny side. The *right* side of the *left* building is on the shady side.

If one focuses on the *right* side (shady side) of the *left* building, during this very short 3 second elapsed time footage, and if you put your DVD player in slow motion, 1/8 or 1/16 if you can, or just "step" through the footage with the pause/still button on your remote control, you can count at least 16 bright white flashes emanating from within the building, several floors beneath the area of the smoke layer. These 16 flashes occur in a short 3 second time frame, from DVD counter 17 minutes, 1 second to 17 minutes, 3 seconds.

I submit that these flashes are visual indications of the "explosions going off everywhere" as reported by so many surviving witnesses.

Good God, what does it take to make a convincing case to allow arrests, trials, convictions and sentencing of these demonic mass murderers in our midst?

150 Marrs, p. 32.

One more thing, Phil, Enigs, and all, this site and these forums are a living, growing document to 9/11 truth being written daily by contributions of witnesses to the truth. It is a compilation of incriminating, prosecutorial evidence that someday will be heard in a court of law. It is however being seen and heard yesterday, today and tomorrow in the Court of Public Opinion.

F/O

> *"He who justifies the wicked and he who condemns the just, both of them alike are an abomination to the Lord."*
>
> (Proverbs 17:15, NKJV)

> *"Pronounce them guilty, O God! Let them fall by their own counsels; cast them out in the multitude of their transgressions, for they have rebelled against You."*
>
> (Psalms 5:10, NKJV)

Returning to remarks of witnesses and survivors of the WTC collapses, Romero further stated the collapse of the WTC was "too methodical" to be the chance result of airplanes colliding with structures. He said it appeared more like the controlled implosions used to demolish old buildings. "It could have been a relatively small amount of explosives placed in strategic points," he said, adding that the detonation of bombs within towers is consistent with common terrorist strategy. "One of the things terrorist events are noted for is a diversionary explosion that attracts emergency personnel to the scene, then detonate a second explosion."[151]

Many have wondered about the witnesses who claimed to have heard multiple explosions within the buildings. One such witness was the head of WTC security, John O'Neill, who stated shortly before he himself became a victim that he had helped dig out survivors on the 27th floor before the building collapsed. Since

151 Marrs, p. 33.

the aircraft crashed into the 80th floor, what heavily damaged the 27th floor?[152]

Another of those mentioning bombs was Louie Cacchioli, a 51-year-old firemen assigned to Engine 47 in Harlem. "We were the first ones in the second tower after the plane struck. I was taking firefighters up in the elevators to the 24th floor to get in position to evacuate workers. On the last trip up, a bomb went off. We think there were bombs set in the building," Cachiolli said, speaking for himself and his fellow firemen.[153]

Auxiliary Fire Lieutenant Paul Isaac Jr. also discussed bombs, telling reporter Randy Lavello that New York firemen were very upset by what they considered a cover-up in the WTC destruction. "Many other firemen know there were bombs in the buildings, but they are afraid for their jobs to admit it because the higher-ups forbid discussion of this fact."[154]

Isaac, who was stationed at Engine 10 near the WTC in the late 1990s, said the higher-ups included the NYFD's antiterrorism consultant, James Woolsey, former Director of the CIA. "There were definitely bombs in the building," he said.[155]

Firefighter Edward Cachia stated, "We thought there was an internal detonation, explosives because it went in succession, boom, boom, boom, boom, and the tower came down... It actually gave at a lower floor, not where the plane hit."[156]

Assistant Fire Commissioner Stephen Gregory reported, "When I looked in the direction of the Trade Center before it came down, before NO.2 came down... I saw low-level flashes. In my conversation with Lieutenant Evangelista, never mentioning this to him, he questioned me and asked me if I saw lower-level flashes in front of the building, and I agreed with him... I saw a flash, flash, flash and then it looked like the building came

152 Ibid.

153 vonKleist.

154 Marrs, p. 34.

155 Ibid.

156 Professor Steven E. Jones, "Why Indeed Did the WTC Buildings Collapse?" www.physics.byu.edu/research/energy/htm7.html, 11/11/05.

down... You know like when they demolish a building, how when they blow a building when it falls down. That's what I thought I saw. He (Evangelista) said did you see any flashes? I said yes, well, I thought it was just me. He said no, I saw them too."[157]

September the 11th survivor Teresa Veliz, manager for a software development company, was on the 47th floor of the North tower when it was struck. "I got off the elevator, turned the corner and opened the door to the ladies room. I said good morning to a lady sitting at the mirror when the whole building shook. I thought it was an earthquake. Then I heard banging noises on the other side of the wall," she said.[158]

Teresa Veliz reached ground level with a co-worker when the South tower collapsed, knocking them down. In near total darkness, she and her co-worker followed someone with a flashlight. "The flashlight led us into Borders Bookstore, up an escalator and out to Church Street. There were explosions going off everywhere. I was convinced that there were bombs planted all over the place..."[159]

Eyewitness Ross Milanytch watched the horror of 9/11 at the WTC from his office window on the 22nd floor of a building a couple blocks away. "I saw small explosions on each floor, and after it all cleared, all that was left of the buildings, you could just see the steel girders in like a triangular sail shape. The structure was just completely gone," said Milanytch.[160]

Another 9/11 survivor, Steve Evans, a reporter for the BBC, was in the South tower at the time of the attacks. "I was at the base of the second tower, the second tower that was hit. There was an explosion-I didn't think it was an explosion-but the base of the building shook. I felt it shake ... then when we were outside,

157 Ibid.

158 Marrs, p. 34.

159 Ibid.

160 Ibid.

the second explosion happened and then there was a series of explosions..."[161]

Fox 5 News in New York City, shortly after 10:00 am on 9/11, videotaped a large white cloud of smoke billowing out near the base of the South tower.[162] Could this be the source of the explosions heard by Steve Evans and other witnesses who survived?

The Fox 5 News commentator exclaimed, "There is an explosion at the base of the building... white smoke from the bottom... something has happened at the base of the building... then another explosion..."[163]

Some of the most compelling testimony came from 9/11 survivor Tom Elliot, who was working in his office at AON Corporation on the 103rd floor of the WTC South tower before the airplanes struck.

Elliot said he was at his computer answering emails when a bright light startled him just before 9:00 am. A rumble shook the building, and he could see flames with dark smoke that appeared to be crawling up the outside of the building. He also felt heat coming through the windows. Strangely, there were no alarms.

"I don't know what's happening, but I think I need to be out of here," he recalled feeling at the time.

Elliot and two others began walking down the building's stairwell when they ran into a few others. The absence of more people and the lack of fire and smoke alarms made them feel they had prematurely panicked. He recalled that when his small group reached the 70th floor, they heard the announcement that the building was secure and there was no need to evacuate. "Do you want to believe them?" a woman said to Elliot. "Let's go!" He followed the woman down the stairs. After descending three more floors, Flight 175 crashed into the South tower. An article in the Christian Science Monitor described what happened next: "Although its spectacularly televised impact was above Elliot, at

161 Ibid.

162 Ibid. p. 35.

163 Ibid.

first he and those around him thought an explosion had come from below. An incredible sound-he calls it an exploding sound, shook the building and a tornado of hot air and smoke and ceiling tiles and bits of drywall come flying up the stairwell."

"In front of me, the wall split from the bottom up," Elliot said. He said people in the stairwell panicked and tried to flee upward until some men pointed out that the only escape was downstairs. By about 9:40, Elliot managed to stumble out of the South tower and make his way to his roommate's office in Midtown, where he broke down sobbing when he learned of the tower's collapse.[164]

Firefighters reporting bombs and explosions. Survivors and eyewitnesses reporting bombs and explosions. News reporters describing explosions and bombs and accompanying smoke near the base of the buildings. All of this should call for a new and complete, impartial and independent, non-Warren Commission like, investigation of just exactly what caused the World Trade Center buildings to collapse.

An article in American Free Press, entitled "*Fire Engineers Challenge Official Trade Center Collapse Theories*," by reporter Christopher Bollyn states that:

"*Fire Engineering* magazine, the 125 year old journal of record among America's fire engineers and firefighters recently blasted the investigation being conducted by the Federal Emergency Management Agency (FEMA) of the collapsed World Trade Center as a 'half baked farce.'

Fire Engineering's editor William Manning issued a "call to action" to America's firefighters and fire engineers in the January 2004 issue asking them to contact their representatives in Congress and officials in Washington to demand a blue ribbon panel to thoroughly investigate the collapse of the WTC structures.

Fire Engineering frequently publishes technical studies of major fires and is read in more than 50,000 fire departments and schools of fire engineering across the nation.

Manning challenged the theory that the towers collapsed as a result of the crashed airliners and the subsequent fuel fires

164 Ibid. pp. 35-36.

saying, "Respected members of the fire protection engineering community are beginning to raise red flags, and a resonating theory has emerged: The structural damage from the planes and the explosive ignition of jet fuel in themselves were not enough to bring down the towers."

No evidence has been produced to support the theory that the burning jet fuel and secondary fires "attacking the fireproofed lightweight trusses and load-bearing columns directly caused the collapses," Manning wrote, adding that the collapses occurred "in an alarmingly short time."

Because no "real evidence" has been produced, the theory that the twin towers collapsed due to fire "could remain just unexplored theory."

Manning visited the site shortly after the collapse and his photographs appeared in the October issue of *Fire Engineering*. None of the photos show load-bearing central steel support columns standing or fallen, which raises the question, what caused those columns to disintegrate?

The steel from the site must be preserved to allow investigators to determine what caused the collapse. Manning said, "The destruction and removal of evidence must stop immediately."

"For more than three months, structural steel from the World Trade Center has been and continues to be cut up for scrap. Crucial evidence that could answer many questions about high rise building design practices and performance under fire conditions is on the slow boat to China, perhaps never to be seen again until you buy your next car," Manning said.

"Such destruction of evidence shows the astounding ignorance of government officials to the value of a thorough, scientific investigation of the largest fire-induced collapse in world history," Manning said.

Nowhere in the national standard for fire investigations does one find an exemption allowing the destruction of evidence for buildings over ten stories tall. Clearly there are burning questions that need answers. Based on the incident's magnitude alone, a full throttle, fully resourced, forensic investigation is imperative.

The lessons about the building's design and behavior in this extraordinary event must be learned and applied in the real world.

"Did they throw away the locked doors from the Triangle Shirtwaist fire? Did they throw away the gas can used at the Happyland Social Club fire? Did they cast aside the pressure-regulating valves at the Meridian Plaza fire? Of course not. But essentially that's what they're doing at the World Trade Center," Manning said.

In a separate editorial; "*WTC Investigation? A Call to Action*" by *Fire Engineering's* Technical Editor, Professor Glenn Corbett of John Jay University in New York City, and two other expert fire engineers, who specialize in high-rise buildings, said the FEMA-led investigation was "superficial and uncoordinated."

"The World Trade Center disaster demands the most comprehensive detailed investigation possible. No event in our entire fire service history has ever come close to the magnitude of this incident," Corbett said.

"Except for the marginal benefit obtained from a three day visual walk-through of evidence sites, described by one source as a tourist trip, no one is checking the evidence for anything. As things stand right now and if they continue in such fashion, the investigation into the WTC fire and collapse will amount to paper and computer generated hypotheticals," Manning said.

Engineers have also complained that they have been shackled with bureaucratic restrictions that prevented them from examining the disaster site, interviewing witnesses and requesting crucial information like recorded distress calls to police and fire departments.

"This is almost the dream team of engineers in the country working on this and our hands are tied," one engineer who asked not to be identified told the *Times*. Members of the team have been threatened with dismissal for speaking to the press. "FEMA is controlling everything," the anonymous engineer said.

Comprehensive disaster investigations mean increased safety. They mean positive change. NASA knows it. The NTSB knows it. Does FEMA know it? No," said Manning.

"*Fire Engineering* has good reason to believe that the official investigation blessed by FEMA and run by the American Society of Civil Engineers is a *half baked farce* (emphasis added) that may already have been commandeered by political forces whose primary interests, to put it mildly, lie far afield of full disclosure," Fire Engineering's editor, Manning said.[165]

I firmly believe one reason why the premier trade journal of fire fighting professionals called the official version of the collapse of the WTC buildings a "half baked farce" is because fire fighters on the scene truly thought the fires were controllable.

An audiotape of New York fire fighters at the scene of the WTC fires made available to the public in mid 2002, indicated that fire fighters managed to reach the 78th floor of the South tower, very near the crash scene at the 80th floor, and seemed certain the fire was controllable. The tape was briefly mentioned by *The New York Times*, but was kept from the public by the U.S. Justice Department.

The audiotape was a recording of radio transmissions made on the morning of September 11th, 2001. The tape was reportedly discovered two or three weeks after 9/11 in the offices of the Port Authority of New York and New Jersey at WTC building 5. Evidently, Port Authority personnel were monitoring and recording the New York Fire Department channel.

Two fire officials mentioned by name in the tape were battalion Chief Orio J. Palmer and Fire Marshall Ronald P. Bucca, both of whom perished when the South Tower collapsed along with 343 other fire fighters, the greatest single loss of fire fighters in history. According to the *Times* article, these firemen "showed no panic, no sense that events were racing beyond their control... At that point, the building would be standing for just a few more minutes, as the fire was supposedly weakening the structure on the floors above him. Even so, Chief Palmer could only see two pockets of fire and called for a pair of engine companies to fight them."

165 American Free Press, August 23, 2004.

Transcripts released provided this statement: "Battalion Seven... Ladder 15, we've got two isolated pockets of fire. We should be able to knock it down with two lines. Radio that, 78th floor numerous 10-45 Code Ones."

As noted by *American Free Press* reporter Chris Bollyn, "The fact that fire fighters had a coherent plan for putting out the two isolated pockets of fire, indicates they judged the blazes to be manageable. These reports from the scene of the crash provide crucial and convincing evidence debunking the federal government's claim that a steel-melting inferno led to the towers' collapse."[166]

I believe another reason why *Fire Engineering* called FEMA's version of the collapse a "half baked farce" is because fire fighters are normally familiar with the types of fires they are fighting and the types of construction of the buildings they may be working in.

A report made by a Lab Director from an Underwriters Laboratories (UL) division in South Bend, Indiana had some interesting comments in correspondence to the National Institute of Standards and Technology (NIST). Kevin R. Ryan of UL wrote to metallurgist Frank Gayle at NIST because NIST was conducting an investigation of the twin towers collapse. Ryan expressed, "The buildings should have easily withstood the thermal stress caused by pools of burning jet fuel." Ryan also pointed out that the steel components would have had to be exposed to temperatures around 2000 degrees Fahrenheit for several hours. "And as we all agree, the steel applied met those specifications. Additionally, I think we can all agree that even unfireproofed steel will not melt until reaching red-hot temperatures of nearly 3,000 F."[167]

Referring to Gayle's own summer of 2003 published metallurgical tests, Ryan noted that "weak steel" was virtually ruled out at that time as a "contributing factor in the collapse."[168]

166 Marrs, pp. 38-39.

167 American Free Press, December 6, 2004.

168 Ibid.

Ryan wrote to Gayle, "Your comments suggest that the steel was probably exposed to temperatures of only 500 degrees (250 C), which is what one might expect from a thermodynamic analysis of the situation." Ryan pointed out that the summary of the findings "states that the perimeter columns softened, yet your findings make clear that most perimeter panels (157 of 160) saw no temperature above 250 C. To soften steel for the purpose of forging, normally temperatures need to be above 1,100 C.[169]

Ryan added, "This story just does not add up. If steel from those buildings did soften or melt, I'm sure we can all agree that this was certainly not due to jet fuel fires of any kind, let alone briefly burning fires in those towers. That fact should be of great concern to all Americans..."[170]

Brigham Young University Physics Professor Steven E. Jones published his study, "*Why Indeed Did the WTC Buildings Collapse*?" He states in part:

"In writing this paper, I call for a serious investigation of the hypothesis that WTC 7 and the Twin Towers were brought down... through the use of pre-positioned explosives. I present evidence for the explosive-demolition hypothesis...

The occurrence of nearly symmetrical, straight-down and complete collapses of the WTC 7 and the Towers is particularly upsetting to the official theory that random fires plus damage caused all these collapses. Even with explosives, achieving such results requires a great deal of pre-planning and expertise.

A symmetrical collapse [as occurred to WTC 7 and the twin towers], requires the simultaneous "pulling" of most or all of the support columns. The second law of Thermodynamics implies the likelihood of complete and symmetrical collapse due to random fires as in the "official" theory is small, since asymmetrical failure is so much more likely. On the other hand, a major goal of controlled demolition using explosives is the complete and symmetrical collapse of buildings...

---

169 Ibid.

170 Ibid.

The observed "partly evaporated" steel members [found in the debris piles] is particularly upsetting to the official theory, since fires involving paper, office materials, even diesel [or jet] fuel, cannot generate temperatures anywhere near the 5,000+ F needed to "evaporate" steel. However, thermite, RDX and other commonly-used explosives can readily slice through steel (thus cutting the support columns simultaneously in an explosive demolition) and reach the required temperatures..."[171]

The observation of molten metal at Ground Zero was emphasized publicly by Leslie Robertson, the structural engineer responsible for the design of the World Trade Center towers, who reported that "As of 21 days after the attack, the fires were still burning and molten steel was still running.[172]

Several other officials also reported the presence of molten metal. Professor Jones wrote, "I maintain these published observations are consistent with the use of the high-temperature thermite reaction, used to cut or demolish steel. Thermite is a mixture of iron oxide and aluminum powder. The end products of the thermite reaction are aluminum oxide and molten iron.

So the thermite reaction generates molten iron directly and is hot enough to melt and even evaporate steel which it contacts while reacting. On the other hand, falling buildings (absent explosives) have insufficient directed energy to result in melting of large quantities of metal. The government reports admit that the building fires were insufficient to melt steel beams-then where did the molten metal come from?"[173]

Jones further asks, "What caused the 47 enormous steel core columns of this building [the North tower] to give way nearly simultaneously?"

In answering his own question, he writes: "Again, use of pre-positioned explosives to cut the core columns first (standard

171 Professor Steven E. Jones.

172 Ibid.

173 Ibid.

demolition practice) provides a simple yet elegant explanation for the observation..."[174]

And so, to summarize, fire fighters at the scene strongly felt the fires were controllable as recorded by the New York and New Jersey Port Authority.

The leading trade journal of fire safety professionals as reported by the editor, William Manning, in *Fire Engineering* called the fire-induced, steel weakening scenario a "half baked farce." UL lab director Kevin Ryan expressed the buildings should have easily withstood the thermal stress caused by briefly burning fires. And BYU Physics Professor Steven Jones expressed his scientific analysis that explosives were used to cut the core columns of the WTC buildings.

The testimony from these professional experts who agree that fire alone could not have brought these buildings down, the fact that in all of history fire alone has never brought down a steel-framed structured building, the accounts of surviving firefighters, witnesses and news reporters discussing bombs and explosions going off everywhere, and the recorded visual indications of explosions by CNN and other news sources should lead reasonable people to conclude that there is more to this story than they've been told to believe and asked to accept.

And now, as the saying goes, for the rest of the story. If bombs and explosions in a controlled demolition, rather than fire-induced steel weakening and gravitational forces, were the primary cause of the World Trade Center towers along with Building 7 collapsing, how could they have been placed in the buildings? Well, with the building's concrete uncharacteristically and unexplainably pulverized to fine powder and the steel beams hauled away before thorough independent analysis could be completed, no one will ever be certain, unless a brave whistleblower comes forward in the near future. But some interesting and plausible explanatory scenarios have been brought forward.

Ben Fountain, a financial analyst who worked on the 47th floor of the South tower, told *People* magazine that in the

174 Ibid.

weeks preceding 9/11, there were numerous and very unusual unannounced drills in which sections of both towers as well as building 7, the Solomon Brothers Building-the three buildings whose destruction closely resembled controlled demolitions as reported by newsmen such as CNN's Aaron Brown as well as many witnesses-were evacuated for "security reasons."These drills could have provided a perfect cover for "technicians" planting explosive devices.[175]

In fact, Larry Silverstein, the lease holder of the WTC buildings, later admitted that after consulting with the NYFD, the decision was made to "pull" building seven, a term professional demolition experts use to describe a typical building implosion.[176]

A PBS documentary home video entitled *America Rebuilds* recorded Mr. Silverstein explaining what happened to Building 7: "I remember getting a call from the fire department commander, telling me that they were not sure they were going to be able to contain the fire. And I said, 'you know, we've had such terrible loss of life, maybe the smartest thing to do is pull it.' And they made the decision to pull. And we watched the building collapse."[177]

Eric Hufschmid, in his video *Painful Deceptions*, describes the "pulling" process: "They use explosives to shatter the joints holding the steel beams together. The explosions are detonated in a sequence that causes the building to fall vertically downward into a tiny pile of rubble. Also, when the building is tall, the explosives are often timed to destroy the interior of the building before the exterior walls are broken, thereby causing the interior sections to fall first. As the internal pieces fall, they "pull" the exterior walls towards the interior. This creates a small pile of rubble with the exterior walls lying on top of the rubble."[178]

Could this be the same or similar process that was used to bring down the North and South towers of the WTC, rather than

---

175 Marrs, p. 37.

176 vonKleist.

177 Eric Hufschmid, "Painful Deceptions," Documentary DVD.

178 Ibid.

controllable "isolated pockets of fire?" The explosions heard and felt by firemen and witnesses and reporters. Watching Building 7 being "pulled" on video, then watching the towers collapse, it looks similar indeed. However, in the case of the North and South towers, it appears the explosives were timed to detonate from the top of the building down, creating the explosive dust clouds surrounding the buildings as they came down.

Professor Jones supports this observation by stating, "... The twin towers appear to have been exploded "top-down" rather than proceeding from the bottom-which is clearly possible, depending on the order in which explosives are detonated. That is, explosives may have been placed on higher floors of the towers and exploded... so as to have early explosions near the region where the plane entered the tower."[179]

After viewing vonKleist's documentary DVD *911, In Plane Site*, and one should watch it multiple times because it is very easy to miss details due to the intensity of the entire documentary, I sent an email to Mr. Chris Bollyn of *American Free Press* to inform him of something else I noticed in the DVD. It reads:

Chris,

Just wanted to point out one more thing I noticed in the 911 In Plane Site DVD. In the Scene Selection menu, if you select the scene "WTC Bombs, Explosions, Demolitions" scene, in the part where they show one of the towers collapsing, just after the group of four NYFD fire fighters describe the presence of detonators, etc., as you watch the tower collapse, if you focus a few floors beneath the top of the dust cloud, but also within the dust cloud, in slow motion, you can distinctly see several bright flashes of light emanating from within the building and throughout the dust cloud. I have counted up to 20 or more of these flashes below the dust cloud; it is difficult to impossible to count the number of flashes within the dust cloud. I thought these flashes could very well be the "detonators" the fire fighters discussed. I just haven't seen this described in any of the articles I've read yet in AFP or

179 Professor Steven E. Jones.

elsewhere. Thought you were probably aware, but if not, thought you may want to take another look...

Chris Bollyn's response:

Glen,

Quite right. If you look at page 60 of Eric Hufschmid's book, "Painful Questions" you see three such orange flashes in the photo of the collapsing tower, well below the level of collapse. Many thanks,

Chris Bollyn[180]

Let's look at one more piece of evidence that supports the explosives strategically placed "pulling" theory of the WTC towers. In an article entitled "Seismologists Have Questions About 'Spikes' at Twin Towers," *American Free Press* reporter Chris Bollyn states in part:

"*The New York Times* recently ran an article about the global network of seismology entitled "Listening for Nuclear Blasts, but Hearing Earthquakes." The article included a graphic of two seismic signatures under the title "Earthquake or Bomb?"

The first seismic signature, that of a nuclear explosion that caused a magnitude 6.6 tremor, "begins with a sharp spike, followed by aftershocks." As AFP reported in September 2002, this is exactly what was seen in the seismic data recorded when the twin towers fell.

An earthquake has a different signature; it starts out with smaller waves, and then increases with the quakes strength, basically opposite to a nuclear signature.

New York seismometers recorded huge bursts of energy, which caused unexplained seismic 'spikes' at the beginning of each collapse.

This would correspond again to CNN's Aaron Brown who reported, "We have just had a huge explosion," as the South Tower began to fall. These spikes at the beginning of each collapse suggest that massive underground explosions may have literally knocked the towers off of their foundations, assisting the causes of collapse, AFP reported.

---

180 Email from Chris Bollyn of American Free Press, January 19, 2005.

"The Palisades seismic record (located 21 miles north of the WTC) shows that-as the collapses began-a huge seismic spike marked the moment the greatest energy went into the ground. The strongest jolts were all registered at the beginning of the collapses, well before the falling debris struck the earth. These unexplained 'spikes' in the seismic data lend credence to the theory that massive explosions at the base of the towers caused the collapses."

And this also corresponds to the Fox 5 news reporter who exclaimed, "There is an explosion at the base of the building, white smoke from the bottom, something has happened at the base of the building..."

"A sharp spike of short duration is how seismologist Thorne Lay of the University of California at Santa Cruz told AFP an underground nuclear explosion appears on a seismograph."

Seismology experts cannot explain why the seismic waves peaked before the towers hit the ground.

When AFP asked seismologist Arthur Lerner-Lam, director of Columbia University's Center for Hazards and Risk Research about these spikes in 2002, he said "This is an element of current research and discussion. It is still being investigated. Only a small fraction of the energy from the collapsing towers was converted into ground motion. The ground shaking that resulted from the collapse of the towers was extremely small. During the collapse, most of the energy of the falling debris was absorbed by the towers and the neighboring structures, converting them into rubble and dust or causing other damage-but not causing significant ground shaking."

So what caused the huge spikes at the beginning of each towers collapse? How did the 1,360-foot tall structures fall at or faster than free fall speed?

In the case of the South tower, the collapse occurred in 10 seconds, while the North tower collapsed in only 8 seconds. A free falling object would take about 9 seconds to fall the same distance."[181]

181 American Free Press, February 7, 2005.

Wouldn't the collapsing floors falling on top of one another in the "pancake" theory slow the falling debris?

AFP also discovered that pools of "molten steel" were found at the base of the collapsed twin towers several weeks after the collapses. The energy source for this residual heat found in these incredible hot spots is another aspect of the towers' collapse that has not been fully explained.

They would not, however, be associated with the short duration jet fuel fires.

Peter Tully, president of Tully Construction of Flushing, NY told AFP that he saw pools of "literally molten steel" at the WTC. Tully was one of the contractors hired on 9/11 to begin removing the debris from the site.

AFP also asked Mark Loizeaux, president of Controlled Demolition, Inc. (CDI) of Phoenix, MD about Tully's report of molten steel on the site. "Yes," he said, "hot spots of molten steel in the basements." These incredibly hot areas were found "at the bottom of the elevator shafts of the main towers, down seven [basement] levels," Loizeaux said. The molten steel was found "three, four, and five weeks later, when the rubble was being removed." He said molten steel was also found at WTC 7, which also collapsed mysteriously on 9/11 and was reported to have been "pulled" by Mr. Larry Silverstein.

"If I were to bring the towers down, I would put explosives in the basement to get the weight of the building to help collapse the structure," Controlled Demolition Inc.'s Loizeaux said.[182]

Again, Professor Jones: "Remarkably the explosive demolition hypothesis accounts for all the available data rather easily. The core columns on lower floors are cut using explosives, near simultaneously, along with explosives detonated up higher so that gravity acting on now-unsupported floors helps bring down the buildings quickly. The collapses are thus symmetrical, rapid and complete, with accompanying squibs-really very standard stuff for demolition experts. Thermite (whose end product is molten

182 Ibid.

iron) used on some of the steel beams readily accounts for the molten metal which then pooled beneath the rubble piles.

I believe this is a straightforward hypothesis... It is quite plausible that explosives were pre-planted in all these buildings, and set off after the two plane crashes-which were actually a diversion tactic. The science is sound. The implications are paradigm-shifting: Muslims are (probably) not to blame for bringing down the WTC buildings after all... The case for accusing ill-trained Muslims of causing all the destruction on 9-11 is far from compelling. It just does not add up."[183]

> *"In the same way, good deeds are obvious, and even those that are not cannot be hidden."*
>
> (1 Timothy 5:25, NIV)

> *"For there is nothing covered that will not be revealed, nor hidden that will not be known."*
>
> (Luke 12:2, NKJV)

183 Professor Steven E. Jones.

CHAPTER THREE
But Inwardly, They Are Ravening Wolves

Ladies and gentlemen, if you are still with me and still reading, then you have obviously kept an open mind. You have read and heard about Operation Northwoods, where *Body of Secrets* author James Bamford expressed that defenders, sympathizers and apologists of the Pentagon have always and will continue to deny any charges of official misconduct or criminal activity or deceit, no matter what evidence or proof to the contrary is set in front of them. And that in light of the Operation Northwoods documents, it is clear that deceiving the public and trumping up and provoking wars for Americans to fight and die in was standard approved policy at the highest levels of the Pentagon.

> *"Hide me from the secret plots of the wicked, from the rebellion of the workers of iniquity,"*
>
> (Psalms 64:2, NKJV)

> *"They devise iniquities: 'We have perfected a shrewed scheme'"*
>
> (Psalms 64:6, NKJV)

For those who may still harbor doubts about the possibility of the existence of large conspiracies, these have been a part of our history going back generations and centuries. From the assassinations of President John F. Kennedy, Martin Luther King, Robert F. Kennedy, and President Abraham Lincoln, to the assassination of peacemaking Israeli Prime Minister Yithak Rabin. To our discussed designed and engineered false pretexts for war: the Northwoods plan, the Gulf of Tonkin episode and the sinking of the USS Maine to list just a few.

In fact, the involvement of a large number of participants in secret plots, schemes and conspiracies have been with us since Biblical times, as recorded in the book of Acts:

> *And when it was day, some of the Jews banded together and bound themselves under an oath, saying that they would neither eat nor drink till they had killed Paul.*
>
> *Now there were more than forty who had formed this conspiracy.*
>
> *They came to the chief priests and elders, and said, "We have bound ourselves under a great oath that we will eat nothing until we have killed Paul.*
>
> *"Now you, therefore, together with the council, suggest to the commander that he be brought down to you tomorrow, as though you were going to make further inquiries concerning him; but we are ready to kill him before he comes near."*
>
> (Acts 23:12-15, NKJV)

So let us put to rest here and now the ridicule of those who are well informed about the existence of conspiracies and the tired, disingenuous, worn-out phrase or accusation of "conspiracy theorist."

You have read former U.S. Army Cpl. and current defense department operative Timothy McNiven's testimony about the 1976 Congressionally commissioned study assigned to his Strasbourg, Germany based unit, and how in that study, it was specifically devised to create the scenario where the WTC towers would be leveled by Middle Eastern terrorists using plastic box cutters and hijacked civil jet transports. That he, McNiven, believes he is still following an order to bring his story to the public in order to expose those who "turned against the American people."

And you have also read and discovered that a growing number of Americans, as well as other citizens of the world I might add, believe the events of September the 11th were an "inside job." And you have seen and read about much of the evidence that supports this scenario. There is a lot of circumstantial evidence, but there is also much physical evidence that supports this charge. And many a criminal have been tried and convicted and sentenced by juries of their peers with less convincing cases.

Before moving on to current legal action in the form of lawsuits that have been filed by survivors of victims against the perpetrators and conspirators of this massive crime against humanity on 9/11, let me just review for you statements made by a previously convicted and sentenced war criminal.

In the nineteenth century, Germany was an arising power with an unbroken string of military victories. It is worth noting here and now how provoking a war can end. From the Third Reich's number two man Herman Goering, at his Nuremberg trial, sentenced to hanging, despite his candor:

"Why of course the people don't want war. Why should some poor slob on a farm want to risk his life in a war when the best he can get out of it is to come back to his farm in one piece? Naturally the common people don't want war, neither in Russia, nor in England, nor for that matter in Germany. That is understood. But, after all, it is the leaders of the country who determine the policy and it is always a simple matter to drag the people along, whether it is a democracy or a fascist dictatorship, or a parliament, or a communist dictatorship. Voice or no voice, the people can always be brought to the bidding of the leaders. That is easy. All you have to do is tell them they are being attacked, and denounce the peacemakers for lack of patriotism and exposing the country to danger. It works the same in any country."[184]

Sound familiar? Goering pleaded that engineering an enemy attack is the STANDARD OPERATING PROCEDURE everywhere to whip up and mobilize people for war. Hitler, Goering and Goebbels were also very likely to have been responsible for

184 Ahmed, p. 334.

the infamous burning of the Reichstag or German Parliament, and they certainly tried to make the most of it. This "communist attack" consolidated their power, in a double play that is a mark of under cover or covert action, creating the illusion of a ruthless enemy, while also conveniently putting the Parliament out of commission.[185] [Just like the anthrax scare put the U.S. Congress out of commission, with impeccable timing for the executive branch, Bush et al.]

This sounds like some kind of universal subterfuge of the rich, wealthy, ruling elite to play against the common, meek people, in their quest for even more power, profit, riches, influence and control. But I feel like I have more in common with the meek and common people of every nation, than I do with the rich, wealthy, ruling elite of any nation, including my own. And remember, in Matthew chapter 5 verse 5, Jesus said: "Blessed are the meek, for they shall inherit the earth" (Matthew 5:5, KJV). And I believe this prophecy to be true. But the meek or the common people of the world, and especially the United States and other countries' common folks who have been deceived enough to join "coalitions of the willing," are going to have to educate themselves about the ways of their rich, wealthy, ruling elite before this prophecy can be fulfilled.

> *"The kings of the earth take their stand and the rulers gather together against the Lord and His Anointed One."*
>
> (Psalms 2:2, NIV)

> *"The wicked in his pride persecutes the poor; let them be caught in the plots which they have devised."*
>
> (Psalms 10:2, NKJV)

And remember, the Book of James Chapter 4 verses 1 and 2 discuss the causes of war. "You lust and do not have. You murder

185 Ibid. p. 335.

and covet and cannot obtain. You fight and war..." (James 4:2, NKJV). And James Chapter 5 verses 5 and 6 discuss the actions of the world's rich oppressors. "You have lived on the earth in pleasure and luxury... You have condemned, you have murdered the just; he does not resist you" (James 5:5-6, NKJV).

And so, with this much evidence, along with supporting scripture that discusses and explains this type of behavior, supporting at least foreknowledge, if not complicity or outright perpetration, responsibility and guilt, surely some course of legal action must be taking place. And yes indeed, there is. And we will get to it very shortly. But the reasons you may not have heard about these developments from say, Dan Rather, Tom Brokaw, ABC's Peter Jennings or Fox News is because these multimillion-dollar salaried mouthpieces and professional propagandists are nothing more than the spokesmen from the corporate-controlled press that also benefit from corporate and government misdeeds. And in the case of NBC, it is owned by General Electric, one of the top ten defense contractors,[186] also known as war profiteers, in the nation.

> *"Lying lips are an abomination to the Lord, but those who deal truthfully are His delight."*
>
> (Proverbs 12:22, NKJV)

> *"A false witness will not go unpunished, and he who speaks lies will not escape."*
>
> (Proverbs 19:5, NKJV)

Thomas Jefferson said about the press, "Our liberty depends on the freedom of the press, and that can not be limited without being lost."[187]

186 vonKleist.

187 Harrison and Gilbert, p. 4.

Well, ladies and gentlemen, I think our mainstream press has long been jeopardized and negatively influenced by forces whose interests long for less than full disclosure a long time ago, as witnessed by one Mr. John Swinton, a New York journalist in 1880 who said, "The business of the journalist is to destroy the truth, to lie outright, to pervert, to vilify, to fawn at the feet of mammon and to sell his country and his race for his daily bread... We are the tools and vassals of rich men behind the scenes. We are the jumping jacks, they pull the strings and we dance... We are intellectual prostitutes."[188] "And now, live from Studio 1A in Rockefeller Plaza..."[189]

"Let's play Hardball." Chris Mathews? Yeah right. Play is the operative descriptor word here.

Indeed, if you feel you have been thoroughly briefed about the pertinent events of the nation's business by listening to the first ten minutes of the evening's newscast, before they get into the other twenty minutes of fluff and corporate sponsorship, then I guess I would have to recommend a little more effort on your part. It would probably be wise to occasionally reference other international news sources or alternative sources other than U.S. mainstream establishment networks. I believe this would help to become more fully and accurately informed. Yes, the truth hurts, and some people can't handle the truth, as Jack Nicholson's character so eloquently stated in *A Few Good Men*.

But as a critical member of our founding fathers expressed, a republic can not survive with an uninformed, an ill-informed or a misinformed populace.

Again, Thomas Jefferson: "In every government on earth is some trace of human weakness, some germ of corruption and degeneracy, which cunning will discover, and wickedness insensibly open, cultivate and improve. Every government degenerates when trusted to the rulers of the people alone. The people, themselves, therefore, are its only safe depositaries. And

---

188 Eric Hufschmid, "Painful Questions, An Analysis of the September 11 Attacks," p. 117.

189 The Today Show, NBC News.

to render even them safe, their minds must be improved to a certain degree."[190]

> *"Happy is the man who finds wisdom, and the man who gains understanding: "*
>
> (Proverbs 3:13, NKJV)

> *"Her ways are ways of pleasantness, and all her paths are peace."*
>
> (Proverbs 3:17, NKJV)

> *"When wisdom enters your heart and knowledge is pleasant to your soul, Discretion will preserve you; understanding will keep you, To deliver you from the way of evil, from the man who speaks perverse things. From those who leave the paths of uprightness to walk in the ways of darkness; Who rejoice in doing evil, and delight in the perversity of the wicked."*
>
> (Proverbs 2:10-14, NKJV)

A question then that comes to my mind is what is the depths of corruption, the limits of wickedness and degeneration that can occur in "every government" on earth?

I cannot more fully recommend a better and more complete news source than the Washington, DC based newsweekly *American Free Press*, which I gave praise to in the introductory pages of this manuscript and which I have used extensively as a reliable reference source throughout this work. Fair and balanced? Not necessarily, but accurate and truthful no matter whose circumcised phallus gets exposed? You better believe it.

The October 4, 2004 issue of *American Free Press*, contains a front page article entitled, "White House Sued; Being Charged

190 Harrison and Gilbert, p. 382.

With 9-11 Complicity," subtitled, "Former high-ranking Republican Says Bush Orchestrated 9-11," by investigative reporter Pat Shannon. Details: that a federal lawsuit has been filed against high-ranking members of the Bush adminitration alleging that President George W. Bush ordered the September the 11th, 2001 attacks as part of an operation in the planning for over 35 years [remember the 1976 Congressionally-commissioned study participated by U.S. Army Cpl.Timothy McNiven] to "gain political advantage" and to push the neo-conservative agenda.

According to the article, Senator Robert Dole's former Chief of Staff, republican attorney Stanley Hilton, has filed a taxpayers' class action civil lawsuit representing 400 members of families of many victims of the attacks as plaintiffs to claim that the Bush administration "violated the constitutional rights of the victims of 9/11."

"This was all planned. This was a government-ordered operation. Bush personally signed the order. He personally authorized the attacks. He is guilty of treason and mass murder," Hilton said.

The suit will be launched under the Federal Fraudulent Claims Act and RICO statutes. Hilton says he has deposed top military officials who assert that high-ranking government officials were complicit in the attack.

He has also gathered documentary evidence as well as sworn statements from agents and informants of the FBI, Pentagon officials and other U.S. military officials that prove that drills and dress rehearsals in mock operations were conducted prior to the actual attack on September the 11th.

Hilton also claims to have incriminating documents showing that President George W. Bush personally signed the orders for the 9/11 attacks on the World Trade Center and the Pentagon.

Hilton has also stated that he has interviewed officials with NORAD, the North American Aerospace Defense Command, which is responsible for monitoring and defending the United States airspace, and other U.S. Air Force officials about the "5 Tripod Drills" that were taking place the morning of September the 11th. One scenario in these drills had planes crashing into the World Trade Center towers and into the Pentagon.

According to Hilton, Vice President Richard B. Cheney was personally leading these drills from a control room on the morning of 9/11.[191]

Remember when Transportation Secretary Norman Mineta testified under oath before the 9/11 Commission, that after he arrived in the Presidential Emergency Operating Center on the morning of 9/11, shortly after the South Tower had been struck, he said, "During the time that the airplane was coming in to the Pentagon, there was a young man who would come in and say to the vice president, 'The plane is 50 miles out. The plane is 30 miles out.' And when it got to be 'the plane is 10 miles out,' the young man also said to the vice president, 'Do the orders still stand?' And the vice president turned and whipped his neck around and said 'Of course the orders still stand! Have you heard anything to the contrary?'"

It certainly sounds as if the vice president was directing "drills" or something on September the 11th.

Hilton said the military, which had been ordered to take part, thought that the criminal events of 9/11 were part of these Tripod drills, and that that was the reason for NORAD "standing down" that day.

Witnesses who have wanted to testify, but have been bound by official gag orders, have stated they will come forward under subpoena, which would override such gag orders, according to Hilton.

Hilton said the neo-conservatives' plans are to continue with more terrorist attacks in order to further their agenda.[192]

When President Bush, during his State of the Union address on January 20th, 2004, told lawmakers that "key provisions of the Patriot Act are set to expire next year," several members of Congress on the opposite side of the aisle began to applaud. Then the president, looking quite perturbed at them and sternly in

191 American Free Press, October 4, 2004.

192 Ibid.

their direction announced that "the terrorist threat will not expire on that schedule."[193] It made me wonder what terrorist threat schedule President Bush might be privy to.

Hilton then went on to express that the neo-conservatives will also continue to whitewash and smokescreen their complicity in these new terrorist attacks.

Attorney Stanley Hilton said he and his staff have been threatened and harassed by the FBI. His office has been broken into and files have been stolen. He said the government is committing obstruction of justice and other crimes to prevent a legitimate civil suit exposing these criminals and their acts of treason and mass murder.

"I've been harassed personally by the chief judge of the federal court, who has instructed me to drop this suit and has threatened to kick me off the court, after 30 years of practicing law," Hilton said. "The word 'terrorist' is now being broadened. It's like the word 'communist' was used for anything during the McCarthy witch-hunt. Anybody can be called a terrorist by Bush's definition. But the irony is that the number one terrorist in the world is living in the White House. I think he deserves the world prize for hypocrisy, chicanery and fraud," Hilton said.[194]

On the evening of September 22nd, 2004, Hilton discovered his Burlingame, California (a San Francisco suburb) office had been ransacked. Police reports showed that Hilton's papers were strewn throughout the office, bookshelves had been overturned, and large files were missing. One officer at the scene reported that it seemed as if "the burglars had wanted to make it obvious that they had been there."

Hilton said he viewed it as a clear act of intimidation, though he was not concerned about any theft of files because back up files had been secreted in multiple locations. However, he does believe that the break in may have had more to do with finding out what was in his files than it did with destroying his records.

---

193 Hilder.

194 American Free Press, October 4, 2004.

On September 21st, the day before the office break in, Hilton's car was broken into, and his checkbook and other personal items were stolen. At the time, he believed it to be a random crime, unrelated to his legal practice. When he discovered his office was also broken into the next day, he thought maybe these acts could be related.

Hilton said prior to these latest incidents, he had been receiving death threats on his cell phone from unknown callers, one of whom identified himself as "Jimmy Tiger." Relation to Tony is unknown at this time. Dirty deeds done dirt-cheap?

Stanley Hilton, former Chief of Staff for Senator Bob Dole, and a longtime republican recounted how during the Pentagon papers case, presidential minions of Richard Nixon broke into Daniel Ellsberg's office and that this type of intimidation and break-ins are "a standard modus operandi of the Republican Party."

Hilton told *American Free Press* that earlier in the summer two United States attorneys visited him from the Disciplinary Committee of the U.S. District Court in San Francisco. They told him that the Chief Judge, Ms. Marilyn Patel, "does not like this case," and wanted him to dismiss it. They then told him if he refused, the Disciplinary Committee intended to take action to prevent him from practicing in the federal court.

Hilton said he refused to drop the case because he was acting on behalf of clients. Hilton said he was told "off the record" that Attorney General John Ashcroft and the Justice Department were now behind the action to stop him, and he was warned not to "go public" with this story.

"This is clearly an attempt to interfere with a legitimate civil rights suit; it is a criminal act; it is a violation of my rights, and it's obstruction of justice, witness tampering and intimidation of an attorney. And they should all be prosecuted," Hilton said.[195]

Attorney Stanley Hilton's taxpayer class action civil lawsuit against the Bush Administration is not the only legal action taking place against them. Another civil lawsuit has been filed

195 American Free Press, October 11, 2004, pp. 1,15.

against top officials of the Bush Administration accusing them of complicity in the September the 11th attacks. According to the November 8th, 2004, issue of *American Free Press:*

Mr. William Rodriguez, a former maintenance worker at the World Trade Center, has also filed a civil lawsuit, his in the Philadelphia, Pennsylvania Federal Court. The suit names President George W. Bush, Vice President Richard B. Cheney, Secretary of Defense Donald Rumsfeld and other Bush team members as being complicit in the 9/11 attacks. Rodriguez claims that these top officials either planned the attacks, or had foreknowledge of the attacks and permitted them to succeed for the purpose of exploiting a "new Pearl Harbor" in order to launch wars against Afghanistan and Iraq.

The lawsuit-Rodriguez v. Bush, et al., Civil Action Number 04 CV 4952-was filed in United States District Court in Philadelphia on October 22nd, 2004.

The phrase "new Pearl Harbor" comes from a declaration of principles stated by the neo-conservative's "Project for the New American Century." In that "Project," the neo-conservatives proposed that an event, similar in magnitude to the Pearl Harbor attack, would be needed to propel American public opinion toward supporting the overthrow of Saddam Hussein and the subsequent domination of the Middle East by the United States.

Attorney Phil Berg is a former candidate for both Governor and U.S. Senator from the state of Pennsylvania, and he is also a former deputy attorney general from Pennsylvania. As William Rodriguez's attorney, he said, "the official story of what actually took place on 9-11 is a lie." Berg, like Stanley Hilton, maintains that many prominent figures in politics, in the military and the mass media consider the official story of 9-11 to be untrue.

"We do not pretend to have put together a full and definitive account of how, and by whom the attacks were carried out. But, information reported in the mainstream media, and viewed in light of common sense, and the laws of physics, demonstrate that the official story, examined closely is not credible."

On September the 11th, Mr. William Rodriguez, a Puerto Rican bom maintenance worker at the World Trade Center rescued fifteen people. He had the master key to the North Tower staircases and unlocked those doors and then led firefighters up the stairwell, aiding in the evacuation of hundreds of additional people who might have otherwise perished on 9/11.

Rodriguez re-entered the building after the first plane struck, and was the last person to exit the North Tower alive, except for those few survivors who were later pulled from the rubble. He survived the collapse of the North Tower by diving beneath a fire truck to avoid the avalanch of concrete and steel. After receiving on site treatment for his injuries, Rodriguez plunged right back into the rescue efforts. The next morning, he returned to the site to continue to aid in the search and rescue efforts.

Later, Rodriguez became an unofficial spokesman for survivors and helped create the World Trade Center Memorial Fund.

When asked why he decided to bring this controversial lawsuit, Rodriguez said that having survived the World Trade Center disaster when so many others did not, he feels compelled to learn the truth of what happened that day. "If what the government has told us about 9/11 is a lie, somebody has to take action to reveal the truth. If suing President Bush is what I have to do to accomplish that, so be it," Rodriguez said.[196]

The October 25th, 2004 issue of *American Free Press* reported that Rodriguez's attorney, Phil Berg, pointed out that the only living Senator who has dared to publicly question even parts of the official story of September the 11th, Senator Mark Dayton, a democrat from Minnesota, had received threats ominous enough that compelled him to shut down his Washington, DC office until after the November 2004 election.

On October 12th, Senator Dayton's Washington, DC office closed until after Election Day due to security concerns. Dayton's Minnesota office said the closure was based on information contained in an intelligence briefing.

196 American Free Press, November 8, 2004.

Mr. Bill Pickle, Sergeant at Arms for the Senate told *American Free Press* that Senator Mark Dayton had shown caution and acted on intelligence information gathered from the previous week.

At congressional hearings on July 31st, 2004, Senator Dayton spoke out and complained about the government's lies and incompetence in the official 9/11 commission report. Speaking about the military's fabrications concerning their failure to respond properly to the "hijacked" planes, Senator Dayton said, "They (NORAD) lied to the American people; they lied to Congress, and they lied to your 9-11 commission to create a false impression of competence, communication, coordination and protection of the American people. And we can set up all the oversight possible at great additional cost to the American taxpayers and it won't be worth an Enron pension if the people responsible lie to us, if they take the records and doctor them into falsehoods, and if they get away with it."[197]

Senator Dayton probably had good reason to temporarily leave his Washington, DC office, after taking those positions publicly, considering what happened to the other Senator from Minnesota, also a democrat, and who wanted to seriously investigate September the 11th, who also opposed the war on Iraq, and who generally stood in the way of President Bush's agenda. Senator Paul David Wellstone died in a mysterious plane crash on October 25th, 2002.[198]

In a book reviewed by James P. Tucker Jr. of *American Free Press* entitled *American Assassination*, authors James H. Fetzer, Ph.D., and Don Four Arrows Jacobs, Ph.D., both college professors (Fetzer at the University of Minnesota, Duluth, and Jacobs at Northern Arizona University), concluded that the Central Intelligence Agency plotted the plane crash that killed Senator Wellstone because he stood in the way of CIA and White House goals.

197 Ibid, October 25, 2004.

198 American Free Press, November 8, 2004.

He was the leading obstacle to war. He might have filibustered the Homeland Security Act. He opposed the White House on tax cuts. He wanted to investigate 9/11. In the Senate, Paul David Wellstone was a major obstacle to the exercise of power, the authors concluded.

Mr. Norman Coleman, the handpicked candidate of Mr. Karl Rove was elected as a Republican to Wellstone's seat in the U.S. Senate.

Fetzer made his case step-by-step, starting with an observation made by investigative reporter Christopher Bollyn of *American Free Press* that the FBI arrived on the scene from the twin cities, Minneapolis-St. Paul surprisingly fast.

"Using very minimal times, I later calculated that for its rapid response team to have arrived on the scene by noon, it would have had to have left St. Paul around 9:30 that morning, about the same time the Senator's plane was departing... which would have been an extraordinary feat of prognostication," said Fetzer.

Thus, the authors make the case that the FBI had advanced knowledge of the impending assassination that also claimed the lives of Senator Wellstone's wife, daughter, three staff members and two pilots.

"The first responders on the scene were ordered not to take photos by the FBI, why? Even the Associated Press photographer who asked us to remain anonymous had a difficult time getting photos and was only allowed fifteen minutes at the crash site, something this photographer said was very, very unusual. You would think that more photographs would be better, since they would provide a more complete record," said Fetzer.

The FBI shoved the National Transportation Safety Board (NTSB), the federal government agency charged with investigating and determining causes of aircraft accidents and incidents, aside. A cover-up would explain the early arrival of the FBI, the prohibition against photographs and the reversal of roles between the FBI and the NTSB, explained Fetzer.[199]

---

199 Ibid.

You see, the way this interaction between the NTSB and the FBI normally works at an aircraft accident site is the NTSB is called out and they begin their investigation. If and when, in the course of their investigation, they suspect or find evidence of foul play or criminal activity, that is when the NTSB requests assistance from the FBI.

The day after the crash, Ms. Carol Carmody, head of the investigative NTSB team, reported that the FBI advised her that there were "no indications of terrorist activity."

"I thought that was odd; since the NTSB had yet to determine the cause of the crash, how could the FBI possibly already know?" Fetzer said.

Fetzer also cited another credible and credentialled Professor at Buffalo State College, Michael I. Niman, who also raised the question that Senator Paul David Wellstone had been murdered. Fetzer said, "Karl Rove, Dick Cheney and Donald Rumsfeld may not have executed this hit, but they were in position to make it happen."[200]

Returning to comments made by William Rodriguez's attorney, Phil Berg said, "Some facts cannot be denied. Clearly 9-11 was carried out by more than one person. Therefore, by definition, there was a conspiracy. What we are arguing here is that the true conspirators have abused their enormous power and the trust of the American people to concoct and to sell the world a false conspiracy theory to justify war and mass murder for economic and political gain. Since the neocons, allied with the president, said in almost so many words that they wished for a new Pearl Harbor, why dismiss out of hand an allegation that they used their undeniably sufficient power to actually bring it about? Why has there been no full and transparent investigation? Isn't it shocking that the federal government grabbed up all the physical evidence, and that no police authority has conducted a true criminal investigation into 3,000 homicides? Instead of due process of law, government officials and the mass media convicted Osama bin Laden and had names and photos of his

200 Ibid.

19 accomplices on the Internet, literally within hours of the attacks."[201]

America Free Press also reported that since the case opened, the federal government has attempted at every turn to have the case dismissed, hoping Berg would run out of energy or financial resources to continue. On April 22nd, 2005, Phil Berg urged the U.S. District Court for the Eastem District in Philadelphia to hear the case despite strong government pleas citing national security concerns as well as the courts lack of jurisdiction to hear such a conspiracy claim.

The court listened to oral arguments and took written briefs from both parties under advisement and is expected to make a ruling in the coming weeks.

Berg said the government's legal motions are baseless and just another attempt to silence "anyone trying to get at the truth behind 9-11."

Berg said, "... the judge gave me great latitude in allowing me to argue my case and permitted me to state critical evidence. However, until these various motions are resolved, we cannot enter into the nuts and bolts of the official discovery process."

Berg told the court bluntly, "If there was no government complicity in the 9/11 attacks, why have defendants lied repeatedly about abundant advance warnings."

Berg claims a web of government deceit and financial backing continued all the way up to the days just before 9-11 as witnesses will testify and records will reveal that the alleged hijackers were actually on the government payroll.

The complaint goes on to say that the defendants deliberately concealed the fact that they had ample warnings of terrorist attacks and failed to act on them in order to carry out a full-blown war on terrorism as a means to justify their neo-conservative political goals.

Regarding 9-11 itself, the Rodriguez action aims to prove that the World Trade Center twin towers, as well as WTC Building 7 were destroyed by a controlled demolition as clearly proven

201 Ibid.

by the laws of physics, and that this demolition could have only been an "inside job." Also, that an unprecedented nationwide "ground stop" order and stand-down of NORAD must have had White House approval since it prevented even the military from flying, allowing the 9-11 attacks to proceed without interruption. And that the defendants conspired to and did allow the attacks to happen by delaying military interceptions of the "hijacked planes."

"Now is the time to stand tall together and bring back our freedoms as they stood under the Declaration of Independence, Bill of Rights and the Constitution of the United States," said Berg.[202]

Attorney Phil Berg is also the representing counsel for Mrs. Ellen Mariani, whose husband, Louis Neil Mariani, died when United Airlines flight 175 was allegedly flown into the South Tower on September the 11th.

On November 26, 2003, Berg announced during a press release, the filing of a detailed amended complaint in the U.S. District Court for the Eastern District of Pennsylvania in the case of Mariani vs. Bush et al, alleging President Bush, and other officials of his administration, including but not limited to Vice President Cheney, Attorney General John Ashcroft, and Defense Secretary Donald Rumsfeld that they:

Had knowledge/warnings of 911 and failed to warn or take steps to prevent.

Have been covering up the truth of 911.

Have therefore violated the laws of the United States, and

Are being sued under the Civil RICO act.

Berg stated, "I will be detailing the charges against Bush and others."

He further expressed that Mrs. Mariani was the first victim family member to bring civil action regarding the events of 911 against United Airlines. Since then, the truth of 911 has not been forthcoming and Mrs. Mariani, for the good of her country,

202 American Free Press, May 9, 2005.

now seeks the truth via this courageous action under the RICO, Racketeer Influenced and Corrupt Organizations Act.

Attorney Phil Berg also expressed that Mrs. Mariani, with her Amended Complaint intends to expose the truth to remember the dead and prevent continued deaths of American military personnel due to President Bush's "Failure to act and prevent" the worst attacks on our nation since Pearl Harbor, and for "failing to act and prevent" the murder of Plaintiff's husband, Louis Neil Mariani, for financial and political reasons and have "obstructed justice" in the aftermath of said criminal acts and omissions.

Plaintiff believes Defendant George W. Bush, is invoking a long standard operating procedure of invoking national security and executive privilege claims to suppress the basis of this lawsuit.

Plaintiff asserts, contrary to Defendant George W. Bush's assertion that Osama bin Laden and his Al Qaeda Network terrorists were responsible for 9-11, the compelling evidence that will be presented in this case through discovery, subpoena power by this Court and testimony at trial will lead to one undisputed fact, Defendant Bush failed to act and prevent 911 knowing the attacks would lead to our nation having to engage in an "International War on Terror" which would benefit Defendants both financially and for political reasons.

Reports have emerged and will be confirmed through discovery that the Carlyle Group, the giant defense contractor, until recently employed Defendant George W. Bush and his father George H. W. Bush. Hence, the "Bush Family" and other defendants financial profiting by war goes to the heart of Plaintiff's RICO Act claim.

Plaintiff further asserts, in the late 1970's and throughout the 1980's, Defendants were allies with both Osama bin Laden and Saddam Hussein during the former Soviet Union's invasion of Afghanistan and Iran-Iraq war respectively, wherein, personal and political deals were made and it is believed upon discovery, these dealings hold the truth about "911."

In sum, Plaintiff will call to trial former federal employees with firsthand knowledge and expertise with military intelligence and other duties to support the underlying RICO act foundational basis to prove Defendants have engaged in a "pattern of criminal activity and obstruction of justice" in violation of the public trust and laws of the United States for personal and financial gains.

Plaintiff will prove, Defendants have engaged our nation in an endless war on terror to achieve their personal goals and agendas. [203]

Mrs. Mariani probably said it best, expressing her grief and her grievances, in her own words, in the following letters to her late husband and her open letter to President Bush:

Dear Neil...

I, as your wife, have searched for sane answers to what happened on that beautiful, sunny, warm Tuesday, September 11, 2001.

You, Neil, were so tanned and fit, happy to be leaving with me before dawn for Boston's Logan Airport. You and I were traveling on separate planes to the California wedding of my daughter, Gina, your step-daughter. You decided to go out for the wedding at the very last minute, and to help pay for the ticket, we held garage sales together.

Neil, I will never forget when we said goodbye at Boston Airport. Neil, you as a gentleman were always carrying heavy items for me, and that morning, you carried inside the terminal two large boxes full of toys for our grand-kids that were to be there for the wedding as flower girl and ring bearer.

You kissed me at the curb and said goodbye. Then you kissed me again inside and said "See you, Ellen. I'll arrive three minutes after your plane lands," and walked away. But suddenly, you came back, gave me a third kiss and a big hug. It was then I noticed you seemed nervous. I thought it was because you were not used to flying. You then said goodbye for the third time, then left. I looked back to catch a last glance at you, Neil, but you were gone and out of sight.

---

203 "911 Victim's Wife Files RICO Case against GW Bush," www.scoop.co.nz/mason/stories/W00311/S00261.htm, 12/22/04.

Neil, you never made it to California for Gina's wedding that September 15, 2001. I left two hours before you and had a scheduled layover in Chicago. It was there that I found out what had happened to you. Your airplane, United Airlines Flight 175, had crashed into the second tower of the World Trade Center. You, my husband, were gone in a ball of fire. The September 15th wedding of Gina's went on in defiance of what had happened on September 11th.

Now as I stood as a new widow of four days, Gina asked me to give her away to be married. I wore two yellow roses, and made a toast in remembrance of you.

Neil, my life as a widow is now very still and has an eerie feeling. I can not hear your voice, or see your handsome face. Many reminders make it hard, like your birthday two days before Christmas. Also, I remember July 30th, which would have been our 14th wedding anniversary.

There is nothing left of you, no resting place or gravesite to visit, just an empty hole in my heart, and the heartache of life without you, Neil. I realize that the sun has shone once again as it did on September 11, 2001, when we parted for the last time, you as my husband, but it does not seem the same. I have wanted to be with you, Neil, so many times since that day and had wished I was with you on that plane, giving each other comfort, like we had done so many times throughout our marriage. This was not to be in the plans God had for us.

Now it is my job to go on without you, Neil. I will always have the memories that we shared together, and I thank God for you being my husband for 13 years. Now I walk all alone for with death did we part. My hope and prayer to God is that we all find peace and comfort and support one another, as we go on living without our loved ones.

Peace and God Bless Us All,

Ellen[204]

And Mrs. Mariani's open letter to President Bush:

Mr. Bush,

---

204 www.911forthetruth.com/pages/EllenNeil.htm, 12/26/04.

This "open letter" is coming from my heart. I want you to know that I am neither a Republican nor a Democrat and that this is not an attempt to "bash the Government."

You Mr. Bush should be held responsible and liable for any and all acts that were committed to aid in any "cover up" of the tragic events of September 11, 2001. As President you have a duty to protect the American people. On September 11th you did not instruct your staff to issue a nationwide emergency warning/alert to advise us of the attack on America. We had to receive the news of the attacks via the news networks.

In the months leading up to the attacks you were repeatedly advised of a possible attack on American soil. During your daily intelligence briefings you were given information that had been uncovered that the very real possibility existed that certain undesirable elements would use commercial aircraft to destroy certain "target" buildings. You never warned the American people of this possible threat. Who were you protecting?

When you took no responsibility towards protecting the general public from the possibility of attack, you were certainly not upholding the oath you spoke when you took office. In that oath you pledged to uphold the Constitution of the United States of America.

On the morning of the attack, you and members of your staff were fully aware of the unfolding events yet you chose to continue on to the Emma E. Booker Elementary School to proceed with a scheduled event and "photo op." While our nation was under attack you did not appear to blink an eye or shed a tear. You continued on as if everything was "business as usual."

In the days following the attacks all air traffic was grounded and Americans, including myself, were stranded wherever they had been when the flight ban was imposed. I was stranded at Midway Airport in Chicago, unable to continue on to California for my daughter's wedding...

It is my belief that you intentionally allowed 9/11 to happen to gather public support for a "war on terrorism." These wars, in Afghanistan and Iraq, have not accomplished what you stated were your goals. Why have you not captured Osama bin Laden? Where are Saddam's weapons of mass destruction? All that has happened is a bill that is passed before Congress for 87 billion dollars to rebuild what you ordered blown to bits. As an American who lost a loved one in the "war on terror" I do pray and support our troops who were sent to Afghanistan and Iraq by you. These troops have and will continue to die for your lies. As an American I can make this statement as it appears that associates of your family may stand to prosper from the rebuilding of Afghanistan and Iraq.

Mr. Bush the time has come for you to stop your control over us. Stop blocking the release of certain evidence and documents that were discovered by the 9/11 Investigation Commission if you have nothing to hide proving you did not fail to act and prevent the attacks of 9/11. Your reason for not releasing this material is that it is a matter of "national security." When in fact I believe that it is your personal credibility/security that you are concerned with. You do not want the public to know the full extent of your responsibility and involvement.

After 9/11 the Patriot Act and Homeland Security Act were passed. Both of these allow the government to tap your telephone, search your home, and seize whatever they feel they need to do on a whim. They can do this without a judge's review or a warrant. I feel that this is in direct conflict with our rights as stated in the Constitution and Bill of Rights.

We the families of 9/11 victims need to have answers to the following questions:

1. Why were 29 pages of the 9/11 committee report personally censored at your request?

2. Where are the "black boxes" from Flight 11 and Flight 175?

3. Where are the "voice recorders" from Flight 11 and Flight 175?

4. Why can't we gain access to the complete air traffic control records for Flight 11 and Flight 175?

5. Where are the airport surveillance tapes that show the passengers boarding the doomed flights?

6. When will complete passenger lists for all flights be released?

7. Why did your brother Jeb (the Governor of Florida) go to the offices of the Hoffman Aviation School and order that flight records and files be removed? These files were then put on a C130 government cargo plane and flown out of the country. Where were they taken and who ordered it done?

It has been over two years since hundreds of our lost loved ones "remains" have still yet to be identified and their remains placed in a landfill at Fresh Kill. We want our heroes brought back and given a public and proud resting place where we can pay our respects and honor them. These innocent people never had a chance as they were taken from us on that sad September Day.

In the court of public opinion Mr. Bush, your lies are being uncovered each day. My husband, all of the other victims and their families and our nation as a whole, has been victimized by your failed leadership prior to and after 9/11.

I will prove this in a court of law!

Ellen M. Mariani[205]

These are very serious charges. To review, Attorney Stanley Hilton, a true republican, not a neo-conservative, the former Chief of Staff of Senator Robert S. Dole, said about the massive crime of September the 11th, "This was all planned. This was a government-ordered operation. Bush personally signed the order. He is guilty of treason and mass murder."

Hilton also said that he has deposed top military officials who assert that high-ranking government officials were complicit in

205 Ibid.

the attack and that he has incriminating documents showing that Bush personally signed the orders for the 9/11 attacks on the World Trade Center and the Pentagon.

And Mr. William Rodriguez, a former maintenance worker at the World Trade Center who rescued many and saved many lives on 9/11, along with his attorney, Mr. Phil Berg, former Deputy Attorney General and former candidate for both Governor and Senator from the state of Pennsylvania, claim that President Bush, Vice President Cheney, Secretary of Defense Rumsfeld and other Bush team members were complicit in the 9/11 attacks. Berg also maintains that many prominent figures in politics, the military and the mass media consider the official story of 9/11 to be untrue.

Berg also said, "... What we're arguing here is that the true conspirators have abused their enormous power and the trust of the American people to concoct and to sell to the world a false conspiracy theory to justify war and mass murder for economic and political gain."

And Mrs. Ellen Mariani along with her attorney, Phil Berg, allege that President Bush and his administration have been covering up the truth of 9/11, that they failed to act to prevent the 9/11 attacks to justify an international war on terror which would benefit the Bush family and other defendants both politically and financially by profiting from war.

I keep thinking about that verse in James 4 about coveting and lusting being the causes of war. Is there a connection here somewhere?

I realize that this material is extremely uncomfortable and upsetting. As the saying goes, the truth hurts. Arthur Schopenhaur once said, "All truth passes through three stages. First, it is ridiculed. Second, it is violently opposed. Third, it is accepted as self-evident."[206]

We all want and almost need to believe in our government, our political system, our way of life, that we support just causes, and in the nation that we celebrate every 4th of July. That this

206 www.letsroll911.org Forums.

could not possibly happen in our land, in our own back yard, and in our time.

But if I were to ask just about everyone if they thought that Adolph Hitler was an evil man, I am confident that close to 100 percent of the time, the answer would be yes. And if that is the case, and I believe it to be, how in the world was he able to commit those atrocities for so long? I think that for a long time, he must have had the support of the populace in Germany. And if he had the support of the German people, either they must have been evil too, or maybe they were entirely deceived by him, or maybe the populace of Germany was too afraid to speak out. And I believe all of these to some degree were contributing factors to his ability to continue for so long his deeds of evil.

But remember, Hitler himself said, "... the great masses of people will more easily fall victims to a great lie, than to a small one."[207] Said another way, the greater the lie, the greater the people that will believe it.

You see, they rely on blind trust, your blind trust, they need your trust. Without your trust, they could not get away with these evil deeds. They take advantage of your trust; it prevents your acceptance of the truth and allows them to continue with the lies and deceit and the evil acts they perpetrate. And the more unbelievable or hideous the act, the easier it is to get away with.

> *"Like a roaring lion and a charging bear is a wicked ruler over poor people."*
>
> (Proverbs 28:15, NKJV)

> *"When the righteous are in authority, the people rejoice; but when a wicked man rules, the people groan."*
>
> (Proverbs 29:2, NKJV)

207 Hilder.

> *"Scoffers set a city aflame, but wise men turn away wrath."*
>
> (Proverbs 29:8, NKJV)

In the first chapter of this text, we discussed some New Testament scripture where in St. Matthew, chapter seven, verses 15 and 16 Jesus said, "Beware of false prophets, which come to you in sheep's clothing but inwardly they are ravening wolves. Ye shall know them by their fruits..." (Matthew 7:15-16, KJV). And in St. Matthew, chapter twenty-four verse 11, Jesus said: "And many false prophets shall rise, and shall deceive many" (Matthew 24:7, KJV).

What does this mean to you and how does it apply to our lives today? Aren't we supposed to learn from the Gospels? Do they or could they still apply to us today?

In Second Peter, chapter two, verses 1 through 3, Simon Peter, an apostle of Jesus Christ, warned us about false prophets in our time. He said, "But there were also false prophets among the people, just as there will be false teachers among you. They will secretly introduce destructive heresies, even denying the sovereign Lord who brought them-bringing swift destruction on themselves. Many will follow their shameful ways and will bring the way of truth into disrepute. In their greed these teachers will exploit you with their stories they have made up..." (2 Peter 2:1-3, NIV).

Is there another connection here somewhere?

> *"And pray that we may be delivered from wicked and evil men, for not everyone has faith."*
>
> (2 Thessalonians 3:2, NIV)

In chapter one of this manuscript, I asked if you thought if you could be deceived, or maybe, just a little bit fooled? Ever fallen for a practical joke? Well, no one likes to be fooled, and this is much more serious than a practical joke. Jesus said many would be deceived, by many false prophets. And the very insidious nature of deception is in the fact that one does not realize the betrayal is taking place. One does not realize it is happening to them, and one's own nature is to believe that it could not happen to them. Then, when evidence of the deception that is taking place begins to present itself to the conscience, ego defense mechanisms kick in and prevent the full realization of the degree or the depth of the treachery that is taking place. This is usually followed by irrational rationalizations like, "Well, they must have had to have done this... for the good of the country... or else..."

Ladies and gentlemen, let me please ask you, if you look at the globe or a map of the world, and consider our nation's short 230-year history, just about everyone and every nation on the face of the planet have been held out to be evil. Whether it was the savage Native Americans, or the evil British Empire, or even those dastardly rebels from the South, or the evil Northern aggressors, how is it these people and their leaders can be evil, but our current leaders cannot? How is it the German people and their leaders, or the French people and their leaders, or the Mexican people and their leaders, or the Cubans and their leader, or the Hondurans or Panamanians, the Colombians, the Puerto Ricans, the Spaniards, the evil empire of the Soviet Union, the Japanese, the Italians, the Chinese, the North Koreans, the Vietnamese, the Filipinos, the Cambodians, the Libyans, the Egyptians, the Saudi Arabians, the Yemenis, the Somalians, the Sudanese, the Iraqis, the Iranians, the Lebanese, the Syrians, the Afghanis and the Pakistanis, the Laotians, the Hungarians, the Austrians, the Nicaraguans, oh yeah, don't forget those evil Palestinians, the obstructers to Mideast peace and evil oppressors of the Israelis- how is it all of these nations, their leaders and their people can be believed to be evil, and their mass media propagandists, but the United States and its best Middle East ally Israel cannot? Does this make any sense?

How do you know that what you truly believe is really nothing more than a true test of the level of the effectiveness of the propaganda that you've been exposed to your whole life?

Remember, it has been said that history is the propaganda of the victors, and written by those who hang the heroes.[208]

In the Temptation of Jesus, in the Gospel of St. Luke, chapter four, verses 1 through 8: "Jesus full of the Holy Spirit returned from the Jordan and was led by the Spirit in the desert, where for forty days he was tempted by the devil. He ate nothing during those days, and at the end of them he was hungry" (Luke 4:1-2, NIV).

"The devil led him up to a high place and showed him in an instant all the kingdoms of the world. And he said to Him, "I will give you all their authority and splendor, for it has been given to me and I can give it to anyone I want to. So if you worship me, it will all be yours." (Luke 4:5-7, NIV)

Jesus answered, "It is written, Worship the Lord your God and serve Him only" (Luke 4:8, NIV).

So, this is how one gets elected.

You'll notice in the passage just reviewed that the devil did not exclude any kingdom or nation; in fact, he showed him "*all the kingdoms*," (emphasis added) during this exchange with Jesus.

And so, as I'm sure you are all well aware, in fact, the United States and its leaders, and its best Middle East ally Israel and its leaders, are entirely capable of acts of evil of the order and magnitude of September the 11th. And the mass media of these nations are capable of self-serving lies and propaganda. Indeed, it was shown to be universal.

Remember Thomas Jefferson stated, "In every government on earth is some trace of human weakness, some germ of corruption and degeneracy... Every government degenerates when trusted to the rulers of the people alone..."[209]

And so, as we continue to explore this scenario, we will continue to present evidence, both physical and circumstantial, that supports this argument. We will continue to make connections that support this thesis.

---

208 vonKleist.

209 Harrison and Gilbert, p. 382.

But just as in the Northwoods documents, many will reject it out of hand, despite the overwhelming and conclusive evidence, because they are conditioned both mentally and psychologically to believe what they believe; in fact, some believe what they are told to believe and nothing else. This is outside of their comfort zone or happy place, and some just will not go there. But once a mind is completely closed and a mind is made up, nothing, not even absolute undeniable physical proof, can penetrate.

Dr. Albert D. Pastore, Phd. further describes this phenomenon in his study titled *An Independent Investigation of 9/11 and the War on Terrorism*. In describing "The Lemming Effect," Dr. Pastore states in part:

"There are of course those who have fallen under the hypnotic spell of the TV talking-heads and 'experts' whom they worship as authority figures. Unaccustomed to thinking for themselves, no amount of truth can sway them from their preconceived prejudices and conditioned reactions. They will even deny that which they see with their own eyes... They become victims of a psychological affliction known as 'the lemming effect.' Lemmings are small rodents who have been observed to follow each other as they charge to their deaths into raging rivers or even off cliffs. Lemminghood is an innate psychological phenomenon, present in most mammals and observable in common people as well as the most sophisticated and educated elites.

Lemminghood is not an intellectual phenomenon-it is psychological. As such, no socio-economic class is immune to its strangulating effect. A grant-seeking university scientist can be a lemming just as much as a fashion obsessed teen-age girl... The power to fit in with one's social peers can be irresistible. To a human lemming, the logic behind an opinion doesn't count as much as the power and popularity behind an opinion. Man, like lemming, behaves collectively... The same lemming effect which enables the masses of a justly governed society to make progress all at the same time, can, in an unjustly governed society, cause the masses to lose their sense of judgement, all at the same time...

Lemmings simply cannot bear the burden of responsibility, or the social discomfort, which comes with thinking independently. They are capable only of repeating that which they hear from the talking heads and 'experts' on TV. Lemmings will not only resist efforts to change their misguided beliefs with all of their mental energy, but they will usually attack anyone who dares to question their myths. Lemmings are absolutely terrified at the thought of being labeled as an 'extremist' or a 'conspiracy theorist.' Ironically, the very same lemmings who instinctively ridicule all 'conspiracy theories,' are always the first ones to blindly swallow the most ridiculous conspiracy theories imaginable when the government and the media present them...

The chains of ideological conformity have too strong of a grip, and breaking them is a difficult task. With the limited resources at our disposal, it is next to impossible to compete with the media-lemming-masters. For this reason, the lie of the emperor is always believed before the truth of the peasant...

Merely being misinformed does not make one a lemming. Anyone can be fooled. There is no shame in being misinformed. But, to persist in erroneous thinking, even in the face of irrefutable evidence and logic, is the height of lemminghood... Those individuals who can muster up these moral and mental virtues will then be ready to accept the truth when it is presented in clear and logical sequence...

The very idea that a Saudi caveman and his band of half-trained, nerdy Arab flight school students orchestrated the most sophisticated terror operation in world history is utterly laughable. And yet, due to the blithering barrage of propaganda and disinformation dished out by the government/media complex, millions of 'patriotic' sheeple now accept this fantastic fairy tale, this moronic mendacity, this silly superstition, this dangerous delusion, with a zealous conviction bordering on mass insanity.

As an admittedly useless public service to my helplessly doomed countrymen, and as a gift to a posterity which will hopefully be more enlightened than my bewildered, blood-thirsty, flag waving contemporaries, I have published this research in the hopes of liberating as many people as I can from the oppressive yoke of media brainwashing and state sponsored lies."[210]

And so, in order to be able to discern facts from fiction, truth from lies, one must absolutely retain an open mind. And the more open, the more light can enter, and the easier and the better one can decipher real truth from official lies.

As Hoosier rocker John Mellencamp sings: "The simple minded and the uninformed, can be easily led astray. And those that cannot connect the dots, hey, look the other way. People believe what they want to believe when it makes no sense at all. So be careful of those killing in Jesus's name, He don't believe in killing at all... So be careful of what you believe in, there's plenty to get you confused. And in this land called Paradise, you must walk in many men's shoes. Bigotry and hatred are enemies to us all. Grace, mercy and forgiveness will help a man walk tall. So walk tall...[211]

Sorry, I'm a big Mellencamp fan, but these lyrics aptly apply here.

And so, with keeping an open mind and carefully considering the evidence and the testimony that has been brought to you so far, how would you decide to proceed if you were a member of a grand jury considering the fates of George W. Bush, Dick Cheney, Donald Rumsfeld, Colin Powell, Ariel Sharon, Paul Wolfowitz, Douglas Feith, Richard Perle, Benjamin Netanyahu, and the rest of the bilateral enterprise?

In the November 8th, 2004, issue of *American Free Press*, there is an article entitled "Citizen Grand Jury Indicts Feds Over Sept. 11 Attacks. Patriots, Researchers Meet in L.A. to Plan Strategy against Elite," written by Christopher Bollyn. It reads in part:

"A citizen's grand jury has voted to indict high officials in the U.S. government for complicity in the events of 9-11 after considering evidence presented by five researchers. The 6 hour

---

210 Dr. Albert Pastore, Ph.D., "An Independent Investigation of 9/11 and the War on Terrorism" http:/letsroll911.orgipw-web/bulletin/bb/viewtopic.php?t=9885, 8/26/05.

211 John Mellencamp, "Walk Tall,"www.lyricalcontent.com/htmlitphp?q=2128&artist=John+Mellencamp&titlt=Walk+Tall, 12/26/04.

event, "Solving the 9-11 Crime-A Citizens Grand Jury" was organized by Lynn Pentz of "911 truthla.us" and held at the Bob Hope Patriotic Hall in Los Angeles during the evening of October 23rd, 2004.

After discussion of the legal and historical basis for the grand jury, it was decided to enlarge the original grand jury to 23 in order to comply with California law.

The grand jury heard much of the evidence presented in this work thus far, presented by researchers Webster Tarpley, Barbara Honegger, Don Paul, Jim Hoffman, and Eric Hufschmid along with Chris Bollyn.

Nay sayers notwithstanding, after hearing the evidence, the grand jury voted to indict President Bush and other high officials of a number of charges of complicity in the 9-11 attacks, and other offenses related to actions taken by the administration in their "war on terror."[212]

At this event, investigative journalist Christopher Bollyn worked alongside Eric Hufschmid, author of "Painful Questions," to create a five-minute video presentation with photographs taken from the Pentagon and the World Trade Center. The photos taken from the Pentagon show extensive decontamination procedures carried out by emergency personnel in full body suits with respirators and scrub downs, indicating the Department of Defense was aware of the danger of depleted uranium contamination at the site. Depleted uranium is extremely dense and is therefore used on the tips of a wide range of missiles in the U.S. arsenal. Missiles tipped with depleted uranium rods are used to penetrate the armored steel of military vehicles and buildings. [213]

Mr. Hufschmid's book, "Painful Questions," contains many important color photographs in large format, not seen anywhere else. As the author, he spent more than $6,000 for the rights to use these photos from Reuters, Associated Press and other sources. Some of these photos show dust and debris being shot

212 American Free Press, November 8, 2004.

213 Ibid

out hundreds of feet, again consistent with widespread reports of explosives by witnesses, firefighters, newsmen, and survivors on the scene, and the top 30 floors of the South tower breaking and tipping, contrary to the commonly accepted fire-induced, gravity collapse scenario. These photos show huge explosions occurring at the breaking point and in both sections simultaneously.[214]

"Painful Questions," now in its second printing, contains evidence that thoroughly debunks the government's conspiracy theory that 19 cave dwelling Arab Templar terrorists with box cutters, with Osama bin Laden directing and choreographing this attack from the caves of Tora Bora because "he hates our freedoms," totally outsmarted the U.S. military, the DIA, the CIA, the FBI, the NSA, the NSC, the NRO, the FAA, the INS, the Federal Reserve, the Secret Service, the US Postal Service and many other federal and local government agencies and caused the devastation of 9-11. Does anybody else think this sounds ridiculous?[215]

Asked about the media's avoidance of the many unanswered questions of 9-11, Hufschmid said, "My guess is that some are there to cover it up, some are afraid to speak the truth, and some are truly ignorant. The mainstream media ignores information they don't want people to know about. TV is the modern weapon. It's better than a bomb. Whoever controls it has the people and the people don't even realize it. (We will shortly cover this issue of who controls the media in the U.S.) This television fantasy world is what we are fighting against. My book and DVD are weapons for the invisible army in this information war."[216]

Asked about the U.S. military's reaction, Hufschmid said, "I would expect our military to be concerned about how they were beaten by such a small group of primitive people. If 19 Arabs with no technology could pull off that attack, and cause that

214 American Free Press, October 25, 2004.

215 Ibid.

216 Ibid.

much destruction, what could 5,000 terrorists with advanced technology do?"[217]

Hufschmid said he couldn't believe that the U.S. military would allow the demolition of the World Trade Center to occur. "It caused such extreme suffering and devastation; it feels to me it was done by extremely selfish people whose primary interest is not America. Some members of the conspiracy took advantage of the attack and demolished the World Trade Center for their own selfish reasons. Without the World Trade Center attack, we basically have a symbolic attack on the Pentagon, similar to what we see in the Northwoods plan."[218]

And so there we have it. A citizens' grand jury that has seen and heard and carefully considered the evidence presented throughout this book, and other sources widely published and disseminated elsewhere, with due credit to other responsible parties, has voted to indict President Bush and other high officials in his administration of complicity, or participation in the 9/11 attacks.

> *"For we wrestle not against flesh and blood, but against principalities, against powers, against the rulers of the darkness of this world, against spiritual wickedness in high places."*
>
> (Ephesians 6:12, KJV)

Before closing this chapter, please allow me to review for you President Bush's responses and answers to parties who questioned how he reacted to the news of the attacks on September the 11th.

But before we review his replies, one should remember that there was no live television news coverage of the first, North tower being struck by American Airlines Flight 11, as this was a "surprise attack." A video did surface later of this first attack by the French film makers Jules and Gideon Naudet, who were in

217 Ibid.

218 Ibid.

New York City, filming a documentary about a typical day in the life of a rookie New York fireman. And to this day, this is the only known video footage of the first tower being struck. But again remember, this was not live TV coverage; it was simply recorded on a movie camera.[219]

President Bush: "I was sitting outside the classroom waiting to go in and I saw an airplane hit the tower, the TV was obviously on, and I used to fly myself, and I said that must be a terrible pilot, and I said it must have been a horrible accident. But I was wisked off and I didn't have much time to think about it. I was then sitting in the classroom and Andy Card, my chief of staff walked in and said a second plane had hit the tower and we, America, was under attack."[220]

This was not the only time President Bush said he saw the first tower struck by American 11 on live TV, which again remember did not exist, unless of course, discreet, closed-circuit video surveillance and feed of the "black-op," for the benefit of the commander-in-chief and other "chicken-hawks" in his administration had been set up, which probably would have been arranged as part of a detailed, covert operation.

But this has been established by timeline. The only live TV coverage of the twin towers being attacked was of the South tower, the second tower to be hit. And if President Bush was in the classroom with the children at this time, then he could not have seen the second tower hit, which again was the only tower hit that was covered by live news. So that means if he did see a tower attack, it would have had to have been the first, North tower, just as he said, which had no live "news" coverage.

On the other occasion when President Bush answered basically the same question, this time by a young child, he answered the same way. The child asked, "What was the first thing that went through your head when you heard that a plane crashed into the first tower?"

President Bush replied, "... Anyway, I was sitting there and my chief of staff, well first of all when we walked into the classroom, I had seen this plane fly into the *first* (emphasis added) building.

219 vonkleist.

220 Hilder.

There was a TV set on and, you know, I thought it was pilot error..."[221]

I think we'll just close this chapter with a little Ozzy along with Black Sabbath:

"WAR PIGS"

Generals gathered in their masses
Just like witches at black masses
Evil minds that plot destruction
Sorcerers of deaths construction
In the fields the bodies burning
As the war machine keeps turning
Death and hatred to mankind
Poisoning their brainwashed minds
Oh Lord yeah

Politicians hide themselves away
They only started the war
Why should they go out to fight?
They leave that all to the poor

Time will tell on their power minds
Making war just for fun
Treating people just like pawns in chess
Wait till their judgment day comes

Now in darkness world stops turning
As the war machine keeps burning
No more war pigs have the power
Hand of God has struck the hour
Day of Judgment God is calling
On their knees, the war pigs crawling

Begging mercy for their sins
Satan laughing spreads his wings
Oh Lord yeah[222]

---

221 vonKleist.

222 "War Pigs," Black Sabbath Online, www.black-sabbath.com/discog/paranoid.html.

CHAPTER FOUR
Ye Shall Know Them By Their Fruits

When investigating a crime, regardless of the enormity, competent investigators must keep the question, "Qui Bono," who benefits, in mind to facilitate the determination of the guilty parties. As we proceed in this chapter, we will investigate why this attack of September the 11th occurred; we will investigate the subsequent wars on Iraq and Afghanistan and the never-ending International War on International Terrorism and why they occurred; and we will investigate "Qui Bono," who benefited and how they are benefiting still from these events.

As far as why this attack of 9/11 and its subsequent resulting wars occurred, we have briefly summarized and reviewed New Testament scripture in Chapter one and elsewhere throughout this book. I would again like to look at the passages in the New Testament Book of James, chapter 4, Verses 1 and 2, which reads, "From whence come wars and fightings among you? come they not hence, even of your lusts that war in your members? Ye lust and have not: ye kill, and desire to have, and cannot obtain: ye fight and war, yet ye have not, because ye ask not" (James 4:1-2, KJV).

And so, to covet, to long to possess something that belongs to another person, entity, or nation, to strongly desire another person's, entity's, or nation's property, land, wealth, or resources, or to lust for power, financial wealth, further control and exploitation for private profit of the world's resources, these then are the causes of war. In short, a land or a resource grab.

How then, did our oil and natural gas get under their sand?

In *Masters of the Universe*, a Daniel Hopsicker produced documentary video about the Federal Reserve Bank, noted author

Michael Collins Piper, of such great and monumental works as *Final Judgment: The Missing Link in the JFK Assassination Conspiracy* and *The High Priests of War* and *The New Jerusalem*, and who is also an investigative journalist for the Washington, DC based newsweekly *American Free Press*, had this to say about war: "There is no question that war is a profit making business. After World War One, Senator Gerald Nye held very famous hearings here in Washington where he dragged in some of the biggest bankers and industrialists and put them on the spot, and just examined profits made by some of these major interests here in the United States alone. And I mean everybody has the image of the arms dealers, well yes, arms dealers do profit from wars. So do the banks that lend money, the international banking houses that lend money to various governments so they can finance their war efforts? Yes, war is a profit-making business. Anybody who says otherwise is a liar or a fool."[223]

Lord George Curzon, the British Foreign Secretary to Russia in Central Asia in 1889 expressed, "Turkistan, Afghanistan, Transcaspia, Persia... are the pieces on a chessboard upon which is being played out a game for the dominance of the world.[224]

According to Nafeez Ahmed, writing in *The War on Freedom*, "The U.S. military industrial complex has been contemplating a prolonged intervention in Central Asia for at least a decade...More specifically, the U.S. war plan to invade Afghanistan has roots in strategic and economic concerns in Central Asia, stretching as far back as 1989. Afghanistan has widely been recognized by U.S. officials as the gateway to Central Asia and the Caspian, and thus to global primacy."[225]

In an article entitled, "Was 9-11 the Excuse Neo-cons Needed for Long Planned War?" reporter Chris Bollyn summarizes that President Bush's crusade against the Taliban of Afghanistan has

---

223 Daniel Hopsicker, "Masters of the Universe," Documentary Video.

224 Ahmed, p. 9.

225 ZIbid. pp. 68-69.

more to do with control of the immense oil and gas resources of the Caspian Basin, then it does with rooting out terrorism.[226]

And this is more aligned and in agreement with the Book of James passages we just discussed. One will note that in those passages of James, nothing was said about removing terrorism or establishing democracies around the world as the causes for war, but plenty was said about covetousness and lustfulness.

> *"Watch out for those dogs, those men who do evil, those mutilators of the flesh"*
>
> (Philippians 3:2, NIV).

Yes, you can hide ravening wolves in sheep's clothing; those would be the wool suites.

The *AFP* article continues to discuss that the economic reasons for the multi-national assault against the Taliban were Uzbekistan, Tajikistan, Kazakhstan and Turkmenistan and their vast oil, gas and other resources.[227] President George W. Bush, whose family is well connected to oil and energy companies, has called for an international crusade against Islamic terrorists, who he says hate Americans simply because they are the brightest beacon of freedom and democracy.[228]

It would be difficult to impossible to mobilize a country for war without a pretext and by honestly informing the nations populace that "exploitation of Caspian and Asian energy markets was an urgent priority for the administration," according to Ahmed.[229]

According to the *American Free Press* article, President George W. Bush's rhetoric about fighting for democracy is masking a less noble, [however a more biblically traditional] explanation for the

226 American Free Press, August 23, 2004, p. B.16.

227 Ibid.

228 Ibid.

229 Ahmed, p. 69.

struggle of control of an estimated five trillion dollars worth of oil and gas resources in the Caspian.

One of the material results of the elder Bush's Desert Storm campaign in 1991 was to secure access to the huge Rumaila oil fields in Southem Iraq, which was accomplished by expanding the boundaries of Kuwait after the war. This allowed Kuwait, a former British protectorate, where American and British oil companies are heavily invested, to double its prewar output.

A similar strategy to control the valuable resources of the Caspian Basin underlies the aggression against Afghanistan, a Central Asian nation that occupies a strategic position sandwiched between the Middle East, Central Asia and the Indian subcontinent.

Central Asia has enormous quantities of undeveloped oil resources, including estimates of 6.6 trillion cubic meters of natural gas waiting to be exploited.

Afghanistan was at the center of the so-called "Great Game" in the nineteenth century when Imperial Russia and the British Empire in India vied for influence and control. Today, its geographical position makes it important to wealthy energy magnates.

Amoco, British Petroleum, Chevron, Exxon Mobile, and Unocal are all engaged in a multibillion-dollar frenzy to extract the reserves of Azerbaijan, Kazakhstan, and Turkmenistan, the three newly independent Soviet republics that border on the Caspian Sea.

On behalf of the oil companies, an array of former cabinet members from the elder Bush administration have been actively involved in negotiations with former Soviet republics. The dealmakers include James Baker, Brent Scowcroft, John Sununu, and notably, Dick Cheney, now the vice president.

Turkmenistan and Azerbaijan are closely allied with Israeli commercial interests and Israeli military intelligence. In Turkmenistan, a "former" Israeli intelligence agent, Yosef A. Maimen, President of the Merhov Group of Israel, is the official negotiator and policy maker responsible for developing the energy resources of Turkmenistan.

This is the great game all over, Maimen told *The Wall Street Journal* about his role in furthering the geopolitical goals of both Israel and the U.S. in Central Asia.

"We are doing what U.S. and Israeli policy could not achieve. Controlling the transport route is controlling the product," Maimen said.

"Those who control the oil routes out of Central Asia will impact all future direction, quantities of flow, and the distribution of revenues from new production," said energy expert James Dorian in *Oil and Gas Journal* on September 10th, 2003.

Foreign business in Turkmenistan is dominated by Maiman's Merhov Group, according to *The Washington Report on Middle East Affairs*.

The Merhov Group of Israel has been contracted to modernize existing natural gas infrastructure and will build new facilities in an oil refinery in the city of Turkmenbashi on the Caspian Sea.

In keeping with Israeli political interests, Maimen's planned pipelines bypass Iran and Russia. Maimen has said that he would have no objection to dealing with Iran if and when Israeli policy allows it, probably after the conquer and subsequent installation of a more "friendly regime" precipitated by another "terrorist attack."

The Merhov Group has hired the Washington lobbying firm Cassidy and Associates and spent several million dollars to "encourage" U.S. officials to push for the Trans-Caspian pipeline.[230]

Yes indeed, war has always been a profitable money-making machine for shrewd investors with foresight, but the extremely close connections of the Carlyle Group, a Washington-based private equity investment firm and war profiteer, to the Bush family raise significant, unavoidable questions of waging war for profit.[231]

230 American Free Press, August 23, 2004.

231 Ibid.

Established in 1987, the Carlyle Group was founded by David Rubenstein, a former staff member in the Carter White House, along with partners Dan D'Aniello and Bill Conway. Today there are eighteen partners in the firm. From the beginning, the founders of the Carlyle Group have recruited former politicians as consultants. Former President George Herbert Walker Bush is among them, along with a host of other Bush cronies.[232]

The Bush connection to the Carlyle Group is nothing short of a scandal, according to Larry Klayman, a notable government watchdog best known for pursuing the scandals of former President William Jefferson Clinton.[233]

"Carlyle is as deeply wired into the current administration (George W. Bush) as they can possibly be," said Charles Lewis, Executive Director of the Center for Public Integrity. The Carlyle Empire owns numerous defense-related companies outright and has considerable business dealings with the U.S. government. Carlyle's directory reads like a Who's Who of high-profile Republicans going back to the Reagan administration. The chairman, Frank Carlucci, is Reagan's former defense secretary. Former Secretary of State, James Baker the third, former Budget Director Richard Darmen, and Arthur Levitt, chairman of the Securities and Exchange Commission through most of the Clinton administration, are all senior advisors to the Carlyle Group.[234]

The Carlyle Group owns so many defense companies, that it is now essentially the eleventh largest defense contractor in the United States.[235] With former Secretary of Defense Frank Carlucci as chairman; it is no surprise that Carlyle is drawn to defense firms. Carlyle owns numerous defense and aerospace firms including United Defense Industries, which makes tanks,

232 Ibid.

233 Ibid.

234 Ibid.

235 Michael Moore, "Fahrenheit 911," Motion Picture Film.

guided missiles, space vehicles, weapons delivery systems and the Bradley Armored Fighting Vehicle.[236]

Carlucci, who is seen as largely responsible for Carlyle's success, said he met in February with his old college classmate Donald Rumsfeld, the new current secretary of defense. He also met with Vice President Dick Cheney, who is also a former secretary of defense under former President Bush, to talk about military business, at a time when Carlyle had several billion-dollar defense projects under consideration.[237]

Well, the September 11th attacks guaranteed that the Carlyle Group, along with United Defense would have a very good year or two, maybe more. Just six weeks after the attacks of September the 11th, the Carlyle Group filed to take United Defense public and in December of 2001, made a one-day profit of 237 million dollars.[238]

In July of 2000, the Carlyle Group bought Northrop Grumman's aerostructures business group in a deal valued at 1.2 billion dollars. The business was renamed Vought Aircraft Industries and remains based in Dallas, Texas. On August 20th, 2000, Vought announced that it had been selected by Northrop Grumman to manufacture the wing for the Global Hawk unmanned reconnaissance system's air vehicle,[239] a weaponized version of which is suspected by many to be the actual aircraft type that was used in the Pentagon attack on 9/11, as indicated in this email this author received from *American Free Press* journalist Christopher Bollyn:

Dear Glen,

Thanks for the photos and the note. Eric (Hufschmid) did forward the photos to me (Photos of Boeing 757). Not a single one of the wheels in the photos resembled the slotted hub found in the Pentagon.

---

236 American Free Press, August 23, 2004.

237 Ibid.

238 Michael Moore.

239 AFP, 8/23/04.

The wheel seen in the Pentagon photo resembles the wheel seen in photos of the Global Hawk. We have not been able to determine the diameter of the wheel from the photo, but judging by the number of wheels seen in the Pentagon (one) and the size of the engine parts, I am pretty sure it was a weaponized Global Hawk that was used at the Pentagon.

One of the eyewitnesses that said the plane flew right over his head, Steve Riskus, told me that he did not recall hearing any sound. This also supports the Global Hawk theory. A 767 or 757 going at full throttle would be incredibly loud... [For that matter, a 757 at flight idle going "right over his head" would be extremely loud.]

I just got home last night from a road trip to Florida. More later.

Thanks again, Glen. Merry Christmas. Christopher Bollyn[240]

"Nothing in recent history seems to approach the success of this group in wholesale conversion of former high government rank to gigantic profits," expressed Dan Thomasson, former editor of Scripps Howard News Service some six months before 9/11, in March of 2001. "To use that influence at the highest levels to garner such enormous wealth and power presents an undeniably unsavory appearance," he said.[241]

Recalling President Eisenhower's words of farewell seems appropriate at this time and place: "... we must guard against the acquisition of unwarranted influence, whether sought or unsought by the military industrial complex. The potential for the disastrous rise of misplaced power exists and will persist. We must never let the weight of this combination endanger our liberties or democratic processes... Only an alert and knowledgeable citizenry can compel the proper meshing of the huge industrial and military machinery of defense with our peaceful methods and goals, so that security and liberty may prosper together..."

And the wise words of Benjamin Franklin, American founding father, "Those who would sacrifice liberty for security deserve

240 Email from Chris Bollyn of American Free Press, December 21, 2004.

241 AFP, 8/23/04.

neither."[242] We must heed these wise words of these learned men as we proceed forward with our study.

In a Memorial Day Tribute to those who have answered their nation's call to arms, *American Free Press* reporter John Tiffany, writing in an article entitled "Soldiers Families Languish in Poverty While Fat Cats Rake in Big War Bucks," truthfully and accurately reports that while life is difficult for the average American military family, the economic outlook is rosy for the next several decades if you happen to be a war profiteer.

Mr. Tiffany expresses that while the war profiteers are rolling in clover, the families of the men and women who fight and die in George W. Bush's [and Ariel Sharon's] imperialistic wars are not so fortunate. For starters, many military families must survive on food stamps and live in low-rent housing.

Whenever the question of a pay raise for the military comes up, they usually get next to nothing. But, if you are a weapons manufacturer, this post 9-11 era is a great time to be in the war business.

Again, this is the same "military industrial complex" that Eisenhower forewarned us against, in his 1960 farewell address.

Northrop Grumman, for example, manufactures planes and bombers, including the B-2 Stealth bomber and the F-14 Tomcat fighter. The company also makes the much-praised unmanned Global Hawk. The 10 million-dollar per copy Global Hawk was deployed to Afghanistan despite the fact that it had not completed its testing requirements.[243]

When Wall Street opened after the September the 11th attacks, on September 17th, 2001, Grumman's stock had risen sixteen percent to $94 a share in anticipation of the coming conflagration. Two days after bombing began in Afghanistan, Northrop Grumman's stock reached a three-year high of $107.60 a share on the New York Stock Exchange.[244]

242 Ahmed, p. 9.

243 American Free Press, Memorial Day Special.

244 Ibid.

Raytheon, another munitions company, is best known for its Tomahawk cruise missile. About 100 of these million-dollar missiles were lobbed at Afghanistan from United States Navy ships, fifty in the opening salvo alone.

Orders for Tomahawk missiles have come in from allies such as Britain, which signed a contract for 48 Tomahawks in an $87 million deal. Raytheon is confident that significant Pentagon orders will follow.[245]

Raytheon is also the designer and manufacturer of the "Bunker Buster" GBU-28, the 5,000-pound earth shaker, and missiles like the TOW, the Maverick and the Javelin, all used in George W. Bush's Gulf War Two.

After taking a severe beating a year and a half before September the 11th, Raytheon is now the biggest stock percentage gainer since the Bush wars, which are anticipated to last for some 40 years by some, began. On September 10th, 2001, the companies stock stood at $26.85; now, as of this writing, it is holding at about $32.80.

And very similar stories can be told of Lockheed Martin and Boeing.

Boeing recently dispatched an army of lobbyists to Washington looking for Congress's help in the form of approval for a set of proposals that make sense if the goal is profits for Boeing, but make no military sense:

Air Force purchase of 60 Boeing C-17 cargo aircraft under a special "commercial" provision that removes financial oversight.

Air Force leasing of 100 Boeing 767 planes to be converted into surveillance planes and mobile command centers for the military.

Protection from billions in potential liability claims stemming from the 9-11 attacks.

Measures to encourage Lockheed Martin to share its $200 billion Joint Strike Fighter deal.

High level officials and advisors in the Bush administration, including Defense Secretary Donald Rumsfeld have claimed the

245 Ibid.

need to revise our armed forces from a Cold War mentality to a modern one.

But the programs earmarked for this additional spending belie such statements. Instead of the funds being dedicated to weapons systems and training that would enable our troops to more effectively fight on the modem battlefields of urban centers, inhospitable mountainous terrain and against enemies who operate in the shadows, the money is to go to such systems as the F-22 next generation fighter and towards the National Missile Defense shield, programs virtually useless in a war on terrorism.

In addition to this bonanza for weapons manufacturers due to this new and increased spending, other war profiteers, usually referred to as innocent "private contractors," have been awarded $680 million in corporate welfare to rebuild Iraq's infrastructure, the same infrastructure blown to smithereens by the previously discussed weapons systems. Contracts to rebuild Iraq's roads, schools, hospitals, and sewer systems, are providing a windfall for the Bechtel Corporation, known jokingly in business circles as Bushtel.

Kellogg Brown and Root, a Haliburtan subsidiary, stands to make a profit of about $490 million rebuilding Iraq's oil wells, financed with public taxpayer funds.[246]

It is currently expected that Iraq will be under U.S. military occupation for at least the next five years. How many extra billions this will cost is unknown.

United States defense companies pay their chief executives on average 50 percent more than other big companies. The typical American CEO earned $3.7 million in 2002, while the typical defense industry top executive raked in $5.4 million.[247]

Perhaps the most disgusting and insidious financial transactions that resulted in enormous profits for some, took place just before the attacks on September 11, and thus indicate that this attack, like the attack on Pearl Harbor, was not an absolute complete surprise to us all, and that those who had foreknowledge took

246 Ibid.

247 American Free Press, Memorial Day Special, p. B.3.

advantage of this to reap huge financial rewards. To summarize, those with foreknowledge profited, and those who profited had foreknowledge. This is the key to Qui Bono, or who benefits, and therefore indicates complicity and guilt.

In an article entitled "Examining Fortuitous 9-11 Stock Trades Could Expose Real Terrorist Masterminds" in the August 23rd, 2004 issue of *American Free Press*, it is reported that manipulators with inside information made huge profits on sophisticated trades as the stocks of the airline and insurance companies plummeted in the wake of the 9-11 disaster.[248] The inside information was so precise that experts have concluded that it could have only come from those who master minded these horrendous attacks, and that they were not members of an Al Qaeda terrorist cell.[249]

This money trail is the closest investigators have come to a "smoking gun" and could lead directly to those who planned the attacks. But with the notable exception of Representative Cynthia McKinney, D-GA, Congress has yet to demand a thorough and open investigation.[250]

This suspicious and unusual stock trading activity indicates that people used inside information to make huge profits. The money made from the trades done with inside information has been estimated to be upwards of $15 billion worldwide.[251]

Selling stocks short involves having your broker sell shares you don't even own, betting, or in this case perhaps knowing, that you can acquire them later at a lower price and supply them to the buyer within a prescribed short time. If you "bet" correctly, the difference in price is your profit. You can lose at this game, but you can also win big and historically, if this shortly precedes a traumatic event, as was the case of 9/11, it indicates foreknowledge.[252]

---

248 AFP, 8/23/04, p. B.14.

249 Marrs, p. 87.

250 AFP, 8/23/04, p. B.14.

251 Ibid.

252 Marrs, p. 87.

"It was reported by the Interdisciplinary Center, a counter-terrorism think tank involving former Israeli intelligence officers, that insiders made nearly $16 million profit by short selling shares in American and United Airlines, the two airlines that suffered the hijackings, as well as the investment firm of Morgan Stanley, which occupied twenty-two floors of the World Trade Center."[253]

The Institute for Counter Terrorism located in Herzliya, Israel, published an article, *Black Tuesday: Worlds Largest Insider Trading Scam?* on September 19, 2001, just one week after 9-11. The author, Don Radlauer, an expert in stock options and derivatives, provided details of the types and volumes of the suspicious trades and said, "Obviously, anyone who had detailed knowledge of the attacks before they happened was, at the very least, an accessory to their planning, and the overwhelming probability is that the trades could have been made only by the same people who masterminded the attacks themselves."[254]

Mr. Radlauer continued, "Tracing the transactions to their real source would be difficult because the trading is sure to have been done under false names, behind shell corporations, and in general to have been thoroughly obfuscated. This doesn't mean that unraveling the threads of these transactions will be impossible, but it probably won't be quick or easy."[255]

City of London broker and analyst Richard Crossley noted that someone sold shares in unusually large quantities beginning three weeks before 9-11. He stated that on the Friday preceding the attacks, more than 10 million shares in the U.S. investment bank Merrill Lynch, were sold compared to 4 million on a typical trading day. He said he took this as evidence that some had insider information and foreknowledge of the attacks.[256]

253 Ibid.

254 AFP, 8/23/04, p. B.14.

255 Ibid.

256 Marrs, p. 88.

"What is more awful than he should aim a stiletto blow at the heart of Western financial markets? But to profit from it, words fail me," said Crossley.[257]

Just prior to 9/11, there were an unusually high number of "put" options purchased for the stocks of AMR Corporation and UAL Corporation, the parent companies of American and United Airlines. A put option gives the bearer the right to sell at a specified price before a certain date.[258] Just like short selling, placing a put option is betting that the stock price will fall.[259]

The American Exchanges that handle options trades, primarily the Chicago Board of Options Exchange, know on a daily basis what levels of put options is purchased.[260]

Among the most conspicuous spikes in trading activity were the huge increases in "put options" placed on the two airlines involved in the 9-11 hijackings, United Airlines and American Airlines.[261]

There was a 9,000 percent jump in United Airlines put options between September 6th, and September 10th, with a huge spike 285 times higher than average on the Thursday before the attack.[262]

"According to Michael C. Ruppert, a former Los Angeles police officer, researcher, and investigator of *From the Wilderness*, an internet news site, between September 6th and 7th, 2001, the Chicago Board of Options Exchange reported 4,744 put options, but only 396 call options on UAL. A call option reflects the belief that the stock price will rise.

American Airlines saw a 6,000 percent jump in put options the day before the attack. On September 10th, there were 4,516 put options compared to only 748 call options. There was no

257 Ibid.

258 Marrs, p. 88.

259 AFP, 8/23/04, p. B.14.

260 Ibid.

261 Ibid.

262 Ibid.

remotely similar trading activity on any other airlines, according to market reports.

'No similar trading in any other airlines occurred on the Chicago Exchange in the days immediately preceding Black Tuesday. That means that someone had advance knowledge that only the stocks of these two airlines would be adversely impacted,' Ruppert said.

There were other questionably suspect stock trades made just prior to September the 11th. According to Ruppert, Morgan Stanley, Dean Witter and Company, which occupied 22 floors of the trade center, witnessed the purchase of 2,157 put options during the three trading days preceding 9/11, compared to 27 per day prior to September 6th."[263]

There was an also unusually high volume of five year United States Treasury Note purchases prior to the attacks of 9/11, including one five billion dollar trade, *The Wall Street Journal* reported on October 2nd, 2001. Five year Treasury Notes are among the best investments in the event of a world crisis, especially one that hits the United States, the report indicated.[264]

"This could very well be insider trading at the worst, most horrific, most evil use you've ever seen in your entire life, or this would be one of the most extraordinary coincidences in the history of mankind, if it was a coincidence," said *Bloomberg Business News* writer Dylan Ratigan.[265]

No United States or foreign law enforcement agency has announced arrests or other pertinent legal developments in the investigation of these trades, the most compelling evidence of foreknowledge, and therefore by year's end, the story of profiting from terrorism had grown cold. Evidently since none of these suspicious transactions could be traced to Osama bin Laded or Saddam Hussein, this news item quietly dropped from sight. But, if these suspicious transactions could not be linked to these "terrorists" where in the world did this investigative trail lead?

263 Marrs, p. 89.

264 AFP, 8/23/04, p. B.14.

265 Ibid.

"Many wondered if it tracked back to American firms or intelligence agencies. This indeed appears to be the case."[266]

According to the *San Francisco Chronicle*, "A source familiar with the United trades identified Deutsche Bank Alex. Brown, the investment banking arm of German giant Deutsche Bank, as the investment bank used to purchase at least some of these options."[267]

Michael Ruppert said that both European investigators and the International Institute for Counter Terrorism tracked the UAL put options to Deutsche Bank Alex. Brown, a firm that was formed by joining the United States' oldest investment banking firm, Alex. Brown, with the German Central Bank.[268]

Until 1998, the Chairman of A. B. Brown was "Buzzy" Krongard, who on March 26, 2001 was appointed executive director of the Central Intelligence Agency. Beginning in 1998, Mr. "Buzzy" Krongard was counselor to the Director of the Central Intelligence Agency, one Mr. George Tenet.[269]

"Mr. Krongard is a man with long-standing and close ties to the financial world. Moving up through the ranks of A.B. Brown, Krongard was elected Chief Executive Officer in 1991 and the Chairman of the Board in 1994. With the merging of A.B. Brown and Bankers Trust Corporation in 1997, Krongard served as Vice Chairman of the Board until joining the Central Intelligence Agency. Bankers Trust acquired Deutsche Bank in 1999, becoming the single largest bank in Europe."[270]

Krongard also served as Chairman of the Securities Industry Association. A native of Baltimore, Maryland, he received degrees from Princeton University and the University of Maryland School

---

266 Marrs, p. 90.

267 Ibid.

268 Ibid.

269 Ibid.

270 Ibid. p. 91.

of Law. He also served as an infantry officer in the United States Marine Corps.[271]

"Understanding the interrelationships between the CIA and the banking and brokerage world is critical to grasping the already frightening implications of these revelations," commented Ruppert.

Mr. "Buzzy" Krongard indeed joined other prominent Americans connected to both the Central Intelligence Agency and Wall Street power. These include Mr. Clark Clifford, who was a key player in gaining legitimacy for the BCCI, a bank that collapsed in scandal. John Foster Dulles and Allen Dulles; Allen oversaw the failed Bay of Pigs invasion and then sat on the Warren Commission, investigating the assassination of President John F. Kennedy, who earlier had fired Dulles from the CIA. Both Dulles brothers were involved with the Bush-Nazi connection. William Casey, who moved to the Central Intelligence Agency after a stint as Chairman of the Securities and Exchange Commission. David Doherty was former general counsel for the CIA and is now Vice President of the New York Stock Exchange. Former President George Herbert Walker Bush was former Director of Central Intelligence, and is now a paid consultant to the Carlyle Group. John M. Deutch and Nora Slatkin, Deutch a former CIA director and his former executive director Slatkin are both now connected to Citibank and Citigroup. And Hank Greenburg, once nominated as the CIA director, is now Chairman of AIG Insurance, representing the third largest pool of investment capital in the world.[272]

No wonder they call the CIA, Capitalism's Invisible Army.

"One of the primary functions of the Central Intelligence Agency, by virtue of its long and very close history of relationships with Wall Street, has been a mandate to track and monitor all financial markets worldwide, and to look for anomalous trades, indicative of either economic warfare or insider currency trading or speculation, which might affect the United States Treasury, or

271 Ibid.

272 Ibid.

as in the case of the September 11 attacks, to look for trades that indicated foreknowledge of attacks like we saw," Ruppert told Online Journal on October 12, 2001. "I am absolutely convinced that the Central Intelligence Agency had complete and perfect foreknowledge of the attacks, down to the date, time, place, and location," he concluded."[273]

"The suspicious stock market trading indicating foreknowledge of the 9/11 attacks only added to the ever-growing proof that people in high positions knew what was coming in September of 2001.[274]

In the opening paragraph of this chapter, we discussed the concept of keeping the question of Qui Bono, or who benefits in mind when investigating a crime, no matter the enormity; that official investigators always primarily consider this concept in order to facilitate the determination of who the guilty parties were. It is directly related to motive.

And we have seen up to this point the main groups who have benefited from 9/11 and the subsequent wars in Iraq and Afghanistan and the International war to make the world safe from terrorism. American und British oil companies like Amoco, British Petroleum, Exxon Mobile, and Unocal. And large business groups like the Carlyle Group, which has had a strong Bush influence and connection, described as scandalous by independent government watchdog groups. Defense related firms have also benefited enormously from the 9/11 attacks, United Defense, Northrop Grumman, Lockheed Martin, Hughes Raytheon, and Boeing.

Also "private contractors" like the Bechtel Corporation where former Secretary of State under President Reagan, George Schultz sits on the board, and Kellogg, Brown and Root, a Haliburton subsidiary with definite strong ties to Vice President Cheney, have also benefited enormously with huge government contracts. [275]

---

273 Ibid. p. 92.

274 Ibid. p. 93.

275 "Windfalls of War"-The Center for Public Integrity, www.publicintegrity.org, 11/11/05.

And we have seen that some major banking interests, with strong ties to the Central Intelligence Agency, were involved in stock transactions concerning airline companies and financial companies that were involved in 9/11 and stood to gain huge financial windfalls. We also concluded that those who gained and who had foreknowledge probably also had a hand in the planning and execution of these massive crimes against humanity.

And it just so happens, that those groups who are charged with protecting the American people, also seem to be the ones who are benefiting the most. At least they seem to be benefiting many times more than Saddam Hussein and Osama bin Laden. Would these guys actually bring the wrath of the U.S. military on themselves and their countrymen? I suggest further thoughtful analysis is in order.

> *"For they do not speak peace, but they devise deceitful matters against the quiet ones in the land."*
>
> (Psalms 35:20, NKJV)

> *"For they eat the bread of wickedness, and drink the wine of violence."*
>
> (Proverbs 4:17, NKJV)

We also briefly touched on a foreign group, which seemed to benefit from energy development in the post 9/11 world in the Central Asian region. The Israeli company, the Merhov Group of Israel, according to its President, Mr. Yosef Maiman, who said, "... Controlling the transport route is controlling the product," when discussing oil routes in the area. And it is this foreign entity, Israel, that also seemed to gain other advantage from the September 11th attacks and where, I think, we should explore and analyze further.

In his book concerning 9/11, *Inside Job, Unmasking the 9/11 Conspiracies*, the author, Mr. Jim Marrs, states that since the September 11 attacks, several media pundits noted that the chief beneficiaries of the terrorism were the Bush administration and Israel. Bush gained welcome relief from bad news in the economy and his own sagging popularity, while Israel found a provocation for unleashing its military against the Palestinians.[276]

And there were also indications that some in Israel had foreknowledge of the attacks.[277]

According to *American Free Press*, a small item that raised eyebrows concerned a broken lease of a tenant at the World Trade Center just days before the 9/11 attacks by a company with close ties to Israel.

One of Israel's largest companies pulled out of the North Tower just days before the attacks of 9/11. The company, ZIM American Israeli Shipping Company, Incorporated broke the lease when it vacated its rented offices on the 16th and 17th floors of the North Tower of the World Trade Center.[278]

The company's World Trade Center office space had been leased until the end of the year and lost $50,000 when they suddenly pulled out in the beginning of September 2001.[279]

The parent company, ZIM Israel Navigation Company is nearly half owned by the state of Israel, and the other half is held by The Israel Corporation. ZIM is one of the world's largest container shipping companies operating an international network of shipping lines, according to *American Free Press.*

American Free Press repeatedly contacted ZIM American Israeli Shipping Company at its new American headquarters in Norfolk, Virginia to inquire about the company's early pull out of its World Trade Center lease, but calls were not returned.[280]

Inquiries on the early withdrawal by ZIM were also routed to the World Trade Center lease owner, Silverstein Properties, which

276 Marrs, p. 94.

277 Ibid.

278 AFP, 8/23/04, p. B.9.

279 Ibid.

280 Ibid.

in turn passed questions to its public relations firm, Howard J. Rubenstein, which also represents the nation of Israel.

A spokesman for Rubenstein said they had no information on the ZIM lease issue.[281]

Despite ZIM's desire to relocate, the company didn't stay in Norfolk very long. Several months after the destruction of its former New York offices in the 9/11 World Trade Center attack, ZIM moved back to New York. Yet the circumstances of its New York to Norfolk to New York adventure seem to have been ignored.[282]

Another interesting, but not yet widely known story concerning Israel and 9/11, began with an article in the September 12, 2001 issue of the *Jerusalem Post*. The headline read, "Thousands of Israelis Missing near WTC, Pentagon." The article stated that, "The Foreign Ministry in Jerusalem has so far received the names of 4,000 Israelis believed to have been in the areas of the World Trade Center and the Pentagon at the time of the attacks. The list is made up of people who have not yet made contact with friends or family."[283]

"It should be emphasized that this 4,000 figure originated in Israel, not with the U.S. news media or Arabic sources. However, the Arab media was quick to seize on it.

A week later, a Beirut, Lebanon television station reported that 4,000 Israeli employees of the World Trade Center were absent the day of the attack, suggesting foreknowledge of the attacks. This information spread quickly across the World Wide Web, but was just as quickly branded a hoax."[284]

However, on September 19, 2001, *The Washington Post* reported about 113 Israelis were missing at the World Trade Center and President Bush on the next day noted more than 130 Israelis were victims. Then 2 days later, on September 22, 2001,

281 Marrs, p. 95.

282 AFP,8/23/04, p. B. 9.

283 Marrs, p. 96.

284 Ibid.

The New York Times stated that amazingly only one Israeli was killed when the World Trade Center towers collapsed.[285]

But would our "best Middle East ally," Israel, other than the savage attack on the unarmed USS Liberty that killed 34 U.S. Navy personnel and wounded 75 more on June 8th, 1967, conduct activities detrimental to us, the United States of America?[286] Let us take a closer look.

In its August 23rd, 2004 issue, *American Free Press* journalist Michael Collins Piper reported that in its October 1, 2001 issue which went to press 9 days after the 9/11 attack, on September 20th, 2001, that AFP was the first national newspaper to make the connection between Israeli intelligence and the 9/11 attacks. For doing so, *AFP* was accused of peddling anti-Israel conspiracy theories. However, events have proven *AFP* right all along.

Shortly after September the 11th, CBS news anchorman Dan Rather appeared on David Letterman's Late Show and said a "cell" of America-hating Arabs had been spotted across the river videotaping the World Trade Center tragedy and were celebrating on the roof of a building. CBS anchor Dan Rather turned out to be completely dead wrong on the identity of those celebrating the tragedy.

Of course, this wouldn't have been the first time the mainstream press erroneously reported erroneous facts.

American Free Press revealed that the "Arab" celebrants were actually a group of Israelis. And in its March 15, 2002 issue, America's oldest and most prestigious Jewish newspaper, *Forward*, has confirmed that these Israelis were connected to Israel's intelligence agency, the Mossad.

Forward has now published information that confirms and elaborates on the details entered into the worldwide news record by *American Free Press* correspondent Chris Bollyn. Here is what *AFP* reported in the October 1, 2001 issue by Bollyn:

---

285 Ibid.

286 Alfred M. Lillenthal, "The Zionist Connection II, What Price Peace?" Veritas Publishing, Bullsbrook, Western Australia, p. 561.

At least three different groups of Israelis-some of whom may have ties to Israel's intelligence agency, the Mossad-were taken into custody after eyewitnesses reported seeing them celebrating in several locations across the river from lower Manhattan in New Jersey.

In two cases, the men were reportedly videotaping the initial kamikaze attack on the World Trade Center in New York. All of the detained Israelis are connected to Israeli-owned moving companies operating out of New York and New Jersey.

One group was reported to have been in Liberty State Park in Jersey City, another was seen in Liberty Park in Union City, and a third group was apprehended on the roof of an Israeli-owned moving company.[287]

The Bergen Record of New Jersey, on September 12th, 2001 provided further insight into the event, reporting that:

"Eight hours after terrorists struck Manhattan's tallest skyscrapers, police in Bergen County detained five men who they said were found carrying maps linking them to the blasts... sources close to the investigation said they found other evidence linking the men to the bombing plot. 'There are maps of the city in the car with certain places highlighted. It looked like they're hooked in with this. It looked like they knew what was going to happen when they were at Liberty State Park,' the source said. Sources also said that bomb-sniffing dogs reacted as if they detected explosives."[288]

Eyewitnesses told police of seeing some Israelis in Union City and Jersey City, both of which have parks named "Liberty"-more than five miles apart. The third group was spotted on the roof of Urban Moving Systems, which is based in Weehawken, New Jersey and from which there is a direct, straight-line view of the World Trade Center site.

A New York Fire Department source told *AFP* that each of these three sites would provide a unique photographic perspective

287 AFP, 8/23/04, p. B.8.

288 Ahmed, p. 350.

of the World Trade Center disaster, suggesting the Israeli agents were working on a photographic record of the tragedy.

The *New York Post* reported as early as September 13th, 2001 about the arrest of the five men, noting also that "the feds declined to release the men's identities or nationalities." The *Post* also reported that officials at Urban Moving Systems claimed to be unaware of what had happened.[289]

Local police had been prompted to intervene after receiving the following Federal Bureau of Investigation alert: "Vehicle possibly related to New York terrorist attack, White, 2000 Chevrolet Van with New Jersey registration with 'Urban Moving Systems' sign on back seen at Liberty State Park, Jersey City, NJ, at the time of first impact of jetliner into WTC. Three individuals with van were seen celebrating after initial impact and subsequent explosion. FBI Newark Field Office requests that if the van is located, hold for prints and detain individuals."

The New York Times and *The Jerusalem Post* reported that angry, suspicious neighbors had mistaken the group for Arabs "going to unusual lengths to photograph the World Trade Center ruins, some with themselves in the foreground smiling, making light of the situation, posing and laughing on and in front of their moving van with the scene of WTC destruction in the background." The *New York Post* reported that witnesses had seen them "cheering" and "jumping up and down" in apparent joy.[290]

The Bergen Record went on to say that the FBI seized the van for further testing and that sources close to the investigation said the men said they were Israeli tourists...[291]

And according to *Jewish Week*, "In the moving van they were driving for their employer, Urban Moving Systems in Weehawken, NJ, the men-ages 22 to 27 and all single-carried box cutters. One had $4,000 in cash, another had a camera, and a third had two passports... They were stopped by police at about 3 p.m. September 11 after two women saw them standing

289 AFP, 8/23/04, p. B.8.

290 Ahmed, p. 350.

291 Ibid.

on the roofs of the moving company and their van, smiling as they took pictures of each other with the burning WTC in the background."[292]

The five suspects who have been officially detained are listed as brothers Sivan and Paul Kurzberg, Oded Ellner, Omaer Marmari and Yaon Shmuel.[293]

The "movers" listed above, were all on tourist visas; they were all employed as a team, without work permits, for an Israeli-owned company.

The FBI, especially after developing their film, suspected them of being Mossad agents, kept them in solitary confinement and wanted to keep them in custody for at least another 90 days. [294]

Why the FBI would suspect that Mossad agents may have been involved in the so-called "Arab terrorist" attack is a question ignored by the mainstream media.[295]

During their confinement, the Israelis, when questioned, refused to give information about their type of former military experience or anything else. Paul Kurzberg, the group's spokesman, reportedly "had trouble" with a seven-hour polygraph test, but "did better on a second try"-in other words, failed them both. According to *The New York Times*, Kurzberg had "refused on principle to divulge much about his role in the Israeli army or subsequently working for people who may have had ties to Israeli intelligence."[296]

And Dominick Suter, the owner of the Weehawken, New Jersey moving company, was also questioned by the FBI, who took documents and computer hard drives, but allowed Suter to go free. A few days later, Suter left the United States for Israel.[297]

---

292 Ibid. p. 351.

293 AFP, 8/23/04, p. B.8.

294 Ahmed, p. 351.

295 AFP, 8/23/04, p. B.8.

296 Ahmed, p. 351.

297 Marrs, p. 97.

On August 23, 2004, *American Free Press* reported that according to an Israeli National News report on October 26th, 2001, the Israeli detainees were suspected of plotting to blow up a New York bridge, although this allegation never reached most Americans who were being told of "Muslim plots" against United States citizens.

An employee of Urban Moving Systems, as told in a follow-up September 15th, 2001 *Bergen Record* report stated that the majority of his co-workers are Israelis and were joking on the day of the attacks. "I was in tears," he said. "These guys were joking and that bothered me. These guys were like, 'Now America knows what we go through.'"

Israeli-connected moving companies seem to proliferate in the events surrounding 9-11. It was not only in the New York-New Jersey area that Israelis working for Israeli-owned moving companies were taken into custody, suspected of involvement in terrorist-related activities. On December 24th, 2001, *American Free Press* reported that two men whom police described as Middle Eastern were detained in the Pottstown area, which is just Northwest of Philadelphia, as reported in the October 17th, 2001 issue of the Pulitzer Prize-winning Pottstown, Pennsylvania *Mercury*. The two men were found with detailed video footage of the Sears Tower in Chicago, widely mentioned as a possible terrorist target.

The Mercury did not identify the men's nationality, but their names were Moshe Elmakias and Ron Kater. "Moshe" is a Hebrew name, which is not likely to have been bestowed on a Muslim or Arab. A woman named Ayelet Reisler, also in their company was detained. The two men worked for a company known as "Moving Systems Incorporated."

Supporters of Israel protested that it was "just a coincidence" that several different suspiciously-acting groups of Israelis would be working for Israeli moving companies and have detailed videos of the World Trade Center disaster and the Sears Tower, another widely suspected potential terrorist target.

American Free Press has learned that there is a connecting network of Israeli-owned moving companies alongside Urban Moving Systems and Moving Systems Incorporated, that have operated under such names as Advance Moving Systems, AAA Van Lines, State to State Van Lines, America's Best Movers and Quality Moving and Storage.

Another connected "moving company" is Moshe's, which maintains a huge brick warehouse just outside the Holland Tunnel in Jersey City, NJ, with a clear view of what was once the World Trade Center. Their 15-story building, solid brick with no windows employs hundreds of young Israelis.[298]

On December 17th, 2001, *American Free Press* reported that there was much more to the story concerning the Israeli detainees who were taken into custody in New York City.

The article reported that Attorney General John Ashcroft has released Paul Kurzberg, an Israeli suspect in the 9-11 terrorist attacks who had trouble with polygraph tests administered by the FBI.

Forward, the New York-based, respected Jewish newspaper, disclosed on November 23rd, 2001, that top-ranking Israeli diplomats had intervened with Ashcroft on behalf of the group, who all apparently are former members of the Israeli Army. The group was released and deported on minor immigration charges. [299]

But again, there is more to the story than just this group of five Israelis. On November 23rd, 2001, *The Washington Post* admitted that among a total of some 60 young Israeli Jews picked up by the FBI in the wake of September the 11th, there were at least a handful actually being held on suspicion of involvement in the terrorist acts.[300]

The Washington Post staff writer John Mintz, pointed out that while most of the Israelis arrested and detained since 9/11 were held on immigration charges, in several cases, such as those in

298 AFP, 8/23/04, pp. B.8-9.

299 Ibid. p. B.10.

300 Ibid.

Cleveland and St. Louis, Immigration and Naturalization Service officials testified under oath in court hearings that they were "of special interest to the government," a term that federal agents have used in many cases involving those who have been detained around the country since September the 11.th[301]

An Immigration and Naturalization Service official said the agency would not comment on the Israelis. He did say though that the term "special interest" means the case in question is "related to the investigation of September the 11th."[302]

"All of the 60 Israeli detainees, according to the *Post*, were supposedly 'observing a time-honored tradition in their country-touring the world after their mandatory service in the Israeli military.' The *Post* said, 'A number of them had served in counter-terrorist units in Israel.'

Although referring to Israel as a 'close U.S. ally in the fight against terrorism,' the *Post* pointed out that although one Israeli detainee, Liron Diamant, said he and his friends had first been mistaken as Arabs, the FBI conducted an 'hours long' interrogation and that they were 'questioned in detail about their Israeli military service.'

Now as a consequence of new admissions by *Forward*, we are learning much more about the one specific group of five Israelis connected to the Weehawken, NJ based Urban Moving Systems, who were picked up in New Jersey."[303]

Urban Moving Systems was "a moving company with few discernable assets" that closed up shop immediately after federal authorities began investigating its activities, *Forward* reported. As previously discussed, the owner of UMS, Mr. Dominic Suter, "fled to Israel" after being questioned by the FBI. *Forward* also said one of its sources admits that Urban Moving Systems was a Mossad-connected operation:

According to one former high-ranking American intelligence official, the FBI came to the conclusion at the end of its

301 Ibid.

302 Ibid.

303 Ibid.

investigation that the five Israelis arrested in New Jersey last September were conducting a Mossad surveillance mission and that their employer, UMS of Weehawken, NJ, served as a Mossad front.

After their arrest, the men were held in detention for two and a half months and were then deported at the end of November, officially for visa violations.

However, a counterintelligence investigation by the FBI concluded that at least two of the men arrested were Mossad operatives, according to the former American official, who said he was regularly briefed on the investigation by two separate law enforcement officials. "The assessment was that UMS was a front for the Mossad and operatives employed by it," the official said.

Forward said the FBI, the Justice Department, and the Immigration and Naturalization Service refused to discuss the case. Forward also reported that its source said that after the United States confronted the Israeli government, Israel privately admitted that the Urban Moving Systems operation was a Mossad front.[304]

And *ABC News* quoted one of the five detained Israelis as saying, "Our purpose was to document the event."[305]

I'll simply ask the reader directly, does this statement seem to suggest foreknowledge in any way, shape, or form? Or, possibly even more than just foreknowledge?

"This is more than enough to wonder whether we didn't have several key culprits in 9/11 behind bars and release them because of high-level U.S.-Israeli intervention," wrote Nafeez Ahmed in his book *The War on Freedom*. "It is worth speculating on the possibilities here. A moving company, for instance, would have been a perfect cover; they could transport equipment in their van, and bring it into the WTC in their uniforms. They absolutely did not cooperate with the police, and in the circumstances, all they had to do was deny everything and wait for help. It came soon, partly in the form of a weepy PR offensive, making them out

304 Ibid.

305 Marrs, p. 97.

as bewildered mama's boys and victims of stern justice," Ahmed wrote.

And it also came in the form of the Justice Department headed by Attorney General John Ashcroft-long known for his fervent affinity for Israel-after top-ranking Israeli diplomats had intervened with Ashcroft on the group's behalf, securing their release on minor immigration charges.[306]

Clearly then, *American Free Press* was on the mark all along. There was a Mossad connection to the events of 9/11, a connection that has yet to be fully and accurately explained.

In a follow up *American Free Press* article concerning the Urban Moving Systems owner, Mr. Dominik Suter, who fled to Israel after 9/11 and initial questioning by the FBI, journalist Christopher Bollyn reported that a leaked FBI Suspect List shows that Dominik Suter is among those suspected of involvement in the terrorist attacks. Despite the presence of an FBI office in Tel Aviv, and the "intimate relationship" between U.S. and Israeli intelligence agencies, Suter apparently remains at large, and the question asked by Bollyn is, why is the FBI ignoring a prime terror suspect?[307]

"The list of suspects is classified 'Law Enforcement Sensitive' and is periodically updated. While Suter's name is on the list, his Israeli nationality is not. Three addresses, two in New Jersey and one in Sherman Oaks, California, are given, as is his Social Security number. The year 1970 is listed as his date of birth."[308]

When *AFP* asked the FBI about the "suspect list," a Bureau spokeswoman said, "Were not going to validate your questions by talking about the list. You are not supposed to have it. It is not for public consumption."[309]

When asked about Israeli cooperation regarding suspects harbored in the Israeli state, Mr. William Carter, chief of the

306 Ahmed, p. 352.

307 AFP, 8/23/04, p. B.11.

308 Ibid.

309 Ibid.

FBI's National Press Office in Washington told *AFP* that Israel was "under no obligation" to turn over suspects and that if they did, it was only as a "matter of good will." Carter then told *AFP* to contact the FBI office in Tel Aviv for information regarding any extradition request for Mr. Suter.[310]

When *AFP* attempted to contact the office of Mr. Robert Geeslin, an FBI agent and deputy legal attaché in the U.S. Embassy in Israel, Geeslin's office refused to discuss the matter.[311]

And Mr. Mark Regev, spokesman for the Israeli government in Washington, DC, told *American Free Press* that the United States and Israeli authorities have an "excellent, on-going, intimate relationship." The "close cooperation" between Israel and the United States includes sharing intelligence information.

However, when *AFP* asked Mr. Regev repeatedly if Israeli authorities would cooperate with the U.S. by apprehending a terror suspect for questioning by the FBI, three times Mr. Regev avoided answering the question.

It should please be remembered that Mr. Dominik Suter owned the Urban Moving Systems business in Weehawken, NJ, that was determined to be a Mossad front for Mossad operatives to conduct Mossad activities as reported by one of the five detained Israelis who, when interviewed on an Israeli radio program stated, "The fact of the matter is we are coming from a country that experiences terror daily. Our purpose was to document the event."[312]

So let us now then take a little closer look at Israel's intelligence agency, the Mossad. It has been reported that top United States Army analysts believe Israel's intelligence agency, the Mossad, is "ruthless and cunning," "a wildcard" that "has the capability to target U.S. forces and make it look like a Palestinian/Arab act," according to an article entitled "U.S. Army Warns: Arabs May Be Framed for Terror" by Michael Collins Piper of *American Free*

310 Ibid.

311 Ibid.

312 Ibid.

Press. Sometimes the most likely suspect in an act of terrorism is actually a "false flag" working for those who are responsible.[313]

This eye-opening assertion about America's supposed closest ally was reported in a first page story in *The Washington Post* on September 10th, 2001-just one day before the terrorist attacks in America that are being blamed on "Arabs" and "Muslims."[314]

"The *Times* reported that this serious charge by United States Army officers against the Israelis appeared in a 68-page paper prepared by 60 officers at the U.S. Army's School for Advanced Military Studies, a training ground for up-and-coming Army officers."[315]

Then, just hours after the terrorist tragedies, a well-known pro-Israel analyst, Mr. George Friedman, proclaimed Israel as the primary beneficiary of the 9/11 attacks.[316]

"Qui Bono?"

"The big winner today, intended or not, is the state of Israel," wrote Friedman, who said on his website at stratfor.com, "There is no question ...that the Israeli leadership is feeling relief" in the wake of the terrorist attack on America as a result of the benefits that Israel will glean."[317]

We haven't heard very much lately about the "Road Map"-the multilateral plan to bring about an independent Palestinian state by the year 2005, the stated timeline by the Road Map participants. Time is certainly growing short to realistically make that deadline.

"Israeli Prime Minister Ariel Sharon's Chief of Staff, Dov Weisglass recently admitted that plans to pull out of Gaza while expanding settlements in the West Bank were aimed to undermine peace plans, stymie the creation of a Palestinian state and halt talks about the right of return for Palestinian refugees.

---

313 AFP, 8/23/04, p. B.7.

314 Ibid.

315 Ibid.

316 Ibid.

317 Ibid.

'The significance of our [unilateral] disengagement plan is the freezing of the peace process. It supplies the formaldehyde necessary so there is no political process with the Palestinians. When you freeze the process, you prevent the establishment of a Palestinian state... Effectively, this whole package called a Palestinian state has been removed indefinitely from our agenda. All of this was done with the United States blessing.'" Weisglass said.[318]

"Considering the United States Army's questions concerning possible provocations by Israel, coupled with this noted intelligence analyst's suggestion that Israel was indeed 'the big winner' on September 11th, a previous report in the August 3rd, 1993 issue of *The Village Voice*, that Israel's Mossad was perhaps involved in, or had foreknowledge of the previous "Arab terrorist" attack on the World Trade Center, takes on new dimensions.

The events of September the 11th do require careful attention in light of the fact that Israel has had a long and proven record in planting "false flags'-orchestrated acts of terrorism for its own purposes and pinning those atrocities on innocent parties.

Perhaps the best-known instance in which Israel used a "false flag" to cover its own trail was in the infamous Lavon Affair. It was in 1954 that several Israeli-orchestrated acts of terrorism against British targets in Egypt were carried out. Blame for the attacks was placed on the Muslim Brotherhood, which opposed the regime of Egyptian President Gamul Abdul-Nasser. However, the truth is found in a once secret cable from Colonel Benjamin Givli, the head of Israel's military intelligence, who outlined the intended purpose behind the wave of terror:

"Our goal is to break the West's confidence in the existing (Egyptian) regime. The actions should cause arrests, demonstrations, and expressions of revenge. The Israeli origin should be totally covered while attention should be shifted to any other possible factor. The purpose is to prevent economic and military aid from the West to Egypt."[319]

318 AFP, 10/18/04, p. 2.

319 AFP, 8/23/04, p. B.7.

Kind of has a "Northwoods" ring to it, eh?

"Considering this one well-documented but little-known historical occurrence, it should be of no surprise that even our own U.S. Army could raise serious questions about the possibility of Israeli intelligence committing acts of terror and planting evidence pointing to the "Arabs."[320] [Especially when one considers our own military brass considered conducting a similar exercise in deception and trickery towards the Cubans.]

There is also evidence of Israel's Mossad providing financing and tactical support for the very "Muslim extremists" presumed to be Israel's worst enemies. In an article entitled "Why Would Israel Fund Terrorism," *American Free Press* correspondent Mike Piper wrote, "The truth is that Muslim extremists have proven useful (if often unwitting) tools in advancing Israel's own geopolitical agenda."[321]

Although many Americans are now aware that Osama bin Laden's early efforts against the Soviets in Afghanistan were sponsored by the U.S. Central Intelligence Agency, the media has been reticent to point out that this arms pipeline-described by *Covert Action Information Bulletin*, September 1987, as "the second largest covert operation" in the CIA's history - was also under the direct supervision of the Mossad, according to former Mossad operative Victor Ostrovsky writing in his book, *The Other Side of Deception*.[322]

Ostrovsky wrote, "A large portion of the mujahadeen's weapons were American-made and were supplied to the Muslim Brotherhood directly from Israel..."[323]

"Former ABC News correspondent Mr. John Cooley, in *Unholy Wars: Afghanistan, America and International Terrorism*, provides confirmation for Ostrovsky's observations. Cooley writes:

---

320 Ibid.

321 Ibid.

322 Ibid.

323 Ibid.

Discussion of the input of outsiders to training and operations in Afghanistan would be incomplete without mention of Iran and the state of Israel...

Several Americans and Britons who took part in the training program have assured the author (Ostrovsky) that Israelis did indeed take part...

What is certain is that of all the members of the anti-Soviet coalition, the Israelis have been the most successful in concealing the details and even the broad traces of a training role, much more than the Americans and the British..."[324]

In addition to this, it should be noted that Sami Masri, an insider in the BCCI, Bank of Credit and Commerce International, told Time magazine journalists, Jonathon Beaty and S.C. Gwynne that BCCI "was financing Israeli arms going into Afghanistan. There were Israeli arms, Israeli planes, and CIA pilots. Arms were coming into Afghanistan and BCCI was facilitating it."[325]

"However, there is much more to the story of the Mossad's ties to the so-called Islamic terror networks that are the stuff of American nightmares today."[326]

In his book, *The Other Side of Deception*, ex-Mossad figure Victor Ostrovsky unveils the disturbing fact that the Mossad had a secret history of supporting radical Islamic groups for its own purposes.[327]

Pointing out that Arab and Muslim-hating hard-liners in Israel and its Mossad believe that Israel's survival lies in its military strength and that "this strength arises from the need to answer the constant threat of war," the Israeli hard-liners fear that any peace with any Arab state could weaken Israel and bring about its demise. In that vein, Ostrovsky wrote, "Supporting the radical elements of Muslim fundamentalism sat well with the Mossad's general plan for the region. An Arab world run by

324 AFP, 5/27/02, p. B.11.

325 Ibid.

326 Ibid.

327 Ibid.

fundamentalists would not be a party to any negotiations with the West..."[328]

Even columnist Mr. Jack Anderson, a devoted news conduit for the Israeli lobby, has bragged of Israeli skill. He wrote as long ago as September 17th, 1972, "The Israelis are also skillful at exploiting Arab rivalries and turning Arab against Arab. The Kurdish tribes, for example, inhabit the mountains of Northern Iraq. Every month, a secret Israeli envoy slips into the mountains from the Iranian side to deliver $50,000 to Kurdish leader Mulla Mustafa Al Barzani. The subsidy insures Kurdish hostility against Iraq, whose government is militantly anti-Israel."[329]

Jack Anderson also wrote: "Israeli agents-immigrants whose families had lived in Arab lands for generations-have a perfect knowledge of Arab dialects and customs. They have been able to infiltrate Arab governments with ease."[330]

And writing in *The New Yorker* on October 8th, 2001, veteran investigative journalist Mr. Seymore Hersh noted that a senior military officer had suggested to him that "a major foreign intelligence service might also have been involved" in the September the 11th attacks.[331]

Fox News reporter Mr. Carl Cameron, in early 2002, broke the story that the U.S. government was holding more than one hundred Israeli citizens with direct links to major foreign military, criminal and intelligence organizations. A bureau spokesperson would not talk about the case but did not deny it either. He referred reporters to the FBI's National Security Division.[332]

Mr. Cameron also said he was hampered in trying to obtain information. "It's very explosive information, obviously and there is a great deal of evidence that they say they have collected." By

---

328 Ibid.

329 Ibid.

330 Ibid.

331 Ibid.

332 Marrs, p. 98.

summer of 2002, the estimated number of Israeli nationals being held in detention had climbed to nearly 200.[333]

Finally, the *Fox News* series detailed the Israeli penetration of U.S. defense and government facilities by a large group of former Israeli military personal who had served in intelligence, surveillance, and explosive ordinance units, and were posing as Israeli art students. An even larger number of Israelis without visas left their "art sales" jobs so quickly after September the 11th that the company that hired them was temporarily closed down.[334]

French intelligence expert, Guillaume Dasquie,' editor of *Intelligence Online*, revealed the contents of a 61-page report, classified, by a United States interagency task force led by the Drug Enforcement Agency, the DEA. Their Office of Security Programs was confronted with reports of "unusual behavior of young Israeli nationals who had gained access to DEA circles."[335]

The Israeli national "art students" are, in fact, members of an Israeli intelligence network operating in the United States, consisting of "around 20 units composed of between four and eight members."[336]

The *Intelligence Online* editor continues:

"A few of the operatives are well known in the Israeli intelligence community. The report cited the names of Peer Segalovitz (military registration number 5087989), and Aran Ofek, son of a renowned two-star general in the Israeli army. The network targeted some of the most sensitive sites in the United States, such as Tinker Air Force Base near Oklahoma City. Indeed the U.S. Air Force's Office of Special Investigation sent a letter to the Justice Department on May 16th of last year to ask for assistance in a case against four Israelis suspected of spying: Yaron Ohana, Ronen Kalfon, Zeev Cohen, and Nãor Topaz."[337]

---

333 Ibid.

334 Ahmed, p. 354.

335 Ibid.

336 Ibid.

337 Ibid.

Furthermore, several of the Israelis involved in this "art student scandal" were observed taking pictures of and reconnoitering United States military bases and homes of U.S. government officials.[338]

Paul Rodriguez of *Insight* magazine reported that the Drug Enforcement Agency's Internal Security unit found that several U.S. military bases had experienced unauthorized entries by some of the Israeli "art students," including two bases from which Stealth aircraft and other super-secret military units operate. Unauthorized photographing of military sites and civilian industrial complexes, such as petroleum storage facilities, were reported to the DEA, documents show and interviews confirm.[339]

The DEA document, whose authenticity is confirmed by official U.S. intelligence sources, states: "The activities of these Israeli art students raised the suspicion of the DEA's Office of Security Programs and other field offices when attempts were made to circumvent the access control systems at DEA offices, and when these individuals began to solicit their paintings at the homes of DEA employees. The nature of the individuals conduct, combined with intelligence information and historical information regarding past incidents may well be an organized intelligence gathering activity." [340]

Paragraph 82 of the DEA document records that MacDill Air Force Base intelligence officers were warned in March of 2001 of the Israeli art students' efforts. United States counter-intelligence officials issued a bulletin on March 23rd, 2001, asserting the existence of an "ongoing security threat" in the form of intelligence agents operating as "Israeli National Art Students that are targeting government offices selling 'artwork.'"[341]

338 Marrs, p. 99.

339 Ibid.

340 Ahmed, p. 355.

341 Ibid.

As previously mentioned, many of these young Israelis formerly served in Israeli military intelligence, surveillance, explosive ordinance and electronic signal intercept units.[342]

Most of them claimed to be art students from Israel's Bezalel Academy or the University of Jerusalem. However, paradoxically, Jerusalem University does not exist, and officials with Bezalel Academy said no names of the "art students" turned up in the school's data bank.[343]

"These people may have been in surveillance, perhaps in preparation of further simultaneous attacks,' which were foiled or called off as it became apparent that September 11 had been quite enough," Ahmed wrote in *The War on Freedom*.[344]

This was the biggest Israeli spy case in the United States since 1984, when naval intelligence officer Jonathon Pollard, an American Jew, was caught giving U.S. military secrets to Israel, reported *Le Monde*.[345]

Unfortunately, these facts have been shoved out of the confines of mainstream cogitations, and are now blithely ignored. "The biggest story of our time, of Israel spying on all branches of the government, on all our intelligence agencies-in the CIA, the DEA, and the White House itself, is not picked up by the leading newspapers like *The New York Times* and *The Washington Post*," observed Mr. Carl Cameron of *Fox News* on *C-SPAN*.[346]

Jane's Information Group, the authoritative military and intelligence analysis service, similarly criticizes the deafening silence on a subject of critical importance to United States national security, not to mention a proper understanding of September the 11th. "It is rather strange that the U.S. media, with one notable exception, seem to be ignoring what may well prove to be the most explosive story since the 11 September attack, the alleged

342 Ibid. p. 354.

343 Marrs, p. 99.

344 Ahmed, p. 354.

345 Marrs, p. 99.

346 Ahmed, p. 356.

break up of a major Israeli espionage operation in the United States, which aimed to infiltrate both the Justice and Defense departments.[347]

"If the major news media in the United States are cowed about negative reporting on Israel, U.S. government officials are probably worse. *Insight* magazine reporter Mr. Paul Rodriguez said one Justice Department official told him, 'We think there is something quite sinister here but are unable at this time to put our finger on it.' Another official flatly stated, 'the higher-ups don't want to deal with this and neither does the FBI because it involves Israel.' *Fox News* reported that 'investigators within the DEA, the INS and the FBI have all told *Fox News* that to pursue or even suggest Israel is spying... is considered career suicide.'"[348] Founder and contributing editor of *Executive Intelligence Review*, Mr. Lyndon LaRouche, believes the September the 11th attacks provided a pretext to implement a plan to strengthen Israel as articulated in a 1996 paper by an Israeli think tank.[349]

The leader of this think tank that produced this paper was Mr. Richard Perle. In 2002, Perle was the chairman of President Bush's Defense Policy Board, which reported to Deputy Defense Secretary Mr. Paul Wolfowitz. Pearle is also a ranking member of the Rockefeller-influenced Council on Foreign Relations and is a key advocate of the "neo-conservative" foreign policy.[350]

Perle's 1996 paper, entitled *A Clean Break: A New Strategy for Securing the Realm*, was prepared for the Institute for Advanced Strategic and Political Studies, a Jerusalem-based think tank with an affiliated office in Washington, DC.[351]

This study paper explains that "Israel can shape its strategic environment... by weakening, containing and even rolling back Syria." The paper continues by stating that "this effort can focus

347 Ibid.

348 Marrs, p. 101.

349 Ibid. p. 102.

350 Ibid.

351 Ibid.

on removing Saddam Hussien from power in Iraq-an important Israeli strategic objective in its own right-as a means of foiling Syria's regional ambitions."[352]

"The ongoing drive to induce President George W. Bush to launch a war against Iraq is a 1996 Israeli government policy that is being foisted on the president by a nest of Israeli agents inside the U.S. government," declared LaRouche.[353]

"This Israeli spy network inside the United States was unable to achieve their objective until President Bush was entrapped by the events of September 11, 2001, and by the falsified account of these events provided by this foreign intelligence apparatus."[354]

On February 19th, 1998, Richard Perle and former congressman Stephen Solarez released an "Open Letter to the President," demanding a full-scale U.S.-led drive for "regime change" in Baghdad. Among the signers of the original Perle-Solarez letter were the following Bush administration officials: From the Department of Defense, Donald Rumsfeld, and Paul Wolfowitz, Dov Zakheim, Douglass Feith and Peter Rodman. From the State Department, Richard Armitage, John Bolten and David Wurmser. From the National Security Council, Elliot Abrams. From the Defense Policy Board, Fred Ikle and from the White House, Zalmay Khalilzad.[355]

LaRouche concluded that "President Bush is being pressured-from inside his own national security apparatus-to adopt an Israeli Likud foreign policy! This is a scandalous hoax, far worse that the Gulf of Tonkin affair of the late 1960s."[356]

This gives even more importance to the recently disclosed developments concerning the classified "Downing Street memo," which stated that "The only way to overthrow it (the regime of Saddam Hussein) was likely to be massive military action," and

352 Ibid. p. 103.

353 Ibid.

354 Ibid.

355 Ibid.

356 Ibid. p. 104.

that "Military action was now seen as inevitable. Bush wanted to remove Saddam, through military action, justified by the conjunction of *terrorism* (emphasis added) and WMD. But the intelligence and facts were being fixed around the policy..."[357]

Well, if "regime change" in Baghdad was policy being formulated as far back as 1996 as documented here, and that a "New Pearl Harbor" would be necessary, and that "terrorism" would be part of the justification, along with WMD for the planned massive military action, and the fact that "intelligence and facts were being fixed around the policy" and that covert black operations used as a pretext for war are part of intelligence operations, would one be way off base to conclude then that President Bush orchestrated the attacks of September the 11th, along with his allies and their intelligence operations in order to implement the stated policy, or is this a rather logical conclusion to the evidence we've seen so far?

In *The High Priests of War*, author Michael Collins Piper noted that "Paul Wolfowitz, Richard Perle, William Kristol and Henry Kissinger, [who once stated that 'Military men are dumb, stupid animals to be used as pawns for foreign policy' according to Woodward and Bernstein in *The Final Days*[358]] are perhaps the most powerful figures in this neo-conservative network that orchestrated this tragic U.S. war against Iraq... These neo-conservatives dream of establishing a world empire and intend to use America's young people as the cannon fodder to accomplish their goals."[359]

The former director general of the Pakistani intelligence services, General Hameed Gul, who worked closely with the CIA during the years of fighting against the Soviets in Afghanistan, said it was his belief that the Israeli Mossad orchestrated the 9/11

---

357 The Sunday Times Britain, "The Secret Downing Street Memo," www.timeson-line.co.uk/article/0,,2087-1593607,00.html, 7/3/05.

358 Hilder, "The Greatest Lie Ever Sold," DVD Documentary.

359 Michael C. Piper, "The High Priests of War," About the Cover.

attacks with the support of their assets [traitors] already within the United States. "This was clearly an inside job," Gul said.[360]

Andreas von Buelow, Germany's former defense minister, who also served on the parliamentary commission, which oversees the German secret services, was a member of the German parliament from 1969 to 1994. He wrote a book, *In the Name of the State*, about the criminal activities of secret services, including the CIA.[361]

von Buelow expressed that he also believes that the Israeli intelligence service, the Mossad, was behind the September the 11th terror attacks. "These attacks were carried out to turn public opinion against the Arabs, and boost military and security spending. You don't get the higher echelons, von Buelow said, referring to the masterminds. The organization doing the planning, such as Mossad, is primarily interested in affecting public opinion. The planners use corrupt guns for hire, such as Abu Nidal, the Palestinian terrorist whom von Buelow called an instrument of the Mossad. The BND (German secret service) is steered by the CIA, and the CIA is steered by the Mossad."[362]

Eckardt Werthebach, former president of Germany's domestic intelligence service, said a sophisticated operation such as displayed on 9/11 would require a state intelligence service behind it, totally unlike the "loose group" of terrorists reportedly led by Mohammed Atta.[363]

Jim Marrs, author of *Inside Job*, *Rule by Secrecy* and *Crossfire*, said in an interview about the September the 11th attacks, "What's amazing when you stop and consider that everyone that they say was involved in the attack, the Al Qaeda network, Osama bin Laden, these are creations of our intelligence agencies. In my book, I detail how Osama bin Laden actually came to the United

360 Marrs, p.104.

361 Ahmed, p. 365.

362 Ibid. p. 366.

363 Marrs, p. 105.

States in the 80s and was given arms, and ammunition and some training."[364]

Former high-ranking FBI official Mr. Ted Gunderson, a 27-year FBI veteran who capped his career as the Senior Special Agent in Charge of the Los Angeles office of the FBI, has his own "inside" knowledge of the Al Qaeda network going back to the days when Osama bin Laden was still officially allied with the United States.

As *American Free Press* reported on January 7th, 2002, Ted Gunderson met Osama bin Laden in the spring of 1986 when bin Laden-traveling under the name "Tim Osman"-visited the United States under State Department and Central Intelligence Agency sponsorship for the purpose of securing arms and aid for Afghan rebels fighting the "evil empire," the Soviet Union.[365]

Marrs continues, "The Al Qaeda people are called a terrorist network. I think they'd be more correctly termed a mercenary or Arab mercenaries. And of course, if you have mercenaries, they were created initially to fight the Russians in Afghanistan. But once you have a group of mercenaries, they'll go fight whoever you order them to fight... Since they were created and working for the CIA, I think the question that has to be asked is, could they still be working for the CIA?"[366]

My understanding is that once you're in the agency, you never really leave the agency.

Remember, back in the first chapter of this text when we discussed Operation Northwoods, how the U.S. generals in the Joint Chiefs of Staff Office considered secretly paying someone in the Castro government to attack us, the United States, in order to provoke by pretext a war with Cuba, a definite mercenary type of operation? Could Osama bin Laden still be on the U.S. payroll, acting as a paid mercenary for the Israeli first neo-con Bush junta?

Germany's former defense minister Andreas von Buelow says the terrorists who actually commit the crimes are the working level.

364 Hilder.

365 AFP, 8/23/04, p. B.1.

366 Hilder.

"The working level is part of the deception," he said. "Ninety-five percent of the work of the intelligence agencies around the world is deception and disinformation, which is widely propagated in the mainstream media, creating an accepted version of events. Journalists don't even raise the simplest of questions... those who differ are labeled as crazy."[367]

Immediately after the attacks of 9/11, Israeli spokesman Mr. Bibi Netanyahu publicly stated, "It is a very good thing" because it would strengthen American support for Israel. And as if to confirm Netanyahu's sentiments, using the 9/11 created war on terror as justification, Israel's Prime Minister Mr. Ariel Sharon soon began escalating the Israeli-Palestinian conflict, pummeling civilian infrastructure, homes, businesses, etc. in the West Bank and Gaza on the pretext of fighting terrorism.[368]

Prime Ministers Ariel Sharon and Ehud Barak both belong to a long line of political generals that started with Moshe Dayan. This breed of generals was raised on the myth of the sanctity of the land. In a 1976 interview, Moshe Dayan, who was the Israeli defense minister in 1967, explained what led, then, to the decision to attack Syria. Syria was conceived as a serious threat to the security of Israel, and a constant initiator of aggression towards the residents of Northern Israel. But according to Dayan, this is "bullshit"-Syria was not a threat to Israel before 67: "Just drop it... I know how at least 80 percent of all the incidents with Syria started. We were sending a tractor to the demilitarized zone and we knew the Syrians would shoot." According to Dayan, what led Israel to provoke Syria this way was the greediness for the land [there's that covetousness thing again]-the idea that it is possible to "grab a piece of land and keep it until the enemy will get tired and give it to us."[369]

Crises are created to torpedo peace talks, and then packaged as Israel's restraint and retaliation by our media. The essential

367 Ahmed, p. 366.

368 Ibid. p. 372.

369 Ibid. p. 369

strategy has been candidly articulated by the Israeli Defense Minister, Moshe Dayan:

"Israel must use the sword as the main, if not the only, instrument with which to keep its morale high and to retain its moral tension. Toward this end it may, no it must, invent dangers, and to do this it must adopt the method of provocation-even revenge and above all, let us hope for a new war with the Arab countries, so that we may finally get rid of our troubles and acquire our space."[370]

I think this would be a good place to review Jesus' teachings about the peacemakers when he was preaching on the mountain in St Matthew chapter 5, verse 9. He said, "Blessed are the peacemakers, for they shall be called the sons of God" (Matthew 5:9, NIV). I think even most Sunday school children could easily and reasonably conclude then by simple reasoning of opposition that, damned are the warmongers, for they will be called the sons of Satan.

At the beginning of this chapter, we discussed the concept of Qui Bono, who benefits, when considering who or what entity or interest or entities or interests may have benefited from the massive crime against humanity that occurred on September the 11th. And I feel assuredly confident in expressing my assessment that the torment, suffering and woe we endured on 9/11, must have been a hookup by traitorous, political harlots -Zionists in Washington, DC with their benefactress allies in Tel Aviv and Jerusalem.

> *"And have no fellowship with the unfruitful works of darkness, but rather expose them.*
>
> (Ephesians 5:11, NKJV)

Cognitive dissonance, described by Walter Chukwa, of 911uncovered.com, is the discomfort felt at the discrepancy between what you already believe, and new information that

370 Ibid. p. 370

conflicts with that belief. This phenomenon is what prevents people from accepting the fact that the U.S. government, along with its best Middle East ally Israel, carried out the 9/11 attacks.[371]

Canadian social philosopher and Professor John Mcmurtry expressed, "To begin with, the forensic principle of who most benefits from the crime, clearly points in the direction of the Bush administration. One would be naïve to think the Bush Jr. faction and its oil, military-industrial and Wall Street Backers who had stolen an election with its man rated in office by the majority of Americans as poor on the economy, and who is more deplored by the rest of the world as a deep danger to the global environment and the international rule of law... Americans are diverted from a free-falling economy to attack another foreign Satan . . . And Israel's apartheid civil war is vindicated at the same time... The more you review the connections and the sweeping lapse of security across so many coordinates, the more the lines point backwards."[372]

Retired United States Air Force Colonel George Nelson concludes about the events of 9/11, "As painful and heartbreaking as was the loss of innocent lives and the lingering health problems of thousands more, a most troublesome and nightmarish probability remains that so many Americans appear to be involved in the most heinous conspiracy in our country's history."[373]

Nafeez Ahmed, writing in *The War on Freedom* states:

The executive branch of the federal government enabled a lethal 'surprise' attack with mass murder against two of the original thirteen states, New York and Virginia. By such an act, the federal government would grossly violate its contract with the states and abrogate its own constitutional rights and privileges.

Like a loose handgun, wielded by a madman, our federal government has backfired on its owners, the states, and the people. The executive has gone to war in defiance of the Constitution, and Congress has abdicated its war-declaring authority on at least 200

371 AFP, 10/11/04, p. 16.

372 Ahmed, p. 275.

373 George Nelson, Colonel USAF, ret.

occasions since 1945. The federal government has proven utterly incapable because of its unwillingness to remedy its chronic and world threatening sickness [Zionism].[374]

American complicity in the rape of Palestine seems to have opened a Pandora's Box that only a shocked and awed America might close again. Instead, mentally lazy attitudes prevail with us: "Why don't the Arabs just pull up stakes and move?" or "they're all crazy there anyway," which amounts to ethnic cleansing justifications. If one manages to explain the intrigues of provocation, one gets, "it's their own tough luck if the Arabs let the Israelis trick them." Such "losers-weepers" rationalizations ignore all our own canons of justice.[375]

We do understand the enormity of our unprecedented loss on 9/11, and even greater losses in past foreign wars. We don't really know who is running foreign policy in our country-our elected representatives or a clique with its own agenda. How can we know for sure our President would be safe taking orders from us, when a popular peacemaking president could be assassinated, without the culprits ever being caught?"[376]

We have no way of knowing what will hit us next, our official color-coded terror threat index notwithstanding, or where our country is being taken. If we do not resolve the problems in our country associated with September the 11th and its subsequent wars, the next calamity will be worse still.[377]

But you can bet your bottom dollar, the accused will be an enemy of Israel, like Syria or Iran, and will be in the way of their own manifest destiny.

We the People are not masters in our own house. A criminal element is running it their way,[378] [our "democratic" four-year cycle of general elections notwithstanding]. Be they CIA or

374 Ahmed, pp. 376-377.

375 Ibid. p. 380.

376 Ibid. p. 383.

377 Ibid.

378 Ibid.

Secret Government, military-industrial-Zionist-banking-oil-mainstream press complex, MI6, City of London or Mossad, it is up to the American people to find them out.

"A true patriot must always be ready to defend his country from its government," an American naturalist once expressed.[379]

To deserve the names of freedom, liberty, democracy and truth, we should have gotten to the bottom of this a long, long time ago,[380] and found whoever these zio-bastards are, and excised this nasty, insidious, oozing, infectious, cancerous growth from our collective national governmental body, before we all expire from its wickedly painful, slow death.

Some have already accepted the death of our once great nation as expressed in this commentary from *The Idaho Observer*. And it somewhat pains me to restate this as I type on July 4th, 2005:

"Nine-Eleven did it. Since the morning after, it has been obvious to many, myself included, that our nation has been irrevocably lost. Not a day in the last 1,200 or so has gone by without some official reminder of how free our people are no longer; and how utterly depraved those in positions of state and federal authority have become.

Once revered by the peoples of the world as defender of freedom and the dignity of the common man, the U.S. is now the nation enjoying the pinnacle of global scorn for its univerally-televised violations of human rights and abuse of military might. The U.S. can no longer lead a humanitarian relief effort without arousing well-deserved global suspicion as to its hidden motives.

Here at home our nation's leaders don't even pretend to hold fair elections anymore and have decided the best way to handle civil liberty is to imprison it. With the world's largest and fastest growing prison population, over half of which are either innocent or convicted of non-violent crimes, we can no longer refer to The United States of America as 'the land of the free.'

379 Oliver Stone, "JFK," Motion Picture Film.

380 Ahmed, p. 384.

Try to write your congressman or pass a needed initiative that isn't instantly emasculated by the sitting legislature if you desire exercising your futility muscles.

Our nation is gone and our leaders have left us with debts that can never be paid. At this time I must announce that I have conceded the nation: What no longer exists cannot be saved.

I will never, however, concede our people. With my last breath, I will inform them. There is no doubt in my mind that we are being taken somewhere as a nation and that we have almost arrived. History has shown that all nations eventually fail. The United States' time has come, that is all. There may be no stopping evil men from destroying our nation, but we can strengthen good people so they can be equipped to build from U.S. ashes a just and honorable society.

If history is our guide, the fall will be chaos-political, social, economic and spiritual chaos. What we are able to accomplish now in the minds of our people will directly affect the magnitude of death, destruction and misery the people of our nation and our planet will be forced to endure after the crash and whether or not the institutions of civilization will be rebuilt in the image of decency or despotism.

At first, conceding the nation feels pretty horrible. 'America dead? She can't be, we must save her! How can we give up on America-what would the Founders think?'

Visions of how we have betrayed the trust placed in us to defend our freedom and fight for the freedom of others torture our thoughts. But after awhile, when emotions subside, the path becomes clear. The Founders even told us that the tree of liberty must, from time to time, be fertilized by the blood of patriots and tyrants, that it is its natural manure, and that, when government becomes bad, we must throw it off and reestablish good government.

It is a relief to know my job is no longer to save a fiction, but to inspire minds of my countrymen with thoughts and ideas that give them strength and fill them with resolve to be noble, reverent beings instead of mindless bickering slaves.

Turning slaves into sovereigns isn't easy, but it's what we have to do because there is nothing left to save us but cach other."[381]

We must proceed with great care. Knowing and defining your true enemies is not as easy as one would think. Wouldn't your true enemies attempt to mislead and deceive you and inform you that they are on your side and direct you against their enemies and your true allies? Be careful the deception and the trickery.

> *"That we should no longer be children tossed to and fro and carried about with every wind of doctrine, by the trickery of men, in the cunning craftiness of deceitful plotting."*
>
> (Ephesians 4:14, NKJV)

Satan is slick and knows no limits. If Satan and his demonic false prophets will come in the name of the Lord, Jesus Christ, I'm sure than that it would not be beneath them to come with the donkeys or the elephants, in the colors of Old Glory, the Union Jack, or even the Star of David, or behind the great Presidential seal itself.

In 2 Corinthians 11:13-15, the New Testament says, "For such men are false apostles, deceitful workmen, masquerading as apostles of Christ. And no wonder, for Satan himself masquerades as an angel of light. It is not surprising, then, if his servants masquerade as servants of righteousness. Their end will be what their actions deserve" (NIV).

> *"The Spirit clearly says that in later times some will abandon the faith and follow deceiving spirits and things taught by demons. Such teachings come through hypocritical liars, whose consciences have been seared as with a hot iron"*
>
> (1 Timothy 4:1-2, NIV).

381 Idaho Observer, "Concede the Nation, Inform our People," www.proliberty.com/observer/20050112.htm, 2/15/05.

"Beware the leader who bangs the drums of war in order to whip up the citizenry into a patriotic fervor, for patriotism is indeed a double-edged sword. It emboldens the blood, just as it narrows the mind. And when the drums of war have reached a fever pitch, and the blood boils with hate and the mind has closed, the leader will have no need to seize the rights of the citizenry. Rather the citizenry, infused with fear and blinded by patriotism, will offer up all their rights unto the leader, and gladly so. How do I know? For this is what I have done. And I am Caesar."[382]

"To sin by silence when we should protest," said E.W. Wilcox "makes cowards out of men."[383]

382 Ahmed, p. 384.

383 Oliver Stone, "JFK," Motion Picture Film.

CHAPTER FIVE
No One Comes to the Father Except Through Me

Years ago, after finishing my aviation degree from Purdue University, back in the late 80s, my first position upon graduation, in order to gain flight time and experience and to eventually join the ranks of the major airlines, was that of a flight instructor at the FlightSafety Academy in Vero Beach, Florida. It was a great place to teach flying to other aspiring pilots with beautiful weather, beautiful beaches, bikinis, and clear blue skies.

I remember most of my flight students, and I tried to be the best flight instructor I could be. But just as students recall teachers who inspired them, I remember one student particularly well who taught me a lot about a troubled geographical area of the world that has had more than its fair share of heartache, strife and turmoil and at times, seems that a just solution and a lasting peace are unlikely if not impossible, and due to design more likely than not.

My friend and flight students name was Musa Hassan, a Palestinian who was probably one of the nicest, most generous and gentlepersons I have ever had the pleasure to know.

I remember one day, as Musa was preparing for one of his ratings, or checkrides as they are known, in preparation for the oral exam, we spent an afternoon briefing as it were, discussing the complex systems on the Piper Seminole, all the factors that affect Vmc or minimum controllable airspeed with an engine inoperative on a multiengine airplane and other related items.

When we had finished briefing, our discussion somehow had turned to the area of his hometown in Palestine, and the troubles of the Middle East region. I had tried to educate myself in the past to understand the problems of this troubled area. You see, there had been "Arab" terror attacks and hijackings and the like, and I was always under the impression that it was always the Israelis who were the victims of this one-sided terror, aggression and violence.

However, realizing that there are always at least two sides to every story, and that neither one is the complete and absolute truth, I believed I had an opportunity to gain a little more of an understanding of that troubled region of the world, through the eyes, insights and personal experiences from someone on the "other side."

Musa said to me, "Glen, let me try to explain this to you in a way that may help you to understand." In my best recollection, he said to me, "Suppose back in 1948, the United Nations had decided that in order to correct the past, and create a better world, the UN would issue a decree that said from this point on, all of Virginia, Tennessee and Kentucky are now going to be a new nation, exclusively for the benefit of one race of people and one religion of people.

"And for the sake of this discussion," he said, "this new nation would be for the exclusive benefit of the Native Americans. Now suppose you had a home or a farm, or a business in this newly designated territory and you were eventually ran off of it, or ethnically cleansed from it, in order to make room for the new settlers and their settlements, to accommodate all the new immigrants to this new nation.

"And let's say this new nation and its leaders imposed all sorts of restrictions on your movement, and you were required to live in refugee camps, and you were treated as second-class citizens in your own homeland.

Musa continued, "Now Glen, suppose after 19 to 20 years of these conditions, this new nation, its immigrants and inhabitants felt and therefore decided they needed more land. So, they decided to take by conquest Southern Indiana, and Northern Alabama, and Mississippi and forced or ethnically cleansed even more of your countrymen off of their farms, homes, businesses and homeland. Now let's suppose, Glen that during this time nobody would recognize this injustice, and nobody intervened on your behalf to assist you with this transgression. And then suppose the United Nations, when they finally attempted to apply corrective measures to this new nation state and have them withdraw to their original borders of Virginia, Tennessee and Kentucky, they were rebuffed and received nothing but complete intransigence and were told by this new nation state that they were not going to leave this expanded area they occupied. And the United Nations seemed virtually prostrate to do anything to apply and enforce correction."

I remember Musa saying at this point, "Glen, I think those boys from Indiana and Kentucky for sure would feel the outrageous wrongdoing in this, and would go to just about any measure required to try and stop and hopefully reverse this trend, and try to provide some dignity and liberty for their people."

I started to get the picture that Musa was trying to paint and was beginning to see the other side of the story.

But then Musa went on and he said, "But Glen, you haven't heard the worst of it. This new nation now wants all of Indiana, Illinois, West Virginia, Maryland and Missouri, along with all of Alabama, Mississippi, Georgia and North and South Carolina."

I began to understand their plight and feel their pain and began to realize that there was indeed more to the story than I had been led to believe through one-sided propaganda and brainwashing.

After Musa finished his ratings and flight courses in Florida, we kept in touch for quite a while. He got a job eventually flying DC-8 freighters.

Over the years, however, we did lose touch, as both of us pursued our careers, moving on from charter, commuter and freight operations to eventually flying for the major airlines.

As my wife, Joy, and I started our family and tried to provide a safe, warm, and comfortable home for our children, it was fairly easy to forget about the troubles in far off lands and in other parts of the world.

But as your children grow up, fast, and approach the age of conscription, and your nation is involved in three wars, two in the Middle East and one never ending international war on terror, and you begin to hear lawmakers and public civil servants discuss the reinstitution of the draft, all of a sudden, things hit a little closer to home.

You realize how evil and slick that Satan is, having us kill one another, misinformed, indoctrinated, and negligent combatants and innocent civilians alike, men, women, boys and girls, and you see his instruments used, false prophets bearing false witness, and using lies as pretext to engage our youth in the worst activity in the world, killing and maiming for life thousands, and you get so frustrated because as plain to see as it is that war is the work of the devil, because certainly Jesus would not have us engaging in these atrocities, sermons are given promoting "justified war" and false prophets preaching in the name of Jesus Christ, just as He said they would, deceive us. And all the while someone, many people, rich, wealthy, powerful people whose own children are safe and secure, profit from this insidious activity, convincing us it is in our "national interest" to "liberate" foreign people from foreign lands, totally against our founders' advice and totally at odds with the Biblical explanations for the causes of war, and totally in contradiction to the teachings of Jesus Christ.

> *"Now the fruit of righteousness is sown in peace by those who make peace."*
>
> (James 3:18, NKJV)

> *"He came and preached peace to you who were far away and peace to those who were near."*
>
> (Ephesians 2:17, NIV)

> *"Depart from evil and do good; seek peace and pursue it.*
>
> (Psalms 34:14, NKJV)

> *"But the meek shall inherit the earth, and shall delight themselves in the abundance of peace."*
>
> (Psalms 37:11, NKJV)

And so, you hope for widespread peace to break out, you pray for peace. And you just do what little you can.

But one also seeks the truth, one seeks wisdom, one seeks a deeper understanding. A parent tries to educate him or herself so they may be able to better answer their children's questions.

And when you feel like you've uncovered a big piece of the truth and causes of global and political strife and turmoil, one feels that he should do his part to help, as you don't want to see anymore of your nation's kids, or any more of God's children anywhere, getting killed for something that is not in their interest, or not really in their nation's interest, and definitely not in the interest of our Heavenly Father.

> *"The Lord will give strength to His people; the Lord will bless His people with peace."*
>
> (Psalms 29:11, NKJV)

In my pursuit to further educate myself, to seek wisdom and guidance, to better comprehend and understand, in order to better answer my children's questions, I came across a little book by a Jewish, Israeli author. His name is Israel Shahak and his book is entitled, *Jewish History, Jewish Religion, The Weight of Three Thousand Years.*

Many of the things I read in this book were truly eye opening and painfully educational; things I have not seen or read anywhere else. In this 103-page text is packed a treasure trove of invaluable information for those who seek to understand the problems of the Middle East and a better understanding of United States foreign policies.

Some of the most enlightening material in this text is where I would like to proceed, further explore and discuss in detail.

On the inside front review pages of this book, Benyamin Beit-Hallami from *Haaretz*, said of this work, "Israel Shahak won fame in Israel by his principled persistence in telling truths which most Israelis don't like to hear."[384]

"This is a remarkable book... It deserves a wide readership, not only among Jews, but among Christians who seek a fuller understanding both of historical Judaism and of modern-day Israel," Ted Schmidt of the *Catholic New Times* reviewed.[385]

"Most disturbing. Shahak insists that the religion, in its classical and Talmudic form, is 'poisoning the minds and hearts.' This controversial attack of Israel by a Jew is bound to alarm Jewry worldwide," the American Library Association Booklist wrote.[386]

"His (Shahak's) message gets to the heart of U.S.-Israeli relations. It is not only Jews who should read *Jewish History, Jewish Religion*, but Christians as well," wrote Grace Halsell from *Middle East Policy*.[387]

And Henry Fischer from *The Link*, stated, "Shahak's book is among the few that are most essential to those of us interested in the Middle East."[388]

In the Foreword to *Jewish History, Jewish Religion*, Gore Vidal wrote:

"Sometime in the late 1950's, that world-class gossip and occasional historian, John F. Kennedy, told me how, in 1948, Harry S. Truman, had been pretty much abandoned by everyone when he came to run for president. Then an American Zionist brought him two million dollars in cash, in a suitcase, aboard his whistle stop train. 'That's why our recognition of Israel was rushed through so fast.'

384 Israel Shahak, "Jewish History, Jewish Religion, Pluto Press, England, Front Review Pages.

385 Ibid.

386 Ibid.

387 Ibid.

388 Ibid.

Unfortunately, the hurried recognition of Israel as a state has resulted in forty-five years of murderous confusion, and the destruction of what Zionist fellow travelers thought would be a pluralistic state-home to its native population of Muslims, Christians, and Jews… I shall not rehearse the wars and alarms of that unhappy region. But I will say that the hasty invention of Israel has poisoned the political and intellectual life of the USA, Israel's unlikely patron.

... From Jerusalem, Israel Shahak never ceases to analyze not only the dismal politics of Israel today but the Talmud itself, and the effect of the entire rabbinical tradition on a small state that the right-wing rabbinate means to turn into a theocracy for Jews only.

... Israel's authorities deplore Shahak. But there is not much to be done with a retired professor of chemistry who was born in Warsaw in 1933 and spent his childhood in the concentration camp at Belsen... He was-and still is-a humanist who detests imperialism whether in the name of the God of Abraham or of George Bush... Like a highly learned Thomas Paine, Shahak illustrates the prospect before us, as well as the long history behind us, and thus he continues to reason, year after year. Those who heed him will certainly be wiser and-dare I say? -better. He is the latest, if not the last, of the great prophets."[389]

Jesuit Fr. John Sheehan once expressed, "Every time anyone says that Israel is our only friend in the Middle East, I can't help but think that before Israel, we had no enemies in the Middle East."[390]

In the Foreword to the second printing of *Jewish History, Jewish Religion,* Edward Said discussed how:

"Shahak endorsed the phrase 'Judeo-Nazi' to characterize methods used by the Israelis to subordinate and repress the Palestinians.

389 Ibid. p. vii.

390 Ahmed, p. 364.

Israel is unique in the world for the excuses made on its behalf: journalists either do not see or write what they know to be true for fear of blacklisting or retaliation...

... Shahak has admonished his compatriots not to forget that an appalling history of antisemitism endured does not entitle them to do what they wish, just because they have suffered....

... But it is as a scholar of Judaism that he towers over so many others, since it is Judaism that has occupied his energies as a scholar and political activist from the beginning..."[391]

And in the Introduction to *Jewish History, Jewish Religion*, Shahak's co-author of his two other books, *Open Secrets: Israeli Nuclear and Foreign Policies* and *Jewish Fundamentalism in Israel*, Norman Mezvinsky writes:

"... This is not a happy book of Jewish apologetics. It is rather a bitter critique of both classical rabbinic Judaism and the Zionist nature of the state of Israel, written by a proud, erudite, courageous Jew who loved the prophetic tradition in Judaism and the positive aspects of Jewish History...

... He focused primarily upon the parochialism, racism and hatred of non-Jews that has continued to plague classical Judaism and much of Jewish society...

Noam Chomsky wrote: 'Shahak is an outstanding scholar with remarkable insight and depth of knowledge. His work is... a contribution of great value.'

... His repudiation of the religious faith in which he had been reared; his conversion to secularism and his later revolt against Zionism did not cause him to reject totally Israeli-Jewish society...

... For thirty-five years he focused mainly upon Israel's denial of human rights and to end oppression of the Palestinians...

... In the early 1970s, Shahak decided that too little was known outside of Israel about the denial of human rights to, and oppression of Palestinians in the Jewish state... Shahak in his talks pinpointed how the Israeli government denied to Palestinian citizens of the Jewish state certain rights reserved for Jews and how Palestinians living in the occupied territories, who were not

391 Shahak, pp. ix-xi.

citizens, were treated far worse... Shahak continually maintained in his analysis that Israeli oppression of Palestinians stemmed from the Zionist character of the Jewish state...

...This book is vintage Shahak and deserves a careful reading by people interested in Judaism, Zionism and Israel and the Arab-Israeli conflict."[392]

So, with that introduction, and Shahak's bona fides well established, let's begin our look at Israel Shahak's work.

Israel Shahak begins *Jewish History, Jewish Religion*, by explaining that "this book, although written in English and addressed to a people living outside the State of Israel, is, in a way, a continuation of my political activities as an Israeli Jew. Those activities began in 1965-6 with a protest which caused a considerable scandal at the time: I had personally witnessed an ultra-religious Jew refuse to allow his phone to be used on the Sabbath in order to call an ambulance for a non-Jew who happened to have collapsed in his Jerusalem neighborhood. Instead of simply publishing the incident in the press, I asked for a meeting with the members of the Rabbinical Court of Jerusalem, which is composed of rabbis nominated by the State of Israel. I asked them whether such behavior was consistent with their interpretation of the Jewish religion. They answered that the Jew in question had behaved correctly, indeed piously, and backed their statement by referring me to a passage in an authoritative compendium of Talmudic laws, written in this century."[393]

The Talmud, the Jewish holy book that explains how the Torah or Old Testament is to be interpreted, is sometimes referred to as the "Shas," a shortened form of the term "Shisha Sedarim" (Six Orders), a reference to the six chapters of the Mishna (codified collection of interpretations of portions of biblical books and other legal material. Together with the Gemara, or commentary on the Mishna, it comprises the Talmud). There are two distinct works known as Talmud: the Yerushalmi (Jerusalem or Palestinian) Talmud, and the Bavli (Babylonian Talmud).

392 Ibid. pp. xv-xvi.

393 Ibid. p. 1.

However, the Babylonian Talmud has greater popularity, so the term 'Talmud' almost always refers to the Bavli. Whoever visits the Israeli Knesset will notice at the entrance a sentence on the wall saying, "Compassion toward a non-Jew is forbidden; if you see him fall into a river or face danger, you are prohibited from saving him because all the nations [goyim] are enemies of the Jews; and when a non-Jew falls into a ditch, the Jew should close the ditch on him with a big boulder, until he dies." This sentence is taken from the Talmud and is typical of the book's attitude toward "goyim" or non-Jews. Some Jews, such as the Karaites, reject the Talmud, but other Jews regard them as idolaters.[394]

"The results of this scandal," wrote Shahak, "were, for me, rather negative. Neither the Israeli, nor the diaspora (dispersed Jewry living abroad) rabbinical authorities ever reversed their ruling that a Jew should not violate the Sabbath in order to save the life of a Gentile."[395]

Shahak continues: "The principle of Israel as 'a Jewish state' was supremely important to Israeli politicians from the inception of the state and was inculcated into the Jewish population by all conceivable ways. When in the early 1980s, a tiny minority of Israeli Jews emerged which opposed this concept, a Constitutional law (that is, a law overriding provisions of other laws, which cannot be revoked except by a special procedure) was passed in 1985 by an enormous majority of the Knesset. By this law no party whose programme openly opposes the principle of 'a Jewish state' or proposes to change it by democratic means, is allowed to participate in the elections to the Knesset... Even this example shows that the state of Israel is not a democracy due to the application of a Jewish ideology directed against all non-Jews and those Jews who oppose this ideology," expressed Shahak.[396]

394 The Barnes Review, "What is the Talmud and What does it say about Non-Jews?" May/June 2005, p. 51.

395 Shahak, p. 1.

396 Ibid. p. 3.

"Another ominous factor," wrote Shahak, **"is that Israeli influence in the USA political establishment is also increasing.**"[397] (Emphasis added)

Shahak goes on to describe the exclusiveness of Israel in a critical fashion: "... Israel 'belongs' to persons who are defined by the Israeli authorities as 'Jewish,' irrespective of where they live, and to them alone. On the other hand, Israel doesn't officially 'belong' to its non-Jewish citizens, whose status is considered even officially as inferior... I suspect that the Jews of the USA or of Britain would regard it as antisemetic if Christians would propose that the USA or the United Kingdom should become a 'Christian state' belonging only to citizens officially defined as Christians.[398]

"The State of Israel officially discriminates in favor of Jews and against non-Jews in many domains of life, of which I regard three as being most important: residency rights, the right to work and the right to equality before the law. Discrimination in residency is based on the fact that about 92 percent of Israel's land is the property of the state and is administered by the Israel Land Authority according to regulations issued by the Jewish National Fund (JNF), an affiliate of the World Zionist Organization. In its regulations the JNF denies the right to reside, to open a business, and often to work, to anyone who is not Jewish, only because he is not Jewish. At the same time, Jews are not prohibited from taking residence or opening businesses anywhere in Israel. If applied in another state against the Jews, such discriminatory practice would instantly and justifiably be labeled antisemitism and would no doubt spark massive public protests."[399]

Shahak continues, "The main danger which Israel, as a 'Jewish state' poses to its own people, to other Jews and to its neighbors [along with young men and women from the United States and any other nation sufficiently deceived to join 'coalitions of the willing,'] is its ideologically motivated pursuit of territorial

397 Ibid.

398 Ibid. pp. 3-4.

399 Ibid. p.5.

expansion and the inevitable series of wars resulting from this aim.

"In 1956 I eagerly swallowed all of (Prime Minister) Ben-Gurion's political and military reasons for Israel initiating the Suez War, until he pronounced in the Knesset on the third day of that war, that the real reason for it is 'the restoration of the Kingdom of David and Solomon' to its Biblical borders."

The Biblical borders of the land of Israel, "which rabbinical authorities interpret as ideally belonging to the Jewish state" include the "following areas: in the south, all of Sinai and a part of northern Egypt up to the environs of Cairo; in the east, all of Jordan and a large chunk of Saudi Arabia, all of Kuwait and a *part of Iraq south of the Euphrates* (emphasis added); in the north, all of Lebanon and all of Syria together with a huge part of Turkey (up to Lake Van); and in the west, Cyprus."

Shahak goes on to say that, "Certainly the late Kahane and his followers as well as influential Jewish, Israeli bodies such as Gush Emunim, not only desire the conquest of these territories by Israel, but regard it as a divinely commanded act, sure to be successful since it will be aided by God. In fact, important Jewish religious figures regard the Israeli refusal to undertake such a holy war, or even worse, the return of Sinai to Egypt, as a national sin, which was justly punished by God. One of the more influential Gush Emunim rabbis, Dov Lior, the rabbi of Jewish settlements of Kiryat Arba and of Hebron, stated repeatedly that the Israeli failure to conquer Lebanon in 1982-5 was a well-merited devine punishment for its sin of 'giving a part of the Land of Israel,' namely Sinai, to Egypt."

"In May 1993, Ariel Sharon formally proposed in the Likud Convention that Israel should adopt the 'Biblical borders' concept as its official policy."[400]

In the December 6, 2004 issue of *American Free Press*, commentator Mr. Charlie Reese states that "the United States is

400 Ibid. pp. 8-10.

bogged down in Iraq because of Israel; that Iraq was perceived as a threat to Israel and certainly not to the United States."[401]

In Chapter four of this text, we briefly discussed the policy paper produced by the neo-conservative network led by Richard Perle for the newly elected Israeli Prime Minister Netanyahu. The policy paper recommended that Netanyahu abandon the peace process, reject "land for peace" and strengthen Israel's defenses in order to confront Iraq and Syria. The document said, "This effort can focus on removing Saddam Hussein from power in Iraq-an important *Israeli* strategic objective in its own right." It is also recommended that Israel use pretexts for pre-emptive attacks.[402]

Now if all this sounds familiar, which it should, it is because Richard Perle, Douglass Feith, and David Wurmser joined other neo-cons in the Bush administration, and Perle was especially vocal in pushing the war on Iraq. They had two pretexts: the attack of 9/11, even though Saddam Hussein had nothing to do with it, and the mythical weapons of mass destruction[403] [the same pretexts the leaked Downing Street memo decisively documented].

I feel it has been thoroughly documented, and we will continue to present evidence that supports the case that our young men and women in uniform are in Iraq on behalf of the Zionist traitors, Israeli firsters and loyalists in the US political establishment and the ill-conceived and illegitimate state of Israel. I'm sorry to say this, but the Department of Defense may as well drape the Israeli flag, the Star of Remphan, on our young men and women's caskets and tell their loved ones back home in the United States at their military state funeral, "on behalf of an ungrateful Israel," because this mad conquest of additional territory is an Israeli objective and not in the United States best interest.

I would like to share comments made by another one of our founding fathers, as recorded by General Charles Cotesworth Pinckney, a delegate to the Continental Congress from

401 AFP, 12/6/04, p. 21.

402 AFP, 9/20/04, p. 19.

403 Ibid.

Charleston, South Carolina. Dr. Benjamin Franklin was one of the five founding fathers, along with John Adams, Roger Sherman, Robert Livingston and Thomas Jefferson, who was appointed to the committee to draw up *The Declaration of Independence*.[404]

Benjamin Franklin was speaking at the Philadelphia Constitutional Convention, addressing the members of the Constitutional Congress in May of 1787 when he asked that Jews be barred from immigrating to America. The following are his exact words as quoted from the diary of General Pinckney:

"I fully agree with General Washington, that we must protect this young nation from an insidious influence and impenetration. The menace, gentlemen, is the Jews. In whatever country Jews have settled in any great numbers, they have lowered its moral tone; depreciated its commercial integrity, have segregated themselves and not been assimilated; have sneered at and tried to undermine the Christian Religion upon which that nation is founded by objecting to its restrictions; have built up a state within a state; and when opposed have tried to strangle that country to death financially, as in the case of Spain and Portugal.

"For over 1,700 years, the Jews have been bewailing their sad fate in that they have been exiled from their homeland, they call Palestine. But, Gentlemen, should the world today give it to them in fee simple, they would at once find some cogent reason for not returning. Why? Because they are vampires, and vampires do not live on vampires. They cannot live among themselves. They must subsist on Christians and other people not of their race.

"If you do not exclude them from these United States, in this Constitution, in less than 200 years, they will have swarmed in such great numbers that they will dominate and devour the land, and change our form of government, for which we Americans have shed our blood, given our lives, our substance, and jeopardized our liberty.

"If you do not exclude them, in less than 200 years, our descendants will be working in the fields to furnish them sustenance, while they will be in the counting houses rubbing

404 Harrison and Gilbert, p. 174.

their hands. I warn you, Gentlemen, if you do not exclude the Jews for all time, your children will curse you in your graves. Jews, gentlemen, are Asiatics; let them be born where they will, or how many generations they are away from Asia, they will never be otherwise. Their ideas do not conform to an American's, and will not even though they live among us ten generations. A leopard cannot change its spots.

"Jews are Asiatics, they are a menace to this country if permitted entrance, and should be excluded by this Constitution." 405

Of course, this quote of Benjamin Franklin's won't be found in any public school history textbooks. These kinds of observations made by our founding fathers have already been censored by the unconstitutional United States Federal Department of Education, which would be also, I presume, under the control of the Jews, according to Israeli Prime Minister Ariel Sharon.

If the reader needs to review other concepts and ideals of our founding fathers, please see again Chapter two of this text.

This may sound a bit extreme or stretching the truth to some. But, in fact, the truth of the matter is even better stated by Mr. Willis Carto, a World War II veteran, a Purple Heart recipient and publisher of *The Barnes Review, A Journal of Nationalist Thought and History*. He writes:

> "As the United States sinks to the status of a colony of Israel's, it is to be expected that our morals and patterns of action will ape those of our superior... Yes, America is a colony of Israel. The purpose of a colony is to supply all its resources and assets desired by the "mother country," and that is exactly America's role to Israel.
>
> Can any other medium in America state this fact openly? None dare speak the truth when it comes to Israel.

405 Benjamin Franklin on Jews, www.compuserb.com/franklin1.htm, 11/8/2005. Also, many internet sources,ie, search "The Benjamin Franklin Prophecy."

> One sure sign of a dictatorship is that the dictator's name can only be spoken with deep deference and praise. How long has it been since you have heard Israel criticized in print or on the air or in the halls of that amphitheater of the absurd, Congress?
>
> As this once-proud nation's corrupt media supports the Bush administrations policy of global aggression, it will never tell the truth: which is that America is a subject nation, totally at the mercy of whatever Israel wants, be it more money or more arms, the invasion of nations perceived as a threat to its hegemonic strategy or groveling praise from the sorry media personalities who pollute the atmosphere. How long America, how long?"[406]

Political commentator Mr. Charley Reese had this to say about our recent past and current national situation:

> "I have long since given up the hope that Americans would wake up and resent the manipulation of their government by a foreign country. The Israeli lobby has been so successful in labeling any criticism of Israel, no matter how justified, as antisemitic that most Americans prefer to stick their heads in the sand. For sure, American politicians and much of the media seem to be terrified by the Israeli lobby, which says more about their cowardice than it does about the power of the lobby itself.
>
> So, suit yourself. Go ahead and spend American blood and treasure for the benefit of Israel...
>
> This whole mess, including the war in Iraq and the terrorist attacks, is a result of the American government's involvement with Israel. It's a dangerous and unhealthy state of affairs..."[407]

---

406 AFP, 1/17/05, p. 10.

407 AFP, 9/20/04, p. 19.

The *Reuters* Washington office reported that the United States has been conducting secret reconnaissance missions inside Iran to identify nuclear, chemical and missile targets as reported in *The New Yorker* magazine.[408]

Seymore Hersh quotes one government consultant with close ties to the Pentagon as saying, "The civilians in the Pentagon [referred to frequently as chickenhawks] want to go into Iran and destroy as much of the military infrastructure as possible."[409]

I believe that this group of civilians is comprised of the same Perle, Wolfowitz, Feith and other double-crossing, subversive, Israeli-first crowd that got us into the Iraq quagmire.

One former high-level intelligence official told *The New Yorker*, "This is a war against terrorism, and Iraq is just one campaign. The Bush administration is looking at this as a huge war zone. Next, we're going to have the Iranian campaign."[410]

Hersh reported that Bush has already "signed a series of top-secret findings and executive orders authorizing secret commando groups and other Special Forces units to conduct covert operations against suspected "terrorist targets" in as many as 10 nations in the Middle East...[411] I also believe that most of these nations are inside the late, Old Testament, "Biblical borders" area of Israel we discussed earlier.

Getting back to Israel, Netanyahu and Iraq, Netanyahu did in fact abandon the peace process as recommended by Perle and the other Bush cabinet neo-cons. And at a cost of over $200 billion and over 2,055 American lives so far and over 15,477 U.S. injured (as of this writing on 11/8/05), Israel did achieve its "strategic objective in its own right"-removing Saddam Hussein from power... and it didn't cost Israel one shekel or one life.[412]

---

408 Yahoo News, 1/16/04.

409 Ibid.

410 Ibid.

411 Ibid.

412 AFP, 9/20/04, p. 19 and www.letsroll911.org, 11/8/05.

One may recall if memory is stretched that before Iraq blew up in our face, President George W. Bush was laying the groundwork to attack Syria, another country Perle and his crowd labeled as a target of Israel. And, as we have just discussed, the other target of Bush and the Israelis-is Iran.[413]

On October 3rd, 2001, not yet a month after 9/11, the Prime Minister of Israel, Ariel Sharon, was quoted as saying, "Everytime we do something, you tell me America will do this and will do that... I want to tell you something very clear: Don't worry about American Pressure on Israel. We, the Jewish people, control America."[414]

On September 21st, 2001, 10 days after the horrific attacks against our beloved nation, Pat Buchanan was quoted in the *Los Angeles Times* as saying, "We are told our enemy is Osama bin Laden, but the war crimes of 11 September were carried out by men who live among us. The enemy is already inside the gates."[415]

Dr. Thomas Sowell, in 1994, exclaimed, "The barbarians are not at the gates, they are inside the gates... and have academic tenure, judicial appointments, government grants, and control of the movies, television, and other media. "[416]

And some 22 years before Dr. Sowell made those remarks, the Reverend Billy Graham was caught on tape making the statement to then President Richard M. Nixon that the Jews had a "stranglehold" on the American media, which needed to be broken because it was ruining the country.[417]

Returning to Israel Shahak's work in *Jewish History, Jewish Religion*, Shahak reported that "Ben-Gurion (the first Prime Minister of Israel) did not pretend that the re-establishment of the Kingdom of David and Solomon will benefit anybody except the Jewish state.

---

413 AFP, 9/20/04, p. 19.

414 Donn deGrand Pre, "The Vipers Venom," Grand Pre Books, Madison, VA, p. vi.

415 Ibid.

416 Ibid.

417 Ibid.

"Historical Judaism and its two successors, Jewish Orthodoxy and Zionism are both sworn enemies of the concept of the open society as applied to Israel."

Shahak continues, "There are two choices which face Israeli-Jewish society. It can become a fully closed and warlike ghetto, a Jewish Sparta, supported by the labor of Arab helots, kept in existence by its influence on the U.S. political establishment by threats to use its nuclear power, or it can try to become an open society."[418]

I think, probably, a little warning is in order before this next section, as when I first encountered this material, I must admit, I was very distressed. I didn't know such attitudes were present as I was always led to believe the "Judeo-Christian" community had so much in common. I think most readers will probably have the equivalent or similar reactions. So, with that, let us please proceed with care and diligence.

According to Shahak's work:

"Before the 13th century, Christian authorities attacked Judaism using either Biblical or general arguments, but seemed to be quite ignorant as to the contents of the Talmud. From the 13th century on, the Christian campaign against the Talmud was apparently brought on by the conversion of Jews who were well versed in the Talmud and who were in many cases attracted by the development of Christian philosophy, with its strong Aristotelian, and thus, universal character."[419]

"It must be admitted at the outset that the Talmud and the Talmudic literature-quite apart from the general anti-Gentile streak that runs through them, contain very offensive statements and precepts directed specifically against Christianity. For example, [here we go] in addition to a series of scurrilous sexual allegations against Jesus, the Talmud states that his punishment in hell is to be immersed in boiling excrement-a statement not

418 Shahak, pp. 12-13.

419 Ibid. p. 20.

exactly calculated to endear the Talmud, or its followers, to devout Christians," [if they only knew].[420]

"Or one can quote the precept according to which Jews are instructed to burn, publicly if possible, any copy of the New Testament that comes into their hands. This is not only still in force, but actually practiced today. As recent as March 23, 1980, hundreds of copies of the New Testament were publicly and ceremonially burnt in Jerusalem under the auspices of Yad Le'akhim, a Jewish religious organization subsidized by the Israeli Ministry of Religions. "[421]

> *"For, as I have told you before and now say again even with tears, many live as enemies of the cross of Christ."*
>
> (Philippians 3:18, NIV)

> *"For many deceivers have gone out into the world who do not confess Jesus Christ as coming in the flesh. This is a deceiver and an anti-christ."*
>
> (II John 1:7, NKJV)

There have been other more recent acts of aggression against Christianity in Israel. As reported in the October 25th, 2004 issue of *American Free Press*, "Two U.S. Christian pacifists were severely beaten by Jewish settlers in the southern West Bank town of Hebron, *Agence France-Presse* reports. Chris Brown and Kim Lamberty of Christian Peacemaker Teams said they were attacked by Jewish settlers as they were escourting Palestinian children to school. 'We were hit with chains, rocks and sticks. The settlers also kicked us,'" Brown reported.[422]

Also reported by *American Free Press* is that Jerusalem's Christian community has demanded that the Israeli government

420 Ibid. pp. 20-21.

421 Ibid. p. 21.

422 AFP, 10/25/04, p. 2.

take action against what they say is growing harassment by extremist Jews. "Some Christians say ultra-Orthodox Jewish students have spat on them or at the ground when they pass. There have also been acts of vandalism against their property, including statues of the Virgin Mary. The harassment peaked recently when a Jewish student spat at Armenian Archbishop Nourhan Manougian and ripped off his crucifix... The Israeli police questioned both men, but no charges were filed."[423]

Another story of anti-Christianity at the hands of the anti-Christians here in the United States was reported by Michael C. Piper of *American Free Press* in a column entitled "Presbyterian Church Threatened by Terrorists; Criticism of Israeli Policy Prompts Arson." Piper reports:

"A violent terrorist threat has been made by an Israeli supporter against one of America's largest mainstream Christian churches.

"A handwritten letter mailed from Queens N.Y.-long been a hot bed of terrorist hate activity by the Jewish Defense League (JDL), was sent to the Louisville, Kentucky based national headquarters of the Presbyterian Church (USA). The letter threatened that if the Presbyterian Church did not reverse its public criticisms of Israel's mistreatment of Palestinian Christians and Muslims and retract its decision to cease church investments in companies that do business with Israel by November 15, 2004, there would be arson attacks on Presbyterian churches during religious services. The letter specifically said the threat was being made in retribution for so-called 'anti-Israel and anti-Jewish attitudes' expressed by Church leaders.

"The Presbyterian leadership-which has been under heavy and repeated attack by leading Jewish organizations such as the Anti-Defamation League (ADL) of B'nai B'rith-is taking the threat seriously and, according to Jerry L. Van Marter, director of the Presbyterian news service, has warned churches to be on the alert," Piper reported.

"There are some 11,200 Presbyterian congregations in the United States, comprising some 2.4 million members.

423 AFP, 11/1/04, p. 2.

"According to *The Christian Post*, an independent, interdenominational Christian media company, the letter even acknowledged that the warning was terrorist in nature: 'I promise violence against Presbyterian Churches-They will go up in flames, bet your ass that's a terrorist threat.'

"The Jewish Defense League (JDL), which the late Jewish-American writer Robert I. Friedman documented, is directed at the highest levels by Israel's intelligence service, the Mossad."

"The ADL officially distances itself from the rhetoric and violence of the JDL. However, it is well known that the ADL acts as a propaganda and intelligence arm of Israeli intelligence and at the same time, has an interlocking base of financial support with the JDL, making the ADL's denunciation of the JDL hypocritical."[424]

At this point, I would again like to return to Shahak's *Jewish History, Jewish Religion*. Referring again to the Talmud, Shahak states that "one can read quite freely-and Jewish children are actually taught-passages such as that which commands every Jew, when passing near a cemetery, to utter a blessing if the cemetery is Jewish, but to curse the mothers of the dead if it is non-Jewish.

"A pious Jew," according to Shahak, "arriving for the first time in Australia, say, and chancing to pass near an Aboriginal graveyard, must-as an act of worship of 'God'-curse the mothers of the dead buried there."[425]

In 1962, a part of the Maimonidean Code, the so-called Book of Knowledge, which contains the most basic rules of Jewish faith and practice, was published in Jerusalem in a bilingual edition, with the English translation facing the Hebrew text. The latter has been restored to its original purity, and the command to exterminate Jewish infidels appears in it in full: "It is a duty to exterminate them with one's own hands." In the English translation this is somewhat softened to: "It is a duty to take active measures to destroy them." But then the Hebrew text goes on to specify the prime examples of "infidels" who must be

424 AFP, 11/29/04, p. 6.

425 Shahak, pp. 23-24.

exterminated, "Such as Jesus of Nazareth and his pupils... may the name of the wicked rot."[426]

> *"Who is the liar? It is the man who denies that Jesus is the Christ. Such a man is the antichrist-he denies the Father and the Son. No one who denies the Son has the Father; whoever acknowledges the Son has the Father also."*
>
> (1 John 2:22-23, NIV)

Shahak continues with more examples of Jewish thought and attitudes towards non-Jews by the Hassidic movement. "Hassidism-a continuation (and debasement!) of Jewish mysticism-is still a living movement, with hundreds of thousands of active adherents who are fanatically devoted to their 'holy rabbis,' some of whom have acquired a very considerable political influence in Israel, among the leaders of most parties and even more so in the higher echelons of the army."[427]

What, then, are the views of this movement concerning non-Jews? As an example, "let us take the famous Hatanya, a fundamental book of the Habbad movement, one of the most important branches of Hassidism. According to this book, all non-Jews are totally satanic creatures 'in whom there is absolutely nothing good'... The very existence of a non-Jew is 'inessential,' whereas all of creation was created solely for the sake of the Jews.

"According to the testimony of Shulamit Aloni, a member of the Knesset, this Habbad propaganda was particularly stepped up before Israel's invasion of Lebanon in March 1978, in order to induce military doctors and nurses to withhold medical help from 'Gentile wounded.' This Nazi-like advice did not refer specifically to Arabs or Palestinians, but simply to 'Gentiles,' or goyim." According to Shahak, many top Israeli and *American*

426 Ibid. pp. 25-26.

427 Ibid. p. 26.

(emphasis added) politicians are ardent adherents and supporters of Habbad.[428]

According to the author of *Jewish History, Jewish Religion*, who as mentioned happens to be an Israeli Jew, and who is openly critical of Israeli policy and Jewish religious attitudes and teachings, "For there can be no longer be any doubt that the most horrifying acts of oppression in the West Bank [and Gaza] are motivated by Jewish religious fanaticism."[429]

Let's take a look at some recent examples of these "horrifying acts of oppression... motivated by Jewish religious fanaticism." Ibrahim Barzak, an *Associated Press* newsman reported on March 16, 2003:

"An American woman in Gaza to protest against Israeli operations was killed Sunday when she was run over by an Israeli bulldozer, witnesses and hospital officials said. Witnesses said Rachel Corrie, 23, from Olympia, Washington, was trying to stop the bulldozer from tearing down a building in the Rafah refugee camp, witnesses said, when she was run over. She was taken to Najar hospital in Rafah, where she died, said Dr. Ali Moussa, a hospital administrator.

"Greg Schnabel, 28, from Chicago said the protesters were in the house of Dr. Samir Masri. 'Rachel was alone in front of the house as we were trying to get them to stop,' he said. 'She waved for the bulldozer to stop. She fell down and the bulldozer kept going. We yelled 'stop, stop,' and the bulldozer didn't stop at all. It had completely run over her and then it reversed and ran back over her,' he said.

"Schnabel said there were eight protesters at the site, four from the United States and four from Great Britain. 'We stay with families whose house is to be demolished,' he told the *Associated Press* by telephone from Rahah after the incident. Witnesses said she was wearing a brightly-colored jacket when she was run over.

"Schnabel said Corrie was a student at Evergreen College and was to graduate this year.

428 Ibid. p. 27.

429 Ibid. p. 29.

"Mansour Abed Allah, 29, a Palestinian human rights worker in Rafah, witnessed the incident. He said the killing should be a message to the U.S. President George W. Bush, who is 'providing Israel with tanks and bulldozers and now they killed one of his own people.'

"Israel sends tanks and bulldozers into the area almost every day, destroying homes and buildings near the Gaza-Egypt border.

"The Israeli military and the U.S. State Department had no immediate comment."

Groups of international protesters have gathered in several locations in the West Bank and Gaza during two years of violence, setting themselves up as human shields to try to stop Israeli operations of this sort.

"Corrie was the first member of the groups... to be killed in the conflict. Several have been arrested in previous clashes with Israeli forces..."[430]

Another atrocity reportedly committed by Israeli soldiers was covered in the November 8th, 2004 issue of *American Free Press*. As reported by Mr. Fred Linguel:

"The execution-style killing of a 13-year-old Palestinian school girl by Israeli soldiers in October... and the killing by an Israeli military sniper of a teenage brother and his sister in May are exactly the types of crimes that fall under war crimes statutes of the UN's International Court of Justice (ICJ), known across the globe as the World Court.

"The facts surrounding the October murder of Iman Al-Harma, who was on her way to school when she was gunned down, horrified the international community but received scant attention in the U.S. media. Al-Harma was in school uniform, carrying a bag filled with textbooks, when an order was given to shoot her as she crossed barren ground in full view of an Israeli command post at the Rafah refugee camp.

"Moments after the unit officer at the post issued the order; the little girl was shot in the leg, forcing the 13-year-old to drop

430 Ibrahim Barzak, Associated Press, "American Women Peace Activist Killed by Israeli Army."www.peacenowar.net Palestine/News/March%2016%2003-News.htm, 01/17/05.

her school bag. She tried to hobble from the scene, but another shot brought her to the ground. The unit commander who has yet to be named in the mainstream press, walked up to her and fired several shots into her school satchel before shooting her several times in the face and head at close range. He then walked away but, as an afterthought, turned back to the child's body and emptied the remaining bullets in his rifle magazine into her body," reported Linguel.

"An autopsy ruled that 17 bullets had struck her, with three fired into her head and face at close range. Even if the unit commander had initially considered her a potential threat, she represented no threat after she was first shot.

"Had she been carrying a bomb, which she was not, she would have had to climb a hill and breach the barbwire fences of the command post in full view of military snipers.

"The Israeli army's disinformation policy unit quickly went into action, telling the media the child had been suspected of carrying a bomb. When that story did not appear to fit the facts, journalists were told she had been used by terrorists to test Israeli military defenses and to lure soldiers into the open.

"When that story also fell flat, several soldiers claiming to have been part of the unit involved in the killing, expressed their outrage to Israeli newspapers under cover of anonymity. There was suspicion that the anonymous soldiers represented a contrived effort to put a better face on the killing.

"To no one's surprise, a week after the child's murder, the unit commander was cleared of wrongdoing," reported Linguel.[431]

Of course, this would be expected when one considers that the Israeli authority looking into this matter had simply to determine that the soldier in question again was acting piously and according to Maimonidean Code, which states "It is a duty to exterminate them with one's own hands," a basic rule of Jewish faith and practice, according to Shahak.

431 AFP, 11/08/04, p. 12.

Might the soldier have received a promotion in rank and pay for his loyal obedience to Jewish law and patriotic Israeli national interest?

Michael Collins Piper, correspondent for *American Free Press*, in a November 1st, 2004 article, wrote:

"Human Rights Watch (HRW) is strongly condemning Israel's excessive use of force against Palestinians, particularly the demolitions of Palestinian homes that have left thousands homeless during the past four years, contributing directly toward the outrage by the Muslim world against the American "special relationship" with Israel, according to Human Rights Watch.

"The pattern of destruction strongly suggests that Israeli forces demolished homes wholesale, regardless of whether they posed a specific threat, in violation of international law,' said HRW, adding that in most cases, 'the destruction was carried out in the absence of military necessity.'

"Hard-line elements within Israel are becoming increasingly more bellicose, for example, Israeli Professor Hillel Weiss declaring: 'The purpose of the armed struggle is to establish a Jewish state in all the territory that will be captured, from the River Euphrates to the Egyptian River (the Nile).'[432]

These Israelis, allied with Bush and his fellow American fundamentalists such as Pat Robertson, Tim LaHaye and Jerry Falwell, who said with such a 'Christian heart' on *CNN's Late Edition* on October 24, 2004 '... blow them all away in the name of the Lord,' (remember the warnings we received about false prophets Jesus gave to us), along with the neo-conservatives who direct Bush, dream of a 'Greater Israel'-one that incorporates substantial portions of Egypt, Iraq and Saudi Arabia, along with all of Syria, Jordon and Lebanon [the late, Old Testament, Biblical borders we previously discussed].[433]

"Rabbi Yitzhak Ginsburg is more candid, saying that 'It is our duty to force all mankind to accept the seven Noahide Laws, and if not, they will be killed.'

432 AFP, 11/01/04, p. 13.

433 Ibid.

"The 'Noahide Laws' refer to rules taught in Judaism that all mankind is, supposedly, morally obligated to follow. There are seven main laws, which include prohibition against idolatry, murder, stealing and homosexuality. Critics of the laws, however, say they are nothing more than an attempt to establish a world order under the Talmud. Christians would especially be affected, as praying to Jesus Christ is forbidden. Anyone who violates these laws would be subject to capital punishment.

"This kind of Israeli fundamentalist rhetoric is hardly, if ever, reported in the American press, which frequently trumpets extremist rhetoric from Israel's critics.

"So while the conflicts within Israel itself, not to mention Israel's endless conflicts with her Arab neighbors, continue to develop, the American political system is being negatively impacted, as a direct consequence. Americans are increasingly divided and confused, and the 'secret' issue of U.S. favoritism towards Israel [in direct violation of U.S. founding fathers principles and guidance] simmers like a pot about to boil over. When and whether well-known American political figures finally dare to speak out remains to be seen."[434]

"In the eyes of the Arab world, the September 26, 2004 assassination of a Hamas leader in Damascus, Syria at the hands of Israeli assassins reflects the principles of the Bush doctrine, promoting 'targeted killings' of enemies anywhere in the world, and further links the United States to the lawless acts of the Israeli government," wrote Mr. Fred Linguel in an October 11, 2004 issue of *American Free Press*.[435]

The killing of Izz el-Deen Khalil outside his home in Damascus, where he lived since 1992, followed a predictable pattern. As he got into his car, his cell phone rang, and when he answered it a booby-trap bomb, concealed under the dashboard exploded.

Israeli authorities immediately said Izz el-Deen Khalil had been the overall Hamas commander.

---

434 Ibid.

435 AFP, 10/11/04, p. 14.

Before the killing, Ariel Sharon's government and the Israeli military had warned they would strike at targets in Syria and were told by the Syrian foreign minister, Farouk Al-Shaara that such threats only served to "exacerbate the deteriorating situation in the region."

For most Middle East observers, the latest assassination was predictable, following statements from Tel Aviv last autumn that Israel was prepared to strike at targets in Syria, Lebanon and Iran.

In the wake of the recent killing in Damascus, some Middle East experts argue that Israel feels it can carry out assassinations in Syria with impunity. They contend that Israeli war hawks have been emboldened by the presence of U.S. troops on the Iraq-Syria border and by neo-cons, who claim a Syrian hand in the Iraqi insurgency.

Those same experts also point to the implied threat of an Israeli attack on Iran's nuclear infrastructure as yet another example of how Israel believes it shares the same foreign policy goals as the Bush White House. There is plenty of evidence to show that each time Israel carries out assassinations, people in Arab capitals see Israeli actions as inextricably linked to the U.S. war on terror.

An acute example of this phenomenon was the outrage across the Arab world after the assassination in March of Sheikh Ahmed Yassin, the nearly blind, quadriplegic cleric who founded Hamas. In Arab newspapers, editorials claimed that Israel had consulted the Bush administration before Yassin was killed along with five other people who were with him.

The killing prompted Egyptian President Hosni Mubarak, considered by the White House as an ally in the war on terror, to warn about the anti-Americanism arising from Israel's actions. He said he had never before seen such levels of hatred of Americans in the region. "People (Arabs) have a feeling of injustice, and, what's more, they see Sharon acting as he pleases, without the Americans saying anything."

A week after President Mubarak made those comments; the U.S. government vetoed a United Nations Security Council resolution condemning the Israeli killing of Yassin.[436]

In the Arab mind, similarities in the tactics and objectives of the Bush and Sharon governments are too obvious to ignore.[437]

The neo-conservatives, who dominate policy in the Bush administration, have accused Lebanon, Syria and Iran of sponsoring terrorism and aiding insurgents in Iraq.

The goal has been to make Israel's enemies America's enemies, making it difficult for the United States to criticize or restrain Tel Aviv's assassination policy and its implied threat to deal with Iran's nuclear ambitions.

The view in Arab capitals is that America and Israel both support targeted killings anywhere in the world and use overwhelming air power in civilian areas, irrespective of the "collateral damage"-the new, antiseptic term meant to obscure the killing of innocent civilians in Fallujah or Gaza.

While there are few figures available for civilian deaths in Iraq-and American television networks make little effort to reflect that aspect of the war-international media coverage points to high civilian casualties from U.S. bombing in Iraq.[438] Recently published figures are higher than 30,000.[439]

The Israelis have never made any pretense that "collateral damage" is merely part of war.

In an open letter to Israeli Defense Minister Shaul Mofaz, a group of prominent Israeli rabbis recently wrote, "There is no war in the world in which it is possible to delineate entirely between the population and the enemy army, neither in the U.S. war in Iraq, the Russian war in Chechnya, nor in Israel's war with its enemies... The Christian preaching of 'turning the other cheek' doesn't concern us, and we will not be impressed by those

436 Ibid.

437 Ibid. p. 15.

438 Ibid.

439 www.letsroll911.Org, 11/8/05.

who prefer the lives of our enemies to our lives." The letter was signed by a number of Israeli rabbis including Haim Druckman, a former Knesset member who heads a large religious youth movement known as the Bnei Akiva Society, Eliezer Melamed, head of a West Bank religious college, and Youval Sharlo, the head of another Talmudic college in Petah Tikva, which combines Talmudic studies with military service.[440]

Continuing our study of *Jewish History, Jewish Religion*, Shahak writes:

"Very many non-Jews, including Christian clergy and religious laymen, hold the curious opinion that one way to 'atone' for the persecution of Jews is not to speak out against evil perpetrated by Jews, but to participate in 'white lies' about them. The crude accusation of 'antisemitism' (or, in the case of Jews, 'self-hate') against anybody who protests at the discrimination of Palestinians or who points out any fact about the Jewish religion or the Jewish past which conflicts with the 'approved version' comes with greater hostility and force from non-Jewish 'friends of the Jews' than from Jews themselves. It is the existence and great influence of this group in all western countries, and particularly in the USA, as well as the other English-speaking countries, which has allowed the rabbis and scholars of Judaism to propagate their lies not only without opposition but with considerable help.[441]

"It is necessary here to dispel at least some of the many misconceptions disseminated in almost all foreign-language (that is, non-Hebrew) accounts of Judaism, especially by those who propagate such currently fashionable phrases as "the Judeo-Christian' tradition or 'the common values of the monotheistic religions.[442]

"For example, it should be clearly understood that the source of authority for all practices of classical (and present-day Orthodox) Judaism, the determining base of its legal structure, is the Talmud, or to be precise, the Babylonian Talmud, while the

440 AFP, 11/8/04, p. 26.

441 Shahak, pp. 29-30.

442 Ibid. p. 32.

rest of the Talmudic literature, including the Jerusalem Talmud, acts as a supplementary authority.[443]

"And it must be remembered that it is precisely the superstitions of classical Judaism which have the greatest hold on the Jewish masses, rather than those parts of the Bible or even the Talmud which are of real religious and ethical value." For example, what is popularly regarded as the most 'holy' and solemn occasion of the Jewish liturgical year and attended even by very many Jews who are otherwise far from religious is the 'Kol Nidrey' prayer on the eve of Yom Kippur-a chanting of a particularly absurd and deceptive dispensation, by which all private vows made to God in the following year are declared in advance to be null and void.[444]

"The Halakhah, that is the legal system of classical Judaism," according to Shahak, "as practiced by virtually all Jews... and as maintained to this very day in the form of Orthodox Judaism-is based primarily on the Babylonian Talmud."[445]

"According to the Jewish religion, the murder of a Jew is a capitol offense and one of the three most heinous sins (the other two being idolatry and adultery)."

"When the victim is a Gentile, the position is quite different. A Jew who murders a Gentile is guilty only of a sin against the laws of Heaven, not punishable by a court. To cause indirectly the death of a Gentile is no sin at all."[446]

Therefore, the Israeli unit commander of the soldier who murdered the 13-year-old Palestinian schoolgirl on her way to school that we discussed earlier, was "cleared of any wrongdoing."

Shahak goes on to say that "a Gentile murderer who happens to be under Jewish jurisdiction must be executed whether the victim was Jewish or not. However, if the victim was Gentile and the murderer converts to Judaism, he is not punished."[447]

---

443 Ibid. p. 39.

444 Ibid. p. 48.

445 Ibid. p. 75.

446 Ibid. p. 76.

447 Ibid.

"All of this has a direct and practical relevance to the realities of the state of Israel. Although the state's criminal laws make no distinction between Jew and Gentile, such distinction is certainly made by Orthodox rabbis [in rabbinical courts] who in guiding their flock follow the Halakhah."[448]

"Of special importance is the advice they give to religious soldiers." According to Shahak, "various rabbinical commentators have concluded that in wartime, all Gentiles belonging to a hostile population should be killed. Since 1973, this doctrine is being publicly propagated for the guidance of religious Israeli soldiers. The first such official exhortation was included in a booklet published by the Central Region Command of the Israeli Army, whose area includes the West Bank. In this booklet, the Command's Chief Chaplain writes: "When our forces come across civilians during a war or in a hot pursuit or in a raid, so long as there is no certainty that these civilians are incapable of harming our forces, then according to the Halakhah they may and even should be killed... Under no circumstances should an Arab be trusted, even if he makes an impression of being civilized... In war, when our forces storm the enemy, they are allowed and even enjoined by the Halakhah to kill even good civilians, that is, civilians who are ostensibly good.[449]

"This same doctrine is expounded in the following exchange of letters between a young Israeli soldier and his rabbi, published in the yearbook of one of Israel's most prestigious religious colleges, Midrashiyyat No'am, where many leaders and activists of the National Religious Party and Gush Emunim have been educated."[450]

The letter from soldier Moshe to Rabbi Shim'on Weiser:

With God's help, to his Honour, my dear Rabbi,

... In one of the discussions in our group, there was a debate about the "purity of weapons" and we discussed whether it is permitted to kill unarmed men or women and children? Or

448 Ibid.

449 Ibid.

450 Ibid. pp. 76-77.

perhaps we should take revenge on the Arabs? And then everyone answered according to his own understanding. I could not arrive at a clear decision, whether Arabs should be treated like the Amalekites, meaning that one is permitted to murder them until there remembrance is blotted out from under heaven, or perhaps one should do as in a just war, in which one kills only the soldiers?

... I conclude with a warm greeting to the rabbi and all his family.

Moshe

The reply of Rabbi Shim'on Weiser to Israeli soldier Moshe:

With the help of Heaven. Dear Moshe, Greetings.

... The non-Jewish nations have a custom according to which war has its own rules, like those of a game, like the rules of football or basketball. But according to the sayings of our sages blessed memory, ... war for us is not a game but a vital necessity, and only by this standard must we decide how to wage it... Rabbi Shim'on used to say "The best of Gentiles-kill him; the best of snakes-dash out its brains."

... We learn the following comment on the Talmudic pronouncement that Gentiles who fall into a well should not be helped out... And if it queried because it was said, the best of Gentiles-kill him, then the answer is that this saying is meant for wartime.

...A distinction must be made between wartime and peace, so that although during peacetime it is forbidden to kill Gentiles, in a case that occurs in wartime it is a mitzvah (imperative, religious duty) to kill them...

Yours-Shim, 'on

The acknowledgment of soldier Moshe to Rabbi Shim'on Weiser:

To His Honor, my dear Rabbi,

...As for the letter itself, I have understood it as follows: In wartime I am not merely permitted, but enjoined to kill every Arab man and woman whom I chance upon, if there is reason to fear that they help in the war against us, directly or indirectly.

And as far as I am concerned, I have to kill them even if that might result in an involvement with the military law...

Greetings-Moshe[451]

Of course, this doctrine of the Halakhah "does exert an influence on the administration of justice, especially by military authorities. The fact is that in all cases where Jews have, in a military or paramilitary context, murdered Arab non-combatants-including cases of mass murder such as that in Kafr Qasim in 1956-the murderers, if not let off altogether, received extremely light sentences or won far-reaching remissions, reducing their punishment to next to nothing."[452]

May I please connect some dots and do a little summarizing here. If Israeli General and Defense Minister Moshe Dayan was true and accurate in his statements that "Israel must use the sword as the main, if not the only instrument with which to keep its moral high and to retain its moral tension. Toward this end... it must invent dangers... it must adopt the method of provocation... let us hope for a new war with the Arab countries, so that we may ... acquire our space."

And if Israel Shahak is accurate in his book *Jewish History, Jewish Religion*, in his description of "... Israel's ideologically motivated pursuit of territorial expansion and the inevitable series of wars resulting from this aim."

And if rabbinical authorities interpret as ideally belonging to Israel the [Old Testament] Biblical borders concept which includes all of Sinai, a large part of Egypt up to the environs of Cairo, all of Jordan, a large chunk of Saudi Arabia, all of Kuwait and the "little piece" of Iraq south of the Euphrates, all of Lebanon, all of Syria, Cyprus, and a large part of Turkey.

And if Ariel Sharon was correct and accurate when he stated "We, the Jewish people, control America." And if Ariel Sharon was also true and accurate when he proposed that Israel should adopt the "Biblical borders concept" as official Israeli policy.

---

451 Ibid. pp. 77-79.

452 Ibid. p. 79.

And if the Maimonidean Code is accurate, which contains the most basic rules of the Jewish faith and practice which says, "It is a duty to exterminate them with one's own hands," referring to the pupils of Jesus of Nazareth.

And if Israeli Professor Weiss is correct and accurate in stating "the purpose of the armed struggle is to establish an exclusive Jewish state from the Euphrates to the Nile."

And if Rabbi Ginsburg is correct and accurate in stating it is Jewish/Israeli, Kingdom of David and Solomon duty to "force mankind to accept the Noahide Laws or they will be killed." And evidently, praying to Jesus is a violation of these laws and subject to capital punishment.

And if the Halakhah is correct and accurate in stating "enemy civilians should be killed."

And if Rabbi Shim'on Weiser is correct and accurate in stating "war for us is a vital necessity" and "the best of Gentiles, kill him." And if it is true and accurate that both Christians and Muslims are Gentiles and all Gentiles are enemies of Israel, or as the entrance to the Knesset says, "All the nations are enemies of Jews."

And if Shahak is correct and accurate in stating "Another ominous factor is that Israeli influence in the USA political establishment is also increasing."

And if it is true that most Americans consider themselves Christian and therefore, most U.S. armed forces are also Christian, or at least Gentile, and since it is also true that the U.S. is at war against terrorism, but everyone knows it is against Muslim countries that just happen to be in Israel's conquest zone, so therefore Christians and Muslims are killing each other, the Gentiles, the enemies of the Jews, are killing each other towards the benefit of the Jews. Is this too simplified, or have we as a "Christian nation" and people been completely fooled and deceived by our treasonous and traitorous politicians and false prophets, who Ariel Sharon said in so many words were under the control of the Jews, and who Jesus himself warned us against?

Have the Jews and the neo-cons in high places, who "control America" and who have control over the news media or more accurately termed American propaganda according to the Reverend Billy Graham, pulled a huge hoax over our Christian eyes and hearts? Have we been neo-conned?

We must become more situationally aware. That's an old pilot concept, knowing your surroundings and environment, keeping your head on a swivel, that kind of thing. We would say to each other "S-A, check 6," meaning to watch your back or what was behind you too.

So then, is there any reason to be alarmed?

No, no reason at all to be alarmed. Go back to watching the NBA, the NFL, or Oprah, or Phil, or that stupid, ridiculous show where girls eat bull penises and all other sorts of other knarly things and try not to puke all over the place.

Your federal agencies and authorities like the 911 Omission Commission have thoroughly looked into all of these matters for you. Thanks a lot Mr. Lee Hamilton, no need to be alarmed here. You're safe here under the yellow caution terrorist code, we'll tell you when to be alarmed. Go back to sleep sheeple, watch Fox news or CNN, they'll keep you accurately informed. Just listen to them though, no reason to ask any questions, we'll tell you when we need to bring back the draft so you can combat and kill more of your fellow Gentile brothers and sisters.

It's the greatest country in the world. I pledge allegiance to the flag, of the United States of America... do that everyday in school and in business meetings, but don't pray to Jesus, that is forbidden according to the supreme law of the land. Yup, they control it. It is painfully obvious to even the most casual observer.

Oops, gotta go now, Blue Collar TV is on, "You just might be a redneck, hahahahaha..." But I digress.

Mr. Ralph Nader, in the November 1st, 2004 issue of *American Free Press*, cited the experiences of an Israeli Air Force officer by the name of Yonatan Shapira. Mr. Shapira, until recently, was a pilot of a Blackhawk helicopter and Captain in the elite Israeli Air Force. He had been dismissed in 2003 because he refused to take part in aerial attacks in areas of the Occupied Territories of Palestine where large concentrations of civilians were liable to become "collateral damage."[453]

In Yonatan's view, such attacks are both illegal and immoral because of the near inevitability of their killing multitudes of innocent civilians. In support of his position, Yonatan cites the fact that of 2,289 Palestinians killed by the Israeli Defense Forces in the recent intifada, less than a quarter, 550, were bearing arms or were fighters.[454]

Yonatan was shocked into his refusal to obey orders by two occurrences, among others. One was the action of a fellow Israeli pilot who fired a one-ton bomb from his U.S.-made F-16 fighter jet, as ordered, at a house in Al-Deredg where a suspected Palestinian terrorist/freedom fighter, depending on your point of view, was staying. Yonatan identifies Al-Deredg as one of the most crowded districts of Gaza and indeed of the world. Besides the targeted Palestinian, 13 local people were killed in that attack: two men, two women, and nine children, one of whom was 2 years old. One hundred sixty other people were wounded in the explosion. A one-ton bomb, Yonatan calculates, has approximately 100 times the explosive power of the type of lethal belts worn by Palestinian suicide bombers. In proportion to the U.S. population and the fatalities of the 9-11 disaster, now an icon and classic measure of terrorist devastation, the fatalities of that single attack on Gaza, population 1.2 million, were greater by 10 percent than the fatalities in America's own 911.[455]

The other occurrence Yonatan cited, that pushed him to refuse orders, came out of a disturbing exchange he had with the commander of the Israeli Air Force, General Dan Halutz, concerning his refusal to serve on a mission in the Occupied Territories. In Yonatan's words: "In the discussion of my dismissal, I asked General Halutz if he would allow the firing of missiles from an Apache helicopter on a car carrying wanted men if it

453 AFP, 11/01/04, p. 12.

454 Ibid.

455 Ibid.

were traveling in the streets of Tel Aviv, in the knowledge that that action would hurt innocent civilians who happened to be passing at the time. In answer, the General gave me his list of relative values of people, as he sees it, from the Jewish person, who is superior, down to the blood of an Arab, which is inferior. As simple as that."[456]

Returning now to the Halakhah, and *Jewish History, Jewish Religion*, Shahak writes: "The obligation of every human being to do the utmost to save the life of a fellow human is of obvious importance in itself. It is also of particular interest in a Jewish context, in view of the fact that since the second world war Jewish opinion has-in some cases justly, in others unjustly-condemned 'the whole world' or at least all Europe for standing by when Jews were being massacred. Let us therefore examine what the Halakhah has to say on this subject.

According to the Halakhah, the duty to save the life of a fellow Jew is paramount. It supersedes all other religious obligations and interdictions excepting only the prohibitions against the three most heinous sins of adultery (including incest), murder and idolatry.

As for Gentiles, the basic Talmudic principle is that their lives must not be saved... Maimonides explains: As for Gentiles with whom we are not at war... their death must not be caused, but it is forbidden to save them if they are at the point of death; if, for example, one of them is seen falling into the sea, he should not be rescued, for it is written: 'neither shalt thou stand against the blood of thy fellow'-but a Gentile is not thy fellow.

In particular, a Jewish doctor must not treat a Gentile patient. Maimonides-himself an illustrious physician-is quite explicit on this; in another passage he repeats the distinction between 'thy fellow' and a Gentile, and concludes: 'and from this learn ye that it is forbidden to heal a Gentile even for payment.... The consensus of halakhic authorities is that the term 'Gentiles' in the above discussions refers to all non-Jews."[457]

456 Ibid.

457 Shahak, pp. 80-81.

The Halakhah also address and discusses the subject of sexual sin and offenses: "Sexual intercourse between a married Jewish woman and any man other than her husband is a capital offense for both parties, and one of the three most heinous sins. The status of Gentile women is very different. The Halakhah presumes all Gentiles to be utterly promiscuous and the verse whose flesh is as the flesh of asses, and whose issue (of semen) is like the issue of horses is applied to them. Whether a Gentile woman is married or not makes no difference, since as far as Jews are concerned the concept of matrimony does not apply to Gentiles. ('There is no matrimony for a heathen'). Therefore the concept of adultery also does not apply to intercourse between a Jewish man and a Gentile woman; rather, the Talmud equates such intercourse to the sin of bestiality. And for the same reason, Gentiles are generally presumed not to have certain paternity."[458]

"According to the *Talmudic Encyclopedia*: He who has carnal knowledge of the wife of a Gentile is not liable to the death penalty, for it is written: "thy fellow's wife" rather than the aliens wife; and even the precept that a man "shall cleave unto his wife" which is addressed to the Gentiles does not apply to a Jew, just as there is no matrimony for a heathen; and although a married Gentile woman is forbidden to the Gentiles, in any case a Jew is exempted. This does not imply that sexual intercourse between a Jewish man and a Gentile woman is permitted-quite the contrary. But the main punishment is inflicted on the Gentile woman; she must be executed, even if she was raped by the Jew: 'If a Jew has coitus with a Gentile woman, whether she be a child or an adult, whether married or unmarried, and even if he is a minor, because he had willful coitus with her, she must be killed, as is the case with a beast, because through her a Jew got into trouble.' The Jew, however, must be flogged, and if he is a Kohen (member of the priestly tribe) he must receive double the number of lashes, because he has committed a double offense: a Kohen must not

458 Ibid. p. 87.

have intercourse with a prostitute, and all Gentile women are presumed to be prostitutes."[459]

The Halakhah also addresses the topic of social status and practice among Jews. "According to the Halakhah, Jews must not (if they can help it) allow a Gentile to be appointed to any position of authority, however small, over Jews." [460]

The Halakhah and the Talmud address Jewish guidance, custom and applicable law towards many other aspects of Jewish life, from testifying in court, to money and property and gifts, to taking of interest and other business practices, to lost property, deception and fraud, to theft and robbery and the subject of Gentiles in the land of Israel. And the author of *Jewish History, Jewish Religion: The Weight of Three Thousand Years*, Mr. Israel Shahak, thoroughly presents, reviews and discusses these areas in an open and candid manner. And I would highly encourage the reader to thoroughly review Shahak's work in detail for him or herself for more information about these topics.

But before closing out this chapter, I would like to further address Jewish attitudes towards Gentiles, Christians and Muslims alike.

Shahak writes: "I would like to discuss examples of halakhic laws whose most important effect is... to inculcate an attitude of scorn and hatred towards Gentiles."

Let us begin with the text of some common prayers. Shahak writes:

"In one of the first sections of the daily Morning Prayer, every devout Jew blesses God for not making him a gentile. The concluding section of the daily prayer opens with the statement: 'We must praise the Lord of all... for not making us like the nations of all lands... for they bow down to vanity and nothingness and pray to a god that does not help.' In the most important section of the weekday prayer-the 'eighteen blessings'-there is a special curse, originally directed against Christians, Jewish converts to Christianity and other Jewish heretics: 'And may the apostates have no hope, and all the Christians perish instantly.' This formula

459 Ibid. pp. 87-88.

dates from the end of the 1st century, when Christianity was still a small persecuted sect. Some time before the 14th century, it was softened into: 'And may the apostates have no hope, and all the heretics perish instantly.' After 1967, several congregations close to Gush Emunim have restored the first version (so far only verbally, not in print) and now pray daily that the Christians may perish instantly."[460]

> *"This is how you can recognize the Spirit of God: Every spirit that acknowledges that Jesus Christ has come in the flesh is from God, but every spirit that does not acknowledge Jesus is not from God. This is the spirit of the antichrist, which you have heard is coming and even now is already in the world."*
>
> (1 John 4:2-3, NIV)

We have mentioned the rule according to which a pious Jew must utter a curse when passing near a Gentile cemetery, whereas he must bless God when passing near a Jewish cemetery. A similar rule applies to the living; thus, when seeing a large Jewish population a devout Jew must praise God, while upon seeing a large Gentile population he must utter a curse. Nor are buildings exempt: the Talmud lays down that a Jew who passes near an inhabited non-Jewish dwelling must ask God to destroy it, whereas if the building is in ruins he must thank the Lord of Vengeance. Under the conditions of classical Judaism, it became customary to spit (usually three times) upon seeing a church, a crucifix or other places of worship of other religions (except Islam).[461]

There are also many rules which effect is to inhibit human friendship between a Jew and Gentile, according to Shahak. For example, a religious Jew must not drink any wine in whose preparation a Gentile had any part whatsoever. "Wine in an open

460 Ibid. pp. 92-93.

461 Ibid. p. 93.

bottle, even if prepared wholly by Jews, becomes banned if a Gentile so much as touches the bottle or passes a hand over it.[462]

According to Shahak, "an Orthodox Jew learns from his earliest youth, as part of his sacred studies, that Gentiles are compared to dogs, that it is a sin to praise them, and so on and so forth."[463]

According to Shahak, the halakhic items discussed throughout this chapter "do represent correctly the teaching of the Halakhah." He says the rabbis and, even worse, the apologetic "scholars of Judaism," know this very well, and for this reason they do not try to argue against such views inside the Jewish community; and of course they never mention them outside it.[464]

And you can safely bet, if "rabbis and apologetic scholars of Judaism" are aware of the teachings of the Talmud and the Halakhah, most "Christian" clergy and "patriotic" U.S. politicians are also in the know. However, they vilify any Jew who raises these matters within ear shot of Gentiles, and they issue deceitful denials in which the art of equivocation reaches its summit.[465]

"Anyone who lives in Israel knows how deep and widespread these attitudes of hatred and cruelty towards all Gentiles is among the majority of Israeli Jews. Normally these attitudes are disguised from the outside world, but since the establishment of the State of Israel, the 1967 war... a significant minority of Jews, both in Israel and abroad, have gradually become more open about such matters. In recent years the inhuman precepts according to which servitude is the 'natural' lot of Gentiles has been publicly quoted in Israel, even on TV, by Jewish farmers exploiting Arab labor, particularly child labor. Gush Emunim leaders have quoted religious precepts which enjoin Jews to oppress Gentiles... as a

462 Ibid. p. 94.

463 Ibid.

464 Ibid. p. 96.

465 Ibid.

devine authority for their own plan to expel all the Arabs from Palestine.[466]

"While many Zionists reject these positions politically... in principle, however, virtually all Zionists... share the deep anti-Gentile attitudes which Orthodox Judaism keenly promotes."[467]

In sum, "Judaism is imbued with a very deep hatred towards Christianity, combined with ignorance about it." This deeply negative attitude is based on two main elements, according to Shahak.

First, on hatred and malicious slanders against Jesus. The traditional view of Judaism on Jesus must of course be distinguished from the controversy between anti-Semites and Jewish apologists concerning the responsibility for his execution.[468]

"According to the Talmud, Jesus was executed by a proper rabbinical court for idolatry, inciting other Jews to idolatry and contempt of rabbinical authority. All classical Jewish sources which mention his execution are quite happy to take responsibility for it; in the Talmudic account the Romans are not even mentioned."[469]

> *"For you, brothers, became imitators of God's churches in Judea, which are in Christ Jesus: You suffered from your own countrymen the same things those churches suffered from the Jews, who killed the Lord Jesus and the prophets and also drove us out. They displease God and are hostile to all men."*
>
> (1 Thessalonians 2:14-15, NIV)

"The more popular accounts-which were taken quite seriously-such as the notorious *Toldot Yeshu*, are even worse, for in addition to the above crimes they accuse Jesus of witchcraft. The very name

466 Ibid.

467 Ibid. p. 97.

468 Ibid.

469 Ibid. p. 98.

'Jesus' was for a Jew a symbol of all that is abominable, and this popular tradition still persists," according to Shahak.[470]

The Gospels, Matthew, Mark, Luke and John, are equally detested and they are not allowed to be quoted (let alone taught) even in modem Israeli schools.[471]

I remember when I was a child in elementary school back in the 60s. We used to walk across the street to a little Christian church for what was called "Weekday Religious Education." The entire classes of the third and fourth grades could partake of this class, although it was optional, as part of the official Indianapolis Public School elementary education program. I believe this practice was discontinued in the 70s as Christian's lost political influence in the US establishment and other anti-Christian groups gained. Since then, we've all witnessed the societal royalty we've achieved.

The second element of this deep negative view towards Christianity is for theological reasons, mostly based on ignorance, according to Shahak:

"Christianity as a religion is classed by rabbinical teachings as idolatry. This is based on a crude interpretation of the Christian doctrines on the Trinity and Incarnation. All the Christian emblems and pictorial representations are regarded as 'idols'- even by those Jews who literally worship scrolls, stones [the star of Remphan], or personal belongings of 'Holy Men.'[472]

The attitude of Judaism towards Islam is, in contrast, relatively mild. Although the stock epithet given to Muhammad is 'madman' ('meshugga'), this was not nearly offensive as it may sound now, and in any case it pales before the abusive terms applied to Jesus. Similarly, the Qur'an-unlike the New Testament-is not condemned to burning."[473]

470 Ibid.

471 Ibid.

472 Ibid.

473 Ibid.

"In the last 40 years the number of non-Jews killed by Jews is by far greater than the number of Jews killed by non-Jews. The extent of the persecution and discrimination against non-Jews inflicted by the 'Jewish state' with the support of organized diaspora Jews [including those in the United States] is also enormously greater than the suffering inflicted on Jews by regimes hostile to them. Although the struggle against antisemitism (and of all other forms of racism [as well as religious discrimination]) should never cease, the struggle against Jewish chauvinism and exclusivism, which must include a critique of classical Judaism, is now of equal or greater importance."[474]

In closing this chapter, I would like to add that I truly hope I have not offended any reader. As I said, many of the teachings and observations I read in *Jewish History, Jewish Religion*, by Israel Shahak were truly eye opening as well as shockingly and painfully educational to me also. In sharing these observations of Orthodox Judaism as presented by Shahak, one risks the application of the label, by the broad brush, of anti-Semite.

But if these observations and teachings of Judaism Shahak has shared with us are accurate and true, and I have no reason to doubt his candid openness and sincerity, then I can honestly say that I am not anti-Semitic. Although we all fail at times, I try to live a Christian life and was taught by Christ's teachings in Matthew, Chapter 6, verses 43 through 45: "Ye have heard that it hath been said, Thou shalt love thy neighbor and hate thine enemy. But I say unto you, Love your enemies, bless them that curse you, do well to them that hate you, and pray for them which despitefully use you, and persecute you; that ye may be the children of your Father which is in heaven..." (Matthew 5:43-45, KJV).

But I will not allow myself or my children as long as I can, or any other person I may be able to reach, to be used as cannon fodder in their quest for a "Greater Israel." There has got to be a better way.

---

474 Ibid. p. 103.

CHAPTER SIX

Blessed are the Peacemakers, for they shall be called the Sons of God

"To contemplate war is to think about the most horrible of human experiences. On this February day, as this nation stands at the brink of battle, every American on some level must be contemplating the horrors of war," said Senator Robert Byrd on the senate floor on the eve of Iraq invasion II.[475]

"Yet, this Chamber is, for the most part, silent-ominously, dreadfully silent. There is no debate, no discussion, no attempt to lay out for the nation the pros and cons of this particular war. There is nothing."

"We stand passively mute in the United States Senate, paralyzed by the sheer turmoil of events..."

"And this is no small conflagration we contemplate... This coming battle, if it materializes, represents a turning point in U.S. foreign policy and possibly a turning point in the recent history of the world."[476]

We will, in this chapter, compare the intentions, words and deeds of those who have truly labored towards peace and freedom by peaceful means, against those "leaders" who have truly, by intentions, words, and deeds, pursued paths of war, destruction, and oppression by evil and tyrannical means.

Senator Byrd continued,

"The doctrine of preemption-the idea that the United States or any other nation can legitimately attack a nation that is not imminently threatening but may be threatening in the future-

---

475 "This is no small Conflagration We Contemplate," Senator Robert Byrd Senate Floor Speech, 2/12/2003, http://byrd.senate.gov/.

476 Ibid.

is a radical new twist on the traditional idea of self-defense. It appears to be in contravention of international law and the UN Charter..."

"High level Administration figures recently refused to take nuclear weapons off the table when discussing a possible attack against Iraq. What could be more destabilizing and unwise than this type of uncertainty...? There are huge cracks emerging in our time-honored alliances, and U.S. intentions are suddenly subject to damaging worldwide speculation."

"Anti-Americanism based on mistrust, misinformation, suspicion, and alarming rhetoric from U.S. leaders is fracturing the once solid alliance against global terrorism which existed after September 11. Here at home, people are warned of imminent terrorist attacks with little guidance as to when or where such attacks might occur. Family members are being called to active military duty, with no idea of the duration of their stay or what horrors they may face."

"The mood of the nation is grim. The economy is stumbling. Fuel prices are rising and may soon spike higher. This Administration, now in power for a little over two years, must be judged on its record. I believe that that record is dismal."[477]

"This Administration has called into question the traditional worldwide perception of the United States as well-intentioned peacekeeper. This Administration has turned the patient art of diplomacy into threats, labeling, and name calling of the sort that reflects quite poorly on the intelligence and sensitivity of our leaders, and which will have consequences for years to come. Calling heads of state pygmies, labeling whole countries as evil, denigrating powerful European allies as irrelevant-these types of crude insensitivities can do our great nation no good..."

"Will we seize Iraq's oil fields, becoming an occupying power which controls the price and supply of that nation's oil for the foreseeable future... Has our senselessly bellicose language and our callous disregard of the interests and opinions of other nations increased the global race to join the nuclear club and

477 Ibid.

made proliferation an even more lucrative practice for nations which need the income?"

"In only the space of two short years this reckless and arrogant Administration has initiated policies which may reap disastrous consequences for years... But to turn one's frustration and anger into the kind of extremely destabilizing and dangerous foreign policy debacle that the world is currently witnessing is inexcusable from any administration charged with the awesome power and responsibility of guiding the destiny of the greatest superpower on the planet."

"Frankly many of the pronouncements made by this administration are outrageous. There is no other word. Yet this chamber is hauntingly silent. On what is possibly the eve of horrific infliction of death and destruction on the population of the nation of Iraq-a population, I might add, of which over 50 percent is under age 15-this chamber is silent. On what is possibly only days before we send thousands of our own citizens to face unimagined horrors... this chamber is silent."

"We are truly 'sleepwalking through history.' In my heart of hearts I pray that this great nation and its good and trusting citizens are not in for a rudest of awakenings."

"I truly must question the judgment of any president who can say that a massive unprovoked military attack on a nation which is over 50 percent children is 'in the highest moral traditions of our country.'"

"This war is not necessary... Our mistake was to put ourselves in a corner so quickly. Our challenge is to now find a graceful way out of a box of our own making..."[478]

Senator Byrd discussed in his senate floor speech the "alarming rhetoric from U.S. leaders," and the "labeling of whole countries as evil," as well as the initiation of "policies which may reap disastrous consequences for years," and the many "outrageous pronouncements" of this administration.

478 Ibid.

Let us now take a closer look at this alarming rhetoric, these outrageous pronouncements, and the potentially disastrous consequences of the policies of this administration.

Just a few short days after September the 11th, on the 20th of September to be precise, President George W. Bush spoke before a joint session of Congress. President Bush said:

"Tonight, we are a country awakened to danger and called to defend freedom. Our grief has turned to anger, and anger to resolution. Whether we bring our enemies to justice, or bring justice to our enemies, justice will be done...

On September the 11th, enemies of freedom committed an act of war against our country. Americans have known wars-but for the past 136 years, they have been wars on foreign soil, except for one Sunday in 1941. Americans have known surprise attacks but never before on thousands of civilians. All of this was brought upon us in a single day -and night fell on a different world, a world where freedom itself is under attack.

Americans have many questions tonight. Americans are asking: Who attacked our country? The evidence we have gathered all points to a collection of loosely affiliated terrorist organizations known as Al Qaeda... Al Qaeda is to terror what the mafia is to crime. But its goal is not making money; its goal is remaking the world-and imposing its radical beliefs on people everywhere... The terrorist's directive commands them to kill Christians and Jews, to kill all Americans, and make no distinction among military and civilians, including women and children...

There are thousands of these terrorists in more than 60 countries. They are recruited from their own nations and neighborhoods and brought to camps in places like Afghanistan, where they are trained in the tactics of terror. They are sent back to their homes or sent to hide in countries around the world to plot evil and destruction..."[479]

Mr. Richard Clarke, the counterterrorism chief to both Presidents William Jefferson Clinton and George Walker Bush,

479 President George W. Bush, Address to a Joint Session of Congress and the American People, www.whitehouse.gov/news/releases/2001/09/20010920-8.html, 5/27/05.

responded to a question shortly after September the 11th from Mr. Charles Gibson on ABC's *Good Morning America.* Gibson asked, "You come in September 12th, ready to plot what response we take to Al Qaeda. Let me talk about the response that you got from the top administration officials on that day; what did the president say to you?"

And Clarke's response, "The president, in a very intimidating way left us, me and my staff, the clear indication that he wanted us to come back with the word that there was an Iraqi hand behind 9/11, because they had been planning to do something about Iraq *before* (emphasis added) they came into office."[480]

This statement by Richard Clarke is supported by a recent disclosure of a Downing Street Memo in *The London Times*, comprising the minutes of a meeting of Prime Minister Tony Blair and his top advisors. These minutes indicate that the United States and Great Britain agreed to attack Iraq well before the invasion and before the president sought Congressional authority to engage in military action and that United States officials were "deliberately manipulating intelligence" to justify war.

The British government document quotes a high-ranking Britsh official as stating that "Bush had made up his mind to take military action."

In addition, the origins of the false contentions that Iraq had weapons of mass destruction remains a serious and lingering question about the lead up to the war. There is an ongoing debate about whether this was the result of a "massive intelligence failure," or the result of intentional and deliberate manipulation of intelligence to justify the case for war. The memo appears to resolve that debate as well, quoting the head of British intelligence as indicating that in the United States, "*the intelligence and facts were being fixed around the policy* (emphasis added)."[481]

480 Michael Moore, "Fahrenheit 9/11," Motion Pictur Film.

481 Rep. John Conyers, Jr., Letter to President Bush Concerning "Downing Street Memo," www.johnconyers.campaignoffice.com, 5/29/05.

"Deceit is in the heart of those who devise evil, but counselors of peace have joy."

(Proverbs 12:20, NKJV)

Charley Gibson then asked Richard Clarke, "What was the reaction you got from the Defense Secretary, Donald Rumsfeld and from his assistant, Paul Wolfowitz?"

Clarke responded, "Well, Donald Rumsfeld said when we talked about bombing the Al Qaeda infrastructure in Afghanistan [you know that monkey bar set they must have taken from an Austin area park on their last state visit that they always show on "the news" when they try to incite anti-Muslim patriotic blood lust], said there were 'no good targets in Afghanistan, lets bomb Iraq.' And we said, 'But Iraq had nothing to do with this...'"[482]

Returning to the president's September 20th, 2001 speech, he said, "Our war on terror begins with Al Qaeda, but it does not end there. It will not end until every terrorist group of global reach has been found, stopped and defeated."[483]

I would now like to also consider the words of a true American hero, although he was also a true hero to the world, who truly changed the world for the better. And these changes have been lasting and permanent, and they were the results of the actions of a true Christian, non-violent peacemaker. The Reverend Martin Luther King, Jr. once said, "The past is prophetic in that it asserts loudly that wars are poor chisels for carving out peaceful tomorrows. One day we must come to see that peace is not merely a distant goal that we must seek, but a means by which we arrive at that goal. We must pursue peaceful ends through peaceful means. How much longer must we play at deadly war games before we heed the plaintive pleas of the unnumbered dead and maimed of past wars?"[484]

---

482 Michael Moore.

483 President Bush, 9/20/01.

484 Coretta Scott King, "The Words of Martin Luther King, Jr." Newmarket Press, New York, p. 83.

George W. Bush: "Americans are asking: How will we fight and win this war? We will direct every resource at our command... every tool of intelligence, every instrument of law enforcement, every financial influence, and every necessary weapon of war..."[485]

> *"Wisdom is better than weapons of war; but one sinner destroys much good."*
>
> (Ecclesiastes 9:18, NKJV)

> *"The work of righteousness will be peace and the effect of righteousness, quietness and assurance forever."*
>
> (Isaiah 32:17, NKJV)

Martin Luther King: "When evil men plot, good men must plan. When evil men burn and bomb, good men must build and bind. When evil men shout ugly words of hatred, good men must commit themselves to the glory of love. Where evil men would seek to perpetuate an unjust status quo, good men must seek to bring a real order of Justice."[486]

> *"In addition to all this, take up the shield of faith, with which you can extinguish all the flaming arrows of the evil one."*
>
> (Ephesians 6:16, NIV)

George W. Bush: "This war will not be like the war against Iraq a decade ago, with a decisive liberation of territory and a swift conclusion... Our response involves far more than instant retaliation and isolates strikes. Americans should not expect one battle, but a lengthy campaign unlike any other we have ever seen. It may include dramatic strikes, visable on TV, and covert operations, secret even in success. We will starve terrorists of

485 President Bush.

486 King, p. 51.

funding, turn them one against the other... And we will pursue nations that provide aid or safe haven... Every nation, in every region, now has a decision to make. Either you are with us, or you are with be terrorists..."[487]

Martin Luther King: "It is time for all people of conscience to call apon America to return to her true home of brotherhood and peaceful pursuits. We cannot remain silent as our nation engages in one of history's most cruel and senseless wars. During these days of human travail, we must encourage creative dissenters. We need them because the thunder of their fearless voices will be the only sound stronger than the blasts of bombs and the clamor of war hysteria.

Those of us who love peace must organize as effectively as the war hawks. As they spread the propaganda of war, we must spread the propaganda of peace... We must demonstrate, teach and preach, until the very foundations of our nation are shaken. We must work unceasingly to lift this nation that we love to a higher destiny, to a new plateau of compassion, to a more noble expression of humaneness.

I have tried to be honest. To be honest is to confront the truth. However unpleasant and inconvenient the truth may be, I believe we must expose and face it if we are to achieve a better quality of American life."[488]

Vice President Richard B. Cheney: "This struggle can only end with their complete and permanent destruction."[489]

ABC News Journalist Mr. Ted Koeppel (referring to the United States Armed Forces): "An awesome, synchronized, killing machine."[490]

George W. Bush: "There are some who feel like that if they attack us that we may decide to leave prematurely, they don't understand what they're talking about if that's the case. Let me

487 Bush.

488 King, p. 89.

489 Moore.

490 Ibid.

finish. Um, there are some who feel like, you know, the conditions are such, they can attack us there. My answer is, 'bring em on.'"[491]

Martin Luther King: "It is still one of the tragedies of human history that the 'children of darkness' are frequently more determined and zealous than the 'children of light.'"[492]

George W. Bush: "Our war on terror is well begun, but it is only begun. This campaign may not be finished on our watch-yet it must be and it will be waged on our watch... It costs a lot to fight this war. We have spent more than a billion dollars a month-over $30 million a day-and we must be prepared for future operations. Afghanistan proved that expensive precision weapons defeat the enemy... and we need more of them. We need to replace aging aircraft and make our military more agile, to put our troops anywhere in the world... Our men and women in uniform deserve the best weapons, the best equipment, and the best training... My budget includes the largest increase in defense spending in two decades..."[493]

Martin Luther King: "A true revolution of values will lay hands on the world order and say of war: 'This way of settling differences is not just.' This business of burning human beings with napalm, of filling our nations homes with orphans and widows, of injecting poisonous drugs of hate into the veins of peoples normally humane, of sending men [and women today] home from dark and bloody battlefields physically handicapped and psychologically deranged, cannot be reconciled with wisdom, justice and love. A nation that continues year after year to spend more money on military defense than on programs of social uplift is approaching spiritual death."[494]

George W. Bush: "We wage a war to save civilization itself."[495]

---

491 Ibid.

492 King, p. 19.

493 President Delivers State of the Union Address, www.whitehouse.gov/news/releases/2002/01/2002-129-11.html, 5/27/05.

494 King, p. 87.

495 Moore.

Martin Luther King: "We will never have peace in the world until men everywhere recognize that ends are not cut off from means, because the means represent the ideal in the making, and the end in process. Ultimately you can't reach good ends through evil means, because the means represent the seed and the end represents the tree."[496]

George W. Bush: "My fellow citizens... at this hour, American and coalition forces are in the early stages of military operations to disarm Iraq, to free its people, and to defend the world from grave danger. On my orders, coalition forces have begun striking selected targets of military importance to undermine Saddam Hussein's ability to wage war."[497]

Secretary of Defense Donald Rumsfeld: "One could almost say it's the mother of all coalitions."[498]

George W. Bush: "You're either with us or against us. You're either evil or your good." "We're gonna smoke him out of his cave... We're gonna smoke them out of their holes."[499]

Martin Luther King: "There is little hope for us until we become tough-minded enough to break loose from the shackles of prejudice, half truths, and downright ignorance."[500]

George W. Bush: "... our Armed Forces have delivered a message now clear to every enemy of the United States: Even 7,000 miles away, across oceans and continents, on mountaintops and in caves-you will not escape the justice of this nation."[501]

Martin Luther King: "I've decided that I'm going to do battle for my philosophy. You ought to believe something in life, believe that thing so fervently that you will stand up with it till the end of your days. I can't make myself believe that God wants me to hate. I'm tired of violence. And I'm not going to let my oppressor

496 King, p. 86.

497 Moore.

498 Ibid.

499 Ibid.

500 King, p. 30.

501 President George W. Bush, whitehouse.gov, 2002 State of the Union Address.

dictate to me what method I must use. We have a power... power that can't be found in bullets and guns, but we have a power. It is as old as the insights of Jesus of Nazareth...

"I am convinced that if we succumb to the temptation to use violence in our struggle... unborn generations will be recipients of a long and desolate night of bitterness, and our chief legacy to them will be a never-ending reign of chaos."[502]

George W. Bush: "Some have said we must not act until the threat is imminent. Since when have terrorists and tyrants announced their intentions, politely putting us on notice before they strike... Let there be no misunderstanding: If Saddam Hussein does not fully disarm, for the safety of our people and for the peace of the world, we will lead a coalition to disarm him. Tonight, I have a message for the men and women who will keep the peace, members of the American Armed Forces: Many of you are assembling in or near the Middle East... Sending Americans into battle is the most profound decision a president can make... We seek peace. We strive for peace... And if war is forced upon us, we will fight with the full force and might of the United States military..."[503]

Martin Luther King: "One of the most persistent ambiguities that we face is that everybody talks about peace as a goal. However, it does not take sharpest-eyed sophistication to discern that while everybody talks about peace, peace has become practically nobody's business among the power-wielders. Many men cry Peace! Peace! But they refuse to do things that make for peace.

The large power blocs of the world talk passionately of pursuing peace while burgeoning defense budgets bulge, enlarging already awesome armies, and devising even more devastating weapons. Call the rolls of those who sing the glad tidings of peace and one's ears will be surprised by the responding sounds. The heads of all the nations issue clarion calls for peace yet these destiny determiners come accompanied by a band and a brigade of

502 King, p. 71.

503 President George W. Bush, whitehouse.gov, 2003 State of the Union Address.

national choristers, each bearing unsheathed swords rather than olive branches."[504]

> *"The wicked have drawn the sword and have bent their bow, to cast down the poor and needy, to slay those who are of upright conduct."*
>
> (Psalms 37:14, NKJV)

> *"You shall destroy those who speak falsehood; the Lord abhors the bloodthirsty and deceitful man."*
>
> (Psalms 5:6, NKJV)

George W. Bush: "The civilized world is rallying to America's side."[505]

Mr. Vince Ryan of American Free Press: "The United States is the laughing stock of the whole world for invading that country which had done nothing to us.' Laughing stock' is too mild. The fact is that the United States is now the most hated country in the world. We used to be the most admired."[506]

George W. Bush: "Freedom from terrorism will come only through pre-emptive war against enemies of democracy."[507]

> *"Let the peace of Christ rule in your hearts, since as members of one body you were called to peace."*
>
> (Colossians 3:15, NIV)

> *"Therefore let us pursue the things which make for peace and the things by which one may edify another."*
>
> (Romans 14:19, NKJV)

504 King, p. 84.

505 Bush, 2003.

506 American Free Press, 9/20/04, p. 21.

507 AFP, 12/20/04, p. 14.

Paul Craig Roberts served as Assistant Secretary of the Treasury for Economic Policy and was credited by President Reagan with a major role in the Economic Recovery Tax Act of 1981. He is a former editor and columnist for *The Wall Street Journal* and was ranked as one of the top seven journalists by the Forbes Media Guide. He was a distinguished fellow at the Cato Institute from 1993-1996 and is a senior research fellow at the Hoover Institution, Stanford University. [509] Mr. Roberts had this to say about the war:

"What world does [President] Bush live in? The United States cannot control Iraq, much less battle the rest of the Muslim world and beyond. While Bush threatened the world with U.S. aggression, headlines revealed the futility of pre-emptively invading countries: 'Pentagon to Boost Iraq Force by 12, 000,' 'U.S. Death Toll in Iraq at Highest Monthly Level,' 'Wounded Disabled Soldiers Kept on Active Duty.'

"Bush's pre-emptive wars are a good way to depopulate the United States and bankrupt our country."

"Why would Bush advocate further pre-emptive invasions (referring to the statement he made on December 1, 2004 in Halifax, Nova Scotia where he said 'Freedom from terrorism will come only through pre-emptive war...') unless he has other Middle Eastern countries targeted, like Iran and Syria..."

"Lacking sufficient military forces to successfully occupy Iraq, how is Bush going to engage in pre-emptive wars against Iran and Syria without bringing back the draft? If eight U.S. divisions can't do the job in Iraq, 16 U.S. divisions won't be enough for Iran."[508]

[They must be considering the use of pre-emptive nuclear strikes or some other form of massive aerial bombardment that would kill thousands of innocent Gentiles.]

"Bush would serve our country and the rest of the world far better by ceasing his aggressive talk and begin working to create trust and goodwill. Bush is a very foolish man if he thinks

---

508 Paul Craig Roberts, www.townhall.com/columnists/BIOS/cbroberts.html, 7/19/05.

America will bear no consequences for his support for Israel's appalling treatment of the Palestinians..."[509]

The Reverend Martin Luther King, Jr. was not the only non-violent Christian peacemaker that was a victim of "more determined and zealous children of darkness." We will continue to revisit Martin Luther King's non-violent approach to human progress and international relations.

But I would now like to review and compare some of the words, intentions and deeds of the late President, John F. Kennedy. As we proceed with the words of the late president, I would kindly ask the reader to please reflect upon the absence of well-meaning intent that has been sorely missing from our national discourse, politicians and pundits alike, as well as presidential monologues.

On June 10th, 1963, President Kennedy addressed the faculty, guests and the president of the American University, which was sponsored by the Methodist Church.

President Kennedy said:

"'There are few earthly things more beautiful than a university,' wrote John Masefield in his tribute to English universities-and his words are equally true today. He did not refer to spires and towers, to campus greens and ivied walls. He admired the splendid beauty of the university, he said, because it was a 'place where those who hate ignorance may strive to know, where those who perceive truth may strive to make others see.'

I have, therefore chosen this time and this place to discuss a topic on which ignorance to often abounds and the truth is too rarely perceived-yet it is the most important topic on earth: world peace.

What kind of peace do I mean? What kind of peace do we seek? Not a Pax Americana enforced on the world by American weapons of war. Not the peace of the grave or the security of the slave. I am talking about genuine peace, the kind of peace that makes life on earth worth living, the kind that enables men and nations to grow and to hope and to build a better life for their

509 AFP, 12/20/04, p. 14.

children-not merely peace for Americans, but peace for all men and women-not merely peace in our time but peace for all time...

Today the expenditure of billions of dollars every year on weapons acquired for the purpose of making sure we never need to use them is essential to keeping the peace. But surely, the acquisition of such stockpiles-which can only destroy and never create-is not the only, much less the most efficient, means of assuring peace. I speak of peace therefore, as the necessary rational end of rational men. I realize that the pursuit of peace is not as dramatic as the pursuit of war-and frequently the words of the pursuer fall on deaf ears. But we have no more urgent task."[510]

At this point, I would like to briefly review for the reader again the pursuits of a racio-religio-politico-nation state, whose leaders have openly stated that war, for them, is a national necessity, and which nation happens to be the United States' "best Middle East ally."

Israel's former defense minister, Moshe Dayan: "Israel must use the sword... to retain its moral tension... it must invent dangers and... adopt the method of provocation... let us hope for a new war with the Arab countries... so we may... acquire our space."[511]

Israeli Rabbi Shim'on Weiser: "... war for us is not a game, but a vital necessity... the best of Gentiles-kill him."[512]

Mr. Nathan Perlmutter, former national director of the Anti-Defamation League of B'nai B'rith, wrote in a 1982 book published by the ADL: "Contemporary anti-semitism lay in the actions of peacemakers... transmuters of swords into plowshares... and nowadays war is getting a bad name and peace too favorable a press."[513]

You know, I prefer to keep things simple when I can. I guess I'm simple minded, but I like to de-clutter, or remove as much

510 JFK speech-American University-1963, www.peace-justice.com/jfk-amer-univ.html, 12/29/04.

511 Ahmed, p. 370.

512 Shahak, pp. 77-78.

513 Andrew and Leslie Cockburn, "Dangerous Liaison. The Inside Story of the U.S.-Israeli Covert Relationship, pp. 189-190.

extraneous material as I can. It helps me analyze so I can see clearly and make up my mind or come to a reasonable conclusion about a matter of thought. It's kind of like the philosopher who said, "I think, therefore I am." Very simple and very conclusive.

And so, this is what I have found. Israel must "invent dangers" and use "the sword" and "hopes for a new war," and for Israel, "war is a vital necessity" and therefore it is recommended for Israel to "kill the best of Gentiles" and also now "peacemakers are anti-Semitic." I can only conclude then that it is "anti-Semitic" to be a peacemaker because if one is actively working towards a condition of peace in the Middle East, one is actually working, unconsciously I would presume, or at least with good intent, against the goals and ambitions of the Jewish state of Israel in their quest for territorial expansion and empire. Their goals and intentions are not just to acquire the land of the Arabs, but to ethnically cleanse the Arabs from that land. And since the United States government, according to Ariel Sharon, is now "controlled by the Jewish people," and the United States Armed Forces are mostly Christian or non-Jewish Gentiles, then what better way to ethnically cleanse your pursued land than by using a foreign army consisting also of your nation's enemies. It's like killing two birds with one stone, or in this case, killing two groups of Gentiles with one never-ending war on terror.

Peacemakers are anti-Semites... really?

> *"But the wisdom that comes from heaven is first of all pure; then peace loving, considerate, submissive, full of mercy and good fruit, impartial and sincere. Peacemakers who sow in peace raise a harvest of righteousness.* "
>
> (James 3:17-18, NIV)

Edgar Steele, writing in *The Barnes Review*, further discusses the condition of the United States today:

"In my lifetime, I have seen America grow and change. I have seen her stand tall, and I have seen her brought low. I have seen the best America can be and now, just recently, I have seen the worst that America can be...

America once was a beacon to the world. She was a beacon of liberty. A beacon of freedom. A beacon of moral strength. That reality became our reputation and a part of our heritage.

Now it is revealed that American troops, under orders from on high, humiliated, tortured and sexually degraded Iraqi and Afghan prisoners of war. American troops shot innocent civilians, more than 10,000 of them so far (recent figures are higher than 30,000 Iraqi civilians dead), many of them women and children.

Our heritage has been squandered for the sake of Jewish empire. Yes-Jewish empire, not America's... Jewish empire. For America has become a Jewish nation in word. America has become a Jewish nation in deed. And America has become a Jewish nation in fact.

Torture is what Israel does. Humiliation is what Israel does. Lying, double dealing and even genocide are Israeli traits, because those things are Jewish traits. "*By deception, we shall do war*"-the motto of the Mossad.

[One can easily recall our own WMD and Iraq's allegiance with Osama bin Laden deceptions for war.] We have become everything that America once stood against...

But we must shake free of the Zionist cabal that rules us today... the same Zionist cabal [that] is cracking down here. The Patriot Act is just the latest installment.

What we've done in Afghanistan; what we're doing in Iraq-killing women and children... bombing churches during services and killing women and children; bombing wedding services and killing women and children; carpet bombing cities like Fallugah (more of which will be discussed shortly) and, now, Najaf; jailhouse torture, humiliation, rape and murder.

We're taking huge U.S. casualties. We're being lied to... Their freedom fighters are defending against a... takeover of their country. We call them terrorists and insurgents. How can you be an insurgent in your own country, fighting an invader? This simply is propaganda at work... (The truth is... the Iraq situation shows every indication of developing into a guerrilla war and a standing conventional occupation army is no match for a native guerrilla force. The Iraqis, be they Shiite, Sunni, Kurd or whatever do not like a foreign occupation any more than you would. And they, as you would, will eventually cleanse their land of this alien force... let's not forget the militia forces in the American Revolution-the sand in the gears of the British war machine'-from our perspective, the most important guerrilla army to defeat an occupying force.[514])

The media is totally under the control of the politically correct today-the 'inner party,' if you will, our Zionist rulers, Jews.

George Orwell's fantasy has become the media's reality. Today... Homosexuality is a desirable lifestyle, Christians are narrow-minded bigots, and patriots are traitors...

Orwell said, 'War is Peace.' Today we have perpetual war to 'keep the peace.' Today, war is peace.

Orwell said, 'Freedom is Slavery.' Today, we yield civil liberties in the name of domestic security. Today, freedom is slavery.

Orwell said, 'Ignorance is Strength.' Today, we accuse those asking questions of being unpatriotic. Today, ignorance is strength.

Orwell's 'Ministry of Peace' waged war. Today, our Defense Department conducts nonstop wars that we start.

We have gone beyond even George Orwell with our version of Newspeak.

There is nothing conservative these days about conservatives. Now, conservative means bigger government and more control.

And there is nothing liberal about liberals anymore-who fall all over one another to surrender personal freedom. Liberal used to mean favoring personal freedom and liberty...

We support totalitarianism, and then call it democracy, both at home and abroad...

We abuse power and call it politics. We ridicule our Forefathers' values and call it enlightenment...

Used to be, we had rights. Today, we posses only privileges, dispensed at the pleasure of our federal government.

514 AFP, 7/18/05, p. 3.

A coup has taken place-and right under our noses. The Patriot Bill was passed by Congress without even being read by any legislator.

Laws already are on the books-as part of the first Patriot Act-that allow the government to visit our local libraries and bookstores to examine our reading habits. Neighborhood watch programs encourage neighbors to spy on one another.

Provisions in Patriot Act II will allow secret arrests, warrantless searches, asset forfeiture and, believe it or not, the stripping of citizenship from Americans so that we can be deported for 'further processing.' Can you say torture and murder...?

Tomorrow's legal system will look like today's military tribunals...

And it is not enough that Zionists control America. They have to reshape it to suit them. Virtually every recent case that involves removal of Christian symbols from society was brought and or prosecuted by a Jew, usually with a Jewish judge presiding.

For the sake of the feelings of 2.5 percent, all the rest of us must yield our cultural heritage. Removing 'under God' from the Pledge of Allegiance; taking down plaques of the Ten Commandments; removing crosses from public venues, taking Christ out of Christmas, first, then Christmas out of year-end holidays altogether. [I remember popular morning news talking heads referring to the holidays last year as 'Christmuka']...

Today, we have a dictatorship with only the illusion of a democracy; not even a pretense of a republic anymore. The judiciary makes laws as directed by the administration. The executive rules absolutely...

The system is broken-irretrievably broken. It can't be fixed, because it won't be fixed. We can't work within the system any more to effect meaningful change because the system won't allow it. As a lawyer (licensed to practice in CA, OR, WA and ID), I'm inside the system. Everyone says the system is broken. You don't know how bad things really are.

If you think Kerry will be different, you are wrong. [He only promised to do a better job of what Bush was already doing. Both

Bush and Kerry were members of the Satan worshipping Skull and Bones Society at Yale.]

We've got to make a change in America...America worked once as a constitutional republic. It can work again...

Together, we can make a difference. Together, we can awaken America. Together, we can take back America...

But we must shake free of the Zionist cabal that rules us today."[515]

Returning to President John F. Kennedy's ideals for our country as expressed in his American University speech, he said:

"Let us examine our attitude toward peace itself. Too many of us think it is impossible. Too many think it unreal. But that is a dangerous, defeatist belief. It leads to the conclusion that war is inevitable-that mankind is doomed-that we are gripped by forces we cannot control.

We need not accept that view. Our problems are manmade-therefore, they can be solved by man. And man can be as big as he wants. No problem of human destiny is beyond human beings. Man's reason and spirit have often solved the seemingly unsolvable-and we believe they can do it again...

Genuine peace must be the product of many nations, the sum of many acts. It must be dynamic, not static, changing to meet the challenge of each new generation. For peace is a process-a way of solving problems.

With such a peace, there will still be quarrels and conflicting interests, as there are within families and nations. World peace, like community peace, does not require that each man love his neighbor-it requires only that they live together in mutual tolerance, submitting their disputes to a just and peaceful settlement. And history teaches us that enmities between nations, as between individuals, do not last forever. However our likes and dislikes may seem, the tide of time and events will often bring surprising changes in the relations between nations and neighbors.

---

515 Edgar J. Steele, "Together, We Can Take Back America," The Barnes Review, Jan. 2005, pp. 12-16.

So let us persevere. Peace need not be impracticable, and war need not be inevitable. By defining our goal more clearly, by making it seem more manageable and less remote, we can help all peoples to see it, to draw hope from it, and to move irresistibly toward it.

Second: Let us reexamine our attitude toward the Soviet Union. It is discouraging to think that their leaders may actually believe what their propagandists write. It is discouraging to read a recent authoritative Soviet text on Military Strategy and find, on page after page, wholly baseless and incredible claims-such as the allegation that 'American imperialist circles are preparing to unleash different types of wars... that there is a very real threat of preventive war being unleashed by American imperialists... the political aims of the American imperialists are to enslave economically and politically the European and other capitalist countries... to achieve world domination... by means of aggressive wars.' [Is this hitting a little close to home?]

...Among the many traits the peoples of our two countries have in common, none is stronger than our mutual abhorrence of war.

... For we are both devoting massive sums of money to weapons that could be better devoted to combating ignorance, poverty, and disease.

... So, let us not be blind to our differences-but let us also direct attention to our common interests and to the means by which these differences can be resolved. And if we cannot end now our differences, at least we can help make the world safe for diversity. For, in the final analysis, our most basic common link is that we all inhabit this small planet. We all breathe the same air. We all cherish our children's future. And we are all mortal.

... For we can seek a relaxation of tensions without relaxing our guard. And, for our part, we do not need to use threats to prove that we are resolute. We do not need to jam foreign broadcasts out of fear our faith will be eroded. We are unwilling to impose our system on any unwilling people-but we are willing and able to engage in peaceful competition with any people on earth.

... Our interests converge, however, not only in defending the frontiers of freedom, but in pursuing the paths of peace... For there can be no doubt that, if all nations could refrain from interfering in the self determination of others, the peace would be much more assured.

... Finally, my fellow Americans, let us examine our attitude toward peace and freedom here at home. The quality and spirit of our own society must justify and support our efforts abroad. We must show it in the dedication of our own lives....

But wherever we are, we must all, in our daily lives, live up to the age-old faith that peace and freedom walk together.

... 'When a man's ways please the Lord,' the Scriptures tell us, 'he maketh even his enemies to be at peace with him.' And is not peace, in the last analysis, basically a matter of human rights-the right to live out our lives without the fear of devastation-the right to breathe air as nature provided it-the right of future generations to a healthy existence?

While we proceed to safeguard our national interests, let us also safeguard human interests. And the elimination of war and arms is clearly in the interests of both...

The United States, as the world knows, will never start a war. We do not want a war. We do not now expect a war. This generation of Americans has already had enough-more than enough of war and hate and oppression. We shall be prepared if others wish it. We shall be alert to try to stop it. But we shall also do our part to build a world of peace, where the weak are safe and the strong are just. We are not helpless before that task or hopeless of its success. Confident and unafraid, we labor on-not toward a strategy of annihilation but toward a strategy of peace." 516

Let us now please return again to some of our current president's words, deeds, intentions and goals for our nation, and our people.

George W. Bush: "Our second goal is to prevent regimes that sponsor terror from threatening America... Some of these

516 President John F. Kennedy, American University Speech-1963.

regimes have been pretty quiet since September the 11th. But we know their true nature. North Korea is a regime arming... Iran aggressively pursues these weapons... Iraq continues to flaunt its hostility toward America... States like these ...constitute an axis of evil, arming to threaten the peace of the world... these regimes pose a grave and growing danger... We are protected from attack only by vigorous action abroad..."

"I'm a war president. I make decisions here in the oval office and foreign policy matters with war on my mind."[517]

> *Do not take me away with the wicked and with the workers of iniquity, who speak peace to their neighbors, but evil is in their hearts.*
>
> (Psalms 28:3, NKJV)

President George W. Bush was addressing his loyal faithful at what appeared to be a black tie fundraising event when he jokingly told his audience, "Those weapons of mass destruction gotta be around here somewhere," followed with a hearty round of inappropriate laughter and applause by his close and faithful supporters. Then he proceeded to say, "Nope, no weapons over there," the inappropriate laughter still present and boisterous. It seemed as if he was presenting some sort of slideshow where in several photos, it looks as if he is bending over, looking for those ever-illusive weapons of mass destruction throughout the oval office. As the joyous inappropriate laughter and inappropriate supportive applause continue, the Commander-in-Chief again says, "maybe under here," "hahaha, clap, clap, clap."[518] Absolutely disgusting.

"We have become everything that America once stood against..."

517 Bush, 2002 State of Union.

518 Moore.

> *"In fact, everyone who wants to live a godly life in Christ Jesus will be persecuted, while evil men and imposters will go from bad to worse, deceiving and being deceived."*
>
> (2 Timothy 3:12-13, NIV)

Martin Luther King:

"I refuse to accept the cynical notion that nation after nation must spiral down a militaristic stairway into the hell of destruction. I believe that unarmed truth and unconditional love will have the final word in reality. This is why right temporarily defeated is stronger than evil triumphant.

I believe that even amid today's mortar bursts and whining bullets, there is still hope for a brighter tomorrow. I believe that wounded justice, lying prostrate on the blood-flowing streets of our nations, can be lifted from this dust of shame to reign supreme among the children of men.

I still believe that one day, mankind will bow before the altars of God and be crowned triumphant over war and bloodshed, and nonviolent redemptive goodwill will proclaim the rule of the land..."[519]

"We are now faced with the fact that tomorrow is today. We are confronted with the fierce urgency of now. In this unfolding conundrum of life and history there is such a thing as being too late. Procrastination is still the thief of time. Life often leaves us standing bare, naked, and dejected with a lost opportunity. The 'tide in the affairs of men' does not remain at the flood; it ebbs. We may cry out desperately for time to pause in her passage, but time is deaf to every plea and rushes on. Over the bleached bones and jumbled residues of numerous civilizations is written the words: 'too late.' There is an invisible book of life that faithfully records our vigilance or our neglect. 'The moving finger writes and having writ moves on...' We still have a choice today: nonviolent coexistence or violent coannihilation. This may well be mankind's last chance to choose between chaos and community."[520]

519 King, p. 91.

520 Ibid. p. 90.

"If you are cut down in a movement that is designed to save the soul of a nation, then no other death could be more redemptive." [521]

In a December 2004 article in *American Free Press*, writer Christopher Bollyn reported that:

"As Americans prepared for Thanksgiving, an estimated 100,000 residents of the besieged Iraqi city of Fallujah, trapped in their homes, struggled to survive without fresh food, water or electricity, reportedly cut off by U.S. forces on November 8th.

On the streets of Fallujah, a city of more than 350,000, dogs gnaw on bloated and rotting corpses that remain unburied for weeks.

Thousands of families in Fallujah were reported to be in a critical humanitarian situation after U.S. forces prevented the delivery of relief supplies. An Iraq Red Crescent Society (IRCS) humanitarian aid convoy was reportedly blocked by U.S. troops for more than two weeks.

Rana Sidani of the International Committee of the Red Cross (ICRC) in Geneva, Switzerland told *American Free Press* on November 30th, 2004, that many civilians were still prevented from receiving aid and medical care. At the beginning of the U.S. operation in Fallujah on November 5th, a hospital was reduced to rubble as a result of U.S. air and artillery bombardments, reported Reuters.

A nearby compound used by the main Fallujah hospital used to store medical supplies was also destroyed. Fallujah's main hospital was occupied by U.S. forces when the ground offensive began. These actions are violations of international humanitarian law.

'Bodies can be seen everywhere. It is very sad. It is a human disaster,' said a spokesman for the IRCS in Baghdad. 'It is difficult to move in the city due to the large number of dead bodies in the streets. The IRCS estimates there are more than 6,000 dead in Fallujah.'

---

521 Ibid. p. 67.

Dr. Said Ismael Haki, the IRCS president said, 'There are no houses left in Fallujah, only destroyed places. I really don't know how the people will return to the city. No one will find their homes.'

As U.S. troops engaged in the most intense urban combat since Vietnam, the controlled, mainstream press scrupulously avoided discussion or footage of the devastation of the Sunni city. For example, rather than discuss and show the widespread devastation of Fallujah, U.S. television news programs focused on a brawl between NBA basketball players from the Indiana Pacers and fans in Detroit.[522]

This should be expected from the mainstream press, as John Swinton, a New York journalist remarked in 1880, and previously addressed: "The business of the journalist is to destroy the truth, to lie outright [or to lie by omission], to pervert, to vilify, to fawn at the feet of mammon and to sell his country... for his daily bread... We are the tools and vassals of rich men behind the scenes ['Live from Studio 1A in Rockefeller Plaza']. We are the jumping jacks, they pull the strings and we dance... We are intellectual prostitutes."[523]

At least 136 U.S. soldiers were killed during November 2004 in Iraq and more than 800 were wounded, mostly in Fallujah, making it the most costly month and operation in terms of U.S. lives since President Bush announced, "My fellow Americans, major combat operations in Iraq have ended, and in the battle of Iraq, the United States and its allies have prevailed," during that publicity stunt aboard the USS Abraham Lincoln aircraft carrier.

"U.S. actions in Fallujah are creating the nightmare that we are seeking to prevent," said Time magazine's Baghdad bureau chief. "I stood there as I saw American boys die. I mean a man shot at close range, blown apart by a rocket-propelled grenade. He dies there in front of you, and I can't help but think, why? For what cause?"

---

522 AFP,12/06/2004, p. 13.

523 Hufschmid, p. 117.

Remember the New Testament Book of James, chapter 4, verse 2, answers that very question, "Where do wars and fights come from among you... You lust and do not have. You murder and covet and cannot obtain, you fight and war..." (James 4:1-2, NKJV).

The New York Times reported actions taken by U.S. forces in Fallujah appear to be prima facie evidence of war crimes. A November 20th, 2004 article reported that U.S. Marines had transformed a mosque into a fortress with machine gunners and snipers perched on the roof. The Times' motto is "all the news that's fit to print," however didn't think its readers needed to know that U.S. forces had cut off water and power to a city of 340,000 people.

The obliteration of Fallujah is a serious war crime, according to Professor Francis A. Boyle, an International Law Professor at the University of Illinois. In his November 15th, 2004 article, *A War Crime in Real Time: Obliterating Fallujah*, he writes: "Article 6 (b.) of the 1945 Nuremberg Charter defines a war crime in relevant part as the 'wanton destruction of cities, towns or villages.' According to this definition, the Bush administration's destruction of Fallujah constitutes a war crime for which Nazis were tried and executed."[524]

One should always maintain hope for appropriately administered justice.

"The chaos of war should never be understated," writes former U.S. Marine and Iraq war veteran, Michael Hoffman. "On the way to Baghdad, I saw many bodies by the road, many in civilian clothing.

You can tell a true war story by its absolute and uncompromised allegiance to obscenity and evil. War is dirty; always wrong... this war is a war that did not have to be fought.

I know this war has nothing to do with protecting my country. My sergeant put it best a week before we left for the Middle East: 'Don't think you're going to be heroes. You're not going

524 AFP, 12/06/2004, p. 13.

for weapons of mass destruction. You're not going to get rid of Saddam or to make Iraq safe for democracy...'

...I wonder how many Iraqi children were killed by my artillery battery, or how many Iraqis were trapped in burning vehicles on the road to Baghdad. These are the thoughts that keep me up at night: the bodies of children and the burned remains of Iraqis....

But those who put all of us there will never understand this ...they need to be judged. But they will never receive the most just punishment: feeling what I and all the other veterans of this hideous war will deal with for the rest of our lives."[525]

On September 25th, 1961, President John F. Kennedy addressed the General Assembly of the United Nations. Relevant portions of this speech are restated here:

"Mr. President, honored delegates, ladies and gentlemen: For in the development of this organization rests the only true alternative to war-and war appeals no longer as a rational alternative. Unconditional war can no longer serve to settle disputes. It can no longer concern the great powers alone. For a nuclear disaster, spread by wind and water and fear, could well engulf the great and the small, the rich and the poor, the committed and the uncommitted alike. Mankind must put an end to war-or war will put an end to mankind.

... Let us call a truce to terror. Let us invoke the blessings of peace. And as we build an international capacity to keep peace, let us join in dismantling the national capacity to wage war.

... But the great question which confronted this body in 1945 is still before us: whether man's cherished hopes for progress and peace are to be destroyed by terror and disruption, whether the "foul winds of war" can be tamed in time to free the cooling winds of reason, and whether the pledges of our Charter are to be fulfilled or defied-pledges to secure peace, progress, human rights and world law.

In this Hall, there are not three forces, but two. One is composed of those who are trying to build the kind of world described in Articles I and II of the Charter. The other, seeking

525 AFP, 12/20/04, p. 7.

a far different world, would undermine this organization in the process.

... For we far prefer world law, in the age of self-determination, to world war, in the age of mass extermination.

Today, every inhabitant of this planet must contemplate the day when this planet may no longer be habitable. Every man, woman and child lives under a nuclear sword of Damocles, hanging by the slenderest of threads, capable of being cut at any moment by accident or miscalculation or madness. The weapons of war must be abolished before they abolish us.

Men no longer debate whether armaments are a symptom or a cause of tension. The mere existence of modern weapons-ten million times more powerful than any that the world has ever seen, and only minutes away from any target on earth-is a source of horror, and discord and distrust. Men no longer maintain that disarmament must await the settlements of all disputes-for disarmament must be a part of any permanent settlement. And men may no longer pretend that the quest for disarmament is a sign of weakness-for in a spiraling arms race, a nation's security may well be shrinking-even as its arms increase.

For fifteen years this organization has sought the reduction and destruction of arms. Now that goal is no longer a dream-it is a practical matter of life or death. The risks inherent in disarmament pale in comparison to the risks inherent in an unlimited arms race.

...As we extend the rule of law on earth, so we must also extend it to man's new domain-outer space.

The new horizons of outer space must not be driven by the old bitter concepts of imperialism... The cold reaches of the universe must not become the new arena of an even colder war."[526]

A documentary that this author could not more highly recommend to the reader is a CSPAN II, *Book TV* program entitled, "9/11 Commission Report Critique."

526 President John F. Kennedy, "Address Before the General Assembly of the United Nations," NYC 9/25/61, http://feralnews.com/issues/jfk/jfk_disarmament speech_to_UN.html, 12/29/04.

Professor Emeritus of the Claremont School of Theology, and author of *The New Pearl Harbor* and *The 9/11 Commission Report, Omissions and Distortions*, David Ray Griffin describes the document, "The National Security Strategy of the United States of America," published by the administration of President George W. Bush in September of 2002.

Griffin states:

"David North says, not unfairly that 'this document asserts as the guiding policy of the United States, the right to use military force against any country it believes to be, or believes at some point may become a threat to American interests.'

Another such document called *Vision for 2020* was published in February of 1997 by the U.S. Space Command. The mission statement at the head of this document reads, 'U.S. Space Command, dominating the space dimension of military operations to protect U.S. interests and investments'-nothing about freedom, democracy and human rights. In the body of the document, in fact, we find this amazingly candid statement: 'the globalization of the world economy will continue with the widening of the haves and the have nots.' The point of this statement is that as the domination of the world economy by the [elite of the] United States and [their] allies increases, the worlds poor will get still poorer, making the have nots hate America all the more. We will need therefore the power to keep them in line.

'The United States can do this,' and this is the documents main message, through full spectrum dominance, which will involve merging space superiority with land, sea and air superiority. Dominance in space will include,' the document frankly says, 'the power to deny others the use of space.'

By speaking only of the Space Command's effort to develop a missile defense system, the Pentagon and the White House like to suggest that its purpose is purely defensive. But the goal includes weaponizing space so as to give U.S. forces, in the words of a more recent document, 'a prompt global strike capability, whether nuclear or non-nuclear, that will allow the U.S. to rapidly and accurately strike distant targets.'

The fact that the U.S. Space Command's program is an aggressive one is announced in the logo of one of its divisions: In your face from outer space."[527]

Are these guys overcompensating for something, or did they not play enough army as young children?

My, we have come a very long way as a civilized society, haven't we? Obviously, there are and were very strong forces that violently opposed President Kennedy's ideals and intentions for a strong, fair, and just nation and peaceful world. For the readers who may be more interested in President John F. Kennedy's assassination, the author could not more highly recommend *Final Judgement, the Missing Link in the JFK Assassination Conspiracy* by noted author Michael Collins Piper, who has also authored *The High Priests of War, The Secret History of How America's "Neo-Conservative" Trotskyites Came to Power and Orchestrated the War Against Iraq as the First Step in Their Drive for Global Empire* and his latest work, *The New Jerusalem*.

Earling Carothers "Jim" Garrison, the former District Attorney from New Orleans who conducted the only trial in the assassination of President John F. Kennedy, expressed in 1967:

"What worries me deeply, and I have seen it exemplified in this case, is that we in America are in great danger of slowly eroding into a proto-fascist state. It will be a different kind of fascist state from the one the Germans evolved; theirs grew out of depression and promised bread and work, while ours, curiously enough, seems to be emerging from prosperity. But in the final analysis, it's based on power and on the inability to put human goals and human conscience above the dictates of the state. Its origins can be traced in the tremendous war machine we've built since 1945, the 'military-industrial complex' that Eisenhower vainly warned us about, which now dominates every aspect of our life. The power of the states and the Congress has gradually been abandoned to the Executive Department, because of war conditions; and we've seen the creation of an arrogant, swollen bureaucratic complex totally unfettered by the checks and balances of the Constitution.

527 David Ray Griffin, CSPAN II, Book TV, "9/11 Commission Report Critique," 2005.

In a very real and terrifying sense, our government is the CIA and the Pentagon, with Congress reduced to a debating society. Of course you can't spot this trend to fascism by casually looking around. You can't look for such familiar signs as the swastika, because they won't be there. We won't build Dachaus and Auschwitzes; the clever manipulation of the mass media is creating a concentration camp of the mind that promises to be far more effective in keeping the populace in line. We're not going to wake up one morning and suddenly find ourselves in gray uniforms goose-stepping off to work. But this isn't the test. The test is: What happens to the individual who dissents? In Nazi Germany, he was physically destroyed; here the process is more subtle, but the end results are the same. I've learned enough about the machinations of the CIA in the past year to know that this is no longer the dream world America I once believed in... I've always had a kind of knee-jerk trust in my Government's basic integrity, whatever political blunders it may make. But I've come to realize that in Washington, deceiving and manipulating the public are viewed by some as the natural prerogatives of office. Huey Long once said, 'Fascism will come to America in the name of anti-fascism.' I'm afraid, based on my own long experience that fascism will come to America in the name of national security."[528]

Returning, once again, to the ideals of the late President John F. Kennedy:

"...And we in this hall shall be remembered either as part of the generation that turned this planet into a flaming funeral pyre or the generation that met its vow 'to save succeeding generations from the scourge of war.'

In the endeavor to meet that vow, I pledge you every effort this Nation possesses. I pledge you that we will neither commit nor provoke aggression, that we shall neither flee nor invoke the threat of force, that we shall never negotiate out of fear, we shall never fear to negotiate.

Terror is not a new weapon. Throughout history it has been used by those who could not prevail, either by persuasion or

528 Ahmed, p. 282.

example. But inevitably they fail, either because men are not afraid to die for a life worth living, or because the terrorists themselves came to realize that free men cannot be frightened by threats...

But I come here today to look across this world of threats to a world of peace. In that search we cannot expect any final triumph-for new problems will always arise. We cannot expect that all nations will adopt like systems-for conformity is the jailor of freedom, and the enemy of growth. Nor can we expect to reach our goal by contrivance, by fiat or even the wishes of all.

But however close we sometimes seem to that dark and final abyss, let no man of peace and freedom despair. For he does not stand alone. If we all can persevere, if we can in every land and office look beyond our own shores and ambitions, then surely the age will dawn in which the strong are just and the weak secure and the peace preserved.

Ladies and gentlemen of this Assembly, the decision is ours. Never have the nations of the world had so much to lose, or so much to gain. Together we shall save our planet, or together we shall perish in its flames. Save it we can-and save it we must-and then shall we earn the eternal thanks of mankind and, as peacemakers, the eternal blessing of God."[529]

529 JFK, UN address.

APPENDIX A
9/11 Video Shocks Sacramento Citizens

August 13, 2004
Posted 1:010 AM Eastern
NewsWithViews.com
http://www.newswithviews.com/NWVexclusive/exclusive34.htm 6/2/05

A new 9-11 video was screened in Sacramento, California, leaving the audience stunned. '911 in Plane Site' is basically presented in two parts. The first segment is 52 minutes and designed for showing on television with the balance of a one hour time slot reserved for commercials. Part II continues with more film and analysis. This video is digitally mastered making details sharp and clear.

'911 in Plane Site' presents actual film from that fateful day and careful analysis focusing on the Pentagon and the two World Trade Center buildings. By slowing down the actual news feeds that day from networks like CNN, FOX, the BBC and others, what you see is quite different from what most people saw in "real time" that day. Live footage from the Pentagon and what was missed by most because of the smoke and confusion was captured up close by the media. Following the showing, a retired vet remarked, "How did we miss this all this time? I've seen media clips of the front of that building [the Pentagon] many times, but I wasn't really seeing what was there. I feel sick."

One particular interview that brought gasps from the audience and many looking around with shock etched on their faces was an interview conducted-live at the time-by FOX News. This intense interview with Mark Burnback, an employee of FOX

News, contains the following narrative, paraphrased: Burnback was close to the path of the second plane and had a good long look at what he describes was not a commercial airliner ... The plane had some kind of blue logo on the front near the nose and looked like a cargo plane. This point was driven to the viewer several times along with the comment from this FOX employee that "this plane wasn't from around here or anything you'd see take off from the airport"

Other footage includes several women who had a very clear view watching the second plane hit were yelling, "That wasn't American Airlines... It wasn't American Airlines going into the building." These interviews were played that morning once on FOX News, never to be replayed again, despite the massive saturation and repetition by the media for many days to come.

Other extremely disturbing segments of this video are the clear, slow motion shots of the second plane going into the towers which show a flash right before the nose of the plane hits the building and a pod attached to the bottom of the plane. This strange flash is clearly recorded from four different angles from four different cameras. While there is only one known piece of film showing the first plane hitting the first tower, in slow motion one can clearly see-as with the second plane-a flash from the nose section right before impact? What caused this?

This video raises extremely disturbing questions about the planes that hit the Pentagon and the World Trade Centers, but no conclusions or accusations are made by the commentator. To date, only one piece of film has been released by DoD of the front of the Pentagon. The question raised in the video is where is all the other film footage from the Pentagon? The heart beat of America's military and security, with a building and perimeter loaded with cameras, but no film for the public to view of events as they unfolded except from one camera?

According to the producers, the purpose of '911 in Plane Site' is to demonstrate that Americans saw one thing that morning that was so shocking, so horrific and so massive, the finer details weren't really picked up. The producer reinforces to the viewer that after one broadcast of many very controversial interviews live on the spot, these particular interviews were never broadcast again, i.e. firefighters on the spot talking about the explosions and bombs inside the towers. Since 9-11, it has been reported that "Building Seven" collapsed because of the two World Trade Center towers collapsing. However, the footage on this video tells a different story and raises more questions.

'911 in Plane Site,' produced by Power Hour Productions, leaves one with many questions as demonstrated by a very upset senior citizen who requested her last name be withheld. Mary asked, "If these weren't commercial airliners, where are those flights? Where are the passengers? My, God what really happened that day?" Indeed, this seemed to be the biggest question expressed by viewers after the lights came back on, but for which there were no answers. Some viewers were visibly upset, angry, and "want damn answers" from the Bush Administration. Others just walked out the door in silence. One upset man commented on the way out of the viewing, "It's time to get this on PBS and every investigative news program on TV. We need answers."

NEW 9-11 FILM NOT WELCOME BY SOME

By: Devvy Kidd
August 15, 2004
NewsWithViews.com
http://newswithviews.com/Devvy/kidd56.htm
6/2/05

NWVs recently ran a news item on a new video titled: '911 in Plane Site. There has been a fair amount of mail to NWVs charging this film is nothing but stupid conspiracy theories by people *who have never seen it.*

Please allow me to provide some additional information not covered in the news item. Besides owning a copy of this film, I also attended the screening of this new video and it was very disturbing.

One critic accused the producers of this film as having some sort of agenda to get Kerry elected. Another stated the producers of this film made it up, creating phony film. Mind you, none of these individuals have seen this video; they only read the news item. Some individuals simply shouted in their e-mail that it was all a bunch of "crap" by "right wing wackos." The usual attack the messenger, obfuscate the message.

This film is being distributed by Power Hour Productions, specifically Joyce Riley and Dave vonKleist. Both are talk show hosts. Joyce Riley has been one of the pioneers in exposing gulf war syndrome; she was a Captain in the Air Force Reserve. Joyce has fought for the truth and gone far and above the call of duty to help countless veterans' througout this country. She is truly one of those relentless seekers of truth; the research she has provided and still produces is always backed up by government documents. The producers of this video are making a complimentary copy available to anyone who lost a loved one on 9-11. There is no money being made off this project, it's just another important step sorting out the truth from theories. I receive no compensation for recommending anyone's videos or books.

Because I personally know Joyce and her husband, I also know that all they have done over the years has been done with love and caring for our vets and not for money. They live very modestly in Missouri. They aren't making big bucks like GOP mouthpiece Shawn Hannity or Democrat cheer leader, Susan Estridge-both of whom revere their party's agenda over truth. There will always be attacks on individuals who speak out against government corruption and tyranny. If you're not taking flak, you're not touching a vital nerve. Ask me. After 14 years I know how the game is played and having been the recipient of a number of serious death threats, it hasn't been much fun.

Of course a plane went into the Pentagon-a big commercial airliner. Why, everyone saw it! Let me point out something about 9-11, at least from where I was sitting that day. I turned on my TV at 5:05 am that morning. Other than food and rest room breaks, I did not leave my desk for close to 16 straight hours. Every station on Comcast in Sacramento-unprecedented-carried non-stop coverage, commercial free on all channels. Not just ABC, CBS, NBC, CNN, but FOX, MSNBC, CNBC, TNT, TBS, BBC and all international channels. Unless one was sitting in a television station with 10 or 20 monitors, it would have been impossible to catch every single minute of coverage that day.

What we all saw was in "real time." This film uses the media feed that day from FOX News, CNN and other conglomerates. It's the same news coverage we all saw in bits and pieces. What the producers of the film did was digitize all this media feed and drop it to slow and super slow motion. What you see is different when presented that way. Your eyes and your brain are able to see things you don't necessarily see in real time. The endless hours I watched live on my television was a horrific event, an act of terror so horrible, it was difficult to comprehend everything at the same time. I don't know about everyone else, but I just sat and watched as events unfolded, speechless with a box of Kleenex. I wasn't looking at the live feeds in slow motion, but "real time."

After I saw the media feed from the Pentagon on this new video, it made me ill. My husband, a retired Army Colonel, was stationed there for four years; we both know that massive building. This new video raised a lot of questions, serious questions that most people will have once they see the film. After seeing the slow motion, frame by frame of both planes entering the two World Trade Center towers, it raised a lot of questions, serious questions that most people will have once they see the film. There is analysis on this video from an expert with paragraphs of credentials on the fuel load of Flight 77, how it should have burned and what you see-rather, didn't see until the smoke clears.

Critics who sent NWVs screeching e-mail that this new film is just "right wing crap," without having seen it, demanding that no one question the events of 9-11, I would like to know who gives those folks the right to demand I not ask reasonable questions based on what I can see with my own eyes. I don't tell people how they should think and I highly resent other people insist that their fellow Americans should be damned for asking reasonable questions.

In the event some of these critics aren't up to speed, here's a news flash: The family members of those killed on September 11th also have unanswered questions-serious ones-about what happened that day. Should I demand that these families not question the government's accounting of what happened that day? Is this what it's come down to in America? Too many things don't add up. I don't know where the passengers might be and the narrator of this video doesn't either, but the question is hanging out there. Once you see the frame by frame, super slow motion from many camera angles of those two planes entering the towers, you *will* wonder and ask the same question. I can tell you that intense efforts are being made to gather more documentation on this issue of the passengers. Because there are no answers, dedicated individuals are making extraordinary efforts to get answers-*no matter what the facts bear out in the end.* Only the truth is what's important; not who is right, but what is right.

My guess is the knee jerk reaction from some people isn't difficult to comprehend: If the official story has big holes in it and concrete proof begins to emerge that things are not what's been sold, Americans will go ballistic over the invasion of Afghanistan and Iraq. The weapons of mass destruction justification hasn't panned out, so President Bush used toppling the dictator, Saddam Hussein, as justification for invading Iraq. As with the situation in the Balkans, Afghanistan and Iraq are a bloody mess. People are concerned and have questions. Apparently, some Americans are offended by such independent thinking-especially during an election year.

There is much more to 9-11 than the average American knows or will endeavor to find out. They don't want to know the truth if it conflicts with the official government story line or interferes with their preconceived notion of what *they* need to believe in order to keep their comfort zone and righteous beliefs intact. Sometimes I wonder how civilization ever progressed if every time someone came along with a different idea or belief, the rest of the people would try to silence them because they didn't like what they were hearing or seeing.

For those who choose to criticize something they have never seen, that's certainly their right. For those who are afraid to see for their own eyes a visual presentation that will raise questions about that day, that's certainly their right. For those who are interested in looking at what was in "plane site," just presented in a different technical format, you can order this video by phone (800) 955-0116. As for me, I would like to see answers to the questions raised on the video.

WHAT REALLY HAPPENED ON 9/11?

Dave vonKleist's Documentary
'911 In Plane Site'
Revisits Disaster, Raises Question Of Cover-Up

By W. Leon Smith
ICONOCLAST EDITOR-IN-CHIEF
http://www.iconoclast-texas.com/News/2004/52news01.htm
6/2/05

VERSAILLES, Mo.-What really happened on 9/11/2001? Dave vonKleist, a champion for veterans' rights, has released a documentary featuring video evidence that raises the spectre of a massive cover-up.

Directed by William Lewis, the original 911 In Plane Site has been reincarnated as 911 In Plane Site-The Director's Cut, offering additional footage.

Said vonKleist, "Due to the overwhelming response of 911 In Plane Site, we were able to collect mountains of new footage and photographs from sources all over the world. We can now say, without a shadow of doubt, that we have undeniable evidence of a massive cover-up."

He added, "From the 16 ft. hole in the outer walls of the Pentagon, to the news reports of bombs, explosions, and potential demolition of World Trade Centers 1, 2, and 7, to the strange attachment on the bottom of Flight 175 and the mysterious flashes caught on videotape by at least five separate sources, it is clear-911 was an inside job."

As radio host of The Power Hour, vonKleist explained that the primary mission of the show is to not only focus on the news "the major networks seem to lose," but to emphasize support for the veterans of the United States.

"We have long reported on the experimentation of our troops that has gone on for over 50 years," he said. "We serve to be a beacon for the truth behind the failure of this country to address the real needs of medical treatment and compensation. We provide a free two-hour video to all Gulf War veterans who write to us and request it," at The Power Hour, P.O. Box 85, Versailles, MO 65084.

The Power Hour can be heard on various stations. Information regarding listings can be accessed at www.thepowerhour.com. The documentary may also be ordered from this site.

In an exclusive interview with The Iconoclast, vonKleist noted that his investigation had raised some serious questions:

How does a plane over 44 feet tall fit into a hole which is only 16 feet in diameter, as shown in the crystal-clear photographic evidence taken at the Pentagon?

Why does photographic evidence taken moments after the event show no wreckage on the lawn of the Pentagon?

Why weren't America and the rest of the world shown the video and photos of the Pentagon, before the outer wall collapsed?

Why is there a "pod" attached to the bottom of Flight 175 and what purpose did it serve in the attacks?

What is the bright flash seen right before impact on both the North Tower and the South Tower, captured on video by five independent cameramen?

Why did a FOX News employee report seeing no windows on Flight 175, a commercial United Airlines jetliner?

Why were there numerous reports of bombs and explosions going off in and around the World Trade Center before any buildings collapsed?

Why did firefighters, reporters, and other on-the-scene eyewitnesses describe a demolition-like, pancake collapse of buildings One, Two, and Seven?

The documentary explores these questions with video, "some of which was broadcast only once as live reports." noted vonKleist, who was able to obtain footage that he says has since been kept from public scrutiny.

During an hour-long question-and-answer session, vonKleist discussed the documentary and the thoughts behind it with the Iconoclast's W. Leon Smith:

ICONOCLAST: Can you tell me about the Power Hour?

vonKleist: Well, we've been on the air for I guess about 4 ½ years now, and we sort of report all the news that they hope and pray you never hear.

I co-host a program with my wife, Joyce Riley, who's been an activist for veterans for many years, has been a spokesperson for the American Gulf War Veterans Association, and has been basically trying to draw attention to the fact that our military has been used as guinea pigs for decades and the first cold war was no different.

We have guys that are sick and dying and continue to be sick and continue to die and who are starting to come back sick and now they're dying, so this thing is happening all over again. But anyway, she and I co-host the radio talk show. She's kind of like the meat and potatoes of the information, and I'm the salt and pepper and occasional cayenne.

ICONOCLAST: Do you have support of a lot of veterans?

vonKleist: Oh, we sure do. We've been in contact with veterans. We offer them free information. We have been since 1995. Any veteran of the Gulf War or even Vietnam that writes to us and asks for information, we'll send them a free video, we send out document packages.

In many cases if they are ill and they're having medical problems, we send them some free products that may help them or may not. We don't want to make any claims, for obvious reasons, but we try to help them out any way that we can because they've definitely been given the short end of the stick by the Veterans Administration and their government officials.

ICONOKLAST: So your wife is the one who got you into this by her being in support of the veterans real strong? Is that what you're saying?

vonKleist: I was sort of into it on my own. I lived up in the north-east. Joyce was living in Houston and I was hosting a radio talk show in Waterbury, Connecticut and I heard her on another radio talk show and called her up and invited her to come on my program.

I've been in broadcasting since the late 70s, so I'm no stranger to broadcasting. I was doing my own radio show when she was doing a radio show in Houston. That's basically how we met, through radio, and eventually joined forces in 1996, and we got married, and we've been fighting together ever since.

ICONOCLAST: What about your background... where did you grow up?

vonKleist: Well, I grew up all over the place actually. My father was in the Air Force. As a child I lived in New York City; Miami, Florida; San Antonio; Anchorage, Alaska; Cape Cod, Mass; and a couple other places in between. I don't even remember at this point.

ICONOCLAST: What called your attention to the 911 situation?

vonKleist: On Sept. 11, Joyce and I were on the air. We had just gone on live at 9:00 eastern time, 8:00 central. At that particular time the north tower had already been struck and all the television coverage was live, so we went on the air at the exact top of the hour and the first thing I did before I even said "Good Morning" was "Ladies and Gentlemen, wherever you are, whatever you're doing, stop, run to your VCR, put a blank tape in, and begin recording any network you can get good reception on."

And as a result we ended up with a lot of video tapes that people copied and sent to us with coverage of all the different networks. Now, at the time we didn't quite know what to do with them. I basically put them aside, put them on the shelf, because I think for the first month America and the world was in shock. I don't think anyone was in a position to really start beginning all kinds of investigations and all that and was basically trying to heal.

In February, I believe, of 2002, there was a website that we came across entitled "Hunt the Boeing! And Test Your Perceptions!" and that was raising questions as to whether or not a 757 had hit the Pentagon.

When I first heard this, I, along with almost everybody else in the country said, "These people must be crazy. These Frenchies are nuts. I've gotta prove them wrong."

So I went to the magazines that we had purchased at the supermarket, People magazine, Newsweek, Time, and all the other commemorative editions. There must have been a dozen of them at one time, and I started going through all the photographs to try to find any photographic evidence that supported the contention that a 757 hit the Pentagon and the more that I looked, the more questions were raised as to whether or not that had actually happened.

So after going through this, I began to come to the conclusion that maybe these questions were very valid ones and maybe we should consider that maybe something else had happened at the Pentagon and that a 757 strike was a cover story.

So I ended up writing an article entitled "From Deception to Revelation." The day that we posted it on our website, powerhour.com, I received an e-mail with a series of photographs that were taken before the collapse of the outer ring.

Now, most Americans have never seen these photographs and, in fact, most Americans see the pictures of the collapse of the Pentagon and assume that that was what happened as a direct result of the strike of 757. Well, the simple fact is that that collapse did not occur until 20 or 30 minutes after "the event." Now these photographs that were taken before the collapse clearly show the firefighters arriving at the scene and pulling hoses off of their trucks and the flame retardant foam being sprayed down on the face of the Pentagon. They also clearly show that there was a small hole about 16 to 20 feet and no wreckage. The question is how do you take a 757, cram it into a 20 foot hole and leave no wreckage outside. So these were very legitimate questions.

I have to assume, Leon, that you've seen all of this information.

ICONOCLAST: Oh yes... About how many copies have you distributed? Is it getting up to the public?

vonKleist: Oh, absolutely. I know that the first release was somewhere between 15 and 20 thousand. The new release is just now getting out there. I haven't even taken a count yet. We're just now starting to get these out. We do have a group in Japan that contacted us a while back and they wanted to make a Japanese translation and distribute it over there, and that's done. As a matter of fact I got a copy in the mail last week. They're already out there with a Japanese translation. There's also a book that goes along with the English and Japanese and photographs. So I mean this is getting very serious legs. It's already been translated into Spanish, and as we speak it's being translated into Arabic, Russian, Pharisee, Korean, Ti, and Chinese. So it's going all over the world right now.

ICONOCLAST: Have any members of Congress or the Senate seen this?

vonKleist: All I can say is that we've sent copies to Washington. We sent them certified return receipts to representatives. One of our listeners in Florida made a donation so that we would send a copy to every one of his state representatives which we did, certified return receipt, and I would say about half of them came back unopened.

So the silence is deafening.

We did send copies to the major agencies in Washington D.C. along with a letter.

If you go to the website, 911 In Plane Site, and look for the heading that says DOD Response, you will see a copy of the letter that we sent along with the copy of the video and you will see a copy of the one and only response that we have received and it just so happens to be sent from Rumsfeld's office and they did not address any of the questions that were raised.

We asked six specific questions in this letter and they didn't address one of them.

The only one that they did touch upon in regard to the Pentagon was a statement that they said, "We are not interested in contributing to conspiracy theories." So they won't address this information. They won't even acknowledge the questions let alone give answers.

ICONOCLAST: If that's the case, then as far as U.S. Congress and Senators, half of them came back unopened?

vonKleist: The ones that we sent out, yes.

ICONOCLAST: What is your goal in this?

vonKliest: I'm trying to avert a global thermo-nuclear catastrophe. We have a president of the United States that thinks nothing about going on worldwide television discussing a possible preempted strike against countries like Iran and North Korea, and yet our country now has been found out to have launched two wars based upon bad Intel.

They said that they had WMDs. We never found them.

They said that they were bringing in materials for developing nuclear weapons. That's turned out to be false. So the information that was given to the American people to justify the current war we're fighting over there in Iraq and the one that we had in Afghanistan were based upon misinformation and propaganda.

The world knows this and yet the United States continues its acts of aggression, so when George W. is on television and talks about a pre-empted strike, I can't help but think that there are many, many, many other countries looking in our direction considering the same option.

ICONOCLAST: So there may be a bad Intel as far as what they may do to us?

vonKleist: Absolutely. Again, we had the Tony Blair issue talking about WMD, the nuclear materials from Nigeria. We had Colin Powell testify before the UN and we know that he was lying too. And this is the information they used to legitimize our launching an attack half a world away.

How can we as Americans say that we love our country and that we're patriotic Americans when we have a government that is willing to lie to launch a war and then when we find out that they were lying we do nothing to them?

ICONOCLAST: As far as the major media goes, have you been interviewed several times or at all?

vonKleist: It depends on what you define as mainstream media.

ICONOCLAST: Well, I would say big daily papers, like the New York Times perhaps or FOX Network or MSNBC.

vonKleist: We've had contacts from them. "Would you please send us a copy of your DVD for a review?" And I'd be more than happy to. We send them off to them and then we never hear from them again.

The mainstream, big time networks, at this point, are just absolutely silent on this subject, with the exception of the past couple of weeks they have had Jimmy Walter on.

My particular take is that the mainstream media are directly involved in the cover-up of all this information. A perfect example in that particular interview with Geraldo, he did show a couple of clips. There were four clips, but they didn't show you the other side of the clip. They cut the clip off each time before we got to the salient point. It's sort of like setting up a joke and not telling people the punch line. They did that four times.

Then, again, if you look at the whole thing at our website you'll see how they handled the clips and you'll see the full clip. They took it off before it showed the full information.

ICONOCLAST: Have you had any repercussions, threats from the public?

vonKleist: We believe that the powers that be do not want this infomation out there. My director, William Lewis, who did a marvelous job with this thing and has been a videographer for years, sent down the master for the duplication of the DVD and for whatever reasons it would not read properly.

So he burned another master and sent that down and we sent it with FedEx and when that one got there it wouldn't read properly either. He had known the person at the duplication plant for some time, and they know each other, and the duplication guy knows that William knows what he's doing. So they got on the phone here and he said well what is the problem?

The duplication guy said he would take a look at this thing on the scope to see what the problem was and it turns out that there was a very lightly etched, very strategically placed laser cut on the surface of the DVD, the master.

This had been sent not once, but twice by Federal Express, so I'm not saying that somebody busted into that envelope and did that, but the disk went from William's machine into the envelope into these guys' hands. So I don't know whether there was sabotage or what but that's basically what happened. Actually there were a total of five different attempts to get this video into their hands. So there's something going on. I don't know what it is. I can't say and I won't say, but there's something wrong in this picture.

ICONOCLAST: So they need to reopen the 911 investigation you think?

vonKleist: What investigation? I don't believe that there was one at all. There's something really wrong in this country when you can spend nearly $800 million investigating Monica Lewinski and a cigar and yet you look at the situation with the Sept. 11 attack and how much they have spent? $60-65 million? What's wrong with this picture?

ICONOCLAST: So you get these out, people become aware of it and what do they do? What needs to happen to remedy this attack?

vonKleist: The general public has no clue as to what it takes to be a patriotic American anymore.

The fact of the matter is that the only way to get a rise out of the American people today is to cancel a beer delivery and one football game We have become so complacent and apathetic that you can have horrendous acts of treason happening right under your nose, such as the case that is going on with our veterans, and yet the people will sit back and do absolutely nothing. They don't want to be the first ones on the dance floor. They don't want to apply elbow grease. They don't want to get their fingernails dirty. They don't want to get involved. They don't want to stick it out.

The sad fact is that we as Americans should be proud to be the first ones on the dance floor to get the party going. And unfortunately that's not the case anymore.

People don't want to know this type of information because along with knowledge comes responsibility and nobody wants to be responsible. Nobody wants to say "Hey, look. I'm gonna have to go to that demonstration." Oh, you know, demonstrations went out in the 60s. People buy into the propaganda or the brainwashing all these years. All the "My vote doesn't count" or "I'm only one person" or "What can I do?" All of this stuff serves one purpose and that's to basically emasculate or neuter anybody from actually getting involved.

Now I hate to coin a phrase that's been demonized by the powers that be, but nonetheless it was said by Thomas Jefferson that the tree of liberty must occasionally be nourished by the blood of tyrants and patriots. And the sad fact of the matter is that we are so far down the road of tyranny in this country it's blatantly obvious; but, unfortunately, most of our countrymen wouldn't recognize tyranny or treason if it slapped them in the face. It's sad, but that's where we are right now.

The whole point of this project is to wake people up, get them involved, and help them to understand how far down the road we have gone and how far away from our Constitution we have strayed.

ICONOCLAST: How long did it take you to produce the tape?

vonKleist: It's been an ongoing exercise. We started really getting involved with this last spring. The initial effort was probably about three months: video taping segments, redoing segments. William Lewis was incredible putting this whole thing together. We put that out there and it came out, I guess it was in July. Maybe it wasn't three months we worked on it, maybe it was two months. Well, right after that we started getting even more information. People found out that somebody had done a project about raising these questions and then we start getting more information, brown manila envelopes with video tapes in there, you know.

ICONOCLAST: Did other people have the same questions?

vonKleist: Well, yeah. People have been asking questions since it happened.

There have been other videos out there seen in certain circles as conspiracy theory videos.

Mine's been lumped in with that, too, and that's why I was very careful to explain specifically the definition of conspiracy theory in the very beginning (of the documentary) and I won't take your time to do that. If you've seen the video you know what that is and I also gave an example of a conspiracy theory in regards to Condoleeza Rice's statement about they'll discuss the evidence in due time. That, by definition, is a conspiracy theory.

When you charge somebody with conspiracy or point a finger at one person, in this case Osama bin Laden and the Taliban, you say "You did Sept. 11. Well, we can't prove it, but you did it. We've got the proof, but we'll show it to you when we're good and ready, but you did it."

If you don't prove it, that is a conspiracy theory. What else can we define it as?

So Rice and the Bush administration has launched two wars a half a world away, they've killed tens of thousands of innocent men, women, and children, they've contaminated the entire Middle East region with depleted uranium to the tune of 4.5 billion years over a conspiracy theory.

Now you tell me who the bad guys are.

It certainly isn't me putting together some sort of a video or anybody else out there that is questioning the absence of our administration.

We have every reason to question them and for them to go on television, and discuss a preempted strike against Korea or Iran. What makes us think that the rest of the world isn't considering the same action toward us? This is why we did this project. Because we are trying to wake up America and the rest of the world as to what is going on in this country and get people to stop the madness. If that means that the Bush administration has to be impeached, whatever, I don't care. This is not a partisan issue. It's not right vs. left, its right vs. wrong. If Al Gore had been elected, and the same thing had happened, we'd be screaming about it against Al Gore.

The official story of what happened on Sept. 11 has everybody scratching their heads, except for those who are purporting the official story.

Anybody out there that has any skill whatsoever is looking at things like the passport that was found at the world trade center. How is this possible? All kinds of information that has everybody shaking their heads saying "This doesn't make sense," but when you factor in the possibility and consider the concept that government officials or agencies or somebody higher up had something to do with the planning of the execution of attacks on Sept. 11, all of a sudden things start to make sense.

Now as they say, those who forget their history are destined to repeat it.

They also say that the definition of insanity is doing the same thing and expecting different results. With that in mind, I want to go visit our history, because I don't want to have to repeat it. Now we just celebrated, if that's the right word, the anniversary of Pearl Harbor. Now Pearl Harbor has now become common knowledge that that attack was not the surprise that we all thought it was. There have been books written on the subject. Retired Lt. Commander Ken Landis has written a book. We had him on as a guest several months ago, so we now know that the attack was not a surprise. They've done television programs on the History Channel, National Geographic, that they knew two days ahead of time that it was going to happen but they did nothing to stop it. The reason is they obviously thought they needed an entry point into Second World War.

In 1964, we come across the North Woods Document drawn up by the joint chiefs in whom they had planned to shoot down our own planes, sink our own battle ships, and conduct terrorist attacks on our own soil so that they could blame it on the Cubans and escalate hostility during the Cuban Missile Crisis.

So if you couple these two factors in, showing that they're willing to sacrifice two thousand of our service personnel, men and women, innocent people, they're willing to sacrifice them to serve their purpose to get into a war. Now you couple that with the idea that they have the mindset where they're willing to shoot down our own planes, sink our own ships, and have terrorist attacks on our own soil, again, killing our own people, why is it so far out of the realm of possibilities that people could consider that they would conduct such an attack with their own country at Sept. 11?

People would ask the question why. Well, let's look at the world situation. How many world super powers are there right now? We're the only one. What is the biggest business in the U.S. if not the world? Defense contracting. So if we're the only world super power and how secure financially do you think that these contractors are feeling right about now? Not real secure. They have to have a war, or else they won't make money. They have to have a threat or they won't make money. You need a bogeyman.

Now you look at Russia. Russia's our biggest friend now supposedly. China's our biggest trading partner. We don't have a world bogeyman. These guys are feeling really insecure right now that have defense contracts. The bottom line here is that these guys are going to benefit tremendously from a war. What's a better war to have than a war with a nameless, faceless enemy with no country that can strike anytime of the day, a war on freedom, a war on terror that Dick Cheney said could go on for decades?

You have to ask the question, "Who benefits?" Now we've got all these different people involved. You mentioned the bin Laden family. How is it that they hopped on these planes and got them out of here? The bin Laden family has been in business with the Bush family since through the Carlyle group for a long time. You look at the Halliburton, Carlyle group, Brown and Root, all of these big businesses. Always the same characters in closed bids that end up with these government contracts. And then we say, well wait a second, if this is all so true, why don't we hear about it on 20/20? How come Dan Rather doesn't tell us about it? Well, for instance, NBC is owned by G.E. #6 defense contractor. See, it's a conflict of interest here.

They took the ceiling off on how many radio stations you can own in the market, so now they've just basically taken over the airwaves. They have taken control. I challenge anybody to read the 10 planks of the communist manifesto and compare them to what's going on today. People will be shocked because we are more communist here in this country than they are in Russia.

At what point do we reach when people start busting out the torches and pitch forks and storm the castle? Now I do not believe in violent revolution, I mean I grew up in the 60s: peace, love, the Beatles, you know. I do not believe in violence at all; however, when you stop and look at the situation here, I mean, Thomas Jefferson did tell us that the most important reason for the second amendment was for the people to allow themselves to be protected from the tyranny of government and you couple that with a bumper sticker I saw that changed my life shortly after Lennon's assassination and it said, "Those who beat their guns into plows will plow for those who didn't." That really hit me between the eyes and I realize now at what point again do we break out the torches and the pitch forks. You can't vote them out. We now know that the voting system is very seriously under question. We now know that we can no longer operate under Constitutional law.

I mean, its common knowledge that we work under a uniform commercial code. We don't have a Constitution anymore. You take that into the courtrooms and the judges laugh at you these days. So if you can't vote them out, and they can't be legislated out. What are we left with? We're in a world of hurt in this country.

ICONOCLAST: How do we get out of it?

vonKleist: I'm of the personal belief right now that the only solution is to let this thing collapse under the weight of its own corruption.

ICONOCLAST: Do you think they're going to wake up?

vonKleist: They're going to have to wait until their own ox is gored and not just gored but gored repeatedly because their own ox is being gored and they're just too dumb to realize it at this point.

That's why I said earlier that the only way to get a rise out of the American people is cancel a beer delivery at a football game. Then maybe they'll get upset.

We have a lot of nerve in this country to sing I'm proud to be an American and most Americans blow the dust off of their flags maybe three times a year during Memorial Day, Veterans Day, and Independence Day and then they stand around and sing patriotic songs and half the words they've forgotten anyway. You know, I'm serious.

How many people can sing along with the Star Spangled Banner when it's played at the beginning of a baseball game?

People have forgotten what their heritage is all about.

They've forgotten about the sacrifices of their founding fathers. They've forgotten what true vigilance is all about.

They've forgotten that this country is supposed to be of, by, and for the people and yet we have public servants that live in mansions as the masters of the country which leaves everyone else living like paupers. What's wrong with this picture?

The governor lives in a governor's mansion. What's wrong with that?

We are sadly brainwashed in this country. And the only way it's going to wake up is to, unfortunately, have some great, big calamity and then the sad thing is that most Americans will be running to the same people for help. They'll go running to the government and say "Help. Help us solve this problem!"

The government will say "(evil laugh) we'll be more than happy to."

It's a mess.

"IT'S THE FLASH, STUPID!"

by Dave vonKleist

http://www.911inplanesite.com/flash_article.htm
6/1/05

The controversies over the events of 9/11 have come to a full boil with the publication of the cover story "Debunking 9/11 LIES" in the March, 2005, edition of Popular Mechanics magazine (PM). The interview with the editor in chief James Meigs on CNN's "Anderson Cooper's 360," and the March 5th interview with Ben Chertoff on the Art Bell radio program, represent perfect examples for the continuing controversy. The fact that the mainstream media has completely ignored some of the most significant photos and video clips that irrefutably challenges the "official story" of 9/11 has simply added more fuel to the fire. The increase of support for "911 In Plane Site" has been overwhelming and Popular Mechanics is now being referred to as "Unpopular" Mechanics!

"The Pod" issue has been a source of debate and division and received top billing in PM magazine. The blatant contradictions made by Ben Chertoff and the PM article should raise red flags with anyone with cognitive skills. For example, the PM article claims that the "pod" is nothing more than a reflection of the sun glistening off of the "fairing." Yet Mr. Chertoff said on the Art Bell program that it was mostly caused by a shadow cast by the engine (the Rob Howard photo published in PM clearly shows the shadow moving toward the front of the plane and off the wing.) How can the "pod" be a reflection and a shadow at the same time? This textbook example of double speak designed to confuse the general public is the very reason why this issue will not go away, and will continue to escalate. *However, the "pod" is secondary in importance to the "flash" issue, which has been completely ignored.*

The "flash" is clearly seen in four video clips in the video "911 In Plane Site." CNN's video clip of the plane hitting the south tower is the most widely available and has not been addressed for reasons that will soon become obvious.

There should be no debate that there indeed was a flash that occurred before the plane burrowed into the building. Two questions are raised that alone challenge the official story. First, what does the "flash" have to do with a terrorist inside the cabin brandishing a plastic knife or a box-cutter? Answer: Obviously nothing, and that leads us to the second question. What caused the Flash? There are four possibilities that come to mind:

a) A reflection
b) Sparks from the fuselage striking the building
c) Static discharge
d) Some type of incendiary (bomb or missile)

Using logical deduction, (Occam's Razor) let's examine each possibility.

Reflection. There are two reasons that it could not have been a reflection. First, a reflection is only seen from one angle, not four. Secondly, the flash occurred on the shaded side of the building. Rule out the reflection.

Sparks. As seen in the video clips, the flash occurred *to the right and below center* of the contact point of the fuselage and is clearly seen in the Camera Planet footage. Rule out sparks.

Static discharge. A static discharge would have arced from the nose of the fuselage to the building at the point of impact. As mentioned above, the flash was seen six to ten feet away from the fuselage and in fact is reflected off the fuselage... Additionally, an electric spark travels at the speed of light and would not likely be captured on several frames on each of the four video clips. Rule out static discharge.

Incendiary (bomb or missile). It is not likely that a bomb could have been placed outside the building so close to the point of impact and timed to detonate at the exact time the plane struck the tower. That leaves a missile. If it was a missile, from where could it have been launched? The flash occurred to the right and below center of the fuselage, *directly in line with the anomaly called "the pod."*

A flash is also seen in the video clip of the plane hitting the north tower, which indicates that there was indeed an event that could not in any way be consistent with a simple hijacking. *The entire hijacking story comes into serious question and cannot stand when factoring in "the flash."*

It should be obvious to the casual observer that the flash issue is by itself devastating to the official story as it not only supports the "pod" issue, but indicates that there is yet another cover-up and a patsy story in place. Until the "flash" issue is acknowledged, honestly debated and explained, the controversy will continue to escalate.

The "flash" issue isn't the only issue that has been ignored. The Pentagon issue also continues to boil and will continue to do so until the media addresses the photos taken *before the collapse*.

PM magazine and the networks have yet, to the best of my knowledge, published or broadcast any of the photos that are the entire reason for the controversy.

The video footage and series of photographs taken before the collapse clearly show no crater, no divot in the lawn, no recognizable wreckage (wings, engines, tail, fuselage, wheels, luggage, seats, etc.) and no hole large enough to accommodate a Boeing 757. *"From my close-up inspection, there is no evidence of a plane having crashed anywhere near the Pentagon..."* Jamie McIntyre, September 11, 2001.

The presentation of the "truth" on broadcasts like "Anderson Coopers 360" or "the Art Bell Show" is at best disingenuous but let's call it what it is: A calculated and deliberate fabrication designed to deflect real issues while ridiculing anyone who dares to think outside their "cage." Ben Chertoff stated, "The wing hit the ground and broke off." If the engine hangs down from the wing, it would have hit the ground first but no mention of this fact was made... He also stated that the plane "liquefied" as it entered the building. If that were the case, how would it have pierced three of the rings so cleanly? The PM report is rife with contradictions as are many of the mainstream media reports.

Numerous times the American Society of Civil Engineers video analysis was cited as the authority when it came to the issue of the Pentagon's collapse. However, the computer-generated video has three glaring errors or omissions. First, they forgot to factor in the 18 ½" steel reinforced exterior wall of the outer ring. Secondly, the tail section remains intact as it enters the building despite numerous photos that show no entry hole. And thirdly, the computer analysis omitted the heaviest, densest and hardest pieces of the aircraft-the engines! With "expert" analysis like this, is there any wonder that the "official" story is being questioned at almost every turn?

What is truly a shame is that there are those in the broadcast media that for whatever reason, continue the farce by labeling those asking these questions as "wingnuts" and hide behind a false veil of fairness while citing these "authorities" as the be all and end all of the "truth." Why is an open debate and a presentation of this suppressed evidence not an option for those claiming a righteous demonstration of "freedom of the press?" I would have welcomed anyone with an opposing viewpoint when I was a guest on the George Noorey program and would do so today. In fact, I would challenge James Miegs, Ben Chertoff or anyone else recognized as an "authority" to debate *these* issues *live* on the air on any radio or television program of their choosing. I commend George Noorey for having the courage to bring me on the air to bring these issues to the attention of the American people and if invited again, would certainly not oppose debate with any "authority." It's not only good radio, it's a way for the people to judge for themselves who is telling the truth and who is not. Art, do you hear me?

America and the world are not as dumb as these people apparently think. The stakes are the highest imaginable and this game is for keeps. Unless this subterfuge ceases immediately the rest of the world will no doubt see the United States as the most manipulated, controlled and dangerous country on earth. God help us.

The issues raised in this article are barely a scratch in the surface of the many inconsistencies in the official story of 9/11.

Until these photographs and video clips are presented to the American people and discussed openly and honestly, the controversy will continue to grow! CNN, FOX, CBS, NBC, ABC, and all news agencies must deal with these issues! They will not go away and neither will those of us demanding honesty from the news networks that claim they can be trusted! It is their integrity that is now in serious question, not those of us asking legitimate questions!

Dave vonKleist
(573) 378-6049
The Power Hour
www.thepowerhour.com
Joyce Riley & Dave vonKleist
877-817-9829

APPENDIX B

Open Letter to Art Bell About the Chertoff's, Israel and 9/11

From: Christopher Bollyn, American Free Press, Washington, D.C.
To: Mr. Art Bell, Coast to Coast Radio

Date: March 4, 2005
Re: *Upcoming Radio Interview with 9/11 Propagandist Benjamin Chertoff, cousin of Michael Chertoff, on Saturday, March 5, 2005*

Dear Mr. Bell,

I see that you will interview Benjamin Chertoff, the 25-year-old "senior researcher" of Popular Mechanics and his research and role in producing the current cover story "Debunking the Lies of 9/11," on your show tomorrow night, Saturday, March 5.

As your Coast to Coast network website says about the upcoming Art Bell show: "Research editor for Popular Mechanics magazine, Ben Chertoff, will discuss the 16 most prevalent claims made by conspiratorial theorists regarding 9/11 and how the staff of Popular Mechanics debunked each of them."

COUSIN OF MICHAEL CHERTOFF

Because Benjamin Chertoff is a cousin of Michael Chertoff, the new head of the Dept. of Homeland Security, a massive bureaucratic security agency created as a result of 9/11, I'd like to ask you a few questions:

Do you condone the flagrant and undemocratic nepotism of the Bush administration, for example this Chertoff connection, whereby a senior government official's cousin has written a propaganda piece supporting the government's seriously flawed and incomplete investigation of the events of 9/11?

This is the kind of thing that Saddam Hussein was known for. This is not very American and at all honest journalism.

Will you ask Ben Chertoff about the journalistic ethics practiced by Hearst Corp. and Popular Mechanics in which a cousin of the "home-land security" czar has produced a major propaganda piece in Popular Mechanics which clearly seeks to discredit the citizens' 9/11 investigation and calls serious researchers like myself, Eric Hufschmid, and Dave vonKleist-liars and extremists?

Will you ask Ben, Popular Mechanics "senior researcher" about how "secondary fires" i.e. burning office furniture, supplies and paper, "induced the collapse" of the twin towers, as the FEMA-Building Performance Study conducted by a team headed by Dr. Gene Corely during ONE WEEK, concluded-including the complete collapse of the towers' 47 central columns? (Source: Executive Summary by Gene Corley, FEMA-BPS 2002)

I would advise you to ask him why the Windsor Building in Madrid endured a 24-hour inferno with temperatures of 1,000 Celsius, without collapsing, on Feb. 12-13, 2005.

Will you, on coast-to-coast radio ask Ben about his relationship with his cousin Michael Chertoff. And will you also ask about Mike's dual-national status as an Israeli national by virtue of the fact that his mother was the first hostess with Israel's El Al airlines and a Mossad operative in 1949-1950 during Operation Magic Carpet?

Tip: Ben's mom told me that Ben is a "cousin" of Michael Chertoff the Sec. of DHS...

Mr. Bell, I will be listening. If you fail to openly address and discuss these essential and troublesome facts, I will be forced to accept the conclusion that you are also part of the 9/11 cover up.

Respectfully,
Christopher Bollyn
American Free Press
Washington D.C.
www.americanfreepress.net

THE HIDDEN HAND OF THE CIA-9/11 AND POPULAR MECHANICS POSTED BY: CHRISTOPHER BOLLYN DATE: THURSDAY, 17 MARCH 2005, 8:29 P.M.

THE HIDDEN HAND OF THE CIA AND THE 9/11 PROPAGANDA OF POPULAR MECHANICS

By Christopher Bollyn
Exclusive to American Free Press

A brutal purge of the senior staff at Popular Mechanics preceded the publication of last month's scandalous propaganda piece about 9/11. Pulling the strings is the grand dame of Hearst Magazines and behind the scene is her obscure husband-a veteran propaganda expert and former special assistant to the director of the C.I.A.

The Reichstag fire, a key event in German history, and the steps that followed en suite leading to the Nazi dictatorship of Adolf Hitler, provide remarkable precedents for what occurred in the United States on 9/11-and since.

The fire that consumed the German parliament building on the night of February 27, 1933, is "widely believed," according to Encyclopedia Britannica, to have been contrived by the newly formed Nazi government to turn public opinion against its opponents and allow it to assume emergency powers.

The day after the burning of the Reichstag, the government headed by Adolf Hitler enacted a decree "for the Protection of the People and the State." Hitler's emergency decree dispensed with all constitutional protection of political, personal, and property rights.

Likewise, a month after 9/11 the U.S. Congress passed, without even reading, similar emergency legislation: the Bush administration's USA PATRIOT Act of 2001. The pre-prepared massive security act's long title is "Uniting and Strengthening America by Providing Appropriate Tools Required to Intercept and Obstruct Terrorism."

Within a month of the Reichstag fire, on March 23, 1933, the parliament passed the Enabling Act, whereby its legislative powers were transferred to Hitler's Reich Cabinet. This act, passed by a vote of 444 to 94, legally sanctioned the Nazi dictatorship.

Another parallel is seen in the way George W. Bush and Hitler came to power. Bush obtained the presidency in 2001 through a Supreme Court decision after a flawed and un-counted election, while Hitler secured the German chancellorship through elections in November 1932 in which the Nazi Party failed to win an outright majority.

Hitler's propaganda minister, Joseph Goebbels, is thought to have let arsonists into the parliament building through a tunnel leading from the official residence of Hermann Goring, Reichstag president and Hitler' chief minister.

Goring then presided over the official investigation, which blamed the communists. In a similar manner, the Bush administration openly opposed an independent investigation of 9/11 and fixed blame on Osama bin Laden and 19 Arab terrorists. Based on this official, but unproven explanation for 9/11 the United States has invaded and occupied two Middle Eastern nations.

"DISINFORMATION AND DECEPTION"

"Ninety-five percent of the work of intelligence agencies around the world is disinformation and deception," Andreas von Bulow, former parliamentary official responsible for the budget for Germany's intelligence agencies, told American Free Press in December 2001.

Like Nazi Germany of 1933, American newsstands today carry a mainstream magazine dedicated to pushing the government's "truth" of 9/11 while viciously smearing independent researchers as "extremists" who "peddle fantasies" and make "poisonous claims."

The magazine pushing the government's 9/11 propaganda, Popular Mechanics (PM), is published by the Hearst family. Its March cover story "Debunking 9/11 Lies," has been exposed by credible researchers to contain numerous distortions and flawed conclusions. American Free Press revealed that Benjamin Chertoff, the 25-year-old "senior researcher" who authored the 9/11 article, is related to Michael Chertoff, the new Secretary of the Department of Homeland Security (DHS). The PM article illustrates how a propaganda method, used by dictatorships, is now being employed by the U.S. government: controlling mainstream media outlets to promote its version of 9/11.

The actions of Michael Chertoff concerning the events of 9/11, the non-investigation that followed, the USA PATRIOT Act, and the propaganda being disseminated in PM, are strikingly similar to actions attributed to the Nazi ministers Joseph Goebbels and Hermann Goring.

While Chertoff is the "czar" of DHS, he is not sovereign at PM or Hearst Magazines, its corporate parent. The president of Hearst Magazines, one of the world's largest publishers of monthly magazines with 18 U.S. titles and more than 100 international editions, is Cathleen P. Black, a 60-year old native of Chicago. Black oversees the publication of 175 titles around the world including Cosmopolitan, Harper's Bazaar, Town & Country, Esquire, Good Housekeeping, and Popular Mechanics.

Black is a former president and publisher of USA Today. In 1983, Black was made president of the new newspaper published by Gannett. The following year she was made publisher and soon became a member of Gannett's board of directors.

"Despite her efforts," her biography reads, "USA Today did not show an operating profit in the eight years that Black was there." The newspaper's non-profitability notwithstanding, Gannett paid Black $600,000 a year for her efforts. USA Today reportedly had a circulation of 1.8 million when Black left in 1991. USA Today is often given away free of charge.

Black left USA Today to become president and chief executive of the nascent Newspaper Association of America (NAA), formed on June 1, 1992. She then became the leading spokesperson and lobbyist for the nation's newspaper industry. Black's position at the NAA carried "considerable political heft," Paul Farhi of The Washington Post wrote, "given that the 1,400 members of her organization control the nation's editorial pages."

In 1995, for an annual salary reported to be "in excess of $1 million," Black was hired by Hearst Corp. to head its magazine division. Named by Fortune magazine as one of the Most Powerful Women in American Business, Black sits on the boards of Hearst Corp., the Advertising Council, IBM, and Coca-Cola. She is also a member of the Council on Foreign Relations.

It is often said that USA Today is controlled by the CIA, which, like the paper, is based in McLean, Virginia. The little-known fact that Black is married to Thomas E. Harvey, an obscure lawyer who became a White House Fellow in 1977 and served as "special assistant" to the Director of Central Intelligence (DCI), provides substance to these rumors. Black's corporate biography does not mention her husband.

President Jimmy Carter made Harvey a White House Fellow in May 1977. "In that capacity," Harvey's biography reads, he "served as special assistant to the Director of the C.I.A Following that he held senior appointed positions within the Department of Defense."

The DCI at the time was Stansfield Turner, who had replaced George H.W. Bush.

Prior to serving the CIA, Harvey worked at the New York law office of Milbank, Tweed, Hadley & McCloy. The international law firm, co founded by Morris Hadley, a 1916 member of Yale University's secret society Skull & Bones, has ties to the CIA and lists William H. Webster, DCI from 1987-1991, as a senior partner. Webster also serves on the Homeland Security Advisory Council.

In the 1980s, Harvey served as General Counsel and Congressional Liaison of the U.S. Information Agency, the former external propaganda arm of the U.S. government. Harvey also served as Deputy Assistant Secretary for the Army and Navy. In 1992, Harvey was personnel director for the Bush-Quayle' 92 Campaign.

Calls to the offices of Black and Harvey for the purpose of this article went unanswered.

THE COUP AT POPULAR MECHANICS

In the months leading up to the Chertoff article in PM, a brutal take-over occurred at the magazine. In September 2004, Joe Oldham, the magazine's former editor-in-chief was replaced by James B. Meigs, who came to PM with a "deputy," Jerry Beilinson, from National Geographic Adventure. In October, a new creative director replaced PM's 21-year veteran who was given ninety minutes to clear out of his office.

A former senior editor at PM, who is forbidden from openly discussing the coup at PM, told AFP that the former creative director was abruptly told to leave and given severance pay of two weeks wages for every year spent at PM. "Three or four" people have been similarly dismissed every month since, he said. He said he was astounded that the coup at PM not been reported in the mainstream media.

PM has long been a supporter of the U.S. military. The magazine ran a full-page ad in support of the troops in Iraq and Afghanistan in May 2003. Since the purge last September, however, PM readers have noticed that government propaganda has replaced scientific writing. A letter to the editor in the current issue says, "I think you guys are just another tool in the government's propaganda machine."

SEISMIC EVIDENCE POINTS TO UNDERGROUND EXPLOSIONS CAUSING WTC COLLAPSE BY CHRISTOPHER BOLLYN

American Free Press
http://americanfreepress.net
August 28, 2002

Two unexplained "spikes" in the seismic record from September 11 indicate huge bursts of energy shook the ground beneath the World Trade Center's twin towers-just as the buildings began to collapse. American Free Press has learned of pools of "molten steel" found at the base of the collapsed twin towers weeks after the collapse. Although the energy source for these incredibly hot areas has yet to be explained New York seismometers recorded huge bursts of energy, which caused unexplained seismic "spikes" at the beginning of each collapse. These spikes suggest that massive underground explosions may have literally knocked the towers off their foundations causing them to collapse.

"MOLTEN STEEL"

In the basements of the collapsed towers, where the 47 central support columns connected with the bedrock, hot spots of "literally molten steel" were discovered more than a month after the collapse. Such persistent and intense residual heat, 70 feet below the surface, could explain how these crucial structural supports failed.

Peter Tully, president of Tully Construction of Flushing, New York, told AFP that he saw pools of "literally molten steel" at the World Trade Center. Tully was contracted on September 11 to remove the debris from the site.

Tully called Mark Loizeaux, president of Controlled Demolition Inc. (CDI) of Phoenix, Maryland, for consultation about removing the debris. CDI calls itself "the innovator and global leader in the controlled demolition and implosion of structures."

Loizeaux, who cleaned up the bombed Federal Building in Oklahoma City, arrived on the WTC site two days later and wrote the clean-up plan for the entire operation.

AFP asked Loizeaux about the report of molten steel on the site. "Yes," he said, "hot spots of molten steel in the basements." These incredibly hot areas were found "at the bottoms of the elevator shafts of the main towers, down seven [basement] levels," Loizeaux said. The molten steel was found "three, four, and five weeks later, when the rubble was being removed," Loizeaux said. He said molten steel was also found at 7 WTC, which collapsed mysteriously in the late afternoon.

Construction steel has an extremely high melting point of about 2,800 Fahrenheit (1535 Celsius). Asked what could have caused such extreme heat, Tully said, "Think of the jet fuel."

Loizeaux told AFP that the steel-melting fires were fueled by "paper, carpet and other combustibles packed down the elevator shafts by the tower floors as they 'pancaked' into the basement."

Kerosene-based jet fuel, paper, or the other combustibles normally found in the towers, however, cannot generate the heat required to melt steel, especially in an oxygen-poor environment like a deep basement.

Eric Hufschmid, author of a book about the WTC collapse, *Time for Painful Questions,* told AFP that due to the lack of oxygen, paper and other combustibles packed down at the bottom of elevator shafts would probably be "a smoky smoldering pile."

Experts disagree that jet-fuel or paper could generate such heat. This is impossible, they say, because the maximum temperature that can be reached by hydrocarbons like jet-fuel, burning in air is 1520 F (825 C). Because the WTC fires were fuel rich (as evidenced by the thick black smoke) it is argued that they did not reach this upper limit of 825 C.

The hottest spots at the surface of the rubble, where abundant oxygen was available, were much cooler than the molten steel found in the basements. Five days after the collapse, on September

16, the National Aeronautics and Space Administration (NASA) used Airborne Visible/ Infrared Imaging Spectrometer (AVIRIS) to locate and measure the site's hot spots. Dozens of hot spots were mapped, the hottest being in the east corner of the South Tower where a temperature of 1377 F (747 C) was recorded. This is, however, less than half as hot as the molten steel in the basement.

The foundations of the twin towers were 70 feet deep. At that level, 47 huge box columns, connected to the bedrock, supported the entire gravity load of the structures. The steel walls of these lower box columns were 4 inches thick.

CENTRAL COLUMNS SEVERED

Videos of the North Tower collapse show its communication mast falling first, indicating that the central support columns must have failed at the very beginning of the collapse. Loizeaux told AFP, "Everything went simultaneously."

"At 10:29 the entire top section of the North Tower had been severed from the base and began falling down," Hufschmid writes. "If the first event was the falling of a floor, how did that progress to the severing of hundreds of columns?

Asked if the vertical support columns gave way before the connections between the floors and the columns, Ron Hamburger, a structural engineer with the FEMA assessment team said, "That's the $64,000 question."

Loizeaux said, "If I were to bring the towers down, I would put explosives in the basement to get the weight of the building to help collapse the structure."

SEISMIC "SPIKES"

Seismographs at Columbia University's Lamont-Doherty Earth Observatory in Palisades, New York, 21 miles north of the WTC, recorded strange seismic activity on September 11 that has still not been explained.

While the aircraft crashes caused minimal earth shaking, significant earthquakes with unusual spikes occurred at the beginning of each collapse. The Palisades seismic data recorded a 2.1 magnitude earthquake during the 10-second collapse of the

South Tower at 9:59:04 and a 2.3 quake during the 8-second collapse of the North Tower at 10:28:31.

The Palisades seismic record shows that-as the collapses began-a huge seismic "spike" marked the moment the greatest energy went into the ground. The strongest jolts were all registered at the beginning of the collapses, well before the falling debris struck the earth. These unexplained "spikes" in the seismic data lend credence to the theory that massive explosions at the base of the towers caused the collapses.

A "sharp spike of short duration" is how seismologist Thorne Lay of Univ. of California at Santa Cruz told AFP an underground nuclear explosion appears on a seismograph.

The two unexplained spikes are more than twenty times the amplitude of the other seismic waves associated with the collapses and occurred in the East-West seismic recording as the buildings began to fall.

Lerner-Lam told AFP that a 10-fold increase in wave amplitude indicates a 100-fold increase in energy released. These "short-period surface waves," reflect "the interaction between the ground and the building foundation," according to a report from Columbia Earth Institute.

"The seismic effects of the collapses are comparable to the explosions at a gasoline tank farm near Newark on January 7, 1983," the Palisades Seismology Group reported on Sept. 14, 2001.

One of the seismologists, Won-Young Kim, told AFP that the Paliades seismographs register daily underground explosions from a quarry 20 miles away. These blasts are caused by 80,000 lbs. of ammonium nitrate and cause local earthquakes between Magnitude 1 and 2. Kim said the 1993 truck-bomb at the WTC did not register on the seismographs because it was "not coupled" to the ground.

Experts cannot explain why the seismic waves peaked before the towers hit the ground. Asked about these spikes seismologist Arthur Lerner-Lam, director of Columbia University's Center for Hazards and Risk Research told AFP, "This is an element of current research and discussion. It is still being investigated."

"Only a small fraction of the energy from the collapsing towers was converted into ground motion," Lerner-Lam said. "The ground shaking that resulted from the collapse of the towers was extremely small."

Last November, Lerner-Lam said, "During the collapse, most of the energy of the falling debris was absorbed by the towers and the neighboring structures, converting them into rubble and dust or causing other damage-but not causing significant ground shaking."

Evidently, the energy source that shook the ground beneath the towers was many times more powerful than the total potential energy released by the falling mass of the huge towers.

TEST FOR EXPLOSIONS?

While steel is often tested for evidence of explosions, despite numerous eyewitness reports of explosions in the towers, the engineers involved in the FEMA-sponsored building assessment did no such tests.

Dr. W. Gene Corley, who investigated for the government the cause of the fire at the Branch Davidian compound in Waco and the Oklahoma City bombing, headed the FEMA-sponsored engineering assessment of the WTC collapse. Corley told AFP that while some tests had been done on the 80 pieces of steel saved from the site, he said he did not know about tests that show if an explosion had affected the steel. "I'm not a metallurgist," he said.

SELLING THE EVIDENCE OVERSEES.

Much of the structural steel from the WTC was sold to Alan D. Ratner of Metal Management of Newark, New Jersey, and the New York based company Hugo Neu Schnitzer East. Ratner, who heads the New Jersey branch of the Chicago-based company, quickly sold the WTC steel to oversees companies, reportedly selling more than 50,000 tons of steel to a Shanghai steel company known as Baosteel for $120 per ton. Ratner paid about $70 per ton for the steel.

Other shipments of steel from the WTC went to India and other Asian ports. Ratner came to Metal Management after spending years with a Sydney-based (Australia) metal trading firm known as SimsMetal.

E-MAIL EXCHANGES BETWEEN CHRIS BOLLYN OF AMERICAN FREE PRESS AND RABBI JONATHAN BARNETT OF WORCESTER POLYTECHNIC INSTITUTE

Sent: Sunday, February 20, 2005 10:14 PM
Subject: RE: Yes, BUT what happened to the core columns?

Dear Jonathan,

First of all regarding the discovery of "molten steel" in the lowest basement of the WTC towers:

This was first reported to me by Peter Tully, owner of Tully Construction of the Bronx, who was one of the four main contractors for the clean up of the WTC site.

I then asked Mark Loizeaux, of Controlled Demolition Inc., about this molten steel. He confirmed it and added the details.

Laymen? Rabbi Barnett, I understand that you are a "man of the cloth" but Mr. Tully and Mr. Loizeaux were at the site when you were not.

From my careful reading of the FEMA-sponsored BPS, I gather that you and your team-mates were at the site for all of ONE WEEK: Page I-2 says, "... the BPS Team mobilized to the WTC site and conducted field observations DURING the week of October 7, 2001.

If this is true, of course you didn't see the molten steel at the bottom of the WTC, because you and your fellow engineers were not at the site.

Rabbi Barnett, Messrs Tully and Loizeaux are not to be so easily dismissed as "laymen," they are professionals who deal with demolitions everyday.

Rabbi Barnett, you seem to be an honest man, why don't you take the bull by the horns and deal with these outstanding questions. You certainly know that the whole truth about 9/11 has not been presented in the BPS.

Do you want to be associated with a bunch of liars who were complicit in hiding the truth about 9/11 from the American people?

I don't think you want to be a part of this nasty cover-up. We know it's a cover-up and that big people and nations are involved. Clearly Israelis had prior knowledge, e.g. Odigo.

We deserve the truth, Rabbi Barnett, and you can help bring that truth to the people.

Let's get to the bottom of this. Enough bull shit.

Best wishes,
Christopher Bollyn

"Barnett, Jonathan Ross" ...wrote:

Chris:

I'll try to explain it again. The fire proofing on some of the core columns was dislodged by the aircraft. As the fires burned, these damaged columns weakened, causing the other columns to carry more and more of the load (this is called load redistribution). Eventually this load redistribution caused one column after another to fail, stressing more columns, until there wasn't enough strength left to support the building, leading to the progressive collapse that caused the towers to fail.

The other difference is that the core in the Windsor building was designed to carry a higher percentage of the wind load then the core of the twin towers. Thus the Windsor building's core was stronger than the twin tower's core. Finally, the Windsor building's core fire proofing was not dislodged by an aircraft. It was reinforced concrete core where the concrete surrounding the reinforcement provided the fire resistance.

There was no sign of molten steel ever found. There were layperson's observations that such steel did exist. But I have yet to see any real evidence; and as a professional, whenever possible, I work with facts, not speculation. There was steel where, due to contamination by sulfur, a eutectic formed which had a melting point of about 1000C which did evidence rapid erosion which looked like it had melted. In any case, this should be expected from the normal fires you would expect to have occurred in the furnishings and debris field as they burned underground (we've' seen this before in sealed mine fires and garbage dump fires).

I don't know how to make this clearer without a face to face meeting. Come visit me in Australia... I'm willing to donate my time and explain things until you understand these concepts.

Jonathan

Sent: Monday, February 21, 2005 1:22 PM
To: Barnett, Jonathan Ross
Subject: What happened to the core columns?

Dear Jonathan,

Thank you for your response. But your answer didn't touch on the KEY question I have been asking since 2001, which is: "What happened in the WTC to cause the 47 central columns to collapse?"

Mr. Barnett, can you tell me why, in your expert opinion, the entire core section of the twin towers, with 47 steel box columns, failed completely?

Why did this core section not remain standing, as in the Windsor Building in Madrid?

Was there an explosive event that severed these columns from the bedrock of Manhattan? What can explain the fact that molten steel was found at the lowest basement level where these columns met the bed-rock?

Best wishes,
Christopher Bollyn
American Free Press

"Barnett, Jonathan Ross"... wrote:

I do not have first hand knowledge of the Windsor building. I was told by an engineer who has a colleague he spoke to in Madrid that the building's steel façade failed due to the heat of the fire which then led to the subsequent fire spread up the exterior face of the building. I do not know how knowledgeable the LA Times reporter is about the building or what he saw or didn't see, but it is certainly possible and very likely that the "charred steel twisted into destroyed shapes" you say he described, was that of the façade's structural steel. This is consistent with the current news that the building is in no danger of collapse, and does not indicate that the building used a steel framed structure.

Regarding your question about steel in concrete: the correct term for this type of construction material is reinforced concrete. Concrete is weak in tension and needs to be reinforced to compensate for that weakness. We typically use materials like steel to provide such reinforcement. The steel is often in the form of long rods buried in the concrete. The concrete surrounding the steel also acts to insulate the steel from heat due to fire. As a result, concrete usually requires no additional fire protection, unlike steel beams and columns which are sometimes protected from the heat of fire by applying an insulating layer of material. In the case of the WTC, as the BPAT suggested and as NIST has confirmed, the insulation was removed from key core columns due to the abrasive action of the incoming aircraft, leaving the remaining, now uninsulated steel exposed to the heat of the fires.

I hope this makes it clear. Bottom line: based on what I now know, the Windsor building was built using a structural frame (the part of the building providing the main support for the structure) consisting of reinforced concrete, the WTC used structural steel. Two different materials of construction with different needs with respect to protection from fire.

I hope this clears things up. Please don't hesitate to ask if there are still some areas of confusion. I know I haven't answered your questions bullet by bullet, but I am trying to clear up the general concepts. It's hard to talk about specifics when there is such a misunderstanding of the global.

Finally, have you read the NIST report? After millions of dollars and two years of study they have filled in some of the details from the BPAT work. I hope you find it of value.

Jonathan

Sent: Sunday, February 20, 2005 8:07 AM
To: Barnett, Jonathan Ross
Subject: 9/11: AFP Questions on Concrete vs. Steel Debate

TO: Jonathan Barnett
Professor of Fire Protection Engineering
Worcester Polytechnic Institute

Dear Professor Barnett,

You say that the Windsor building is "a concrete framed structure but what are you saying about the steel framing that supports the concrete? Are you saying that the construction of the Windsor Building and the World Trade Center differ in a way that prevents the performance of the buildings from being compared?

This is how the steel framing in the Windsor Building has been reported:

"As the fire burned into the night, all that was visible of the upper parts of the building was the flaming, gutted remains of steel-reinforced concrete floors."

"The morning light exposed the damage from the spectacular fire that lit up the night and attracted thousands of onlookers. The top floors were little more than charred steel twisted into destroyed shapes. Everything else was burned away." (L.A. Times)

And a non-published source:

"Again, as hammer dog would say-what are you talking about, enough of your damn vague references for us to guess responses to. The Madrid building was steel with concrete floors-concrete is less stable during fire than steel-so WTF is your point? and post it, don't allude vaguely to it!"

O.K.

I understand that the core of the Windsor Building had more concrete than the periphery, so was the case in the WTC. The WTC core of the towers had 5" thick concrete floors while the outside areas were 4."

Is it that the central support columns of the Windsor Building are clad in concrete? Is that the case, and if so, is that the primary difference? Is it not the case that the central columns of the WTC were also clad, but with dry wall?

But the fundamental question that I have been asking since September 2001 is: "What happened in the WTC to cause the 47 central columns to collapse?"

This is the key question that the BPS does NOT answer.

If we accept the theory that the fires caused the trusses to weaken and fail, this still does not explain what caused the 47 huge box columns to fail-at the below-ground level.

Why did the central columns and core section of the WTC collapse COMPLETELY, while they remained standing full length in Madrid?

Are you saying that concrete is the difference. Does concrete perform this much better in extreme fire conditions?

Many thanks,
Christopher Bollyn

"Barnett, Jonathan Ross". ... wrote:

In addition to my earlier reply... I learned today that the Windsor building is a concrete framed structure, not steel as you reported. There is little to compare to 9/11... sorry

Sent: Friday, February 18, 2005 6:14 AM
To: Barnett, Jonathan Ross
Subject 9/11 Collapses-Open Letter to Dr. Gene Corley
From: Christopher Bollyn, American Free Press, Washington, D.C. To: Jonathan Barnett, Worcester Polytechnic Institute

9/11 COLLAPSE-OPEN LETTER TO DR. GENE CORLEY

Posted By: Christopher Bollyn
Date: Thursday, 17 February 2005, 12:27 p.m.

From: Christopher Bollyn, American Free Press, Washington, D.C.
To: Dr. W. Gene Corley, Senior Vice President

Construction Technology Laboratories, Skokie, IL
Note: Dr. W. Gene Corley was Team Leader of the FEMA-Sponsored building assessments done by engineers of the Murrah Federal Building, Oklahoma City (1995) and the World Trade Center, New York City (2001)
RE: Comparison of Performance of World Trade Center Towers and Windsor Building (Madrid, Spain) After Intense and Prolonged Fire of Feb. 12-13, 2005
Date: February 17, 2005

Dear DR. Corley,

In the executive summary of the FEMA-sponsored study entitled World Trade Center Building Performance Study (BPS-2002), you wrote that "secondary fires" caused the twin towers to collapse (p.2):

"The heat produced by this burning jet fuel does not by itself appear to have been sufficient to initiate the structural collapses," you wrote. "However, as the burning jet fuel spread across several floors of the buildings, it ignited much of the buildings' contents, causing simultaneous fires across several floors of both buildings.

"Over a period of many minutes, this heat induced additional stresses into the damaged structural frames while simultaneously softening and weakening these frames. This additional loading and the resulting damage were sufficient to induce the collapse of both structures."

In the section that deals with the collapse of the twin towers, the BPS says (p. 2-37): "Because the aircraft impacts into the two buildings are not believed to have been sufficient to cause collapse without the ensuing fires, the obvious question is whether the fires alone, without the damage from the aircraft impact, would have been sufficient to cause such a collapse... it is impossible, without extensive modeling and other analysis, to make a credible prediction of how the buildings would have responded to an extremely severe fire in a situation where there was no prior structural damage."

Dr. Corley, do you agree that the Windsor Building fire in Madrid provides an excellent real-world model to show how the twin towers should have responded to "an extremely severe fire" alone?

The Windsor Building has central support columns in its core section, which is similar to the construction of the twin towers. As you know, the central core supported the gravity load of the twin towers.

Why did the 47 central columns of the WTC towers fail completely while similar columns in the Windsor Building remain standing-even supporting a building crane as the attached photo shows?

Respectfully,
Christopher Bollyn
American Free Press
Washington, D.C.

IS MITRE CORP. THE TROJAN HORSE OF 9/11?

Posted By: Christopher Bollyn
Date: Friday, 1 April 2005, 1:38 p.m.
IS DEFENSE CONTRACTOR MITRE CORP
THE TROJAN HORSE OF 9/11?

By Christopher Bollyn
American Free Press
http://www.americanfreepress.net

Did a central controller with "super user" privileges of the command and control systems of the Department of Defense, NORAD, the Air Force, and the FAA, control the aerial attacks of 9/11? There is only one agency that has that capability-a little-known private company known as MITRE Corp.

There are basically two versions of events surrounding the terror attacks of September 11, 2001. There is the government version, propagated by the controlled media, which claims that 19 Arab terrorists, organized by Osama Bin Laden in Afghanistan, hijacked 4 passenger aircraft and used them to attack the World Trade Center and the Pentagon. This version, used to launch the "war on terror" and two invasions in the Middle East, is challenged by a lack of evidence.

On the other hand, a host of unofficial explanations, based on available evidence, make up what can be called the "inside job" or anti-government version. This version basically claims that agents embedded within the U.S. military and intelligence organizations conspired to carry out the terror attacks.

The two foreign nations most often implicated in the unofficial explanations of 9/11 are Israel and Britain. Both countries are supporters and beneficiaries of the Bush administration's "war on terror."

For the Israelis, Iraq, a major threat, was drastically reduced in power and put under military occupation. For the British, a oil-rich territory, Iraq's southern region of BASRA, which it originally occupied in 1914, was reoccupied and its immense oil assets put under control of the Crown.

Royal Dutch Shell and BP, formerly named British Petroleum, are two companies said to be controlled by the Crown, which have posted record profits since 9/11.

While both Britain and Israel have substantial assets and powerful organizations in the United States, proponents of the anti-government version have not explained how a foreign power could manipulate the computer systems of the Federal Aviation Administration (FAA), the North American Aerospace Defense Command (NORAD), and the U.S. Air Force, and thereby control the aerial attacks of 9/11.

When American Free Press interviewed Eckehardt Werthebach, former president of Germany's domestic intelligence service, in December 2001, he said "the deathly precision" and "the magnitude of planning" behind the 9/11 attacks would have required "years of planning."

Such a sophisticated operation, Werthebach said, would require the "fixed frame" of a state intelligence organization, something not found in a "loose group" of terrorists like the one allegedly led by Mohammed Atta. Many people would have been involved in the planning of such an operation, Werthebach said. He pointed to the absence of leaks as further indication that the attacks were "state organized actions." "

Andreas von Bulow, who served on Germany's parliamentary commission and oversaw the three branches of the German secret service, told AFP that he believed that Mossad, Israel's intelligence service, was behind the terror attacks. The attacks, he said, were carried out to turn public opinion against the Arabs and boost military and security spending.

"You don't get the higher echelons," von Bulow said, referring to the "architectural structure" which masterminds such terror attacks. At this level, he said, the organization doing the planning, such as Mossad or British intelligence, is primarily interested in affecting public opinion.

In a recent article in AFP, "The Perfect Terrorist Plan To Level the Twin Towers Created In 1976" by Greg Szymanski, it was reported that the U.S. Army devised a plan in 1976 to bring down the towers using commercial airliners and box cutters as weapons.

At the time, George H.W. Bush was head of the CIA and Martin R Hoffman was Secretary of the Army. Hoffman told AFP that he did not recall being involved in this planning reportedly done by the U.S. Army.

An architect, even of destruction, needs a contractor. Proponents of the anti-government version of 9/11 provide evidence to support their claims, but do not explain how the U.S. military and civil aviation control systems could have been hijacked to allow the aerial attacks to occur. Because the attacks involved systems used by the FAA, NORAD, and the U.S. Air Force, the conspirators would have needed "super user" access to the command and control centers of these three separate organizations.

Super user means the most privileged user on a computerized data system. The super user has complete access to all files on the system. For the previously mentioned agencies, and virtually all other U.S. defense and intelligence organizations, there is one such possible super user: a little-known private not-for-profit organization, based in Bedford, Mass., known as MITRE Corp. MITRE also has a headquarters in McLean, Va., on a campus it shares with Northrop Grumman.

The MITRE Corp. is a major defense contracting organization headed by the former Director of Central Intelligence (DCI), Dr. James Rodney Schlesinger, who was reportedly made DCI at the request of Henry Kissinger in 1973, later served as Secretary of Defense.

Schlesinger, a former director of strategic studies at the RAND Corp., was described in a 1973 biography as a "devout Lutheran," although he was born in New York in 1929 to immigrant Jewish parents from Austria and Russia. Schlesinger earned three degrees from Harvard University.

Schlesinger's father, an accountant, founded the accounting firm Schlesinger & Haas, and was a trustee and chairman of the budget of the Stephen Wise Free Synagogue. His father was also a member of the New York State Grand Lodge of Masons.

The MITRE Corp., of which Schlesinger is chairman of the board of trustees, is connected to the Massachusetts Institute of Technology (MIT). MIT's Lincoln Laboratory and Mitretek Systems of Falls Church, Va. Schlesinger is a senior advisor for the Lehman Brothers investment firm and a member of the Defense Policy Board and advisory council for the Department of Homeland Security (DHS).

The MITRE Corp. has provided computer and information technology to the FAA and the U.S. Air Force since the late 1950's. MITRE is a Federally FUNDED Research and Development Center (FFRDC) for the Dept. of Defense, the FAA, and the Internal Revenue Service.

The chairman of the board of trustees of Mitretek Systems, a spin-off of MITRE Corp., is Martin R. Hoffman, who served as Secretary of the Army when the "perfect terrorist plan" was reportedly prepared in 1976.

MITRE's Command, Control, Communications, and Intelligence (C3I) FFRDC for the Dept. of Defense was established in 1958. The C3I "supports a broad and diverse set of sponsors within the Department of Defense and the Intelligence Community. These include the military departments, defense and intelligence agencies, the combatant commands, and elements of both the Office of the Secretary of Defense and the office of the Joint Chiefs of Staff," according to MITRE's website. "Information systems technology," it says, "coupled with domain knowledge, underpin the work of the C3I FFRDC."

The U.S. Air Force maintains its Electronic Systems Center (ESC) at the Hanscom AFB in Bedford, Mass. The ESC manages the development and acquisition of electronic command and control (C2) systems used by the Air Force.

The ESC is the Air Force's "brain for information, command and control systems," according to Charles Paone, a civilian employee of the ESC. It is the "product center" for the Air Force's Airborne Warning and Control System (AWACS) and Joint Surveillance Target Attack Radar System (J-STARS), Paone said.

Asked about MITRE's role at the ESC, Paone said, "MITRE does the front-end engineering. It's basically our in-house engineer." MITRE employees operate the computer systems at Hanscom AFB, Paone said. MIT's Lincoln Laboratories, the parent of MITRE, is located on the Hanscom AFB.

A second FFRDC, the Center for Advanced Aviation Systems Development (CAASD) provides computer engineering and technology to the FAA. MITRE's support of the FAA began in 1958, when the company was created.

The FAA's Airspace Management Handbook of May 2004, for example, was written and published by the MITRE Corp.

Jennifer Shearman, MITRE's public relations manager for "corporate identity" in Bedford, told AFP that MITRE is a "trusted mentor" for the FAA and is a "unique" provider of "objective and independent" information for the U.S. civil aviation authority.

MITRE's Bedford headquarters are located near Boston's Logan airport where the two planes that struck the World Trade Center supposedly originated. Bedford lies directly under the flight path of westbound flights leaving Logan.

MITRE developed the technology "to aid controllers in solving problems while keeping aircraft close to their route, altitude, and speed preferences." Shearman was unable to say why the MITRE technology apparently failed on 9/11.

Indira Singh, an "IT consultant" who previously worked on a Defense Advanced Research Project, and who was employed by

J.P. Morgan on 9/11, in risk management, pointed to MITRE's role at the FAA during the 9/11 Citizens' Commission hearings in New York last September. "Ptech was with MITRE Corporation in the basement of the FAA for two years prior to 9/11," Singh said. "Their specific job is to look at interoperability issues the FAA had with NORAD and the Air Force in the case of an emergency. If anyone was in a position to know that the FAA-that there was a window of opportunity or to insert software or to change anything-it would have been Ptech along with MITRE."

A representative of Ptech could not be reached. [Ptech appears to have been a Mossad front company created to provide insecure Trojan Horse software to the U.S. military and intelligence agencies. Ptech has the typical Arab owners and financiers-and Mossad operators.]

For example, see Michael Goff, former marketing manager at Ptech, Inc. http://www.goffpr.com/about.asp

Schlesinger bio info: http://www.mitre.org/about/bot/schlesinger. html

HOW MOSSAD DECEIVED THE U.S. MILITARY ON 9/11

Posted by: Christopher Bollyn
Date: Friday, 1 April 2005, 11:13 p.m.
In Response To: Is MITRE Corp The Trojan Horse of 9/11? (Christopher Bollyn)

Mossad, Israel's military intelligence agency, infiltrated the most sensitive computer networks in the United States through a little start-up company known as Ptech, in Quincy, Massachusetts.

Most notably, it was this infiltration that allowed the events of September 11, 2001 to occur.

If the crimes of 9/11 had been properly investigated, these people would have been investigated and booked long ago. The Mossad connection is obvious; read on:

In order to facilitate the computer network penetration, Mossad set up a IT consultancy and software provider named Ptech using Lebanese and Arabs as the front-man financiers and founders and keeping their Jewish American "sayan" in a secondary, but critical position.

First a note of background on what Ptech did, from the January 2005 article "Michael Chertoff and the sabotage of the Ptech investigation" on the Rigorous Intuition weblog:

"Joe Bergantino, a reporter for WBZ-TV's investigative team, was torn. He could risk breaking a story based on months of work investigating a software firm linked to terrorism, or heed the government's demand to hold the story for national security reasons. In mid-June, Bergantino received a tip from a woman in New York who suspected that Ptech, a computer software company in Quincy, Mass., had ties to terrorists. Ptech specialized in developing software that manages information contained in computer networks.

"Bergantino's investigation revealed that Ptech's clients included many federal governmental agencies, including the U.S. Army, the U.S. Air Force, the U.S. Naval Air Command, Congress, the Department of Energy, the Federal Aviation Administration, the Internal Revenue Service, NATO, the Federal Bureau of Investigation, the Secret Service and even the White House."

"Ptech was doing business with every federal government in defense and had access to key government data," Bergantino said.

Source: http://rigorousintuition.blogspot.com/2005/01/michael-chertoff-and-sabotage-of-ptech.html

The Mossad handler at Ptech was, in my opinion, an American named Michael S. Goff, who is disingenuous about what he did, when he worked at, and when he left, Ptech.

It should be noted that Ptech "got on its feet in 1994." Goff implies that he left Ptech when Goff Communications began in 1994; certainly not true.

Here is what Michael Goff's website says about his work there: Michael was marketing manager at Ptech, Inc., a leading provider of business process modeling, design and development software. In this capacity, Michael managed various marketing programs and activities including public relations, direct mail, Web development, collateral, trade shows and seminars. Additionally, Michael worked closely with the Ptech sales organization to perform competitive analysis as well as manage lead tracking fulfillment activities.

When Michael first joined Ptech, he shared responsibilities between marketing and information systems for the company. As information systems manager, Michael handled design, deployment and management of its Windows and Macintosh, data, and voice networks. As part of this effort, Michael developed Lotus Notes-based systems for sales and marketing lead tracking and IS service and support requests. Michael also performed employee training and handled all procurement for software, systems and peripherals.

See: http://www.goffpr.com/about.asp

From Goff Communications website, you will notice that one of his current prize clients is an Israeli company known as Guardium. Guardium is less than 5 miles from Hanscom AFB, site of MIT's Lincoln Labs and about the same distance from Boston's Logan Airport. The Israelis are all over MIT and Boston.

See: http://www.guardium.com/

Guardium, a "database security" firm, is clearly a Mossad operation working in a critical area-the same area that the two planes that hit the World Trade Center originated-Boston's Logan Airport.

Don't take my word for it, look who finances Guardium:

http://www.guardium.com/investors.html

Three firms, all Israeli, and all manned by Mossad agents. It should be noted that Mossad's headquarters are in Herzeliya. It is clear that the three firms, Cedar Fund, Veritas Venture Partners, and StageOne, are all Mossad funding outfits.

So, with Ptech, what we had was an American "sayan" [i.e. Jewish agent who works with the Mossad when necessary], Michael S. Goff, who had Mossad agents feeding him information and directing him WHILE he worked with his Lebanese Muslim "partners" in Ptech.

Now why would a young American lawyer working with a good law firm in his home town suddenly leave the practice of law and work with a dodgy start-up software company owned and financed by a Lebanese and a Saudi? Get the picture? Am I making sense?

Mossad asked him to do it. For the good of the Jewish people, etc, etc.

Under Goff, Ptech software loaded with trapdoors and Trojan Horses was sold and loaded onto the MOST sensitive computer systems that failed miserably, or performed well (depending on your view), on September 11, 2001.

Goff's father and grandfather, Samuel, were accountants who belonged to Worcester's "Commonwealth Lodge 600 of B'nai B'rith," whatever that group does for the American people. They were both 32nd Degree Masons. Does an apple fall far from the tree?

IMPORTANT NOTE to the non-corrupted FBI and U.S. Law enforcement agents: If you take a close look at the individuals who are running Guardium, and those behind the three companies who are financing this outfit, and interrogate them in Guantanamo for a few weeks, we will get to the bottom of who pulled off 9/11. I guarantee it.

Christopher Bollyn
American Free Press

TARGET SYRIA
DID ISRAEL KILL RAFIK HARIRI WITH A PRECISION PENETRATOR BOMB?

By Christopher Bollyn
American Free Press

The U.S. media is indulging in war mongering "yellow journalism" by repeating baseless allegations that Syria is behind the "car bombing" of a popular Lebanese nationalist, while the evidence suggests that the assassination was carried out using a guided missile launched from a plane-a precision penetration bomb-a "targeted killing" technique perfected by Israel.

"An enormous car bomb blasted the motorcade of former Prime Minister Rafik Hariri," The *New York Times* reported with authority from Beirut about the Valentine's Day massacre of Lebanon's billionaire ex-premier and at least 11 others, including 6 of his bodyguards. The *Times,* however, presented no evidence to support its allegation that a "car bomb" had killed the popular Lebanese nationalist. The bomb had directly struck Hariri's car in the motorcade and "ripped a 30-foot crater in the street" of one of Beirut's wealthiest sections.

Hariri was a well-known philanthropist and "the symbol of both Lebanon's political and economic renaissance," *The Daily Star*, Lebanon's English language paper wrote, "and his shocking death leaves the country facing an uncertain economic future."

Hariri was the driving force behind the return of foreign investment after Lebanon's 15-year civil war. Solidere, the company he founded, played a key role in rebuilding Beirut's downtown area. "Ironically," the *Star* reported, Hariri was killed in the waterfront hotel district he had rebuilt.

In addition to being behind Lebanon's reconstruction, Hariri was credited with stabilizing the Lebanese pound for the first time in 14 years. He kept inflation low and investments flowing in. Lebanon hosted more than 1 million Arab visitors in 2004 and had recovered its status as the Arab world's preferred holiday destination-largely thanks to Hariri.

"Responsibility for the bomb was uncertain," *The Chicago Tribune* opined, "but everything points to Syria and its agents." The *Tribune* ran the *Times* article on its front page. As for what "everthing" was that "points to Syria," the *Tribune* presented its evidence: "The timing and the sheer size of the explosion-an estimated 650 pounds of dynamite that left a crater 30 feet wide and 9 feet deep-point to Syrian involvement," the *Tribune* wrote. "This was no amateur job."

MOB-AND U.S. MEDIA-BLAME SYRIA

"Mob blames Syria for Hariri assassination," ABC News reported. "[Lebanon's] Interior Minister Suleiman Franjich, [a Maronite] suggested that, based on the crater in the middle of the road and preliminary reports, the attack may have been carried out by a suicide bomber who rammed Hariri's motorcade with a vehicle laden with explosives," the U.S. mass media network reported.

However, no evidence has been found to indicate that a "suicide bomber" or "a vehicle laden with explosives" were involved in the killing of Hariri.

A now-missing Palestinian living in Lebanon taped a claim of responsibility on behalf of a previously unheard of group called "Victory and Jihad in Greater Syria." Military experts, however, quickly dismissed the Palestinian's claim saying the magnitude of the blast suggested it was the work of a technically sophisticated group, with access to high-tech explosives.

The U.S. administration of President George W. Bush was quick to point fingers at Syria. "We condemn this brutal attack in the strongest possible terms," White House spokesman Scott McClellan said. "This murder today is a terrible reminder that the Lebanese people must be able to pursue their aspirations and determine their own political future free from violence and intimidation and free from Syrian occupation," McClellan said.

That Syria was the "target" of American criticism was "unmistakable," the *Times* reported, although McClellan and other administration spokesmen admitted they had no concrete evidence of Syrian involvement.

"NO EVIDENCE"

"We're going to turn up the heat on Syria, that's for sure," a senior State Department official told the *Times*. "It's been a pretty steady progression of pressure up to now, but I think it's going to spike in the wake of this event. Even though there's no evidence to link it to Syria, Syria has, by negligence or design, allowed Lebanon to become destabilized."

On February 15, the UN Security Council requested an urgent report into the "terrorist" assassination and urged Syria to pull its 14,000 troops out Lebanon. While Lebanon wants a Swiss investigation, the UN will reportedly send its own investigation team.

Bush ordered the U.S. Ambassador in Damascus, Margaret Scobey, to return. Before she left, Scobey delivered a message of "concern and outrage" to the Syrian government.

"U.S. officials were careful not to lay public blame for the atrocity directly on Syria," *The Times* of London wrote, "... but they left little doubt as to whom they viewed as the ultimate culprit."

WHO IS THE ULTIMATE CULPRIT?

But is Syria the ultimate culprit? Why would Syria murder Hariri, the architect of Lebanon's post-war reconstruction and prosperity? And why would anybody, let alone Syria, murder Hariri in such a spectacular way?

Like the 9/11 attacks, the murder of Hariri appears designed to influence world public opinion and provide a necessary *casus belli* to build a case and justify aggression against Syria. Why would Syria want to bring condemnation and war upon itself? Who is really interested in destabilizing Lebanon and Syria?

The assassination "has cast a giant cloud over Lebanon's immediate political future," *The Daily Star* wrote. "This outrage brings back memories of 1975 and the death of popular leader

Maarouf Saad, who like Hariri came from Sidon. The murder of Saad came just three months before the start of the civil war and is still seen by many as the catalyst to the apocalyptic events which enveloped this country for 15 years."

While Israel was briefly mentioned as a possible suspect in the bombing, the mainstream media has completely ignored that possibility. The evidence, however, indicates that the Hariri bombing may have been a guided missile attack from the air, a common method of "targeted killing" perfected by Israel.

Israel has killed an untold number of Palestinians in the Gaza Strip and the West Bank with precision guided bombs and missiles launched from the air. Last March, in one such targeted killing, the Israeli military used a guided missile to kill the quadriplegic and wheelchair-bound spiritual head of the Palestinian militant group Hamas, Sheikh Ahmed Yassin.

"Reports from the scene said Sheikh Yassin was being pushed in his wheelchair when he was directly hit by a missile," the BBC reported on March 22, 2004.

Israeli Prime Minister Sharon dismissed accusations that Israel was involved in the murder of Hariri.

"I think that it will be unnecessary at all to answer what has been said about the Israeli participation or responsibility to what is going on in Lebanon," Sharon said when asked about the charges.

AN UGLY CRIMINAL ACT

Syrian Foreign Minister Farouk al-Sharaa strongly condemned the attack. "This is an ugly criminal act," al-Sharaa said. "We condemn those who are sowing sedition in Lebanon. We hope that the Lebanese people in these difficult times will be cohesive and strong and reject any internal sedition or outside interference."

Syria's President Basher Al-Assad "expressed his deep sorrow" and described the assassination of "a man Syria considered a friend and an ally in the region" as a "horrendous atrocity." Hariri's legacy is that of "a man who helped rebuild a nation ravaged by civil war and a protector of peace between his people," a Syrian government statement said.

"This heinous act," the statement read, "... aims at destabilizing Lebanon and creating chaos, hostilities, and a sense of insecurity... This tragedy is not only a national loss for Lebanon but also for Syria and the Arab world."

While the U.S. media portrays Hariri and Syria as foes, his last press release, issued on the day of his death, suggests otherwise: "We are most keen on preserving relations with Syria and protecting its interests," Hariri said, "this stems from our deeply rooted national and pan-Arab convictions."

WHAT CAR BOMB?

The bombing of Hariri's motorcade occurred in broad daylight in an exclusive section of Beirut's waterfront known as the Cornice. There are, however, no eyewitness reports or physical evidence to substantiate the claim that is a suicide car bomber attacked Hariri's car.

Based on the size of the crater, estimated to be 30-50 feet across and 9-10 feet deep, an expert told *American Free Press* that the car bomb would have had to have been several tons in size, not the reported "650 pounds of dynamite."

The crater also shows that a ruptured water pipeline, dirt, and rubble were thrown up and out from the center of the crater, suggesting that the actual detonation occurred at some depth below the surface of the street.

Keith A. Holsapple, an expert on craters and professor of engineering mechanics at the University of Washington, examined the photographs of the Beirut crater for AFP. "There is no doubt," Holsapple said, "at least a several ton bomb would be required if it were delivered by a vehicle and detonated above the surface."

"A 50-foot crater in a wet soil would require on the order of 6 tons of ANFO (ammonium nitrate fuel oil) if the explosion were just above the surface," Holsapple said. "If the bomb was detonated just below the surface, that bomb weight is reduced to about 2 tons, and if a penetrator weapon was used, the weight would be on the order of 1 ton, to within a factor of two." A larger bomb would be required if the soil was "essentially dry at depths at the time of the event," he added.

But there is no evidence that a large vehicle carrying tons of explosives smashed into Hariri's vehicle and it is highly improbable that someone buried two tons of explosives under the street hoping that Rafik Hariri would drive by. So where was the bomb?

DEATH FROM ABOVE

There is some evidence indicating that the explosion that killed Hariri detonated under the street directly below his car.

The crater that resulted suggests that a precision guided aerial bomb struck Hariri's car, passing through it and penetrating into the road-before exploding. This is also indicated by the condition of Hariri's corpse. The lower part of his body was reported to be badly mangled and damaged while his head and torso were recognizable.

"If a penetrator weapon was used," Holsapple said, "the weight would be on the order of a 1 ton, to within a factor of two." A penetrator weapon is an aerial bomb, such as a bunker-buster type, which is a guided weapon that is designed to penetrate the surface before exploding.

On an information webpage entitled, "Bombs for Beginners," the Federation of American Scientists (FAS) explains how aerial bombs create craters: "The cratering effect is normally achieved by using a GP [general purpose] bomb with a delayed fuzing system. This system allows bomb penetration before the explosion. Since the explosion occurs within the surface media the energy of the blast causes the formation of a crater," it says.

A 1-ton penetrating bomb, silent and unseen, would explain the huge crater and the fact that there is no evidence of a truck bomb attacking Hariri's motorcade.

Sam Hamod, an expert on Middle Eastern affairs, wrote, "We must do as they do in other criminal cases, look at who had the most to gain from the assassination of Prime Minister Hariri. The Lebanese had a lot to lose, as did the Syrians.

"No matter where else you look, no one else had anything to gain except Israel and the U.S.," Hamod wrote. "America quickly pointed the finger at Syria, as did Israel, which was tantamount to convicting themselves because they are the only two countries that would gain by creating unrest in Lebanon."

E-mail From Chris Bollyn

Sent: Sunday, February 20, 2005 3:58 PM

Subject: Bollyn Questions on Hariri Bombing Photos-Warning: Graphic Photos

I have written about the murder of Rafik Hariri. My guess is that Hariri's convoy was hit by an Israeli missile or guided bomb which targeted Hariri's car and penetrated the ground under or in front of his car and blew him up.

Some people are saying that this was a "micro-nuke" that was in his car or even planted in the road beforehand.

Please look at the attached photos of the smoke and condition of Hariri's body and tell me what you think.

(Original photos attached in e-mail not available for publication) Questions:

What does the light color of the smoke tell us at the top of the plume?

If the car bomb was in the vehicle, or another vehicle, wouldn't the smoke be dark from the beginning? Even blackish?

Could this be the sand that has been thrown into the air from the detonation in the sandy soil of the Corniche (beachfront)?

Is this the signature of a high-explosive bomb?

If a micro-nuke were planted in Hariri's car would his corpse be in such good shape?

Best wishes,
Christopher Bollyn

E-mail From Chris Bollyn

Sent: Friday, March 11, 2005 12:04 AM

Subject: The Balkanization of Iraq-Was it a Suicide Bomber or an Airstrike?

Check out this short BBC video of the latest bomb, or air strike, in Iraq. This attack killed scores of Shiites at a funeral.

From BBC new page:

http://news.bbc.co.uk/1/hi/world/middle_east/4337363.stm#

Click on "Disturbing Video" in top righthand corner: "Disturbing scenes as bombers target Shia funeral"

NB-You will hear it reported that some of the eyewitnesses said it was an airstrike. But it is being passed off as a suicide bomber.

On what evidence? How do we know it was a suicide bomber? Nobody saw him. The media always says it was a suicide bomber. This is what they have been doing in Israel for years-calling it a suicide bomber after they remove the car that exploded. (e.g. Jerusalem a couple years ago.)

"He" even left a crater.

I think that most of these "sectarian" bombs are actually missile airstrikes being carried out to foment civil strife and ultimately civil war. Precision targeted missiles are unseen and silent. Nobody can see them. Balkanization of Iraq, divide and conquer, is clearly the strategy being employed in Mesopotamia.

Christopher Bollyn

IF FLIGHT 93 LANDED IN CLEVELAND, WHAT CRASHED IN PA?

Posted By Christopher Bollyn
Date: Tuesday, 22 March 2005, 12:11 a.m.

IF FLIGHT 93 LANDED IN CLEVELAND,
WHAT CRASHED IN SHANKSVILLE?
OR
THE DELETED REPORTS FROM
THE HISTORIOGRAPHY OF 9/11

By Christopher Bollyn

As any journalist or historian knows, when a major catastrophe occurs it is extremely important to monitor the first news reports because they often describe a very different version of events than those produced after government spin doctors have gotten their fingers in the story. The earliest reports, which are often more candid and honest than those that follow, need to be preserved for history.

The complete journalistic record and the eyewitness testimony of the events of 9/11 form a body of historical writing, known as the "historiography," of the terror attacks that have changed the course of American history. To remove or delete articles or reports from this body is a crime against history.

There are, however, at least two very important stories from the September 11, 2001, which have been effectively deleted from the historiography of 9/11.

The two stories, one from Cleveland and one from Albuquerque, are essential to understanding what happened on that awful day, but both have been excised from the publicly accessible body of historical writing about 9/11.

FLIGHT 93 LANDED IN CLEVELAND

The first story, posted at 11:43 a.m. on September 11, 2001 by "9News Staff" of Cincinnati's WCPO-TV, reported that United Airlines Flight 93 had landed in Cleveland. This is an up-to-the-minute news report about the flight that supposedly crashed in a reclaimed mine near Shanksville, Penn. at 10:06 a.m.

"A Boeing 767 out of Boston made an emergency landing Tuesday at Cleveland Hopkins International Airport due to concerns that it may have a bomb aboard," said Mayor Michael R. White.

"White said the plane had been moved to a secure area of the airport, and was evacuated."

"United identified the plane as Flight 93. The airline did say how many people were aboard the flight."

"United said it was also 'deeply concerned' about another flight, Fight 175, a Boeing 767, which was bound from Boston to Los Angeles."

"On behalf of United Airlines," CEO James Goodwin said: "The thoughts of everyone at United are with the passengers and crew of these flights. Our prayers are also with everyone on the ground who may have been involved. United is working with all the relevant authorities, including the FBI, to obtain further information on these flights."

This small, but extremely significant story of 147 words, which can still be found at the station's archives, has been purged from the historical record.

The original story is here: http://web.archive.org/web/20021109040132/ http://wcpo.com/ specials/2001/americaattacked/news_local/story14.html

A search for the story on WCPO's website brings up a page with the title, but no story. This is what one finds:

Plane Lands In Cleveland; Bomb Feared Aboard

Reported by: 9News Staff

Web produced by: Liz Foreman

9/11/01 11:43:57 AM

This story has been removed from WCPO.com.

It was a preliminary AP story, and was factually incorrect.

http://www.wcpo.com/specials/2001/americaattacked/news_local/ story14.html

This is very odd. A seemingly well-documented story about the actions of one of the four planes involved in 9/11 has been simply deleted from the historical record because it was deemed to be "factually incorrect?"

Who decided that?

United Airlines personnel and the mayor of Cleveland are quoted in the story, yet it is later judged to be "factually incorrect?" What's really going on here?

EXPLOSIVES IN THE TOWERS

A second story that has been deleted from the public archives of 9/11 was written on September 11, 2001, by veteran journalist Oliver Uyttebrouck of the Albuquerque Journal.

This story was based on a telephone conversation between Van Romero, an explosives expert from New Mexico Tech and the Journal. The conversation occurred shortly after the towers collapsed.

Uyttebrouck's article began:

"Televised images of the attacks on the World Trade Center suggest that explosives devices caused the collapse of both towers, a New Mexico Tech explosion expert said Tuesday.

"The collapse of the buildings appears 'too methodical' to be a chance result of airplanes colliding with structures," said Van Romero, vice president for research at New Mexico Institute of Mining and Technology. "My opinion is, based on the videotapes, that after the airplanes hit the World Trade Center there were some explosive devices inside the buildings that caused the towers to collapse," Romero said.

"Romero is a former director of the Energetic Materials Research and Testing Center at Tech, which studies explosive materials and the effects of explosions on buildings, aircraft and other structures."

The article was published on-line under the title "Explosives Planted in Towers, N.M. Tech Expert Says." An archivist at the paper told American Free Press that the article was published "on page A2" in an extra edition of the paper that came out later in the day on September 11, 2001.

The 9/11 extra edition of the paper was archived in the usual manner, Judy Pence, librarian for the Albuquerque Journal, told AFP.

The Uyttebrouck story of 9/11, however, is not found in any of the public archives of news articles from September 11, 2001. AFP asked NewsBank, Inc. of Chester, Vermont, why the Uyttebrouck article does not appear in their data banks of news articles.

"We checked with the Albuquerque Journal," Lisa Veysey of NewsBank wrote, "and learned the paper did not submit that article to the archive. We do not have control over the content in the online archive. The paper sends us the content to be archived and we have to archive exactly what they send. We can't add or remove any articles."

The text of the original article and Romero's subsequent recantation is here: http://www.public-action.com/911/jmcm/ABQjournal/

Romero had told Uyttebrouck that "the collapse of the structures resembled those of controlled implosions used to demolish old structures."

"It would be difficult for something from the plane to trigger an event like that." Romero said in a phone interview from Washington, D.C.

"Romero said he and another Tech administrator were on a Washington-area subway when an airplane struck the Pentagon."

"He said he and Denny Peterson, vice president for administration and finance, were en route to an office building near the Pentagon to discuss defense-funded research programs at Tech."

It appears that Romero's first opinion did not agree with the spin masters in Washington. Although it was published in the extra edition of the Albuquerque Journal under the title "Use of Explosives Believed," it was withheld from the electronic material sent to the national newspaper archives.

Apparently the editors of the paper were advised by a higher authority to keep the story from being added to the public archives that have become the historiography of 9/11.

Is this America's "free press" or is this Soviet-style censorship?

The Uyttebrouck article concluded:

If explosions did cause the towers to collapse, the detonations could have been caused by a small amount of explosive, he said.

"It could have been a relatively small amount of explosives placed in strategic points," Romero said. The explosives likely would have been put in more than two points in each of the towers, he said.

The detonation of bombs within the towers is consistent with a common terrorist strategy, Romero said.

"One of the things terrorist events are noted for is a diversionary attack and secondary device," Romero said.

Attackers detonate an initial, diversionary explosion that attracts emergency personnel to the scene, then detonate a second explosion, he said.

Romero said that if his scenario is correct, the diversionary attack would have been the collision of the planes into the towers.

Tech President Dan Lopez said Tuesday that Tech had not been asked to take part in the investigation into the attacks. Tech often assists in forensic investigations into terrorist attacks, often by setting off similar explosions and studying the effects.

"FIRE, NOT EXPLOSIVES

For a person investigating the events of 9/11 today, this is what the Journal has about Van Romero in an article titled "Fire, Not Extra Explosives, Doomed Buildings, Expert Says," written by John Fleck dated September 21, 2001:

"A New Mexico explosives expert says he now believes there were no explosives in the World Trade Center towers, contrary to comments he made the day of the Sept. 11 terrorist attack.

"Certainly the fire is what caused the building to fail," said Van Romero, a vice president at the New Mexico Institute of Mining and Technology.

The day of the attack, Romero told the Journal the towers' collapse, as seen in news videotapes, looked as though it had been triggered by carefully placed explosives.

As for Romero, he was awarded with presidential favors, including an appointment to serve on the President's Advisory Commission on Education Excellence for Hispanic Americans. The commission was created by President George W. Bush on October 12, 2001.

Romero was also credited for procuring some $56 million in federal funds to New Mexico Tech in 2003. Romero reportedly was influential in making his university "first in the nation" among institutions of higher education for receiving federal funds.

APPENDIX C

The following email was sent by the author in January of 2005 to both Chris Bollyn of "American Free Press" and to Dave vonKleist of "The Pour Hour" and producer of "9-11 In Plane Site."

Subject: Important Allied Pilots Association Contact for 9-11 In Plane Site

Dear Chris and Dave,

I just spoke with the Director of Communications for the Allied Pilots Association, the union that represents the pilots of American Airlines. I spoke with him about the contents of 911 In Plane Site and he said he was going to order it. I think it would be very wise for you both to contact him. His name is Gregg Overman. He can be reached at (800) 323-1470, extension 2269. I also think it would be wise, whether he orders it or not, to send him copies of the DVD as he is the Director of the APA national communications department.

I also left a message with the President of ALPA, the Air Line Pilots Association, the union that represents most other airline pilot labor groups, including ATA, my employer, and United, Northwest, Delta, USAir, and many others. His name is Captain Duane Woerth. He can be reached at (888) FLY-ALPA, select option two and spell his last name. I told him about the DVD and the website (www.911inplanesite.com). He should also be contacted and provided copies of the DVD.

Here locally, I talked with a good friend of mine who is on the retirement and insurance committee here at ATA ALPA. I am going to show him the DVD in an attempt to raise support to show it at a local council meeting.

I've also left copies with school administrators and teachers in an attempt to show it at PTO meetings and hopefully, eventually high school students.

Anyway, hope you both are well and I look forward to hearing from you.

Sincerely,
Glen Stanish

Sent: Tuesday, January 18, 2005 4:48 PM
Subject: Re: Important Allied Pilots Association Contact for "9-11 In Plane Site"

Dear Glen,
Thanks for the note. It sounds like you are reaching the right people with the DVD and information. I will call these contacts ASAP.
More later,
Christopher Bollyn

Sent: Monday, January 24, 2005 7:07 AM
Subject: 911 In Plane Site

Dear Glen,
Thank you so much for your take charge approach! I sent a copy to Mr. Woerth at the ALPA after talking to his office. Please let me know if you get any feedback from the meeting tomorrow night. Your efforts are a textbook example of how everyone on the "Power Team" is affecting change!

Keep in touch.
Dave
The Power Hour
www.thepowerhour.com
Joyce Riley & Dave vonKleist

From: Glen R. Stanish
To: "Dave vonKleist"
Cc: William Lewis; "Chris Bollyn"
Sent: Monday, February 07, 2005 12:02 PM
Subject: Response from APA

I just got a call from Mr. Gregg Overman, the Communication Director for the Allied Pilots Association, the union that represents the American Airlines pilots. He said to the best of my recollection that the APA would not have an institutional response to 911 In Plane Site. That he did view it. That 911 was a sad day for the APA. Basically their response is no comment.

I then asked him if he would like to share his personal response and he declined that also, although he did say he may contact me to discuss this some other time when he visits family here in Indianapolis. I told him I'd buy him lunch and a beer and that I would very much like to discuss this any time he may care to.

At ALPA National, I'm still waiting to hear back from Mr. Keith Hagy, Director of Engineering and Air Safety.

Any updates from you all would be greatly appreciated.

Sincerely,
Glen R. Stanish

From: "Glen R. Stanish
To: "Chris Bollyn"
Cc: "Dave vonkleist
Sent: Saturday, January 22, 2005 11:01 AM
Subject: 911 In Plane Site Presentation to Senior ATA Flight Personnel

Chris and Dave,

I just spoke to an old friend who happened to be my primary flight instructor 20 some plus years ago. He just happens to be the B-757 Fleet Manager at ATA Airlines. I spoke with him about the contents of the DVD and he is putting together an audience of senior flight management personnel to view 911 In Plane Site on Tuesday, the 25th. Just wanted to let you know, but if there is anything specific either of you would like me to add in addition to the DVD, please let me know. Thanks. Have a good weekend.

Glen

From: "William Lewis"
To: Glen Stanish Sent: Monday, January 24, 2005 10:29 AM
Subject: RE: 911 In Plane Site Presentation to Senior ATA Flight Personnel

Dear Glen,

My name is William Lewis, I am the executive producer for "911 In Plane Site." I have one question that I would like for you to ask.

Just before you press the play button, ask the entire room for a show of hands if they believe that 911 was carried out by hijackers. Ask for a (public) show of hands.

At the very end of the documentary ask the question again. How many people still believe that the events of September 11, 2001 were carried out by a select group of box-cutter wielding, Islamic hijackers?

If you wouldn't mind doing that for me and let me know what the results are. Dave and I have found in the past that you almost have a complete, 100% reversal of opinion when asking that particular question. (Plus it helps us to evaluate the effectiveness of the film)

Thanks for all that you are doing. We need more people like you.

Best Regards,
William Lewis
BridgeStone Media Group

From: Glen R. Stanish
To: William Lewis Sent: Monday, January 24, 2005 11:00 AM
Subject: Re: 911 In Plane Site Presentation to Senior ATA Flight Personnel

Dear Mr. Lewis,

I will be more than happy to conduct that brief introductory survey and I'll get back with you as soon as possible afterwards... If there is anything else I can do, please let me know.

You and Dave have put together a fantastic DVD and I am sharing it with as many people as I can. I'm trying to target people in positions that may have the greatest effect. Dave informed me that he was able to speak to the office of the President of the Air Line Pilots Association. I gave him another name of a leadership position of the APA, the Allied Pilots Association, the union representing the American Airlines pilots. His name is Gregg Overman and he is the Director of Communications at APA. He can be reached at 800-323-1470, ext. 2269.

I also thought it would be a good idea to contact the head of the AFA, the Association of Flight Attendants. Her name is Ms. Pat Friend. I left her a message the other day and gave her the name of the DVD and the 911inplanesite.com website. She should probably also be contacted, as their union membership I think is larger than ALPA. If you just punch in Association of Flight Attendants in your search engine, their website will come up and a phone contact will appear.

I haven't had the opportunity to contact the leadership of the IAM, the International Association of Machinists and AMFA, these are both unions that represent airline mechanics and ramp and agent workers, but I think they would be worthwhile contacts.

Also the Teamsters union represents some pilot labor groups.

Also Southwest Airlines has there own independent in house union. I think its abbreviation is SWALPA or SWAPA. I think they would be good contacts too.

Anyway, I'll get back with you as soon as I can after the presentation with the results of the pre and post survey and other pertinent details.

You guys are truly inspiring and I hope to some day meet you all.

Take care,
Glen R. Stanish

From: William Lewis
To: Glen R. Stanish
Sent: Monday, January 24, 2005 3:15 PM
Subject: RE: 911 In Plane Site Presentation to Senior ATA Flight Personnel

Excellent job. Thank you again. I will review the new contact information that you sent.

Best Regards,
William Lewis
BridgeStone Media Group

From: Glen R. Stanish
To: William Lewis
Cc: Dave vonKleist
Sent: Thursday, January 27, 2005 4:27 PM
Subject: 911 In Plane Site Preview by 757 Fleet Manager
William and Dave,

My friend... The B-757 Fleet Manager at ATA Airlines came by today to pick up a copy of the DVD to preview it before sharing it with other senior flight management personnel. He said he would get back with me later tonight to give me his feedback. But I feel better now thinking that the rest of the management team will soon see it also.

Any progress with the APA or ALPA?

I called again Pat Friend, the President of the AFA, I didn't talk with her but left her a message to check out the website and dvd, that it was important information for our industry as well as our nation.

Anyway, I'll keep you posted.

Take care,
Glen

From: Glen R. Stanish
To: Dave vonKleist
Cc: Chris Bollyn; William Lewis
Sent: Wednesday, February 02, 2005 4:12 PM
Subject: ALPA Initial Response

Dave, William, and Chris,

Wanted to send you a little update. The B-757 Fleet Manager at ATA, did pick up and view 911 In Plane Site. He said it would probably take a long time to get an audience of other management flight personnel together to view it together so he said he was going to make several copies and pass them around the flight dept.

He did say he was impressed by it and that he felt the coverage of the Pentagon was conclusive or some other similar descriptive and that he could tell there was something underneath the South tower aircraft. We'll probably talk again soon. If you would like Dave, I could give him your phone if you would like to speak with him.

On the ALPA National front, I called the office of Captain Duane Woerth, President of ALPA, today and spoke with his secretary. I said I was calling on your behalf. She told me that Captain Woerth has not seen the documentary yet, but forwarded it to the Director of Engineering and Air Safety, Mr. Keith Hagy

I spoke with Mr. Hagy and again said I was an ALPA member and that I was calling on your behalf and was wondering if ALPA could respond officially (to the documentary, 911 In Plane Site) in writing or email, that I felt one was in order since they had been provided a complimentary copy. Mr. Hagy was very professional and kind and said he had forwarded it to Chris Baygh, not sure of the spelling, in Accident Investigation for a closer look, that ALPA was involved in the initial investigation.

I told Mr. Hagy that while I was with TWA that there was much controversy surrounding the TWA 800 accident, and that I had flown with many Captains that understood there was much more to the story of that "accident"

Anyway, Mr. Hagy took my phone numbers and he said he would call again after Accident Investigation had looked further into it, but I do expect an official response from ALPA eventually. I will keep in touch with these gentlemen,

I also heard back today from Senator Lugar's office. A young man named Chris Geeslin called. We talked about some of Stanley Hilton's and Phil Berg's comments along with the editorial of Fire Engineering magazine. I basically told him I thought 9-11 was a current day Northwoods Operation. He assured me that it was not and I told him I felt much better after he called. HaHa. Anyway, keep in touch and I will provide any and all updates that come my way.

Glen

From: Glen R. Stanish
To: Dave vonKleist
Sent: Friday, February 18, 2005 9:55 AM
Subject: ALPA Accident Investigation Response

Dave,

I spoke with Chris Baum in ALPA accident investigation on 2/16/05. He said ALPA had a very limited role in the 9/11 investigation since this was a criminal act.

He also said that he viewed 911 in Plane Site, that he wasn't sure if ALPA would have an official response, but he would try to encourage Captain Woerth, the President of ALPA, to respond. He said he was a retired military pilot, never an airline pilot and his response was basically that he felt the documentary was "one-sided" and that this was a low priority for ALPA due to the dismal state of the airline industry.

I then asked him if he felt 9-11 was in any way related to the state of the industry.

Anyway, I don't seem to be having much luck in getting responses from people in official positions. I never considered myself abrasive or my personality to be detrimental to assisting the cause. I'll keep pressing on in any and all capacities I consider appropriate. If there is anything else you can think of that I can do, I'll certainly try. Please let me know. Any responses I get from other pilots, I'll pass along.

I did go to the Central Library yesterday and made several enlarged photocopies of the 9/24/01 issue of "New York" magazine, the photo of the 767 approaching the South Tower. Something that should not be there is definitely there.

One more thing, I'm trying to get together with a recently retired Air Force officer who viewed the documentary with a friend and fellow ATA pilot I shared it with and who burned a copy. He said he has some information he would like to share with me as Mark, my friend told him I was working on a book containing much 911 material. I'll get back with you on that. We were shooting for lunch Monday, the 21", but my kids are out of school for Presidents Day/Winter break. We'll reschedule asap. Take care Dave.

Glen

From: Glen R. Stanish
To: Chris Bollyn
Cc: Dave vonKleist
Sent: Wednesday, January 19, 2005 10:59 AM
Chris,

Just wanted to point out one more thing I noticed on the 911 In Plane Site dvd. In the Scene Selection menu, if you select the scene WTC Bombs, Explosions, Demolitions scene, in the part where they show one of the towers collapsing... just after the group of four NYFD firefighters describe the detonators, etc., the second time, as you watch the tower collapse, if you focus a few floors beneath the top of the dust cloud, but also within the dust cloud, in slow motion, you can distinctly see several bright flashes of light emanating from within the building and throughout the dust cloud. I have counted up to about 20 of these bright flashes and I thought they could very well be the "detonators" the firefighters discussed. I just haven't seen this described in any of the articles I've read in AFP or elsewhere. Thought you probably were aware, but if not, thought you may want to take another look.

Also, I plan on contacting the President of the Association of Flight Attendants, the International Association of Machinists, and AMFA, the unions for flight attendants and airframe and powerplant mechanics respectively and inform them about the dvd and website. I may forward them your way if you don't mind, or at least get back to you again with their responses. Maybe these little ripples will gain some strength.

Please keep in touch. Thanks Chris.

Glen

From: Glen R. Stanish
To: Chris Bollyn
Cc: Dave vonKleist; William Lewis
Sent: Sunday, January 30, 2005 8:23 AM Subject: 911 In Plane Site

Wanted to let you know... yesterday, Saturday the 29, my daughter had a gymnastics competition. I saw a young man wearing an NBC, Channel 13 (Indianapolis) jacket so I introduced myself. He had a daughter there at the state fairgrounds competing also. We got to talking and he told me he was a helicopter pilot for NBC Channel 13 and so when I told him I was a pilot for ATA Airlines, we started talking about 9-11. I gave him the website and the name of the DVD, but he told me that he flies with some ex-Vietnam helo pilots and that they were familiar with the material on 911 In Plane Site ...

Take care,

Glen

From: Glen R. Stanish
To: The Power Hour Radio, Dave vonKleist
Sent: Thursday, March 17, 2005 12:04 PM
Subject: Glen R. Stanish Biographical Info for Radio Show Introduction

Dave,

I am looking forward to being a guest on your program. Thank you so much for having me on.

I am currently employed with ATA Airlines as a Boeing 737 First Officer or copilot. I have been in this position for two years.

Prior to ATA, I was an MD-80 F/O for TWA and American Airlines

I was with American Airlines on 9-11, I was with TWA and AA for six years.

Prior to TWA, I flew six years for a USAir regional airline, Jet stream International now known as PSA

Prior to the USAir regional position, I flew Lear jets and twin Cessna aircraft for a Charter company here in Indiana.

Prior to the Charter pilot position, I was a Flight Instructor for four years at FlightSafety in Vero Beach, FL and at Purdue University and at Mt. Comfort here in Indiana.

I am a 1989 graduate of Purdue University, majoring in Aviation Technology, the Professional Pilot Program.

I became aware of your documentary, 911 In Plane Site after discussing an article in the American Free Press with Christopher Bollyn. I read this article several months ago in which Chris wrote about the documentary, and also discussing that there was no identifiable wreckage of a B-757 at either the Pentagon or the Shanksville, PA locations. When I read this, I contacted Chris Petherick, the editor of AFP and told him I was a professional pilot, that during our training with the airlines, whether during new hire training or at our annual recurrent training, we are required to cover CRM or cockpit or crew resource management. During this training, we cover aircraft and airline accidents, there causal factors and as crew members how or what we would do differently to prevent these types of accidents.

We are shown slides or video of these aircraft accidents and there are always large pieces of identifiable aircraft wreckage. For example, the TWA 800 accident, the B747 out of JFK to Paris, they recovered and rebuilt the entire aircraft in a Calverton NY hangar. Pan Am 103 over Scotland, a large piece of the cockpit remained and is recorded in many photos, USAir flight 427, a 737 that crashed near Pittsburgh, large pieces of wing and tail with flight controls still attached and landing gear was recovered, the United DC-10 that crashed in the cornfields of lowa, large pieces of wreckage remained, the Delta flight that crashed at DFW, the L-1011, large tail section was identifiable, there was an American Eagle ATR turboprop that crashed in Northern Indiana on a Halloween night, again positively identifiable wreckage remained, the Valujet crash in the everglades, you can go on and on but the one constant when an airline hull is lost, wreckage remains. They do not disintegrate to the molecular level.

When I discussed this with Chris Bollyn, he contacted you and I was provided a copy of 911 In Plane Site. I must say, you have produced a masterpiece. I have shared this dvd with several other pilots. I have contacted the Allied Pilots Assn., the union that represents the American Airlines pilots. I have contacted ALPA, the Air Line Pilots Assn. and I am doing what I can to help get this information out to as many people in the industry as I can. I am trying to schedule a public showing at the local library here on the south side of Indianapolis.

Anyway Dave, I'm looking forward to the show and I hope to meet you all some day soon.

Glen R. Stanish

"Glen R. Stanish" … wrote:

Dear Dave, William, and Chris,

Hello. How are you all doing?

I'm trying to schedule a public showing of 911 In Plane Site at the Johnson County, White River Library. I spoke with the Manager of the library and he told me I needed two things in order to show this documentary.

First, he said I needed a release form from the producer to show it in order to cover licensing requirements.

Second, he said the community room is for groups of five people or more…

By the way, I spoke with… the 757 Fleet Manager here at ATA. He told me that just about everyone in the Flight Department at ATA has seen the film. He said many flight managers were impressed by the film but reactions were either they believed in the material or that it was a liberal propaganda piece. He also said staff in the scheduling department were viewing it currently. So it is making its rounds here at ATA.

By the way Chris, I really appreciate you including me in your email news distributions. Please keep me on your list and keep the updates coming.

I hope you are all well and I appreciate your help in getting this film shown to the public here in Greenwood IN…

Glen

From: Chris Bollyn

To: Glen R. Stanish; Dave vonKleist

Cc: William Lewis

Sent: Tuesday, March 15, 2005 11:09 AM

Subject: Re: Public Showing of 911 In Plane Site

Glen, et al:

I am having a 9/11 discussion/presentation of the evidence on March 26 at the Schaumburg Township District Library in Schaumburg, Illinois. This is about 25 miles NW of Chicago. The Library is on the SW comer of the intersection of Roselle and Schaumburg Roads.

The event is from 2 to 5 p.m. in the library's Rasmussen Room on the second floor.

I will be discussing and presenting the evidence found in Eric Hufschmid's book and Dave vonKleist's video.

Dave: Do you want me to sell a few of your DVD's directly or should I advise how to get in touch with you?

Eric has put together a few minutes of footage for me on a DVD to open the eyes of the audience.

Dr. Gene Corley was invited but said he has another obligation. Phil Jayhan plans to attend the event.

Christopher Bollyn

CHRISTOPHER BOLLYN AND ERIC HUFSCHMID PRESENT 9/11 THE EVIDENCE OF A HOAX

Chicago Area Event
Schaumburg Township District Library
March 26, 2005
2-5pm.

Official Version:

19 Arab terrorists hijacked passenger jets and flew them into the World Trade Center and the Pentagon on September 11, 2001 causing the destruction of three towers and killing some 3,000 people. Secondary fires caused the steel and concrete towers to collapse in clouds of dust.

Fact or Fiction?

WHAT REALLY HAPPENED ON 9/11?

A Presentation and Discussion
of the Evidence
Schaumburg Township District Library
South Rasmussen Room
Presented by:
Christopher Bollyn, Journalist
American Free Press
Eric Hufschmid, Author
Painful Questions:
An Analysis of the September 11th Attack
Invited Participants:
Dr Gene Corley, Team Leader
World Trade Center Building Study (FEMA)
Phil Jayhan, 9/11 Researcher
www.letsroll911.Org

PRESS RELEASE
July 19, 2005
Christopher Bollyn
American Free Press
Washington, D.C.

To honor the memory of the victims of 9/11, William Rodriguez, last survivor from the World Trade Center, will speak at the Schaumburg Township District Library, near Chicago, on Sunday, August 21, 2005, from 2 to 5 p.m.

On September 11, 2001, Rodriguez, custodian of the stairwells of the North Tower, helped save hundreds of lives at the World Trade Center by leading firefighters up the stairwells and opening the fire doors with his master key. Disregarding orders from his superiors, Rodriguez repeatedly returned to the building to assist those trapped within the burning tower. He is the last person known to have escaped from the North Tower and miraculously survived the collapse by diving under a fire truck that was parked near the entrance.

For his heroic efforts Rodriguez has been honored by the White House and made a national hero by the legislature of Puerto Rico, his homeland.

The event at the Schaumburg library is the only scheduled event in the Chicago area in which Mr. Rodriguez will appear. He will be available for interviews with the press on Saturday, August 20, and respond to questions after the event, which will begin promptly at 2 p.m.

On July 18, the library board voted unanimously to provide Mr. Rodriguez with the largest possible forum. The Rasmussen Room at the main library accommodates about 200 people. The event is free and open to the public.

The three-hour event is being organized by Christopher Bollyn, a long-standing patron of the library and independent journalist who writes for the *American Free Press* of Washington, D.C.

As president and member of the board of several victims' groups, Rodriguez was instrumental in the creation of the 9/11 Commission-and providing it with subpoena power. He was one of the last witnesses to testify before the commission but none of his testimony appears in the commission's final report.

William Rodriguez is a twenty-year veteran employee of the World Trade Center and survivor of the 1993 bombing. He knew every inch of the buldings and was in the burning tower saving lives from the time it was hit until seconds before it was demolished. His story is one of the most compelling you will ever hear of the events of 9/11.

In addition to Mr. Rodriguez, other 9/11 researchers have been invited to this historic event, including:

- De Gene Corley, structural engineer and team leader of the official WTC Building Performante Study
- Deve vonKleist, co-host of The Power Hour and producer of *911-In Plane Site*
- Phil Jayhan, webmaster of www.letsroll911.Org

American Free Press has made a donation to make this event possible.

For more information about the event or to schedule an interview please contact Christopher Bollyn at: afp_europe@yahoo.com

PRESS RELEASE

American Free Press

Presents a

PUBLIC SYMPOSIUM on 9-11

Featuring

The amazing and important eyewitness testimony of a survivor and hero from the World Trade Center

William Rodriguez

The Custodian & Master Key Holder who miraculously survived the destruction of the World Trade Center after saving hundreds of lives Other Invited Speakers

- **Dr. Gene Corley,** Construction Engineer and Team Leader of FEMA-sponsored *World Trade Center Building Performance Report*
- **Eric Hufschmid,** Researcher and Author of *Painful Questions: An* Analysis of the September 11 Attack
- **Phil Jayhan,** Researcher and Webmaster of letsroll911. Org
- **Dave vonKleist,** Radio Host and Producer of 9/11 video "*In Plane Site*"

Presented by Christopher Bollyn, Journalist, *American Free Press*

SUNDAY, AUGUST 21, 2005

From 2 to 5 p.m.

SCHAUMBURG TOWNSHIP DISTRICT LIBRARY

130 S. Roselle Road, Schaumburg, IL

www.stdl.org

Pre-event press interviews with William Rodriguez can be done by phone at (210) 537-4826. He will also be available in person for interviews with the media on Saturday, August 20.

For more information contact: afp_europe@yahoo.com

WILLIAM RODRIGUEZ, A 9-11 SURVIVOR

By Deanna Spingola
August 25, 2005
www.spingola.com/william_rodriguez.htm

This past week I had the great pleasure of meeting William Rodriguez, a humble man from Puerto Rico who worked at the World Trade Center. He looked healthy in spite of suffering from many 9-11 related problems.

The occasion was at a special meeting at the Schaumburg, Illinois Township Library in the Chicago suburbs. This informative presentation served as a memorial for the many victims as we approach the fourth year anniversary of 9-11. In addition to William Rodriguez other knowledgeable and well qualified individuals presented their thoughts: Phil Jayhan, Dave VonKleist and Christopher Bollyn, a journalist with the American Free Press. This event, where there should have been standing room only, was sponsored in part by the American Free Press as well as Jimmy Walter and Eric Hufschmid, a physicist and author of Painful Questions.

A press release was sent to all of the print media in the Chicago area about a month in advance of this event. There was a very tiny isolated notice about the event in one of the Chicago papers. Surely, we could hope that the local newspapers would wish to interview all of the participants about such an important subject as 9-11. But, only one Hispanic television station sent a journalist and a camera. So we must assume that the other Chicago news organizations, affiliates of a much larger cabal, have already determined exactly what their readers are supposed to believe about 9-11. Let's not deviate from the government version and confuse people with the truth!

William Rodriguez gave an outstanding, sensitive discourse about his experiences on that fateful day. He appears to be a genuinely warm, gentle caring human being and it is easy to believe that his working relationship with his many fellow employees was much more-they were also his long time friends. Daily, he met with them for breakfast in the Windows on the World Restaurant on the 106th floor. Nearly two hundred people, many of them William Rodriguez's friends, were in that restaurant that morning. None of them survived. Not only did he lose his job on 11 September 2001, he lost most of his friends. William Rodriguez would have also perished had he been in the restaurant that morning but he arrived at work at 8:30 a.m. rather than his usual time of 8:00 a.m.

William Rodriguez had worked at the World Trade Center for about twenty years. He was in charge of the three stairwells, A, B and C in the north tower designated as WTC1, a class "A" building. The stairwells were narrow, steep and without windows. There were also 97 passenger and 6 freight elevators in the building. On a typical morning, he would finish breakfast then begin at the top of the building and methodically work his way down. Arriving at 8:30 on the morning of 9-11 he went to the maintenance office located on the first sublevel, one of six sub-basements beneath ground level. There were a total of fourteen people in the office at that same time. As he was discussing the day's tasks with others, there was a very loud massive explosion which seemed to emanate from between sub-basement B2 and B3. There were an additional twenty-two people on B2 sub-basement who also felt and heard that first explosion.

At first he thought it was a generator that had exploded But the cement walls in the office cracked from the explosion. "When I heard the sound of the explosion, the floor beneath my feet vibrated, the walls started cracking and everything started shaking." said Rodriguez, who was crowded together with fourteen other people in the office including Anthony Saltamachia, his supervisor for the American Building Maintenance Company.

Just seconds later there was another explosion way above which made the building oscillate momentarily. This, he was later told, was a plane hitting the tower at about the 90 floor. Upon hearing about the plane, he immediately thought of the people up in the restaurant. Then there were other explosions just above B1 and individuals started heading for the loading dock to escape the explosion's resulting rampant fire. When asked later about the first explosions he said: "I would know if an explosion was from the bottom or the top of the building." He heard explosions both before and after the plane hit the tower.

A fellow worker Felipe David came into the maintenance office. "He had been standing in front of a freight elevator on sub-level 1 about 400 feet from the office when fire burst out of the elevator shaft, causing his terrible injuries." The skin on his face had been peeled away by the heat of the blast and he was horribly burned on thirty-three percent of his body. "He was burned so badly from the basement explosion that flesh was hanging from his face and both arms." William asks: "How could a jetliner hit 90 floors above and burn a man's arms and face to a crisp in the basement below within seconds of impact?" William led Felipe David outside to safety and medical assistance. William continued to hear people screaming and returned to the building in spite of police orders. There were people encased in the many elevators. There were frantic people who needed help.

There was a swooshing sound coming from the freight elevators on B2 and B3. Water from the fire sprinklers from all of the floors had gone into the elevator shaft. There were two individuals trapped below who were in danger of drowning. Rodriguez was able to secure a long enough ladder to extend into the shaft to facilitate their escape from a certain watery grave.

He had possession of just one of the five master keys that opened all of the stairwell doors at each of the floors in the 110 story building. The other four key holders were trained for emergencies. They had already left the building. Firemen from New York City Unit Six arrived. Each fireman, in addition to their heavy protective clothing, had about 70 pounds of equipment.

William, who now had the only key, led the firemen up stairwell B. Firemen were struggling up the stairs as victims were hastily descending.

The firemen made it up to the 27th floor but were exhausted from the burden of their equipment. As William had ascended the stairwell he, as well as the firemen, had heard explosions from the 20th through the 30th floor. Chunks of the building were falling down all around them and they could literally hear the creaking in the building. Yet, the firemen continued to climb -to give aid, support and direction to the lost and the terrified. The firemen rightfully assumed, from past experience, that the fire was isolated at the location where the plane entered. This rupture and the resulting damage would not affect the integrity of the rest of this well designed steel building. That assumption, and unknown factors, probably related to the explosions, would cost the lives of many of these dedicated firemen.

On the 33rd floor, William was able to procure some dust masks from a maintenance office. The air was thick with suffocating smoke. On the 33rd floor he found a women laying on the floor in a fetal position. She didn't know where to go or what to do. They had fire drills twice a year but because of employee turnover, not everyone had a clear view of emergency procedures. While some individuals intuitively respond appropriately in an emergency, others are absolutely paralyzed by their fears.

Strangely, while William was on the 33rd floor he heard lots of very loud noise as if someone was moving heavy equipment and furniture around on the 34th floor. The reason this is interesting is that the 34th floor was empty. Elevators did not stop at the 34" floor. It was off limits due to a construction project. The new security chief, John O'Neill had his new office on this floor. William said that this was the first time that he felt fear. They continued to ascend to the 39th floor. This is as far as William got before he was turned back by the firefighters. As he began his descent he heard the plane hit the south tower.

He made it back down to the chasm where the large metal framed front doors were before they were blown out. Just the bottoms of the elevator doors were blown partially open indicating the source of the powerful pressure-from beneath. The large ornate pieces of marble that covered the walls were now resting where they landed. It resembled a war zone. He couldn't breath, his eyes burned, his leg was burned. Someone yelled: "Don't look back!" William, like most of us would, looked back momentarily. The building was coming down. He then raced for the first cover he saw-a fire truck. That is where he was found, under the truck and buried in rubble. Pulverized concrete mixed with asbestos and smoke created a dark pervasive cloud of doom. Flashlights were necessary. William received temporary medical assistance and then went to work trying to find survivors.

The mangled bloodied bodies of the jumpers blanketed the ground. William will never forget the anguish he felt or the sight of this senseless horrific carnage. This was evidence of desperation-people desperate to escape possible death by suffocation or by fire chose death by jumping. The fire created by the jet fuel was contained and isolated yet the building came down. Something else had occurred in that building. Much of the initial flame actually burned outside of the building instantly upon impact. The fire was spent-even at the giant gaping hole where the plane breached the building where people worked, talked with friends and felt relatively safe.

William Rodriguez saved lives that day. Currently he is attempting to alert the public to what actually happened. He is a courageous witness to those terrible events. The controlled censored media doesn't really appear willing to report the real news but rather they promote whatever the propaganda ministry wants the masses to believe. It takes continuous courage to go against such opposition but that is the kind of man he is. He says that he owes it to his friends-those that were slaughtered for some covert political agenda.

William spent hours testifying behind closed doors in front of the 9-11 Commission. His testimony as an eye witness does not appear in the 576 page report. But after all, Bush confidently told us within mere hours exactly who the perpetrators were, so why go to the trouble to examine the evidence or talk with the people who were really there-the hundreds of witnesses. The only agency that was immediately allowed to investigate the circumstances of the event was FEMA, the Federal Emergency Management Agency.

The National Institute of Standards and Technology (NIST), an independent investigative group was also allowed to scrutinize the circumstances. He contacted them four times but never got a response. NIST was funded by the government which gives you a pretty good idea of just how subjective their findings were. They were paid $35 million dollars and the investigation lasted two years. The taxpayers certainly did not get their money's worth.

William Rodriguez also contacted the FBI who never followed up. The media was not interested. CNN spent a day filming and interviewing him at his home but when it was shown the following day it was thoroughly edited. Some reporters have subtly warned Rodriguez to keep quiet as his words could jeopardize his life. They said, "You do not know who you are dealing with!" He had already defiantly looked death in the face and he will probably continue to courageously tell his story. He is speaking for his friends who were forever rendered speechless. He says: "I am living on borrowed time since I probably should be dead anyway."

William Rodriguez is the lead plaintiff in a RICO lawsuit filed against George W. (warmonger) Bush and others. He is alleging conspiracy to commit murder and other crimes. So not only is he speaking for his friends but he is seeking justice for all of the victims, both those who died and those who were injured.

The World Trade Center twin towers were erected by the Port Authority of New York and New Jersey from 1968 to 1972. To adequately fireproof the buildings a mixture of asbestos and cement was sprayed during the construction. However, this fireproofing technique was banned in 1971 by the New York City Council. By then there was already hundreds of tons of this material in the building. Later, some of this material was removed yet there was still about 100 tons of asbestos remaining. Asbestos was used in other areas that would not leave the harmful residue unless there were extraordinary circumstances such as those that occurred on 9-11.

William Rodriguez says: "I have tried to tell my story to everybody, but nobody wants to listen. It is very strange what is going on here in supposedly the most democratic country in the world. In my home country of Puerto Rico and all the other Latin American countries, I have been allowed to tell my story uncensored. But here, I can't even say a word." Thank goodness for the alternative media where one may still discover the truth.

In spite of millions of dollars spent on gathering intelligence, our intelligence either was not effective or totally ignored-it failed to protect the taxpayers who paid the ultimate price. On 11 September 2001 the defense systems of the most powerful nation on the earth failed. Our defense communications, NORAD failed. Our commander-in-chief, intent on a child's goat story, failed to appropriately respond after knowing about the first plane hitting the north tower. His actions could have saved others. The twin towers, symbols of our economic status, failed. They collapsed-the only known steel frame buildings in history known to have failed because of fire. Many other steel frame buildings have burned for hours and hours yet they did not collapse. Of course, we do not know the cause of their failure as the evidence was rendered unavailable for independent investigation-either it was sold immediately or otherwise withheld. There was also the failure of the local authorities to warn the people about the highly toxic air that burned their lungs and blanketed there offices and homes and would create life long health problems. They were told that there was no problem.

After 9-11 there was a failure to discover exactly who made millions of dollars on all of the put options on American Airlines and United Airlines. There were so many failures yet I haven't heard of one person reprimanded or thoroughly investigated for inefficiency.

There were also successes which involved enormous sacrifices:

There were about 350 firemen who gave their lives-crushed in the totally unexpected and unprecedented building collapses. There were medical people who tenderly treated the trauma struck victims. There were more than two thousand injured souls. The policemen, about 75 of whom died, did not fail to do their job. There were thousands of volunteers who searched for the dead and dying who did not fail to think of others. There were trained search and rescue dogs who did not fail to gallantly perform-many of whom have since died of cancer as a result of burrowing through the toxic waste. And William Rodriguez did not fail. He made selfless saenfices for others. He acted appropriately-just like a man of integrity and courage should act. He did not hesitate-unlike others-those who have sworn allegiance to our constitution, our country and to the citizens. They each should have responded as their elected offices demanded. They should have responded like the patriotic Christian Americans they claim to be. It takes more than just rhetoric-it takes action. If William Rodriguez ever runs for office-I hope you vote for him. He can be trusted!

IGNORING 9-11
MAINSTREAM PRESS AVOIDS SEPT. 11 HERO'S TESTIMONY

By Christopher Bollyn
American Free Press, americanfreepress.net
September 5, 2005

Schaumburg, Illinois-In amazement and awe, audiences hang on to every word of William Rodriguez when he speaks about his experiences of Sept. 11, 2001. The compelling testimony of the former custodian of the World Trade Center, in which he clearly describes a huge explosion occurring in the basement of the North Tower seconds before the plane struck the building, demolishes the government version of events as completely as the explosions that pulverized the twin towers.

The 40-minute testimony of Rodriguez, a national hero, presents listeners with an inescapable dilemma. Either Rodriguez is making it all up or the official explanation of what caused the destruction of the two 110-story steel and concrete towers is a pack of lies.

Because the corporate-controlled press cannot square the Puerto Rican custodian's testimony with the official version, they simply have to avoid him entirely.

To pursue the truth in a public forum is why *American Free Press* invited Rodriguez to participate in its 9-11 Symposium in Schaumburg, a suburb of Chicago, home of the world's first skyscraper constructed with steel girders.

Dr. Gene Corley, structural engineer and team leader of the Federal Emergency Management Agency (FEMA) report on the destruction of the WTC, was invited well in advance to participate in the symposium and defend the fire-induced gravity collapse theory. Corley chose not to.

As team leader of the official engineering study about the damaged towers Corley wrote: "... absent other severe loading events such as a windstorm or earthquake, the buildings could have remained standing in their damaged states until subjected to some significant additional load."

"The large quantity of jet fuel carried by each aircraft ignited upon impact into each building. A significant portion of this fuel was consumed immediately in the ensuing fireballs [outside of the buildings]. The remaining fuel is believed either to have flowed down through the buildings or to have burned off within a few minutes of the aircraft impact. The heat produced by this burning jet fuel does not by itself appear to have been sufficient to initiate the structural collapses," Corley wrote in the executive summary of the "World Trade Center Building Performance Study."

According to Corley, neither the impact of the planes nor the burning fuel caused the towers to collapse.

"Over a period of many minutes," Corley wrote, "secondary fires, such as burning office supplies and furniture set alight by the burning fuel, induced additional stresses into the damaged structural frames while simultaneously softening and weakening the frames."

"This additional loading and the resulting damage were sufficient to induce the collapse of both structures," the FEMA-sponsored study concluded.

Corley, a senior vice president with Construction Technology Laboratories in Skokie, has his office 20 miles from the Schaumburg library where the 9-11 Symposium was held on Sunday, Aug. 21.

Corley told AFP that he is quite willing to discuss the findings of the official report, but during the entire month prior to the event he failed to respond to several written invitations. AFP finally called Corley's office two days before the event and was told he would be in Memphis.

Corley played a key role in authoring similar technical reports about the Pentagon, the Alfred P. Murrah Federal Building in

Oklahoma City, and the Branch Davidian compound disaster in Waco, Tex.

In addition to Rodriguez and Corley, three other researchers were invited to participate in the symposium.

Dave vonKleist of "The Power Hour" radio show and producer of the video *In Plane Site*, traveled from Versailles, Mo.

Phil Jayhan, author of the letsroll911.org web site, came from McHenry, Ill. and Eric Hufschmid, the California-based author of *Painful Questions: An Analysis of the Sept. 11 Attack*, donated books, videos and funds to the event.

MAINSTREAM MEDIA ABSENT

Although the news departments of every major media network in the Chicago area were informed well in advance of the event, the only news outlet to attend was the Spanish-language Univision television channel, which interviewed Rodriguez for the nightly news. Thus, while Rodriguez, a national hero who has been honored at the White House five times, delivered his testimony to a full house at the conference, not a single reporter from the English-language media or *The Chicago Tribune* bothered to attend.

The suburban *Daily Herald* told AFP that they "lacked the resources to cover the event," and featured a front-page story about adult dodgeball the following Monday.

Peter Hernon, chief of *The Chicago Tribune's* Schaumburg office, told AFP that he was unaware of the event although his bureau had received numerous notices by post, fax, email and phone. The *Tribune*, which has a bureau only two miles from the library, had even published an announcement of the symposium the Friday before the event.

Likewise, Richard Wronski, news desk editor on the day of the event, said he had not heard of the event.

Hernon and Wronski were less than completely honest because a fellow editor at the Schaumburg office told AFP two days before the symposium that while the paper was well aware of the event, it had decided not to cover it.

Puzzled by these responses, AFP asked N. Don Wycliff, public editor at the *Tribune*, how the decision was made not to cover what was probably the most significant 9-11 event ever held in the Chicago area. The Tribune Company is one of America's largest media networks owning print, television and radio outlets in the nation's three largest markets of New York City, Chicago, and Los Angeles.

AFP told Wycliff about how Rodriguez had returned to the burning tower several times and led firefighters up the stairwells opening the locked fire doors with his master key allowing many trapped workers to escape.

Wycliff then asked what Rodriguez had to say that might add to the public understanding of what happened on 9-11.

Told of the tremendous explosion that Rodriguez and others felt in the basement of the North Tower at 8:46 a.m., before the plane hit the building, Wycliff said, "The fact that three or four years later this guy comes out with these revelations doesn't strike me as news."

It is a fact, however, that Rodriguez has been saying the same thing since he was pulled from under a fire truck buried under the rubble of the North Tower. His testimony to the official 9-11 commission, however, was not included in the final report.

Peace Takes Courage

If You're Not OUTRAGED,
You're Not Paying ATTENTION

Request for a Letter of Confirmation
Written by: Paul Sheridan

http://peacetakescourage.com/articles/sheridan.htm 8/30/05

Paul Sheridan was selected as one of 2005's Civil Justice Foundations Champions (along side 2004 Vice-Presidential nominee John Edwards), an award given to those who make a difference to consumers in the United States. Sheridan also joined a list of well-known whistle blowers and victims advocates honored by the Civil Justice Foundation, including Erin Brockovich.

Paul Sheridan wrote a letter to Secretary of Defense Donald Rumsfeld on July 22, 2005. This letter was received on July 25, 2005, at 9:24 in the morning. What Mr. Sheridan asked for was simple-A simple, straight-forward letter that was authored and personally signed by Secretary Rumsfeld confirming that there was no doubt in his mind that American Airlines Flight 77 crashed into the Pentagon on September the 11, 2001.

Mr. Sheridan has not received a reply at all, which makes us all wonder if our Government is telling the truth about what really happened at the Pentagon on September the 11, 2001.

Mr. Paul Sheridan's letter to Secretary Rumsfeld follows:

22 July 2005

Honorable Donald H. Rumsfeld
Secretary of Defense
1000 Defense Pentagon
Washington, DC 20301

Subject: Request for a Letter of Confirmation
Reference: September 11, 2001 and the Events at the Pentagon in Washington, D.C.

Dear Secretary Rumsfeld:

I was pleased by your recent rejection of a suggestion by Senator Edward Kennedy that you tender your resignation as Secretary of the Department of Defense. We, the taxpayers, need you to remain in your current post for the duration of the current administration.

Regarding us taxpayers, we sometimes internalize the impression that U.S. government employees, especially those 'inside the beltway,' feel that we, the taxpayers, work for them. I have never felt that you engender that impression, but I would like to emphasize that one context of the subject is the fact that you work for me, a taxpayer. Again, I do not believe you have forgotten that fundamental fact.

Background

I am from New York, New York. I am a 'New Yorker' and always will be a 'New Yorker.' Family members reside in the New York metropolitan area. Indeed, a close relative is a high ranking official in the New York Metropolitan Transportation Authority (MTA), and previously reported directly to then Mayor Rudolf Giuliani. (On the morning of September 11, 2001 we temporarily lost cell phone contact with this relative, but all was/is "well."). For these and all other obvious reasons, the events of September 11, 2001 will remain, for me, a permanent issue of deep patriotic and personal grief.

Current Discussion

As you are aware, the taxpayers are constantly being bombarded with direct and indirect discussions regarding the events of September 11, 2001. A prominent recent discussion which reemphasized the ongoing relevance of September 11, 2001 came from President George Bush on June 28, 2005 during the address to his (and your) subordinates at Fort Bragg. By not-later-than the third paragraph of his talk, which mostly dealt with the war in Iraq, President Bush exclaimed:

"The war reached our shores on September the 11th, 2001. The terrorists who attacked us-and the terrorists we face-murder in the

name of a totalitarian ideology that hates freedom, rejects tolerance, and despises all dissent."

The carnage in Madrid of March 11, 2004, and the recent catastrophe in London of July 7, 2005 again prompted a bombardment of the taxpayer which specified the ongoing relevance of September 11, 2001. As the Fort Bragg audience was told, September 11, 2001 is not "behind us."

Paraphrasing President Bush, we are very fortunate to live in a country that loves freedom, encourages tolerance and has, as a pretext to its very existence, dissent. Indeed, President Bush's nominee for the 109th Supreme Court Justice, Judge John Roberts, refers to our nation as a "constitutional democracy."

September 11, 2001 and the Events at the Pentagon in Washington, D.C.

On November 10, 2001 President George Bush made the following statement to the United Nations:

"Let us never tolerate outrageous conspiracy theories concerning the attacks of September the 11th, malicious lies that attempt to shift the blame away from the terrorists themselves, away from the guilty."

It is by the grace of God that you were both present at the Pentagon and not killed by the event there on September 11, 2001. You demonstrated a patriotic integrity, for all to see, by walking to that area of the Pentagon that had been struck by that aircraft. In the effort to assist in any way possible, you personally were at the crash site within minutes of the event.

Certainly, from your first-hand witnessing, there are no "conspiracy theories" about what crashed into the Pentagon. The official rendition was that American Airlines Flight 77 crashed into the Pentagon, killing all crew and 58 passengers. The DOD Armed Forces Institute of Pathology (AFIP) issued a report on November 16, 2001 which states that, by use of bodily remains, all Flight 77 crash victims were positively identified. Given that separable, individual bodily remains survived the conflagration of Flight 77, to such an extent as to allow positive identification of the victims, certainly 60 tons of Boeing 757 aircraft components also survived at the Pentagon; a scene that you personally observed on September 11, 2001. It is in this context that I make a simple but specific request.

Request for a Letter of Confirmation-Background

The aforementioned taxpayer bombardment includes the allegation that a Boeing 757 did **not** crash into the Pentagon on September 11, 2001. This allegation is the central issue of my request. Clearly this allegation is designed to "*shift the blame away from the terrorists themselves, away from the guilty.*" I have read innumerable documents and reports on the events of September 11, 2001. This readership includes the 'National Commission on Terrorist Attacks Upon the United States' which was closed on August 21, 2004. I noted that all ten 9/11 Commission Members signed their names to the report. As public servants working for the taxpayer, the Commission Members believe what is stated in their report. Ironically, unlike yourself, the Commission Members were not present at the Pentagon on September 11, 2001. And yet despite that lack of direct personal witnessing of the Pentagon event, the Commission Members unabashedly signed the report, doing so in the patriotic spirit of the proverbial *John Hancock*. My request involves similar behavior on your part.

Request for a Letter of Confirmation-Specific Request

My request is very simple. I would like to receive from you a simple, straightforward letter, that you author and personally sign, that confirms and states that there is no doubt in your mind that American Airlines Flight 77, which utilized a Boeing 757 passenger aircraft, crashed into the Pentagon on September 11, 2001. I request that this letter of confirmation be received at my address listed above not more than 30 calendar days subsequent to receipt-signature of the instant letter at the Pentagon.

What I Will Not Accept

So that my request is not subject to misinterpretation, I will review the specific and general responses that are not acceptable. I will not accept a letter authored and signed by a member of your staff. I will not accept proposals, of any kind, that suggest that in-the-alternative I review various reports, computer simulations or engineering reviews: I am already thoroughly familiar with those sources of information. In general, I will not accept diatribe about "conspiracy theories." (Indeed, the underlying theme of this request is your assistance with obviation of these allegations, theories, etc.) In general, I will not accept a response that is not directly from my Secretary of Defense, Mr. Donald H. Rumsfeld

Request for a Letter of Confirmation-Reiteration

Many have said, and I agree, that you are probably the most well-known Secretary of Defense in the history of the United States of America. Your actions prior to, on the very day in-question, and after September 11, 2001 are part of the justification for that place in history. Again, the American taxpayers and the world need you to remain at your current post. Certainly you would agree that the American taxpayer has earned and is deserving of a simple and personalized confirmation, from their Secretary of Defense, that the Pentagon event of September 11, 2001 is not questionable or worthy of "malicious lies." In the context of national security, and the need for ongoing public confidence in the integrity/honesty of the Administration, your proverbial *John Hancock* is requested on a letter of confirmation.

I look forward to hearing from you. Please do not hesitate to contact me at any time.

Cordially,
Paul V. Sheridan

cc: President George W. Bush
Secretary Michael Chertoff
Secretary Norman Y Mineta
Senator Edward M. Kennedy
Ms. Renata B. Greenspan
Mr. Gerald J. Arpey
Mr. Glenn F. Tilton
Mr. Martin C. Jischke

16 August 2005

Senator Mark Dayton
Suite 298
Federal Building
Fort Snelling, MN 55111

Subject: My Letter to Secretary Rumsfeld of July 22, 2005

Dear Senator Dayton:

Thank you very much for your efforts regarding the 911 Commission Report. I too have been very concerned about this and related issues.

In this regard I am sharing with you my letter to DOD Secretary Donald Rumsfeld. As you can see from the FedEx enclosures, my letter was signed-for on July 25, 2005. Note that on page-3 I specify that the Secretary is to respond within 30 calendar days of receipt-signature. That would be August 25, just before the Labor Day holiday, and the return of Congress.

(For clarification, the last four courtesy copies at the end of my letter to Secretary Rumsfeld are as follows:

Ms. Reneta B. Greenspan	Director at AFIP	See Page 2 of letter
Mr. Gerald J. Arpey	Chairman, American -Airlines	
Mr. Glenn F. Tilton	Chairman, United-Airlines	
Mr. Martin C. Jischke	President of Purdue University	Location of ASCE

It was the Purdue American Society of Civil Engineers (ASCE) that had released, sometime in 2003, a controversial report and related computer simulation involving the event at the Pentagon.

I am also enclosing the documentary dvd *In Plane* Site. It runs approximately 61 minutes, but is worth every second. Viewing this dvd will provide part of the context for my Rumsfeld letter.

Please reference my name with Senator John Edwards. He and I, along with Father Patrick Doyle, were co-winners of the 2005 Civil Justice Foundation award. At the conclusion of the award gala in Toronto on July 26, 2005, 1 handed a copy of the *In Plane Site* dvd to the Senator; he promised to view it.

If or when Secretary Rumsfeld does not respond to the subject, I would like you to forward it to him requesting a response. Please feel free to contact me at any time.

Respectfully,
Paul V. Sheridan

enclosures

18 August 2005

Senator Joseph R. Biden, Jr.
Suite 2000
1105 North Market Street
Wilmington, DE 19801-1233

Subject: My Letter to Secretary Rumsfeld of July 22, 2005

Dear Senator Biden:

Thank you for your efforts regarding Iraq and the Joe Wilson/ Valerie Plame issues. As you can see from my "*What the Boss Wanted to Hear?*" editorial, I too have been very concerned about these issues.

In this regard I am sharing with you my letter to DOD Secretary Donald Rumsfeld. The FedEx enclosures indicate that my letter was signed-for on July 25, 2005. Note that on page-3 I specify that the Secretary is to respond within 30 calendar days of receipt: that would be August 25, just before the Labor Day holiday, and the return of Congress.

I am also enclosing the documentary dvd *In Plane Site*. It runs approximately 61 minutes, but is worth every second. Viewing this dvd will provide part of the context for my Rumsfeld letter.

If or when Secretary Rumsfeld does not respond to the subject, I would like you to forward it to him requesting a response. Please feel free to contact me at any time.

Respectfully,
Paul V. Sheridan

Enclosures

P.S. Please reference my name with Senator John Edwards. He and 1, along with Father Patrick Doyle, are winners of the 2005 Civil Justice Foundation award. On July 26, 2005, at the conclusion of the award gala in Toronto, I handed a copy of the *In Plane Site* dvd to the Senator, and he promised to review it.

*For clarification, the four courtesy copies at the end of my letter to

Secretary Rumsfeld are as follows:

Ms. Reneta B. Greenspan	Director at AFIP	See Page 2 of letter
Mr. Gerald J. Arpey	Chairman, American -Airlines	
Mr. Glenn F. Tilton	Chairman, United-Airlines	
Mr. Martin C. Jischke	President of Purdue University	Location of ASCE

It was the Purdue American Society of Civil Engineers (ASCE) that had released, sometime in 2003, a controversial report and related computer simulation involving the event at the Pentagon.

UNCLE SAM'S CHRISTIAN PATRIOTS
GLEN STANISH

Where is America heading? There is only one way to find the course for America's future and that is to remember America's past. Author Glen Stanish walks us through history and into the future in Uncle Sam's Christian Patriots. This investigative book studies recent global events against a backdrop of politics, religion, and history. How does the pursuit of truth in America measure up against the Word of God? What were the intentions of the Founding Fathers as they painstakingly wrote our Constitution? Glen pleads a case for peace in a world ravaged by terror, asking the reader to think outside the box in Uncle Sam's Christian Patriots.

Impressive & Thorough... A masterpiece of research and documentation.

William Lewis
Executive Producer of the documentaries 911 In Plane Site
and Beyond Treason
BridgeStone Media Group

Interesting and informative... really made me think... brought to light many things that I was not aware of.

Captain Don Hein, L-1011, B-737
ATA Airlines, Air Line Pilots Association Member

Author Glen Stanish received a Bachelor of Science degree from Purdue University in Aviation Technology, the Professional Pilot program. Until recently, he was employed as an airline pilot for fifteen years. He currently resides in Indiana. Glen has been married for 16 years, and he and his wife have been blessed with two wonderful children. Glen enjoys jogging, playing the drums when everyone else is out of the house, reading, music and sports. Although he loves coaching and umpiring little league baseball, he enjoys spending time with family most of all.

Milton Keynes UK
Ingram Content Group UK Ltd.
UKHW022109171123
432796UK00005B/97